In my second night of college, I was raped. Shattered and al[one], [t]o the Mexican border and headed north through 2,650 miles of desert [a]nd mountains to Canada, walking the height of America in search of [h]ome. This is the story of how my recklessness became my salvation.

"BEAUTIFUL AND SO WILDLY ENGAGING." —LENA DUNHAM

GIRL IN THE WOODS

ASPEN MATIS

a memoir

GIRL IN THE
WOODS

WILLIAM MORROW
An Imprint of HarperCollins*Publishers*

GIRL IN THE
WOODS

A Memoir

ASPEN
MATIS

Photo Insert Credits

Photo on page 5 *(bottom)* courtesy of Kat "Censored" Jimenez.
Photos on page 5 *(top)*, 6, 7, 8, 10 *(bottom)*, 11, 12 and 13, 14, 15 *(top)* courtesy of Aspen "Wild Child" Matis.
Photos on page 8 and 9, and 10 *(top)* courtesy of Stephanie "Trainwreck" White.
Photos on page 15 *(bottom)* and page 16 *(top)* by Larry Brunt.
Photo on page 16 *(bottom)* courtesy of Jill Rothenberg.

Portions of this book have previously appeared in the *New York Times, Tin House,* and *Psychology Today.*

HarperCollins books may be purchased for educational, business, or sales promotional use. For information please e-mail the Special Markets Department at SPsales@harpercollins.com.

FIRST EDITION

Designed by Jamie Lynn Kerner
Map designed by Brittany Gray
Trees on title page and part title pages by © MattGrove / Getty Images

Library of Congress Cataloging-in-Publication Data has been applied for.

ISBN 978-0-06-229106-6 (hardcover)
ISBN 978-0-06-239061-5 (international edition)

15 16 17 18 19   OV/RRD   10 9 8 7 6 5 4 3 2 1

For all girls told they cannot be the heroes of their own stories

And for Susan Shapiro, my narrative heroine

Trauma is not what happens to us, but what we hold inside in the absence of an empathetic witness.

—Peter A. Levine, *In an Unspoken Voice*

Contents

PART III: THE WAY THROUGH

GIRL IN THE

WOODS

Canada

21

Washington

20

PACIFIC
OCEAN

19
18
17
16

N
NW   NE
W   E
SW   SE
S

15

Oregon

the
Pacific Crest
Trail

14
13

12

California

11

10
9

1. lake morena
2. warner hot springs
3. oriflamme mountain
4. fuller ridge
5. big bear city
6. hiker heaven
7. casa de luna
8. kennedy meadows
9. aspen meadow
10. muir trail ranch
11. sierra city
12. etna
13. ashland
14. crater lake
15. bend
16. the bridge of the gods
17. trout lake
18. the knife's edge
19. packwood
20. stehekin
21. manning park

8

7
6
5
4
3
2

1   Mexico

PROLOGUE

JUNE 18, UNKNOWN PLACE, THE NORTHERN HIGH SIERRA, MILE 1170

I emerged from trees to a field of dense snow sheened with ice. I walked out onto it, feeling exposed, stepping carefully across the uneven sun-cupped surface of last year's snow, an ocean of shallow bowls, slippery and round. I tried to step only on the pockmarks' glossy rims. The holes' bottoms were soft snow, melting out. Step there, and you might fall through.

I was in the High Sierra. I had walked into this snowy spill of mountains from desert. Two months earlier, I'd stood in the shadow of the rust-brown corrugated metal fence that rippled along the Mexican border as far as I could see. The desert dipped and swelled like the sea, and among the dusty waves I saw no one. I'd begun at the soundless place where California touches Mexico with five Gatorade bottles full of water and eleven pounds of gear and lots of candy. My backpack was tiny, no bigger than a schoolgirl's knapsack. Everything I carried was everything I had.

From California's deserted border with Mexico, I had walked more than a marathon a day. Yesterday I had hiked twenty-five miles. Today I'd hiked seventeen miles, already. The miles flowed beneath my quick feet, a river of pale gravel, a river of branches against sky, of stones on stones, of snakes, of butterflies and inchworms and dead leaves that smell as sweet as black rich mud. For days I'd seen no one. But I wasn't scared of the solitude. Peopleless wilderness felt like the safest place.

The snowfield sloped downhill, and I began to run. My gait was wild now, careless, heels punching the glassy ice. My hard steps shot cracks through the ground like a hammer to windshields; my impact shattered the world again, again. I was enjoying the *pop* sound of cracking ground, the jolt of breaking through that extra inch.

Then I fell through, into the snow, up to my neck.

My heart stopped. I wriggled to free my arms. They wouldn't budge. The snow's coarse grain abraded me, tearing painfully into my limbs. I had to make it out of this girl-deep hole. I struggled. I squirmed. I needed to fight. With all my power, I had to free myself.

And then in one slick thrust I popped my two arms free. They were throbbing, snow-scraped and red. I was wearing only thin black running spandex and a polypro short-sleeved shirt. I hadn't planned to be stuck fifteen minutes in the snow.

I tried to push myself the rest of the way free, but my legs were stuck. I couldn't shift my feet, even an inch. I couldn't feel my heels. I thrashed; it did no good. I pressed my hip left, into the snow; even as it burned me, I held my core against it until the hole melted wider, harder, into dripping ice. As the hole widened my body heated; my right foot cooled, freezing and then burning. I struggled to move a toe, feel the brush of one shifting against another. I knew how easily I could lose my foot. In an instant the mountains had morphed from my playground into my death trap. Even with all the survival skills I'd mastered in my thousand miles of walking, past basking rattle-snakes I'd stepped over like sticks, the glass-eyed bears, the shame and weight of my secret, after everything, this silly threatless snowy spot could be where I—just nineteen years old, a dark dot of a body in boundless whiteness—would end.

I violently wanted to live.

Chinese proverb says that a journey of a thousand miles begins with a single step. This journey had begun with the coercion of my body, with my own wild hope. I'd walked into the desert alone in search of beauty and my innocence lost—and strength. I had taken two and a half million steps in the direction of those things, to get to here. Now, up to my neck in a hole in a field of snow in remote mountains, all I felt was stuck.

This is the story of how my recklessness became my salvation.

PART I
Terrible Seeds

CHAPTER 1

The Garden City

I lived my first eighteen and a half years in a white Colonial in the idyllic town of Newton, Massachusetts. Newton is the Garden City, statistically the safest place in America, only one murder in my entire lifetime. It is a beautiful old town, where the spring light rests on yards' tangerine-orange and violet pansy beds, on marigolds, sugar maples, crab apple trees, white houses, brick houses clutched in curled fingers of Dutch ivy.

I never had to move, was never shaken or uprooted. My parents were married happily, my neighborhood was wealthy, sidewalks clean. My mother and father both went to Harvard Law School. They were accomplished Boston lawyers. We had plenty of money. I had two older brothers. I was the baby of the family. No one I'd ever loved had died.

I was extremely close to my mother, and the people who lived on the streets around our house would have recognized me as the little girl who was always walking with her mom. We walked together several evenings a week, past Whole Foods Market and the Little League field, Mason Rice Elementary and the glass-still lake. The suburban night was quiet and very dark. Tranquil Crystal Lake gleaming in streetlamps, decaying leaves slippery on the sidewalks snaking its rim. The waterfront mansions all glowed the same soft yellow. We walked side by side over roots pushing through the concrete sidewalk, talking almost exclusively about me. I'd tell her how my day was, the homework I had to do, upcoming tests, goals, even college. Our evening stroll was three to seven miles, when we crossed the main streets, we held hands; I loved it.

Later, when we were back, my father would come home. Usually I'd be alone at the kitchen table eating a dinner my mother had made just for me. Often, she made a different dinner for each of us, whatever we said we wanted; during the day she'd call each of us to ask.

My father didn't talk to me about myself like my mother did. Some days he'd arrive back home and say, "Debby. Tell me something brilliant." No matter what I said he'd declare to my mom, "She's a genius." I'd feel giddy, drunk with the security of love. It thrilled me when he called me "art smart" and encouraged the silly stories I wrote. But other nights I'd place myself in an old wooden kitchen chair waiting for him to come home, and when he'd come, I'd say, "Dad," he'd say, "Hello," and walk through the room, past me, up the stairs. Each step would creak beneath his weight. I could never predict his mood, but I'd always hope it would be good and he'd look at me and kiss me, request a kiss back, want my love, want me.

Hidden in his home office, whitewashed wood door shut, he'd write. By the time I was in high school he'd written thirteen sprawling books, his thickest 2,600 single-spaced pages. He also sometimes played guitar up there, his Gibson acoustic—a lovely sunburst model to replace the one stolen from his Dodge when he was twenty-one and newly married to my mom.

On nights when my father was "good," about three or four nights a week, he would go on an exercise machine he had in his room we all called the Ski Machine for an hour. It was very old and loud, wooden with two old skis sliding on metal tracks. As he worked out, Dylan or sometimes Springsteen blasted from his bedroom's speakers, singing "You're a Big Girl Now," singing songs he loved and that

I grew to love, so loud his music played in every room. He told me he had every single song Dylan ever recorded. Whenever anyone asked me what music I liked best, I'd answer, "The music of my father's generation."

I always desperately wanted him to see me. Freshman year, I joined Newton South High School's Nordic ski team, but just as I began to get good and score in races, Dad threw the Ski Machine away, replaced by a soundless treadmill.

He paid much more attention to my brother Jacob, who was five years older, popular, a dedicated baseball player. My father had always been a poor athlete, introverted and nerdy; he was small and wore thick glasses. My mom always used to say, "I'm raising Debby, Steve has Jacob." Hanging out with Jacob, my dad got to be one of the guys for the first time in his life. Dad glowed with the athletic boys' affirmation. He loved that his own son was athletic and well-liked.

And my big brother Jacob was easy to like. He was sprightly and uncommonly good looking, with a quiet, magnanimous confidence that attracted people. He was my hero, too, and I listened to him. He gave me lots of wise advice. He told me to put myself in win-win situations, and that, "You have to know what you want, and you have to get it." And when I was little, restless, that advice had sounded profound. Figure out what you want. Know what you want. Get it. Jacob had figured it out, was working to get it. He wanted to be a baseball player. He worked to improve both his speed and his strength, ate lean meats and whole grain breads and pastas and fresh vegetables and fruits—no junk; no treats. It was monkish. In high school, he played on the varsity baseball team all four years, and his senior year he was captain. He taught me how wildly hard work pays. I was attracted to his unshakeable diligence.

I loved that my classmates thought that he was amazing. In kindergarten, when he was in fifth grade, I would see him for a moment each day on the playground when our class lines passed each other. Sometimes, in front of everyone, he'd lower his hand and high-five me as he passed. I remember the thrill of the smack, the security I felt.

When Jacob was nine, my mother began to allow him to walk to the Mason Rice baseball field in Newton Centre, all alone. His bravery startled me. I felt a small surge of thrill for him. On days that he had a game, my mom and I would walk together to the field, Jacob and my dad would already be there—he'd leave the office early; he scored all of Jacob's games—and as a family we watched him play.

I would wave my Go Jacob! posters. I'd draw #4, his number, with Magic Markers and decorate them with all different-colored glitters. Sometimes my poster would read I Love #4. Sometimes it'd say, more thoroughly, I Love #4 (He is my brother).

I'd wander the fields around his game, picking buttercups, showing all the mothers my posters, asking the prettiest ones if I could please borrow their lipstick. The moms would always laugh and slide lipstick from their sleek purses and slip it to me, and laugh more, harder, as I drew it onto my tiny mouth.

My mother was constantly worried about my self-esteem. She always feared that innocuous things my father or my brothers said would hurt my self-esteem. My father would say, "Debby, stop talking for a minute," and I would, and my mother would be worried.

"Steve!" she'd say, "Let Debby tell her story." She'd turn to me. "It's a very, very good story," she'd say to whatever I'd been talking about, regardless. Then she'd talk to my dad, in front of me, about my very fragile self-esteem. "Self-esteem is so important for her."

My mommy had to grow in harsher circumstances. She would tell me how her own mother, my grandma Belle, used to dictate how many squares of toilet paper was the right number to use; she was extremely frugal; she said you were using too much toothpaste, the wrong telephone, you were ungrateful; you were ruining her life. She yelled. She was controlling and arbitrary. My mommy told me that Grandma Belle was a cold mother.

My grandmother had rarely kissed her girls. So to be better, my mommy kissed me when she woke me every morning, at the end of every day, when she picked me up from school or dropped me off. She was wonderfully affectionate. She always said yes when I asked if a friend could sleep over that night, or if I could have this or that arts-and-crafts thing I wanted, or if I could go to this-or-that place with her—to pick apples or downhill ski or swim. Yes, yes, yes; we could. We could do anything together.

Both my parents were extremely generous, paying for years of ballet lessons and private painting classes, ceramics, Nordic ski team—supporting all my "productive" activities, anything I said I wanted to do. When I was sixteen, they had my oldest brother Robert "publish" my first "book"—an illustrated children's book called *In the Garden,* filled with watercolors I'd made in my private painting lessons. They had two thousand hardback copies of the book printed. They always encouraged my art.

My mom would tell me that the escape from her chilly childhood home was college. She fled to school two thousand miles away.

She earned a graduate degree from Harvard; she argued on behalf of a neglected child before the Supreme Judicial Court of Massachusetts and contributed precedent-setting articles to law books and had two boys, then me. I was born when she was forty-three, a full twenty years older than my grandmother had been when she'd had her. I was her youngest, her baby girl.

My mother called me Doll Girl. She physically dressed me every day of elementary and then middle school, then high school—scrunched up my pants and slipped them over my pointed feet and pulled them up and instructed me to arch my back, *clip-clipped* shut my bra. At sleepaway camp without her for the first time the summer following fourth grade, I didn't change my clothes for the entire month and never once brushed my hair, and so by the end of the season my curls were tangled into one dry rat's-nest dread. Before that summer, I'd never washed my own hair and was, in the face of the tiny task, paralyzed. She took this as evidence that I couldn't be trusted to take care of myself and immediately took over showering me again once I returned home, instead of leaving me to wash my own hair.

As a kid, I used to make lists of all the things I couldn't do. I'd lie on my stomach on my bedroom's polished wood floorboards, my elbows propping me up, and carefully write:

1.   Ride a bike
2.   Put in contact lenses
3.   Make my hair look better
4.   Lose ten pounds forever
5.   Be likable
6.   Lovable
7.   Swallow a pill. Not even a Tic-Tac!!

These were not things I wasn't allowed to do; my parents were actually very permissive. They were things that I believed I wasn't capable of, that were out of reach for me. When I'd finished, I'd usually toss the list in the recycling so no one would see it, but I knew it by heart.

One day, twelve years old and feeling brave, I told my mother I was going to walk all by myself to Mason Rice and back, but she said, "I'm coming."

I was prepared, argued "Jacob could."

She looked at me, feigning confusion, up and down. I'd heard many times before that I had bad judgment, couldn't be trusted to take care of myself. "Jacob has a baseball bat," she said and then awkwardly left my room.

I knew that wasn't the true reason, but I dropped it.

The first time I walked alone, thirteen, I was terrified. A twig snapped under my shoe; my heart revved wildly. I'd walked these sidewalks a thousand times with my mom, yet I was scared by all her fears. Don't talk to strangers, walk quickly past parked cars, look both ways, all ways, always. Be alert. There was so damn much to remember to stay safe.

After about ten minutes, about halfway to Newton Centre, I turned and ran, reached the driveway sweaty, hot and dizzy, impossibly relieved to be back home.

The safest summer place was Colorado. My mother's parents, Grandma Belle and Grandpa Mel, lived in a small ranch house in Colorado Springs, and each August we'd go visit for two weeks. The house was modest, one story, exotic blood-red throw rug over silvery olive green carpet, packed with thousands of old fragile trinkets, old gold clocks and porcelain songbirds, wings painted yellow. It was exciting there, the air clean and bright and smelling of red clay. Jacob and I'd have lots of free time to wander and play cowboys and Indians, Davy Crocket, Bigfoot—whatever games we wanted. Once when my dad was videotaping Jacob juggling, my grandma took me out to the backyard to pick mint leaves that grew in the shade behind the house. She taught me how to recognize the plant. We rinsed the leaves of their dirt, scooped vanilla ice cream, ate it with the fresh mint on top. I'd give her my drawings of trees and the mountains above us.

At each summer's end, we'd kiss Grandma Belle and Grandpa Mel goodbye, drive away from Colorado Springs, its twinkling gold lights fading, black mountains growing. Mommy, Daddy, Jacob and I'd drift soundless toward mountains and go backpacking.

We'd hike through aspen forests, along high ridges, down to valley-lakes. The trails were veins, the mountainscape a body infinitely beautiful and novel. And it was our home—at least for seven perfect days each year.

My father would catch fish. He'd stand in the center of a creek, in the calm below the churning rapids, and cast and cast and cast his line until a sharp tug told him we had food. He'd reel it in and say, "All right. Some trout." And then he'd grip its core and slam its head against a rock. I'd hold out my warm palms, the fish still twisting, flapping madly. Fluttering like a shot-clipped bird.

It would fall into my palms' small softness, dead.

By the time I'd hopped from rock to river-rock and then up the trail to our camp, the fish would be limp, its eyes bulging. I'd give it to my mom. She'd have already smashed Wheat Thins with a spoon expecting it, and without a word about the fish—it was always about us, if we were cold or too warm or in need of any thing—clean out the guts and roll it in the shards of cracker.

And then beneath the strung-gem Milky Way, brightening in the blackening sky, she'd heat the pan over a tiny stove, the oil hopping, searing hot. I'd stand close to her, smelling the fat, smelling the granite-chilled air so cold and piney. The fish would fry till golden and my father would be back and my brother would need food. He'd be doing crunches in the dirt.

We'd eat the fish together: all there. All fed. It was always crisp and flaky, sometimes a little fishy, drip-wax white and wild. We'd caught this food, I'd think. We would eat it all, translucent bones the only bits left on our plates, so white in the moon's light, as thin as dried-up veins.

Each cluster of stars like city lights in fog. Too many specks to ever really see.

And I would always think: we are a tribe, foraging for berries, catching fish. Crushing wheat thins so the fish tastes good.

If we all did what we should, we would survive.

Our fire flared and wavered, found a new pine limb and slipped across it quick as an ink drop bursts in water, huge, growing beautifully. Snapping and spitting. Burning my white cheeks.

My very best memory with my dad is from one of those Colorado summers. I was eight or maybe nine. He took me—just me—on a drive through Colorado Springs, up to The Bluffs. I hardly ever got to be alone with him. We walked, he first, me following.

We didn't talk. I imagined he was William Clark and I was Captain Meriwether Lewis. I'd watched a documentary on them in school and read some thick, gorgeously illustrated picture books, and I loved the story: they discovered new places no one had ever seen; they were professional explorers who got to discover new landscapes for the President, which is what I wanted to be when I grew up and got to choose my job. I told my dad this. He said, "Eureka! I don't think no one-body's seen this here territory, young Lewis."

I nodded, solemn, "Ain't nobody, Clark. Just us." I made a sun shield with my flat hand and squinted, slow and dramatic, looking down on the park's green soccer fields and softball diamond and pearl-gold wildgrass, gleaming in a silent strip of resting sun. Above us the redrock rose sharply upward, right to low clouds; the clouds were infinite, like the glinting light on ocean's restless swells. "It's colorful," I declared. "I'm gonna here name it Co-lor-*ado!*"

My Clark-dad clapped one hard loud clap. "You's brilliant! You'll have to write that down later, so as you don' fo-get."

I followed him up and down dry hills, declaring all kinds of victory, takin' note of the deergrass and the newts, up, nearly high as the vast cloud-ceiling, up to the top of Co-lor-*ado* Springs. From the very top I noticed a faraway green patch. I spoke slowly, still in character, "That thar's par-dice," then, again myself, said, "Daddy, look." I pointed best I could at the patch, emerald in late summer's golden light.

He squinted, cupped his brow. His hands were brown from sun. "That's just a school, Colorado College."

The name meant nothing to me, not good or bad, I'd never heard it before. He started to walk back down the bluff's pale red dust path, and I asked, calling after him, "Like Harvard?"

But he kept walking. He didn't answer, and we moved on in silence, me speeding past him, back down the dry red bluffs. Quickly I got ahead, slipped on gravel. "Don't get hurt," my dad's voice called after me, speeding to rejoin me. "Please."

The emerald patch was out of view now. I wouldn't forget it. I'd remember how I'd seen it like a green gemstone.

When it came time to think about colleges I applied to only one, that Eden glimpsed while hiking with my father: Colorado College.

CHAPTER 2

Terrible Seeds

Ten years later, my parents flew from Boston out to Colorado to help me settle into the dormitory.

Going to college here was a fight I'd won; my father thought I could have done better. Now, seated in the backseat of the rental car, I found myself in the beige otherworld of Colorado Springs. It was the paved front range, a vast and continuous strip mall. One grand field of Carl's Jr.s and Taco Bells and EZ Money Pay Loans and Starbucks, repeating. The streets were straight and wide. It seemed in fashion to have a little American flag fastened to your car's antenna. This artless red-white-and-blue town was my new home. Liberal me. It made me laugh. I was in the flats. The mountains were out there, somewhere beyond the concrete plains.

The college was a supposed oasis in the city. The campus itself was verdant, tree-shadowed—a liberal arts school nestled amid the sprawl of this conservative military town. The year before I applied, the Princeton Review ranked us the number 3 reefer school; here weed was more popular than alcohol. Students were attractive and artistic; we could study modern dance and filmmaking; we had galleries. Studio Art was actually a major. The Princeton Review described the school's vibe as "Intellectual and all-around chill." Nothing bad should have happened here.

There's a story about the start of her college days that Mom used to tell me in my childhood bedroom, as I relaxed into my dreams—a true story. On the second day of my mother's freshman orientation, at a crowded mixer in the student union, my mom somehow got pushed up against the wall. A boy was pushed up next to her, and they glanced at each other. He said something to her. "It was not romantic like the scene in *West Side Story* in which Maria and Tony spot each other from across the gym floor," she would say to me. Sometimes she'd laugh. "We probably talked about where we came from. When the boy said he was from the Bronx, I probably said, 'My mother was from the Bronx, too.' I don't remember if we danced at all. I don't remember when or if he and I even ever had a formal date." There are many bits of the story she doesn't quite remember.

What my mother does remember is that they would study in adjoining carrels in the university library, which closed each night at eleven o'clock, though freshman girls had to be back in their dorms, safe and sound, by ten. Boys were not allowed in the women's dorms, except for in the living room areas during certain hours. My mother lived in Capen House, an old Victorian with about twenty freshman girls chaperoned by an old woman, the widow of a professor. After they left the library, the boy would walk her back to the dormitory. Each night she signed in just on time, with a time stamp.

My mother typed his papers; she did his laundry. They went together for late-night pizza or sometimes ribs and rice at a restaurant named Bobo's, which was in Ball Square, a short walk away and open late. Some days she brought him food from the dining hall because his parents couldn't afford the meal ticket. On weekends girls had until midnight before they had to sign in. My mom and the boy used to make out on the roof of the library.

One night while they were up there above the city, all the lights of Boston went completely black. "We just saw the whole lit city disappear," she said, and the whole world was just the two of them. The boy was my daddy. That was the story's punchline.

On the old library's roof, in pupil-darkness, my parents made love.

The next day was The Blackout. "A bunch of guys like Daddy brought out guitars," and they celebrated in the darkness.

They were married the night before graduation.

My mother cleaned my new dorm room with vigor. She got down on her knees and scrubbed the floor, the pale linoleum checkers. The room had already been cleaned by the college and smelled of new plastic mattress cover and bleach, but she washed everything all over again. I only stood and dumbly watched her. She bent over; my father grabbed futilely at her butt—he couldn't reach—and mumbled something loving, calling her "Arthur Bad," a bastardization of "awfully bad," one of their pet names. She darted around us, washed around our feet, sterilizing everything.

I blinked, lethargic, said half-heartedly, "My room's already clean, Mom. You can stop washing." She answered, "But you have allergies," kept scrubbing, taking care of things for me as she always had.

I knew there was no point in arguing with her—she had always been deaf to my "No."

At sixteen I declared that I would like to dress myself from now on.

She paused. She said, "You won't get to school in time." I couldn't do it.

When she still tried to dress me now I'd flinch; I'd say, "Stop it. I'll do it." I'd say, "Get the fuck out. I need some privacy." I would fight her.

Her behavior wouldn't change. She would again dress me in my sleep, again; next morning, again. I'd wake; I could say anything. She wouldn't hear me.

Mine were hollow words.

In our arguments, we'd had our typical script. I would say something in protest, she'd say nothing. I'd say, "Did you hear me?" She'd say, "Yes." She'd turn on NPR if we were in the kitchen or the car, or turn on the faucet and start brushing her teeth. Tomorrow she'd do the same thing—buy more food "for me" than I could possibly eat, dress me for school so I could get there in time, slip in and out of the bathroom freely while I was in the shower.

I would snap at her; sometimes I'd call her a bitch. Once, I asked her to leave me alone in the bathroom, she didn't listen, and I scratched her, like a wild cat—furious. I hit her on the breast with an open hand.

That time she yelled—called me a bitch back. She left the bathroom, but the next day was the same, as if she had forgotten.

Sometime in middle school, I realized that our dynamic—her helping me put on my clothes, me submitting and allowing it—wasn't common. I had realized it wasn't normal—none of my peers needed their mothers to dress them. In all conversations I omitted it. I'd pretend that I dressed myself for school—lying—overcompensating and mentioning how I'd put my shirt on, apropos of nothing.

I knew I had an embarrassing secret.

I grew to believe it—I needed her help. I would fail without it. I forfeited myself to this conclusion. This understanding was my greatest shame.

I began to feel rage—hate for her. Desire to break from her and prove to her, and to the world, and to myself that I was my own valid person.

When I finally confronted her about her need to control and "handle" things for me, she would say, "I thought I was just being nice."

She was adamant: I would be late to school. "*Then* you'll have real problems."

I felt underestimated. I hated how out of control and powerless I felt.

Arguing was ineffectual, trying felt pointless.

Now my dad and I sat together on the dorm-room bed, out of Mom's way in the small room, feeling useless.

My dad leafed through my course booklet; he seemed focused.

He pointed out one smiling face, a political science professor, and told me he knew him. Before my dad had gone to Harvard Law, he'd studied the French political thinker Alexis de Tocqueville at the University of California's Berkeley campus, and he had a whole past there I hardly knew about. I never knew the right time to ask him. I was about to then, but my mom bent down to scoop a mound of my clean clothes into a big black trash bag, and Dad patted her butt, and the moment was over; I just smiled and looked away. I liked seeing that my parents were still so much in love.

The school had given me a single in a very large newly constructed dormitory, my top choice on the New Student Housing form. I'd fudged the housing questionnaire to make myself seem nocturnal and loud, impossible to live with. I'd never shared a room, and the notion seemed overwhelming.

Outside my dorm the sky's pure blue was deepening; day's light was darkening. My mother hung my fall dresses in the closet, folded my shorts and shirts and underwear and shut them all neatly out of sight. I sat on the vinyl mattress, watching as she separated out a pile of tank tops and cotton panties and tossed them into a fresh black garbage bag.

"Did we bring too many extra clothes," I asked, confused. "Are you taking my underwear back home?"

"No," she said. "We are going to rewash these pieces of clean clothing together, in order to teach you how to do laundry." She strode down the hall, and called back at me, "You need to know how to use a washer and a dryer."

"Mom no, it's clean," I said, following her, unheard.

As she washed them all again, I didn't even try to help. She didn't give me room. I was always in her way. I just wanted her to go. It was time to finally be free of her.

She handed me four hundred dollars, cash, and a credit card that she and my dad would pay. She looked at me. She was squinting, but her eyes looked at the same time widely opened.

"What?" I said.

The dryer rattled. "If a boy tries to give you champagne," she said slowly, as if she were speaking to a child, as if I were stupid, "he is trying to get you drunk." She enunciated each word; she had planned to say this.

I watched the dryer turn. My underwear tumbled over themselves, stuck in their places in the spinning bulk: white, nude, dark cherry red. I said back to her, too loudly, stuck in her unending unrelenting overprotectiveness, "Mom, you're insane. No one drinks champagne. That doesn't happen. You're being crazy. Please can you just leave."

She handed me another wad of twenties, squeezed me, and left me.

It was the last day of August, Sunday the thirty-first, the new school year would begin tomorrow morning. I felt as free as if I were falling. I knew not a single person at Colorado College. I was happily anonymous, liberated from my humiliating past. I felt unbound and defiant. I was determined to prove to my parents—and to myself—that I could take care of myself, once and for all. I could keep myself safe. I didn't need them. They'd finally see that all their worry about me was needless. Dusk swallowed the stately brick and stone buildings, curled lines of ivy gripped the stone like a giant's long black fingers, spreading.

I'd flown to campus from the borderline of California and Oregon only a few days earlier, from a walk along a wild footpath through mountains I'd taken alone in an attempt to shake myself from my mother's grip.

I'd first learned about the path at seventeen, when I'd found *Travels in Alaska*—a brittle and browning, 1979 trade paperback edition of John Muir's classic—among flat basketballs and insecticide in my family's garage. When I'd opened it, the spine cracked in two. I felt a swell of compassion for my parents to think that they had bought this wild old book. They had once fostered desire for something distant, something large—a seed they'd buried, abandoned.

In the weeks after I'd first uncovered the book in the garage,

I read it over and over, imagining John Muir writing letters and essays describing the grace of his found-home, so beautiful that even wealthy tourists began to venture out to see. He was an escapee, a pioneer of conservation in a time when industrial production was new and booming. I wanted to know Muir, meet him, catch his joy. Go where he'd gone. Be as free and euphoric as he was when he was discovering for himself Alaska, glissading, traversing boundless snow, alone. I wanted his life route, his sure footprints to follow instead of those my mother had decided on for me.

And then I'd learned that I could do just that. His wandering path is marked. A two-foot-wide, 211-mile-long continuous footpath from Happy Isles Trailhead in Yosemite Valley, south through the High Sierra of California, to the summit of Mount Whitney—14,505 feet tall, the highest peak in the lower forty-eight. And this great trail is just a small section of a much longer trail that extends from Mexico to Canada. This long footpath is called the Pacific Crest Trail.

I decided I had to walk it.

That summer, I'd lied to my parents, knowing they would never let me go alone—told them that instead of camp I was going to California with some kind of Outward Bound alumni group I'd put together through e-mail—and, by myself, I'd hiked the 211-mile John Muir Trail through the High Sierra Mountains.

They did find out, they were both worried and my father especially felt terribly betrayed, and the summer I was eighteen, again with their credit card, I returned to California and again hiked the John Muir Trail. This time, I didn't stop at the John Muir Trail's northern end but instead kept walking north until my trail converged with a longer wilderness footpath—the Pacific Crest Trail. I kept walking and walking. The summer before college started, I hiked just shy of one thousand miles.

These summers had been my great rebellion. I'd spent the months before college happy, glowing with my new independence. It was so fucking fun, I was so wildly free. I had wanted to take a gap year and keep going, walk the trail all the way to Canada. I told my mother I was going to, she said no. She said I would be older than everyone at college then, and it would be harder to date. I would be a year behind and too old.

So I walked one thousand miles and then came to school. I flew straight from Medford, Oregon, to Colorado College. The freedom of the woods lingered in me here; I felt lighter. I hoped to be changed by it, allow this seeding independence to root in my childhood Eden's soil and grow until at last it was undeniable.

New freshmen wandered along the quad's walkways. I watched clumps cross from dining hall to orientation video dance party to campus-safety lecture without certainty or friends or direction. Their dark bodies were tentative, posture bad. I straightened. I wandered, too, but alone. I knew nobody; no one knew who I was. I was the only student from Newton South High School to go here. More than anything—the mountains, the good English literature program—anything—I had chosen Colorado College, a tiny school two thousand miles from my home in Massachusetts, for the anonymity it would provide me.

Now, finally at college, I felt quiet, giddy and lonely. Suddenly here, and already completely lost. I saw myself taking long walks over the campus paths each evening, alone. I'd always been such a damn loner. I'd never met anyone I fit with. I wanted a boyfriend to hold hands with. Tonight was my second night away at college. I thought about my mother pushed against my father. That couldn't possibly happen to me, I thought, no.

My new room was still tidy, T-shirts and sweaters folded, summer dresses hung in a line in the closet—my mother's good work. There was almost nothing left for me to do. Tomorrow morning classes would begin. I was sitting on the navy plastic-covered mattress of my bed, opening my cardboard box of books when a shrill alarm startled me. It stopped me on the bed, *ereh-ereh-ereh*, my heart revving. It was the fire alarm. I've never been good in emergencies; *Stand*, I thought, and I stood. I thought, *Walk*. Outside the air was hot and very still. A line of fire trucks turned their red and silver lights, changing the color of a field of freshman faces. It smelled of cut grass and of stone.

Kids dashed in and out of the sprinklers outside. The fire trucks' spinning red and silver lights brightening the mud, the sprinkler-sprays, dizzying me. I saw a girl was looking at me. She was pretty. Her skin was very pale, moonlit, a serene lunar blue. Closer, she was sprayed with freckles, galaxies, and I saw worlds in her. She walked toward me. I was paralyzed. I actually shut my eyes.

"Hey there," she said to me, "you're in Slocum?"

Slocum was the dormitory. I opened my eyes. "Yes, am."

She told me her name was Katherine. A man's voice echoed through a bullhorn speaker. I couldn't understand what he was saying.

I told her I was Debby. I said, "I can't hear what he's telling us, can you?"

I don't remember if she said she could. I remember she asked me if my roommates were cool, and I said I had a single, and she said she had a single, too, and declared us "singles sisters," and I think we actually hugged.

In a blissed hour—I'd broken in, found my first friend—freckled-porcelain Katherine slipped into my room followed by a skinny boy with black hair and wooden drumsticks in the back pocket of his jeans who also happened to be my neighbor, followed by a thicker redheaded boy I'd never seen before. Katherine didn't really know them, none of us knew anyone yet really, but she did know a boy who'd said he met the redhead, and that he was cool. The redhead's posture was very confident. He was handsome in a smug-boy way: popped collar, khaki shorts. So Ivy League. His hair was red and wiry, his lips plump and melon pink. His name was Junior. The other boy was Zach. All four of us were freshmen, all new here.

Someone had the DVD of *The Breakfast Club*. I don't remember how we decided on my room for watching it. It all happened very quickly. There's a lot I don't remember, just the details that struck me.

I saw myself in the tall mirror stuck on the back of my dorm room's blond wood door. The room's color switched erratically: pale blue, pale yellow. My pink shorts were too high waisted to be cool. *The Breakfast Club* kids talked and laughed—they were distorted on the mirror's edge, shrunken and flipped—applied dark lipstick using only cleavage to hold it steady, smoked weed and bonded, became the greatest friends, lovers.

Junior rolled a joint. I took a hit, then another. I tried not to inhale too deeply; I didn't want to lose myself completely. My room still smelled like bleach. We all four were sitting on my bed without removing our shoes, muddy from the fire drill, it was my second night at motherfucking college, and I felt euphoric. It was the second time in my life I had ever smoked weed. In the mirror my shorts were tiny; they looked good. My lipstick was dark as blood. Junior told me something that I couldn't hear.

I wondered what he'd said but felt stupid asking him to repeat it, so I didn't. Katherine and my neighbor passed the joint; they were staying sober. A burgundy lipstick stain glared on the lumpy joint.

Junior placed his palm softly on my inner thigh. I noticed his hands were thick and very pale.

I thought: What am I doing here? In suburban Colorado, wearing lipstick. Smoking weed.

And I thought: What am I doing here? What am I doing here? What *am* I? I wanted to feel like a pretty girl, even out in Colorado with no one who knew me. To be beautiful. To live beautifully. I drew on maroon Make Me Blush lipstick.

The champagne comment my mother had made earlier in the day seemed even more bizarre now. No one drinks champagne, I thought again, deciding she was tragically insane.

Somebody was drumming his pencil on his shoe-sole rubber, and the shy girl in the movie kissed the boy—this was freedom—and then the movie ended suddenly and the room was darker, and then blindingly light.

The thin boy got up and walked into the quiet hall with Katherine. I followed them out and hugged the girl and then the boy—he was flushed—and walked back in. I was happy Junior had stayed, I liked him. I wanted him to want to kiss me. My thick door clicked.

I sat down on the shiny linoleum floor, unsure what space was best to go to. Junior was still on my bed. My new bed was dirty from our shoes, patterned with dry crumbs of mud. Junior crushed one to dust in a pinch. We sat in silence and I felt a throbbing knocking softly in my collarbone—I'd broken it as a kid—I was a little turned on, we were together, alone. When the boy who remained turned to me, I'd smiled at his red hair; I happily kissed him. He had seemed easygoing, poised. He placed his hand lightly down on my inner thigh. I froze. I was suddenly afraid. I said, "Thanks for coming over. I'll see you soon, all right? Okay?"

He pressed his hand down on my leg—clutched so it hurt—and I twisted out from under it and stood—I was standing on my bed, felt like jumping!—and he rose up on his knees and I said, "'Bye! I'm going to go to bed." I was excited. I was scared.

But he did not leave. He didn't seem to hear me at all, or care.

He tried to put his hands in my shorts; I told him, "Slow down." He didn't. I compromised; I didn't want him to touch me below my shorts, told him instead he could titty-fuck me; everywhere above my pink short shorts, he could kiss me. I tried to give him one thing so he might leave without taking everything—so that the boy won't be angry; become threatening. He took what I'd offered, then found my waistband again. I felt guilty that I'd led him on, but I asked him to get up and go. He didn't look handsome to me now.

He jerked my shorts down, below my hips, without unbuttoning them. The fabric cut into my hip. I heard the plastic button hit my room's linoleum floor. The clip-sound was chilling. I said, "Stop it." His deafness maddened me. I remember bracing myself. Stiffening and feeling still as dead soft wood. I only whispered, "Stop," though I'd tried to scream. The entire time, he'd only ever looked at my body, never at my face, his empty eyes hungry, never seeing me at all. I wasn't the presence of a person, but a body. I could have said anything, he wouldn't have heard me. He'd never responded, not by stopping, not with his words.

I'd trusted him, thought he'd stop if I said, "Wait." Thought he'd go, leave, after The End. After the movie's boy and girl kissed, flicked to black. Instead, he'd touched me. The slice of sky in my cracked window had glowed black, dense as a bomb.

Afterward, I asked him if he wanted to stay. To sleep over. I desperately wanted to feel I'd wanted this, that what happened was not what happened. I begged him to stay.

He told me I was "fucking crazy"—I was crazy to ask for that. Those were the only words he'd spoken to me since Katherine had left. He knew what he'd done. My plea scared him. But he was lucky. My irrational request would later fog the clear act and save him from expulsion and conviction and shame.

I was the one who felt shame.

In six weeks, I'd gone from virgin to rape victim. When I met Junior, I was not a virgin, but I'd only had sex with one man, only once, in a trailside town before leaving the California mountains to begin school.

Just a few weeks before flying to Colorado, I'd made the decision that I was going to lose my virginity, and I had. I wanted to lose it before college, didn't want to be that weird girl who'd never had sex. I just wanted to get it out of the way.

I had had four rum and Cokes. The man's name was Tyler. He had a shaved head, a black bumblebee beside the number 66 tattooed on his muscular neck. I didn't know then that it was a gang tattoo. He and I met in a dive bar, me stumbling, playing pool against myself. We talked, he leaned in, and we were both staying at the exact same Motel 6, both traveling through, not from this SoCal town. He was about 850 miles into his PCT journey, walking away from his past in the gangs of Florida, hoping to figure out what work could be more fulfilling for him. I sensed a desire for something better in him. Amazing, I'd drunk-thought; we had so much in common.

"You're mad sexy," he said, and I was flattered he'd noticed me, thought I must be his type. We walked along the highway, back to our motel together. He never took my hand but placed his flat palm against my bottom, held it there, occasionally patting as I stepped, pushing sometimes as I slowed.

That night he undressed me fast and without care, tossed each item of my clothes on the bed, the rug, the beige-tile floor of his motel room's bathroom as he nudged me in. We had sex on the cool linoleum. There were three other guys in the motel room, asleep. When I gasped he thought it was from pleasure and covered my mouth with his hand and told me to shut up and thrust thrust thrust my hip against the toilet's cold base until he saw the blood and said, "*Fuck*. Period," and I said, "No. It's my first time," and he stopped thrusting, stopped.

He said, "No. Really, why?"

I thought I should have told him before, felt bad and whispered "Sorry," sorry. I didn't say that I'd been putting it off, saying no for years, waiting for someone I loved so it would mean "I love you," so I wouldn't feel sorry after.

He asked if I wanted to keep going. I said, "Yes, until you come," because that was the thing to do, I thought. Because I didn't want to have to say that, my first time, the guy didn't even like me enough to come.

I was never cool. I loved Kay Ryan poems and solitude and snow. I loved wildflowers, wilderness, running fast. Winter more than summer. The music of my nerdy father's bygone days. I'd allowed one irrational fear—a stupid thought—to hurt me, take me, stain me forever: the thought that I'd be taunted in college if I were still a virgin. The thought that anyone would care one plum, care at all.

The ridiculous belief let me give it all up, give up, loosen my grip.

As I curled up in my bed that second night of college, I kept wondering: what if sex with Tyler allowed Junior into me? I hadn't been too drunk to say no to Tyler; I could have stopped it. He hadn't forced me. I just hadn't wanted to be the girl I was: innocent, a child. And like that, that fast, after years waiting, saying, "Wait," keeping it, it was gone to a stranger. No love. Just terribly sorry. Motel 6. My blood. I would never, ever be spotless-me again. I'd rot, was rotten, felt sick, dizzy, mad.

Maybe, if I hadn't lost it to Tyler, I would have gotten Junior to leave. What if my compliance, then hesitation, would have instead been stiffness and great, penis-taming rage. What if sex with Tyler took from me not just my virginity but my mind, my judgment, my facility to say no and sound convincing. What if—and this seemed too true to refute—had I not had sex with Tyler, I'd not have ended up alone, stoned, with a boy I didn't know. If the first sex hadn't happened, the rape wouldn't have happened, either. I would never have let Junior stay.

I wanted to be clean and safe, in control of my sexuality. I associated such security with virginity. If I hadn't tried to be so cool, so okay with being alone with a boy and drugs and night, none of this would have ever happened.

After the boy left that night, I pulled back on the same underpants and slept in them, and in the morning found two red-black spots of blood on the white cotton, the only physical sign I'd been raped, altered physically forever. The floor was still quiet, it was early and dark, and in a stall in the dormitory's huge girls' bathroom I removed them, held them in my hands under the bright fluorescent lights, my face hot and my hands hot. I did not move. The sun came up. Two, three hours passed and the sky lightened and went blue. Other girls came in and out, laughing, brushing their teeth. I sat on the toilet in my stall with the underwear in my hands, staring at the marks of blood. I couldn't erase the image in my shut eyes of these two terrible seeds that stained them.

The proof.

On their second night at college, my parents met.

On my second night at college, I was raped.

The next day, I saw him on the big green field for our freshman class photo. There were five hundred of us, but I saw only him. I didn't know what to say. I said, "Hi." He didn't look at me and didn't say anything and wandered away as if he were just deaf and dumb as a mopey dog. I told Katherine what had happened after she left and Junior stayed. She gently hugged me. She asked me if I wanted her older boyfriend to beat Junior up for me. I didn't.

I had never been taught how one was supposed to handle rape. The plain word—"rape"—felt unreal to claim.

I didn't call my parents.

Two dim weeks later, I went to the college's rape counselor.

She was sure she could help. She offered me a blue lollipop—I placed it under my tongue—and said, "Sit, hon." The office was tidy but windowless, and I remember she had three colorful boxes of Kleenex, lined up on the little table beside my chair. I remember her modest gold wedding band, her plump lips and chocolate eyes. She was beautiful. I told her everything. She encouraged me to pursue the matter through the college's mediation process. It was too late for physical evidence of rape to still exist, she explained, and so the police would be unable to help me. But we would get a "conviction." Junior would get expelled.

She typed up my account of the night, gave me peach-colored tissues to absorb my soundless tears.

I hugged my sides and rocked myself in her plush "guest" chair.

CHAPTER 3

Blood on the Tracks

I had no proof that Junior had raped me. I had to testify at an internal Colorado College hearing, in a beige conference room at a long folding plastic table with the rape counselor and the mediator and the mediator-in-training (she was observing)—and me. The mediator confirmed, "You smoked dope with him." She confirmed with me, "Nobody else saw it."

But of course there were no witnesses with us when it happened. I had no evidence. No physical signs of my rape existed anymore. My body had already purged them. That was the irreversible reality.

I told her yes, it was true. "We smoked a little, but I tried not to inhale."

She wrote something down. She held her eyes firm on the pad. "Marijuana is a hallucinogen," she said softly.

The implication: I had hallucinated a rape.

That was completely ridiculous. I wanted to cry out. I couldn't speak. I couldn't even swallow. The rape counselor handed me Junior's testimony.

Junior's testimony described graphically how I said he could titty-fuck me. I was shivering; my throat was closing, my cheeks burning. Though he'd lied in his omissions, all these things Junior described were true. I gasped to breathe. I felt horribly guilty, horrified I had asked him to do that, that I'd believed if I offered him that, he wouldn't take more. I'd be safe. Now in daylight, sober, it made no sense. I felt in my gut I'd done something absolutely unforgivable. I had offered, "You can titty-fuck me if you want to." Now how could this be rape?

But Junior did not claim that we'd had consensual sex. He wrote I'd wanted him to lie with his head on my breasts; he'd done that. Then I had wanted for him to titty-fuck me. He wrote he'd thought to himself it was strange of me to want for him to titty-fuck me, but he'd done that for me. He'd never been asked to do that before. He'd done it. Then he had left. We had not had sex. I probably wanted to, but he didn't. Instead he'd left me in my new room, safe and alone. That was the very most astonishing part of everything he wrote. I couldn't process it. He wrote simply that we had never had sex at all.

The mediator spoke. She said that, by her judgment of the events of that night, what exactly had happened was "inconclusive." I was softly humming as she said it, thinking, "Oh I know where I can find you/In somebody's room/It's a price I have to pay/You're a big girl all the way" from *Blood on the Tracks*, lyrics of "You're a Big Girl Now." I realized she was finding Junior innocent of rape. That meant that I was guilty of lying. I hardened my cheeks and the little muscles behind my eyes. I saw dust suspended. I couldn't see my hands. I could not move. I was not sure what the next move was. I didn't think there was a next move.

In the bed he'd raped me in, I curled into the fetal position. My box of books from home was just feet from my limp body, still unopened. I couldn't cry. I stretched and touched my phone. I lightly pushed MOM, listened to the ringing, breathed. I would tell her. I had to.

I honestly hadn't been thinking about how sad or horrified my mother might feel, learning that her Doll Girl had been hurt—but of how I knew, in her eyes, I had just completely confirmed all of her fears about me. And I was devastated I had.

Her assessment was that I had poor judgment, and my rape had immediately confirmed it. I believed that the rape had erased all of the progress I'd made in my time hiking and proved my mother right. Immediately. I was hurting with not only the shame of the rape, but also the shame of feeling I'd wanted to prove myself a valid, independent person—but I couldn't.

I told her only, "I said, 'Slow down' and then, 'Stop it.' I was frozen." I left out the marijuana. I left out the titty-fuck.

She was absolutely silent as I spoke. I imagined her in our Newton home. She was sixty-two, still agile, hair now mourning dove gray. I waited through a muteness. I worried learning her baby daughter was raped had startled her. I worried it had killed her. Slow moments passed. But then she spoke.

"You need to speak about this with a counselor," she said flatly. "My mother knows a psychologist who's on Weber Street." She told me she would find the information for me immediately.

Immediately—now I remained quiet through the line.

"Debby?"

"That isn't necessary." I said, "I've already spoken to someone at school."

Her tone changed, I sensed it in her breathing: inaudible, as usual—lighter. I waited for her to say something more. I didn't want her practical support, I wanted comfort. At last she spoke again. "Did you have a good dinner?"

I felt I'd just been slapped. I quickly shut my phone.

I couldn't believe her strange irrelevant question. I wished I hadn't told her. I wished I could go back in time and decide not to. The air in my room tasted rancid, of damp dirty socks and old dried period blood. But I wasn't on my period. I couldn't breathe this air. My phone lit up—MOM—but I didn't answer. I had to go outside, get out, right away.

I wandered up the block to the Conoco convenience store and

bought a one-pound bag of Jolly Ranchers, the pink watermelon kind, and chain-popped them as I walked to the river. It was sleek and black, carving gracefully north to Denver. I imagined not stopping, just stepping north, reaching all the way to Denver, sleeping whenever I got tired, in the river's silent bushes, hidden, unmonitored— the insanity and liberation in that. White aspens and the yellow dirt path falling: swallowed up by night.

I had expected my mother to be sad, hurt—devastated. This wooden reaction was not what I was expecting at all. Her stiffness hurt. It shocked me as much as my rape had.

I thought of my brother Jacob, wanted his advice.

Going into my first year of middle school, awkward and terrified, I'd asked Jacob what would happen if no one liked me; he'd told me to sign up for lots of clubs, to try new things and try to learn as much as I could. When I'd been nervous the new school would be too hard for me, Jacob had assured me: I'd been one of the smartest kids at Bowen Elementary, and I'd be one of the smartest kids at Oak Hill, too. It would be the same kids. I would be okay.

That made good sense to me. I took great comfort in this. Jacob was right. I could trust my brother.

Now Jacob would know what to do.

Four weeks after the rape, Jacob flew out to Colorado Springs; I couldn't wait to finally see him. We'd had a fight the last time we'd talked, and I was nervous—the air between us had felt cold— but I hoped we could move past it now. I needed him. I hadn't told him about what happened my second night at school. He remained happily ignorant. And I knew that truly he'd come out to Colorado not for me but to campaign for Obama—it was late September 2008, and Colorado was a swing state—and autumn was Jacob's off-season, after the baseball year had ended, before the beginning of spring training in February. But I believed maybe he'd chosen Colorado Springs because I was there.

I planned how I would tell him—in my grandparents' old baby blue Cadillac, on a long drive through golden, trembling aspens, up in mountains the color of morning sky. I'd tell him: some bad news. *Very* bad news. He'd listen, and wind would rustle the aspens, their bark impossibly white, and the season's first snow would slip down, gracefully like a car spinning off on ice and into a soft snowbank. Bright flakes would pile in long mounds on the colorless aspen branches. The roads of frozen yellow dirt crisscrossing outward in a wild, infinite system of ways to go.

I'd imagined he'd listen, saddened, heartbroken, and say, "I'm sorry. I love you. This doesn't change a thing." He'd squeeze my shoulder and rub my back, and we'd sit in silence, in comfort in the still car's heat, snowflakes gliding in the wind. My big brother would make me feel protected again.

It didn't happen like that. He'd arrived while I was away, backpacking in Canyonlands, Utah, with a small pack of freshmen on an Outdoor Recreation Club orientation trip. He stayed at my grandparents' ranch house, three miles off campus, his first couple of nights and then, the night I got back, he met me on the green. I was carrying my backpack, all my stuff dusty with desert dirt. He hugged me and I held him. He was here to campaign for Obama. I needed him here, for me. I was safer knowing he was here. For a moment on the green, dusty and exhausted under the yellow walkway lamps, I felt better, good, like things were on the upswing, like Jacob could fix things.

I did tell him in the baby blue Cadillac. We were not in aspens, but on the Colorado College campus. We were talking about where to get dinner—José Muldoon's Tex-Mex or just sandwiches. He did listen, quiet. We were parked on the southern edge of the campus, near my freshman dormitory. An ambulance's lights were spinning red and bright blue in the distance, a far-off catastrophe. We sat isolated from it, in the car, the heat humming, not hearing the siren or knowing or caring all too much about whoever out there needed help.

"Can I tell you something?" I'd said, knowing already that I'd started wrong; my tone was casual, creating dissonance. Jacob had seemed irritated tonight, hungry, and we'd been talking about nothing substantial. I already regretted starting now, this way. Though I couldn't unspeak.

He waited. "Yeah?"

"I got raped on my second night at school," I said fast, so fast I was unsure he would hear it.

"Like," he said, his face tinted red, then blue, then red, silently changing in the ambulance's far light. "Like, how?"

My eyes watered. I didn't know the right thing to say, now.

"I'm sorry," my brother said, "but how did that happen?"

I didn't want to tell the story. I didn't know how to tell the story.

Jacob asked me if I'd kicked him. I whispered, "No." I was crying, though I didn't know if my brother saw. He wasn't looking at me. He was looking out the windshield, toward the darkness, maybe at the ambulance, which was still there, lights spinning on, taking too long.

"Did you even scream?" he asked. He couldn't understand how it had happened, how I had let it happen, how someone could rape me, how I could be alone with someone who would rape me.

I was silent. I felt I'd just been erased, whited out like an embarrassing typo, my mouth filling with snow.

Then, he asked, "Do you want me to beat him up for you?"

All I said to that, all I could say, was "No."

I hardly saw Jacob for the rest of his six-week stay in Colorado Springs. He was very busy, but he tried to make time for me. I tried to avoid him. I was still angry—I hated that he'd made me feel I had to defend myself when I told him about my rape. But before he left, we took a nighttime walk around Colorado College's campus.

Strolling the green beside him, I felt frumpy and fat—I felt almost apologetic about my appearance. My hair was a tangled brown mess of curls, and I was wearing the same sweatpants I'd had on for days, maybe a week. I confessed to him—I'd felt unattractive since middle school. I told him I was now absolutely ugly, since the rape.

He told me I had to be blind. "Debby, you were a cute kid," he said. He told me his girlfriend had seen a picture of me from when I was a little girl and commented how pretty I was. "You look the same now."

I squinted at my brother. I'd never worn makeup, always wore glasses. High school boys at Newton South had never seen me. They weren't sweet to me. They didn't treat me special, hold doors or pick up my dropped pencils like they did for the more popular—prettier—girls. I told him, "I've actually always been ugly."

Jacob told me I was simply wrong. "You're just not pulling out any of the stops."

The "stops," apparently, were getting contact lenses, a better haircut, and maybe mascara or something like that. "What girls wear," he said. "Like lipstick."

"Like lipstick," I repeated. I had done that.

That I could do.

But I couldn't put contacts in. I could not do it. No one would get to see what Jacob saw: that, secretly, I was pretty. It was something only Jacob knew, and he told me, and I heard and smiled but didn't yet believe that it was true.

"You're beautiful," he said.

He was sweet and affirming. I remained cold.

I said that he looked different now—he looked shorter to me.

He had wanted to be the bigger person, and, in my hurting, in bitterness I'd cut him smaller.

For the rest of his six-week stay in Colorado Springs, Jacob slept at my grandparents', in my mother's childhood bedroom. He became a manager at Obama's Manitou Springs headquarters. I hardly saw him, just two more times. He was very busy.

When Obama won, Jacob had his own party to go to—one for his campaigners. I wasn't invited. Then he left and drove back east. He would play professional baseball that summer under bright lights before exhilarating crowds. I wouldn't go to any of his games.

They allowed Junior to stay on campus. Then, just weeks after he had been found innocent, the college removed him from his room in the other big dorm on the other side of campus—they didn't explain why—and moved him into my dorm, a single on the floor above me. On the stairs I sometimes saw him. I passed him in the hall; he lived next door to Katherine, who had become my only friend. I saw him on my way out to class, at breakfast or in the middle of the day when I came home to put down my class stuff and lie down. He never seemed to notice me.

The college's rape counselor helped me to find new housing. I had an "immediate need." Campus Housing called me. "There's no singles in the dorms left," said a husky alto voice. I could choose between a forced triple—three girls in a double—or a room of my own off campus, farther from him.

I said, "The one farther away, I think."

She said, "Great! That's good. Okay." Then she hung up.

And so Junior remained on campus, in my building. I dumped the contents of my dressers into heavy-duty trash bags, stuffed my dresses like garbage into the bags, hangers and all. I was promptly relocated into the Colorado College Inn, an off-campus "space" for students who got bad numbers in the housing lottery—or kids who got not-so-bad numbers but really, really wanted to be alone. Students had named it the Cinder-block Palace. I hauled my trash bags one by one to my new room by myself. By bag three, halfway between the two rooms, my arms were trembling. I dragged it for a minute more and stopped, sat down on the wide sidewalk with my stretch-marked garbage bag. I was wearing sweatpants I hadn't washed in months, a stained yellow sweatshirt that said Colonials—my big brother's old college baseball team—in faded cursive letters.

Moving in my belongings, I saw few people in the hallway, not one single girl. A boy, here and there. Near-all the rooms in this building, it turned out, contained young men. My neighbor, a skinny hermit, had fake blood smeared across his hallway window. I hoped I'd never see him.

My new room was my cave among strange stranger-students' caves: all shadowed and dank, a motel for hiding in darkness. White paint peeled off the wooden toilet lid and exposed bleached naked wood; the paint that still clung to the lid cracked and separated from the wood and rippled, bile yellow near the crack edges. I felt as yellow as this place, as fucked, as sad.

The bedroom was carpeted with short gray-blue loops of the roughest weave—part plastic—sealed to the cinder-block walls with a black-tar rubber. I would lie on my back in the narrow bed and stare for hours at the blank ceiling, the whitewashed cinder-block walls, thinking about why I was here, why I'd been moved to the CC Inn. I felt banished, punished for what he'd done. I'd been tricked—this horrid place was, in fact, not even far from my old dorm. It was just across the street, behind the Conoco gas station, always in the shade. It didn't feel safer. It didn't feel safer at all.

I lay there, angry and scared, realizing finally that my school would not help me. The rape counselor didn't. My parents couldn't. I had to help myself. I had to leave this place.

More than anything, I thought about my mommy. I felt she abandoned me.

In my lightless room I dialed the Rape, Abuse & Incest National Network's hotline. The line rang; a nameless woman quickly answered. The hotline was anonymous, the voice could have been any woman anywhere; I could have been anybody, too. She wouldn't know. So I told her about the weed, my momentary attraction to Junior, his thick pink fingers, the titty-fuck thing—everything. I confessed: before he'd raped me, I'd liked him.

My heart revved as I said it. My judgment must be awful, she would think. My mother was right; I had bad judgment. I had told him he could titty-fuck me; everywhere above my pink short shorts, he could kiss me. How could I have wanted that? How could I have trusted a rapist? Somehow I had. I used the woman on the hotline like a priest.

She stayed on the line with me for hours as I spoke, listening; she whispered, "I'm here," as I cried. Her invisible presence softened the hard pain that gripped my stomach. She told me that my rape was not my fault, that I should feel no shame, that—simple as it may sound—I hadn't caused it. No one causes rape but rapists. No one causes rape but rapists. No one causes rape but rapists. It was true. And it had not been obvious to me. And hearing it from someone else, a professional, someone who should know, helped me believe that soon I would believe it.

My shoulder blades unclenched. I felt like it was night and I was lost, but I at last had a path out of the woods, and dawn was going to break. It always did.

It wasn't my fault, it wasn't my fault, it was not my fault.

The spring semester began; I enrolled in new courses. It was a fresh semester, a new year. Soon I would turn nineteen. I would try to have a party. People would begin to notice me.

My classes were exactly the subjects I'd wanted. They sounded interesting; lucky me. Things weren't so awful. I tried hard to feel grateful and relieved. I was *lucky*. I was back at school, free; I was okay. I was.

My tasks were manageable, miniscule: study cool things with smart people; pass the exams. Each morning, brush your teeth; repeat each night. Remember to eat. Sleep when you're sleepy. I went to my class each morning, punctual, prepared for discussions. I read my readings, watched the required films. It was regimented and very clear; it was easy.

I would call my mom and tell her how well I was doing, how I was in control, handling things.

She would act happy, but her questions would always make me feel out of control. She would tell me how I should budget my time to finish my work on time.

The season warmed and frost-gemmed walls slowly thawed: dulled by winter's old dirt. I tried to act cheerful. I felt only exhausted, numb.

The spring brightened like a Technicolor fever and I dutifully studied for Film Theory, but by then I hated class. The films and critics' essays didn't captivate me. The clinical white walls of my dorm depressed me. I could watch the films in my room on my lit laptop, but I couldn't escape into them. I needed different stories. I needed stories of escape.

I flicked my pocketknife open. My dad had given it to me when I turned ten; I'd been a Girl Scout then. The blade was dirty, gunked with gray stickiness, though I hardly used it. I knelt; the walls of my room were at once purely white and very dim. I cut open the dented box of books I'd brought from home, labeled "Debby's Books— Personal." It was filled with the adventure books my mommy had once read me. Then I noticed, shoved in a back corner of the box, a cracked, brown spine marked *Travels in Alaska*.

My breathing stilled as I picked it up in my dark dorm room, so far from the life I imagined when I found this book, from the freedom I'd felt on Muir's trail only months ago. I looked out my window and saw the Conoco gas station that blocked my sight of the trees. There was no trace of nature around me. I'd come to this college hoping to be close to the wilderness, close to my favorite camping grounds, close to my happiest memories, and I had none of it now.

I reopened *Travels in Alaska*.

I was so comforted and hopeful, having it in my hands again, and I reread it with a headlamp through the night. He wrote, "Come to the woods, for here is rest. There is no repose like that of the green deep woods. Sleep in forgetfulness of all ill."

Dawn broke. That next day I felt better, hopeful and entirely safer. I remembered family hikes on trails through aspen forests, along high ridges, down to valley-lakes. The trails were veins, the mountainscape a body infinitely beautiful and novel. My family was harmonious in the woods. I longed to return to them, to then. My wild little tribe.

That morning, giddy, having just finished rereading the old copy of *Travels in Alaska,* I called my father. I told him that I'd taken the book. I asked him where it had come from, what it'd meant to him and Mom. Maybe years ago, when they'd picked up this book, they would've understood my longing to walk into the wilderness.

He said: "You have it?" He repeated back to me: "By Muir?" Then he said he'd never read it, hadn't known they'd had it. He'd never even heard of it.

I had been called to adventure since childhood, always; I heard the call. I thought back to the freedom of my summer—my happiness, alone in mountains.

Muir promised: "In God's wildness lies the hope of the world—the great fresh unblighted, unredeemed wilderness. The galling harness of civilization drops off, and wounds heal ere we are aware."

Slowly I began to picture myself finally walking the Pacific Crest Trail, the 2,650-mile-long continuous footpath from Mexico to Canada, the path through America's last long, quiet strip of wilderness. The Pacific Crest Trail. In that sad winter that path was the place my mind fixed on. I thought of Goethe: "At the moment of commitment, the universe conspires to assist you."

Muir whispered: "Go quietly, alone; no harm will befall you."

I answered yes. Yes! I would go.

CHAPTER 4

The Things I Carried

The Pacific Crest Trail crosses California, Oregon, and Washington state—from Mexico all the way to Canada. It would take a person of average height and gait about six million steps to walk the footpath's length. It passes through twenty-six national forests, seven national parks, five state parks, and three national monuments—the terrain varies wildly.

Class was nine A.M. to noon every day, and each day straight after, I'd stride past my idle peers to my motel room—my laptop—to google the PCT.

I learned that ideally the time to hike across the desert was in winter. But then I'd reach the foothills of the High Sierra in the springtime—too early. If I entered into the Sierras prematurely—before mid-June—the mountains would be buried beneath mounds of winter's accumulated snow—impassable. The time to begin at Mexico was spring, to set myself up to arrive in Sierra Nevada in the middle of June. But I had to move quickly—by October the trail through Washington would be erased by new snowfall, the pine trees bent, snapping below snow's weight. In late September or early October each year, hikers who haven't yet crossed into Canada are snowed out.

That meant I had twenty-two available weeks to attempt to walk

2,650 miles. Five months. I'd have to average over twenty miles per day. But of course I would have to face some storms; I could expect that in the Sierras and Cascades I may have days I could walk all day but only cover ten or fifteen miles. Which meant, on the easier sections of trail, I'd need to hike thirty-mile days. This weather window seemed almost impossibly narrow.

I googled: "Hike the entire PCT. When to begin?" To my shock I found there was a real answer. It was a send-off party in the remote desert directly on the Pacific Crest Trail, about twenty miles north of the Mexico border. It was called Kickoff, an annual massive party timed to match the melting snow, where people hoping to walk the whole trail began. I wasn't the only one.

The party was always in late April, always at a dry campground in the desert called Lake Morena County Park. I clicked through photos of rows of little olive green tents, of red coolers of canned beer, hamburgers grilling, potato salad slopped in tin baking pans atop checkered red-and-white-draped picnic tables—all swarmed by men in sun-faded dress shirts, fueling up and braced to attempt the same journey I had just conjured from this blank-walled shit-motel.

It seemed so remarkably—impossibly—perfect: a big send-off party for people who wanted to do exactly what I wanted to do.

I read dispatches from the wilderness—from people I wanted to find and join and walk with north. From this suffocating space I escaped into the Mojave Desert: vast and windblown, petrified, my laptop the only light in the dank dim room.

There was a PCT vernacular. I wanted to become fluent in it. If you attempt to walk the entire trail through in one continuous hike, you're called a thru-hiker. Thru-hikers accept help from trail angels, kindly local folks who live in the tiny trail-towns.

Every new thru-hiker gets a trail name, but you can't give one to yourself; it must be earned—bestowed on you by another thru-hiker, or a trail angel. You usually get your name from some defining characteristic of yours or from something stupid you've done. This was the custom. I read about one man who sewed and stuffed his own goose down sleeping bag, except his stitches were loose and too spaced out, so every morning he'd wake up covered with little goose down feathers. That was Chicken Fucker.

I discovered a lively online discussion forum on which hikers and "armchair thru-hikers" debated in a frenzy all things Pacific Crest Trail-related. It seemed the most-referenced gear guru was a man named Ray Jardine, the granddaddy of ultralight theory. His idea: less is better; carry just only what's necessary.

I joined the Facebook group Pacific Crest Trail Class of 2009. *Classes*, like college.

I Facebook-friended people who had thru-hiked the trail—"PCT Class of 2008," "PCT Class of 2007"—and messaged them question after question as they occurred to me. Dozens of hikers gave me dozens of tips. I always wrote back and I always said "thank you" and meant it truly. I asked: "What should I carry to filter the creek water—a pump?" (Nothing. Trail water's pretty clean.) "Is it safe for me to go the whole way alone?" A man who called himself Never-Never had publicly answered: *Alone is safe,* and then he'd found me on Facebook and requested to be my friend. I'd accepted him.

He had hiked a long and rugged segment of the Continental Divide Trail, which also extends from Mexico to Canada, but through the states in the middle of the country—and next he planned to thru-hike the PCT. We chatted happily about long trails. I escaped into the stories he told.

We began to talk on the phone. In the real world he was an aspiring photographer, and also a line cook at a burger joint. He was in his middle-twenties, lived in a coastal town in New Jersey. We talked about our lives, and our dreams, why we didn't belong where we lived, why wilderness would be better. We were both mountain people in our hearts. The PCT was a solid path out of our lives, a place that existed—and Never-Never knew the way.

It turned into phone sex. I'd pretend with him that I was wearing sexy clothes I didn't actually believe I'd look good in. He'd ask me what I was doing, I faked breathy orgasms, told him how I touched my clit, wanting freedom, the mountains, beautiful sunsets and fire, I wanted the world, wanting terribly to be a feral child.

I liked knowing that it was wild of me.

In the privacy of my motel room, I'd click through his profile photos, writing him back, as night darkened around my untouched bed, as the cicadas silenced and the streetlights blinked out, sometimes even until dawn. On Valentine's Day a huge red velvet heart-shaped box of Godiva chocolates came in the mail with a note that said his real name on it: Phillip. Next he sent me two inflated photographs of places I had seen online and said I liked, already framed. He'd taken them. I sent him clear marbles I'd "made" by baking them in the oven and then dropping them immediately into ice water; the insides would crack, the outsides would remain undamaged.

He ended it. He called our correspondence "too much of a roller coaster" for his heart—and it had shocked me how little I'd felt. I didn't cry, or even feel like I'd lost someone. In truth, I felt relieved. I had been telling him about other boys who liked me who hadn't existed. I'd invented them because the idea that I would someday have to meet this man in flesh had begun to scare me. I'd become worried about what he might expect once we met offline.

I wanted to start fresh when I arrived at Kickoff, a new and unknown girl. I was happy to have stumbled upon a subculture with its own language, vibrant, distant, exotically and seductively different from suburban Colorado.

The Pacific Crest Trail. I searched for it again. Again the simple red-stricken black-and-white drawing appeared, and I selected it again, a simple path, the original image of the journey I had seen. It was unforgettable: that jagged bright red line through shades of gray. In lonely night dreams I heard the pat of feet on a shadowed forest path leading over slick rocks, past rare ruby birds that would whistle dissonant tunes like the music in dark fairy tales and swoop down to rest on my open palm, a message for me encrypted in their song.

A tribe of one, I'd cowboy-camp, body relaxed, right on dirt trail, or curl up nights in a field of buttercups glowing gold beneath a snowdrift-colored moon, floating low, impossibly huge.

The sky in my tinted hallway window blushed, lightened. Days bled into one other until I wrote in my journal, *This is my last Friday at CC.*

I was cupping a hot white mug of steaming peppermint tea, and I stepped outside in the same sweatpants and sweatshirt I'd worn the day before and day before that. I walked over a new dusting of snow in my running shoes, happy for the first time since I'd arrived out here for school. I had decided: I was going to hike the whole Pacific Crest Trail. I was done here, free of Colorado College.

I felt the seed of something strong sprout something real in me and felt a surge. I'd be in the woods, homeless, walking north with my fellow self-exiled desert pilgrims. I'd be a dropout.

I had nothing left to lose.

I had many things to determine, and quickly.

I would set off north from the Mexican border three days before Kickoff, I decided; I could walk the twenty miles from the border to Kickoff with time to spare.

I needed to decide what I'd carry with me for the next five months, what weight was worth bearing on my back. The daunting reality was that, in order to keep moving and slip through the narrow weather window, I would need my backpack to be very light.

Thru-hikers need to carry base weight—the heft of everything in your fully packed backpack that isn't edible—plus the weight of all their food and water. The amount of water on my back would vary from none (where frequent streams gush) to up to a gallon— eight pounds!—in the desert. I estimated each day I'd need to eat roughly two pounds of food, maybe an ounce or so less. So my starting pack weight each leg of the hike would be my base weight plus two pounds of food per day and that day's water weight. The strain of additional weight rapidly makes backpacking painful and, in some cases, damaging to tendons and ligaments. So every ounce, every gram of weight you carry has to be necessary.

The question is: what is necessary?

The trail-alumni's list of things I shouldn't carry was exactly everything I'd believed I'd need:

1. *Don't wear hiking boots.* If you walk in heavy leather boots, three pounds each and stiff, you will get blisters. Thru-hikers wear modified running shoes that weigh one pound apiece.

2. *You don't need extra food, extra water, extra clothing for extra warmth—anything extra. You don't need soap or deodorant.*

   Everything you carry you should need daily. Take an ultralight sleeping bag, know you'll be chilly some nights, leave the sweater home—if you're cold you'll get into your sleeping bag. No change of clothes or a bar of soap (which pollutes the streams)—everybody will smell like themselves.

   The only item worth carrying that won't be necessary every day is a heavy-duty trash bag with a head hole cut out. This is "rain gear."

3. *Don't bring a stove or a pot*—the type of freeze-dried food you could have cooked on the trail is disgusting and not as nutritious and calorie efficient as nuts, cheese, dark chocolate.

4. *You don't need a headlamp or a flashlight, or batteries. You don't even need a knife, or a first-aid kit.*

5. *You don't need maps. No compass.* The path will be clear.

   That one perplexed me.

   I'd just have to trust that one.

I doubted I could survive in the woods without these very basic things to help me. It seemed like a tremendous leap of faith to forsake the tools I'd always been told I needed.

And yet leaving college to walk was such a massive leap of faith already, and nothing I'd ever trusted and believed in seemed true any longer.

There was someone whom I did still trust, though. He came to me and I felt instantly safer.

John Muir.

I rushed back to Muir, his books, maps of his treks. I found that when Muir hopped cities' fences and ventured up into foothills, to mountains, he took with him just a blanket and a loaf of bread and sometimes a small "quantity of tea." He made it sound so easy. Clean and simple. It sounded impossible, impossibly liberating. I felt the pull of ultralightness, desire to not need things, to go light, to be lighter. I was drawn to John Muir's minimalist approach to preparing for adventure, the faith, the magic: trust the mountains and they will foster you.

I was five feet four, and weighed about 120. My comfort weight was about twenty-four pounds. That was all the weight I could bear to carry to Canada. That meant my base weight should be eleven. In reality, if I carried a burden much greater than Muir's, I wouldn't make it.

Me, and wilderness, and eleven little pounds of things.

With so little to depend on, this walk would teach me how to take care of myself. I'd learn to build my tent and sleep in the shelter I had made. Each cold morning I would dress myself. There'd be no one to do it for me. I hoped through all this, I would lose the post-rape fat I'd gained. I hoped to learn why my mother couldn't hear me. I'd felt despair and needed her wisdom and love. I wanted the trail to carry me to answers that would restore everything sacred, obliterate my confusion and my shame.

Already, this little-walked gigantic trail through my country's Western wilderness held in my mind the promise of escape from myself, the liberation only a huge transformation could grant me. This walk would be my salvation. It had to be.

In spring it rained. Mornings in the Cinder-block Palace I awoke to a threatless blue sky and by afternoon each day the sky was bruised with clouds and dark. Then it would rain fat drops. The biggest raindrops I'd ever seen. This smacking would last for two hours or maybe three, and on the third straight day of afternoon rain I came home from class and the carpet was marshy from halfway down the hall, water spreading from under my locked door. I opened it. What seemed like a foot of water poured into the hall. My lamp reflected in the carpet like the moon.

I called my mom.

In the rain I told her my room had flooded—I was yelling so I could hear myself—and to hold on, hold on; let me get under the sheet-metal awning, here, the gas station. Okay. Yes, Mommy, *come.*

She said she loved me and she missed me all the time, and of course she would come back out to me. She'd get a ticket to Colorado, the next available.

Then I yelled over the downpour, an afterthought, a thought I'd had a thousand times but now intensely believed was the truth: "I'm leaving school, Mom. I'm going hiking on the Pacific Crest Trail, 'kay, 'bye!" I hung up before she could answer.

I jogged through the warm rain, huge drops breaking, breaking on me, hitting, harder, mixing with my streaming tears, entirely obscuring them.

From the shelter of the student union I called my father to tell him I was unimpressed by school and cold in Colorado, even in April. It still felt like December. I told him I needed a physical task, something concrete to do. I had never talked about my rape with him, but I assumed he knew. I believed that my mother would have told him. I told him flatly that I was dropping out. I was quitting college to walk from Mexico to Canada and be alone.

My father inhaled, exhaled loudly; I waited. He inhaled again, everything suddenly audible, the student union was largely empty— pool table set up for play, the colored balls balanced in a tidy triangle, poised to be hit—and I felt like I was shrinking. "You're doing that," he said finally. "Debby, tell me what you expect will happen."

What did I expect. I had to make a case. There were a thousand past permutations of me that I hated. I thought immediately of my body. I wanted to shed it, be fit, transform: revert backward to what it had once been. I wanted to traverse America's wilderness—great and fresh, unblighted, unredeemed—and become powerful.

I wanted to shock my mother. To terrify her; that satisfied me. I felt wickedly defiant. I'd shed my dependence on her, would fully, purely and completely escape her.

Yet I also wanted to revive my bond with her. I wanted her to once again see me as her Doll Girl, beautiful again, lovable. Not damaged, marred and shameful. I saw all the best moments of my childhood. The trail seemed the only path back to them.

The raindrops had stopped falling. I stepped out of the student union's glass doors, someone had propped them open, out to the open green. By the brick admissions building, desert roses were opening, the softest silky pink, beads of rain on their curled petals glistening like gems in the new sun. The ivy that gripped the brick had turned electric green.

The shock of spring saddened me. This was the time of year I'd be studying madly, being tested, excelling, elegantly completing my first year away with As. I felt robbed of all the achievements I'd failed to earn. All the friendship and the love I hadn't found.

I answered my father only, "I expect to become happy eventually."

A cold wind gusted and the tiny roses rained. I wondered at what point in our call the downpour had finally stopped. To my shock he answered that he'd drive me to the Mexican border.

Then we said goodbye and also said, "I love you."

I slept that night on a couch in the common room of the old big freshman dorm where I'd been raped, feeling immune, my time here ending.

I woke to my phone ringing. It was my mother; she was already here for me. She'd flown directly into Colorado Springs' tiny airport and arrived on campus before I'd even woken. From the minute I'd called, it had taken her just twenty hours to get to me. "Doll Girl, good *morning* Deb-Deb," her voice cooed.

I was prepared to tell my mother I really was leaving.

My parents, both lawyers, had four advanced degrees between them. My oldest brother, Robert, was in law school. Jacob graduated from college an All-American and was promptly drafted by the New York Mets. I thought how both my parents and both my brothers not only went to school but earned prestigious distinctions, whereas I couldn't even finish my first college year. I wasn't finishing. I was dropping out of freshman year with only just five weeks left. I would be the family dropout, the failure. I was fucking up the whole family legacy.

My mother would resist. Any mother would. I knew I'd have to fight her. This time I had to beat her.

When I told her again in person, we were in the all-you-can-eat dining hall, having a wordless dinner. She was eating a bright plate with greens and beets from the local section of the salad bar. She had tried to make me one, too, but I had said no. I swallowed French fries with ketchup and chocolate cake with white soft-serve ice cream on top. She watched me. She'd never seen me eat like that.

I had gained ten pounds. She could see. She said so. She said, "You'll lose it on the trail, plus more. So you can eat however you want."

I looked up at her. So she was letting me go. It seemed impossible, remarkable.

She repeated again, again, again that I would lose it.

The next day we packed. In my ruined room my mother lunged from task to task, dried-out book to crusty mug, frantic, cleaning. Taking care of things.

In the hallway's hollow gray light I looked down at my belongings: clothing, plastic flip phone and its charger, laptop, all of my shoes. My things entirely blocked the hallway out.

I left a whole dorm room full of stuff and took only candy and Make Me Blush lipstick and myself.

It would be another year before I learned that what happened to my room was not caused by rain—the rain was merely a coincidence. The water that filled my room was not rain but waste. A sewage pipe had burst.

My mother took me to the R.E.I. on Colorado Springs's outskirts, and loaded the cart up with heavy unbreakable Nalgene branded water bottles, mittens, fleece hats she wanted to buy me—and I unloaded them all. On family backpacking trips my backpack had weighed half as much as I had. My parents wore gigantic backpacks, fifty pounds each at least, so heavy they'd be bent forward under the bulk. My dad had a bad back now. On this walk, I would carry none of that. I unloaded it all.

My mother stiffened, startled. Her eyes were open, huge and frantic. "They're water bottles, Debby," she said. "You'll need water?"

"No, fuck," I said. I was rude. "Just no." I told her thru-hikers use Gatorade bottles. Nalgenes are unnecessarily heavy. The backpack I insisted I wanted was a tiny neon green nylon knapsack.

Of course she didn't understand. She refilled the cart with everything I'd unloaded and bought it all, even as I insisted I would carry none of it.

We stayed back in my grandparents' ranch house, and my mom cooked for me; she'd cleaned up all my things, everything wrecked. I needed a one-way ticket to Los Angeles. She bought it for me. She took complete care of me. Yet she never asked how I was feeling, how I was coping, if the rape was screwing with my mind and self-image, if a mute space had formed in my head. I focused on a raindrop stuck on the side of a rusty pole, or my damp gray shoelaces.

I slept in the old house's basement; it was cool and smelled like turpentine and clay, it was drafty like a tornado shelter, wind knocking hard desert shrubs against the high strips of filthy window. A thousand trinkets, backyard's mint plants spreading like kindly weeds. The dirt in the yard smelled dank and sweet, of red rock, red clay, dust, thundershowers, childhood. That would be my last night in Colorado.

My mother drove me to the airport, told me, "Daddy will be waiting at the gate." He was using his vacation days to drive me to Mexico. It would be a father-daughter road trip to the border.

I told her this sounded good. I didn't ask her why she'd said nothing comforting back when, months before, I'd said: Mom, that's rape.

I landed in Los Angeles wearing my small knapsack filled with trail mix and granola bars and chocolate and cheese, an ultralight tent, sleeping bag and sleeping pad. My face was hot from crying in the air, my cheeks taut with dried tears. My dense pack was heavy and unwieldy on me, pulling me side to side. I swayed under it.

My father was at my gate, as promised. He looked smaller, stood leaning forward, crooked, in the car sat artificially straight as if he had been given an order he could not defy. He had slender limbs and a firm bulge of a gut, a curly mess of greasy mud black hair. Green eyes and puffy lips. Looking at him, I saw his lips were mine, my slender fingers his too. I saw myself in him, how far I was from him.

In the car we didn't talk much. We referred to my sadness, never "rape."

We stopped in San Diego, not on the way, but my dad thought it would be nice to see the water. We parked by a big and busy beach. Lots of surfers. I remember the sun, red at its center, golden white along its rim.

Swimmers bobbed in the water, their little heads dipping and rising and dipping, black shadows against that big red sun. The water looked drugged: black shot with pink and the silver you see in game shows.

My dad and I walked out, out a half mile at least into the ocean on a concrete jetty. We had squeezed through a gap in a chain-link fence, ignored a sign that said: Stop. Do Not Walk High Tide. Was it high tide? We weren't sure. The jetty was twenty feet wide at least and plain concrete like a flat sidewalk over the ocean, God knew how far out.

We just went.

We both noticed the water climbing up and up, our distance from the massive black surface shrinking. But we kept walking out. The flat, wide concrete disappeared. It looked like we were walking on water.

When the water splashed at our ankles, we turned back.

The rising ocean thick under our stepping shoes. The concrete no longer visible, only trackable by feel. With one long step—I'd thought I had been walking cut-blade straight—I raised a foot and dropped it off the edge. Fell back onto the jetty, soaking myself. My heart rushing. I was a five-minute run from the beach. If I'd stepped off all the way I could have drowned.

My father gasped, paused over me, gave me a hand up, and strode with me, pushing water, at my side.

We were almost swimming.

The rest of the way back I dragged my rubber shoe sole along the concrete corner-edge often, remembering it was there, remembering it was there. We made it back on land in a surge of adrenaline, in silence, the ocean lapping at our calves.

For dinner that night my dad and I went to an Italian restaurant at the bottom of a flight of big stone stairs. It felt fancy, but we were in a basement. Dad laid out for me the conditions of this walk. He explained that Mommy had a satellite telephone for me. I had to lean in to hear him. He said that it would work in desert, on remote glaciers, in Africa—anywhere—and Mommy would mail it to the post office in Warner Springs, the first little town the PCT would pass through, out in the Anza-Borrego Desert. It had cost my parents $1,500, so I should keep it protected in a waterproof bag. With it, I would be able to call my parents and report to them my GPS coordinates nightly, no matter what.

This was their only requirement. They would pay for my gear, mail me new running shoes to remote post offices along the trail, boxes of trail-food to far-off places, continue to pay off the credit card they'd given me for college. All I had to do was call them. Could I do that for them? I could, of course, Daddy.

I'd never slept in a room alone with my dad before that trip, and I felt his desperation, how desperately he wanted to keep me safe, to be my keeper, but that wasn't his job anymore. He was going to leave me in the desert. That was the only job for him now.

I knew leaving me at Mexico's edge would pain him. I didn't care.

Morning light glared like a spotlight on my face in my hotel bed. I blinked awake. Dust spun in the hot light, my hair was damp with sweat. Even in this clamorous air-conditioning. Outside must have been smoldering. I felt out of shape and lethargic, gently rocked my whole body, gaining enough oomph to sit up. I felt drained of energy. The desert sprawls from the Mexico border to the southern edge of the High Sierra Mountains—702 parched sun-scorched miles. It was dusty and expansive. I was in no shape to walk across it. But I was sitting up. Then, standing.

My dad was still sleeping, breathing deeply, his lips parted. My pack sat, open, gaping, empty of the eleven pounds I'd fill it with.

In the hotel room's bathroom, my dad still snoring, I stripped naked. My body was too pasty. I'd grown to hate it. It was time to dress myself in the clothing I would walk in.

I stepped into pink cotton Soffe shorts. I wasn't wearing underwear. I'd abandoned underwear eight months earlier, the morning after Junior had raped me. He had yanked them off me and so, the next morning breaking, in my little stall, I had yanked them off myself. I hadn't worn them since.

I pulled on socks, running shoes, laced them. I hooked my bra. I hated sports bras, they smushed breasts and made me feel at once confined and fat, and so I would hike in something I felt better in—a new wire-supported bra I'd found in a mall in Colorado Springs, at Victoria's Secret. It was lilac satin, a tiny white silk bow at the front clasp. I'd feel prettier in it. Then I pulled on a black long-sleeved half-cotton, half-synthetic running shirt, covering it. Put on a baseball cap from Jacob's old college team. In my pack I had a picture of Jacob on a baseball field, his stately profile. It would be the only photograph I carried.

Finally, I put on my prescription sunglasses. I'd worn glasses since third grade, each new year's pair thicker than the last, the glass distorting my huge child-eyes. With the glasses, the little compliments my mom would give me about my eyes became rare. My dad would sometimes say, sweetly teasing, "Let me see what you look like in your contact lenses," and I would take my glasses off, and he would say, "Looks good!" I would stand like that, holding my glasses awkwardly, not putting them down, walking around clumsily bumping into things, until after a minute, every time I would have to put them back on.

He'd sometimes tell me, "Men seldom make passes at girls who wear glasses." The verse was from a Dorothy Parker poem, and I used to think it was written by my grandma, my dad's mother, because she was Dorothy Parker, though her name was only a coincidence.

I grew to see glasses as unattractive.

I understood: if I could only wear contacts, I would look better. Until I could learn to touch my eyes, I feared I would never be seen in the way I might have been.

Now, instead, I looked at myself through the dark lenses. I would only carry the one pair—tinted—so that no one would know they were prescription.

I had the sense that something was missing. I looked like a girl ready to jog to a soccer scrimmage, not like a trans-country backpacker. Not like I was setting off to hike 2,650 miles through mountainous wilderness, alone. The only items of clothing I would take with me that I wasn't wearing were black spandex leggings and a fleece-lined wool hat.

Dressed in everything I thought I needed, I kneeled on the milk-colored carpet and transferred songs from my chunky white laptop on to my iPod. Songs were light. I added album after album I had loved. The Red Hot Chili Peppers, Ben Folds, Springsteen—but mostly Dylan. Albums uploaded quickly, more than a thousand songs. Songs weigh exactly nothing. I could carry all the ones I wanted to hear.

I added "Mississippi," "Moonlight," "Hurricane." I added "Date Rape" by Sublime, in which the rapist gets eternally anally raped in prison for what he did—the judge "knew he was full of shit"—a modern sort of ballad.

I hummed to myself. I was trying to stop hearing my dad's soft snoring.

There was so little I wanted to carry. Packing my backpack took me all of four minutes.

At the Tijuana-California border, my father filled my empty Gatorade bottles with water from a big jug he'd bought in San Diego.

They were a liter each, and I had five of them, as in the desert the air was dry and hot and water would be scarce. I sat on the minivan trunk and ate cold pizza left over from the night before in the candlelit Italian basement, took big bites too fast, my dad still filling up every water bottle I had.

He hugged me. I held him back, hopping awkwardly down. He had to leave me now. I would stay. It was what I had wanted. It was time.

My father started the rental car. He drove up the dirt road, north, away, his dust trail hanging, fully obscuring him. I was at Mexico's edge, alone, my own master, and the sky was boundless and empty and so intensely blue, sunspots deep red in my vision, my eyes straining to see better.

A big sandstone monument marked the southern terminus of the Pacific Crest Trail. The path looked unexceptional, just a three-foot-wide rut snaking through the dust, over a sandy hill and out of my range of vision. This was the beginning of something almost unending. I stepped down it.

Instead of walking, I ran. North along the dusty trail. I was out of shape and knew that my fast pace was not sustainable, but I wanted to get north fast, to get somewhere, and so I ran fast then slow then fast again—fiercely unsure—like a scared kid fleeing a house I suddenly hated.

The trail was marked with rusty signs. Scattered insects and reptiles basked in the sun. I felt I'd discovered a tiny unknown country: hills of dust like open ocean's swells.

The most gorgeous views appeared in rows like windows into my history. My vision seemed to brighten fiercely, as if it had awoken fully. Sunlit desert, uneven mountains in the distance. The ground I walked on was dried mud, cracked intricately like a window shattered but still intact. Touch it, and it would collapse to dust.

The bottles my father had filled felt heavy, the water still cool from CVS air-conditioning. I paused and unscrewed the top of one of the bottles, took a swig, wiped my full girlish lips, and tipped it and poured it out into the dust. The thread of water falling caught the sun like a band of silver as it slipped to the dry ground. The dirt was so dry and packed that it couldn't absorb the water. It beaded and then pooled up, lying in a small depression like a plate of sun. I poured out the next one, and then the next one, until my five liters had become just two.

Because this is what I knew: The first water source on my path was Hauser Creek, a small creeklet sixteen miles up the trail. It was one thirty in the afternoon, sun high and hot, air dry, ground dry and white as chalk. Now I had to walk sixteen miles through the desert to Hauser Creek. It wasn't a choice any longer. It was what I had to do now not to die.

I was running, faster. The notion of running to Canada from Mexico was ridiculous, I knew that, but then of course the notion of walking to Canada from here was almost equally ridiculous. It was all ridiculous. I was on a journey to solve a problem that had no solution. Matted, dirty hair and sunburn and sore quads—and deprivation—would be fun for a weekend, but this was a lifestyle. I'd chosen to be homeless for five months, to live in a tent, to be filthy and lonely. I couldn't walk off the rape, my brother's callous questioning, my mother's long deafness. My over-loving mother had become a wall. My easy road had become the Pacific Crest Trail. My soft pink feet would become callouses, my soles would harden, they'd feel no tenderness as they stepped.

I could go someplace gorgeous where nobody knew me and start over. I might feel something there, even if that thing were burning, blistered feet. I wanted to walk the whole great trail, this trail, tip to distant tip. The path unfolded beneath my stepping feet.

I would walk it until it faded in the mist and lush of northern Washington, then ended. I would walk the height of the country. I would walk off my fat, my sadness, the year of my rape. The PCT would lead me to an otherworld, through the sadness I felt here, out of it.

CHAPTER 5

The Dangers of the Desert

Sunspots blotted my vision. The desert was white as light and boundless. The sky limitless. No birds. Not one smoky puff of cloud. Though I had the crazy sense that I was being watched.

In the bends of crossing trails, tangled in bushes and in the bases of sharp yucca, empty chip bags and soda bottles and candy bar wrappers quivered in the death-heat, catching the sun, not yet sun-faded. This trash was fresh. I'd imagined I'd be out here alone, yet clearly people had eaten at this spot, and recently. Then I noticed, slung on a cactus right beside me, two pairs of border booties—homemade shoe sleeves made of cut-up old carpets that obscure illegal immigrants' shoe prints in the dust. Like an inexplicable shadow on the bedroom wall, the trash triggered mirages of unseen danger. Like my fallen plastic button. Evidence of some other presence.

Then out down the bone-white path I noticed a figure moving slowly—a man. He was breathing hard, nearing me—no, only just a boy. He looked about fourteen. His brown hair flop-flopped on the back of his neck; he twisted to more clearly see me. I stopped and stood still to see him better too, and he stared and kissed the air at me and then walked right off of the trail, out, into the spiny plants and boundless dust of open desert. No one was with him. He was carrying nothing.

We were about seven miles north of the border, and I wondered if he knew where he was headed. My own long dusty path looked straight and led out into open desert. The established trail was frightening enough. The boy was smaller now, again a brown speck. I really hoped this boy would make it okay.

I stared down the footpath, pale dust rising in the infinite sunlight. The trail didn't end. I stepped by more carpet booties, tossed off like plaster masks after a masquerade. I felt unsafe. There were people near me, I was sure, but I couldn't see them. I passed a yellow square sign, like a road sign: *"¡Cuidado! No exponga su vida a los elementos. ¡No vale la pena!"*

There was no English translation, but I could tell that it said: "Warning! Do not expose your life to the elements. Not worth it!"

And there was an illustration of a sun, a cactus, a rattlesnake, and water waves in a circle with a slash through them: no water. These were the dangers of the desert, and people confront them and sometimes die on their journeys to live in this country. I thought then of the stories I would have to someday tell my own children: dropping out of college, raped. Self-exiled, walking across the desert. I felt in a hotspot in my gut that I might be a dropout, ever after.

A sole cloud drifted like a balloon; the sun blinked. In shadow I saw the dry hills more clearly. I could enter this gorgeous world where nobody knew me and start over. The path unfolded beneath me, and I followed it, jogging, faster, smelling the dust, feeling the sunshine heating my dry cheeks, legs, burning, burning.

I bit into a green apple, then saw I'd nearly stepped on a rattlesnake, just skimmed its edge; the snake lay across the trail like the shadow of a branch, at least three feet long. Its brown and beige mosaic stark and distinct against dust. I shrieked.

The snake rushed over the bone-colored dirt with impossible speed and into a hard-leafed creosote bush, its rattling fast and hollow, more menacing than any human sound. I ran back south a hundred yards; I was fine. I stood and breathed a minute, then walked back north, kept walking, watched my feet quickly move.

Again I bit my apple, breathed, chewed—my last piece of fresh food; everything else was processed or salted or junk. I already regretted eating the fruit so soon.

The path ahead would be dangerous, I couldn't deny that. I stepped along the trail, over another snake, unsure what kind it was. It was skinny and dusty; I stepped; I heard no rattle. I stepped over another, gasped; I nearly hadn't seen it. Another. The snakes were endless, the venom of their bite deadly. The Mojave Green Rattlesnake, a pit viper native to the deserts of the South Western United States, is infamous for its potent, debilitating neurotoxic venom. Chance of survival is good if medical attention is sought within minutes of a bite—fair if within an hour. But after that serious symptoms rapidly develop: Vision abnormalities and difficulty swallowing and speaking. Skeletal muscle weakness leads to difficulty breathing: respiratory failure. In cities, fatality is uncommon—antivenom is effective—but the untreated bite of a Mojave Green is fatal. Which meant, for me, a bite would be fatal.

So many things can happen to hikers in this mountainous desert, frightening things. I recalled something dark I'd read about the hot springs out here—warm swimming holes of gleaming black water—the pools' bottoms silty, so soft they were almost slimy. That softness is a slick algae. It coats rocks and as tired hikers slip their toes over the stones, puffing up sediment, opaque clouds rise in the clear black water. These hot springs host *Naegleria fowleri*, an amoeba that invades the human central nervous system through the nose, climbs along nerve fibers, up through the floor of the cranium, into the brain. With a "unique sucking apparatus," it eats cells of the brain. Such invasions are rare but most always end in death. Ninety-eight percent of infected humans die within half a month. The 2 percent who live through the invisible attack will be brain-damaged and nerve-damaged. Their taste buds will mutate and food will smell repulsive. They'll vomit, nauseated at the odor of baked bread, or of bacon frying—every odor. They'll grow confused, hallucinate and suffer through seizures. Their bodies will live on, out of their control. Then, the prognosis is bleak. There is no cure. *N. fowleri* will be discovered postmortem. There is no vaccine.

Rape had also stolen my control over my body, but at least it was survivable. And there were other things too; things I couldn't so clearly avoid:

Lyme disease, waterborne illness, dehydration. These dangers were common. *Giardia,* a microscopic parasite that swims in water tainted by cow patties or rodent scat—or any animal feces—is a constant sickness risk. Hikers have to drink water from streams, mountain lakes and springs, there's really no other option, but water sources contaminated with *Giardia* can cause hikers intestinal illness—abdominal cramps, nausea, and debilitating, dizzying dehydration that leaves hikers demobilized. Treatment for *Giardia* requires an antibiotic available in town—and somehow you need to get to town.

Along the Pacific Crest Trail, I would only encounter small mountain-towns where I'd get to shower and wash up about once a week. I'd stride and sweat; I'd stink. My backpack would absorb my back sweat, reek worse than a gym bag. My brown synthetic T-shirt would fade tan, salt crusted, its armpits black. I would carry bacteria. A complete community of independent maladies, hitchhiking on me. We all could make it, if we all behaved. I prayed on specks of twirling dust, on the first shooting star I would see that desert night: no ataxia. No bacteria that eats brain and body cells. I prayed: behave. Behave.

Yet looking up that dusty path into desolation, basking snakes and bacteria didn't concern me, they weren't threats I considered. In retrospect, it's stunning to think how the most damaging threats were also the most common and how easy it was to die. Only about five hundred people arrive each spring at this trail from Mexico to attempt to hike the whole way to Canada, and fewer than half of those—some odd two hundred—will make it all the way. In all of history, fewer people on the planet have walked along the Pacific Crest Trail the whole way from Mexico to Canada than have summited Mount Everest. And each year—every single year—some hikers die.

For three hours I walked briskly without stopping. The walking itself was shockingly easy, the trail gradually descending, ascending, a smooth dusty path through fields of brittle grasses, hard chaparral shrubs, and graying cacti. Lonely blue mountains so pale they were almost ghosts against the sky spread at the western horizon. I now stepped over basking snakes as if they were only sticks. It amazed me how quickly I'd gotten used to them and I didn't know if I was brave or reckless.

In a blink the trail became green. The dry grasses and waxy plants vanished. A canopy of trees quivered above my head, and I heard the sound of running water and noticed a person: a man. My first instinct was to turn off the trail, slyly step without sound around him so he wouldn't notice me. But then I thought: how crazy. How absolutely unnecessary. I would have to trust that this man wouldn't hurt me.

This was the other danger I couldn't ignore and had in fact always known: Most people who attempt to thru-hike the PCT are men. I had signed myself up for this. If men were the truest trail danger, I would soon be dead as sundried wood.

The man was leaning against a big white rock and drinking water out of a Nalgene water bottle—not a Gatorade bottle, the much lighter option. I was disheartened to notice that his backpack was massive. Mine was little as a schoolgirl's knapsack. Now, looking at the huge size difference, I doubted the sufficiency of my tiny pack, I doubted everything.

The man nodded at me.

I stopped walking. He looked to be in his midtwenties, very tall and pasty, his backpack like a second body beside him.

"You thru-hiking?" I asked. I wanted explanation of all the stuff he was lugging. Really, I wanted confirmation from a fellow hiker that I was carrying the right things, too—that I could make it. In that motel room with my father, I'd been more focused on putting together my playlist than on the things that were going into my pack to keep me alive, and now, standing in the desert at the trail's beginning before a man with a huge backpack, my intent focus on my dad's music seemed misguided. Maybe I should have packed more things.

The man squinted at me, said, "Hey. Left Field."

It took a moment to realize that he was telling me his name. "You're Left Field?" I asked him, squinting also. Even in shade, the air was impossibly bright. "What's that from?"

"From the A.T. 'cause I'm just really random. And sometimes I'm off in left field, so . . ."

So he had already hiked the Appalachian Trail. So he probably knew what he was doing.

"When you finishing?" he asked.

"What?"

"When you plan to finish the trail?"

I found this question surprising. I didn't really know. "Oh. Late August? Somewhere 'round there. School starts in late August, so I have to be done by then."

To really finish by the end of August, I would have to average twenty-something miles a day with not one day of rest. If I'd actually believed I'd be finishing in last August, I was lying to myself. I would be crazy. The truth was I didn't know. I wasn't then thinking about life after the trail; life after the trail seemed more a wish than a plan.

"Then I won't see you," he said. "I'm not gonna finish till October, probably."

I scooped water from the small creek with an empty bottle and we said bye, bye to each other, and I kept walking and he stayed there. He hadn't mentioned my tiny knapsack, and I'd never asked him about all of the things he was carrying, and if I needed them too.

Again I ran. Up, up to the top of a hump then down its back side, fast; again the place was desert. No more shade. As fast as I had entered: out of that tiny and sudden oasis hugging that loud stream. Singing to myself along the dusty trail, thinking: I'm okay. Left Field's okay.

I really never did see Left Field again.

The sun was low when I finally took my first break, stopped walking and sat in the center of the trail—no sharp things there. Soft dust. No birds above. The sky endless, a blank mask, and I felt energized, not tired, impossibly all right. I chugged the last of my water. Not hungry, but wanting lime or green apple, any tart juice. My tongue felt weirdly rough. My taste buds were raised like goose bumps. Even hydrated with that extra water from the creeklet, I needed to make it to Hauser Creek at mile 16 to drink water tonight.

That first dusk was sudden, like the sharp darkness after a lightning strike. The sky had been clear all day, but walking over sand I smelled rain, felt electricity in my hair and fingers. I was very thirsty, smelling water, wishing for it. The earth softened suddenly, the dirt no longer compacted, small reddish dead leaves scattered on the ground like brittle hands. Tufts of real green grass appeared, the type you'd see on an unkempt baseball field's outfield. Then I noticed dark, damp stones laid out in a row. Euphoria hit. It was Hauser Creek. I had gotten on the trail at 1:30 P.M. with sixteen miles to hike and by that first dark walked those sixteen miles. I'd made myself make it all the way to water. I'd made it. I'd accomplished my ambitious afternoon's goal. Now, I would have only four miles to Lake Morena—to Kickoff—in the morning, and I was very proud.

I set up my tent alongside Hauser Creek, among the tents and tarps of hikers I didn't know. Some lit from inside by headlamps, glowing golden. It was a small encampment of hopeful new thruhikers, but it surprised me how I didn't feel the need to meet them. Each of them wanted to do the same thing I wanted to do, but now—able to meet them in the flesh—I no longer wondered why. In a black clump on a slab of rock, a group of hikers talked softly, laughed together in bursts. I didn't join them.

I climbed into my tent alone. Lying against the smooth cool nylon of my tent floor, I realized I'd imagined I would mostly be alone. Desert wilderness had seemed to me the safest place because it was peopleless, and people hurt me, but here I was, my first night sleeping on the trail, a girl in a tent among tents of laughing strangers. I knew that mostly men attempted this walk, but I wasn't sure if I should expect to be alone for days and then to see a man, or if boys would surround me in swirling packs, migrating north with me. From the bed I slept in in the Cinder-block Palace, I'd dreamed the Pacific Crest Trail would provide me solitude, but now I considered more realistically the omnipresence of men, the single danger I couldn't will myself to ignore. I'd be in wilderness not alone but within the society of my fellow desert pilgrims, a girl among wayward men.

I ate a dinner of Wheat Thins and mini Snickers inside my tent, knowing as I munched that I wasn't supposed to eat where I would sleep, as food scents attract wild animals. I didn't have energy to brush my teeth, just lay down, back against the cool tent floor. I wouldn't need my sleeping bag tonight, I thought. The air was warm. My spine relaxed into the nylon-covered ground, and I craved creamy comfort food, an ice-cream sundae, a glass of cold chocolate milk. Since the rape I had lived purely off junk. My seven teenage years of eating chicken breast and broccoli now seemed pointless. Monkish. Entirely exhausting. I lay flat on my back, breathing, chain-popping juicy Starbursts, unwrapping them one by one, watermelon Jolly Ranchers, Atomic Fireballs for spice. Lay's chips for salt. The crap food I loved as a kid but hardly ever indulged in. Now I could have it all. My tent felt safe.

I pulled out my backpack and rummaged through the things I brought. Just eleven pounds and three ounces. John Muir wrote: *I went alone, my outfit consisting of a pair of blankets and a quantity of bread and coffee.*

I became obsessed with this new truth: I needed so little. But for all the so-called necessities I left behind—underpants, a first-aid kit, extra batteries, a warm jacket, a single change of clothes, deodorant or soap, or even a map—I needed to bring lipstick and my new lacy bra. I needed candy. I needed to feel like a woman, to be pretty, even out here in this new world, with no one I knew. Especially here. I needed the candy from my childhood, the sweets I had banned for so long.

Eleven pounds, three ounces was all I needed to survive, and looking at it in this tent that belonged just to me, I knew I could make it. I'd survived Junior and I didn't doubt that I'd survive this, too. I didn't fear that I would die out here. I carried impossibly little, but this was wilderness, the safe playground of childhood summers, and I was strong and also smart, sure that the eleven pounds of things I carried was exactly all that I would need to survive.

I found my cell phone at the bottom of my backpack. I wanted to call my mom and tell her I had water and shelter, and I was safe. But I had no signal—the satellite phone she mailed me was a five-day walk away, up in Warner Springs. I felt guilty; she'd be so worried tonight she wouldn't fall asleep. If I had no service tomorrow too, she'd really worry. I curled up small in my tent. I imagined her back in Newton, trying to sleep.

I pulled my stuffed sleeping bag out and wiggled inside. I made note: the desert is cold at night.

But I couldn't fall asleep. I felt chilled. I skimmed my hand over the cold tent floor, feeling for my iPod, hoping the old lyrics of treasured songs would transport me somewhere warm. I pictured a rocky beach, late-summer trips to the Cape with my mom, the smell of sunscreen and washed-up dead crabs and salty air. Dylan, Springsteen, Buffalo Springfield, good old Avril played, randomly ordered. My Pacific Crest Trail playlist. I'd put it all together, desperate to blast away, the soundtrack of escape.

CHAPTER 6

Unbound Ghosts

APRIL 21, HAUSER CREEK, THE DESERT, CALIFORNIA, MILE 16

I woke that first morning to my body shivering; I was uncomfortably cold, even curled inside my sleeping bag, wearing all my clothes—in southernmost desert. Temperatures wouldn't get much milder than this, I knew. I hoped I wouldn't be so cold every night. I opened my eyes to pale green: my small tent's ceiling. My skin was prickled with goose bumps, my fingernails lilac, the air lonely, smelling of sage and dust, so silent I heard ringing.

I emerged that day to a pale sky and took my tent down in silence. The aluminum tent poles glittered in the early light—frost clung to them. Even so close to Mexico, the night had really frozen. I used my bandana to shield my hands from the poles as I pulled them apart. The rods gleamed, beautiful; cold metal burned me. I slipped my hands under my shirt and pressed my icy fingers to my stomach. I inhaled and quickly folded them with a metallic clatter and slipped them inside my pack to carry. I packed up my eleven pounds of things into my little lime green gem of a knapsack.

I was gone before anyone had woken.

The sun broke over the faraway mountains, now a hazy beige as if stamped on the milky sky, this world an old postcard from bygone years. My shoulders burned even through my thin cotton T-shirt, the sunshine ruthless. Days and nights were distinct creatures now.

I jogged over the shoeprints of people who'd passed over this ground yesterday, perfectly preserved: the Nike check mark, the swirl of imprinted polka dots. They were stamped into the dust, jeweled with beads of ice and glinting in the new sun. A strong wind would erase them, but the air was still. The footprints all clearly pointed north. The California desert spans a thousand miles, and the PCT twists across seven hundred sun-hardened and dusty miles of it, and it was mesmerizing to consider that I was one in a loose pack, walking the same path.

I was approaching long-awaited, long-dreamed-of Kickoff, the clotting spot of this dispersed bunch of people, the nomads' gathering ground. Following this endless path of tracks, hearing their delicate crunch, ice crystals breaking under my weight, I inhaled and felt the thrill of migrating northward through America. Among these tracks might be hidden the ones of a friend, a lover to traverse this mammoth desert with—a tribe. These were my fellow self-exiled American explorers. My new family.

I felt a pang of longing. I felt hopeful. Back the way I'd come, my train of dust hung in air like solid sun, a personal jet stream. Ahead, unseen, was my long-awaited Lake Morena. Tomorrow Kickoff would begin, and I would have a second chance at my first day at college.

It was terrifying.

The California desert was immeasurable, and already I was lonely. In under an hour of jogging, descending, I'd reached Lake Morena, the gathering grounds. But I had been so quick and efficient, so eager to arrive, that I had reached the party grounds thirty-six hours early. Now there was nothing to do but wait.

I saw no lake, just the sign: Lake Morena. It was nailed to a dead tree, flaking paint on wood. A wet lawn sprawled golden in the morning's still coolness, its patchy yellow grass and pale dirt dewy. Old wood picnic tables sat with nothing on them; iron barbecue grills, planted beside each vacant table; campsites marked by two-foot gray wood posts: 1, 2, 66. Eighty-six altogether. This would be the place, but nobody was here yet. I was the first. It was its own sort of barren Eden, no apples to pick.

I stood there on Kickoff's grounds, hoping to feel heightened—wonderful and empowered; instead I felt dizzied, overheated. I was potently uncomfortable in my pale chubby body. I felt transported back to my childhood, the summers of taunting and rejection. More than anything, this felt like the first day of sleepaway camp, my first time away from my mother. She had packed T-shirts and cotton shorts and socks and bucket hats and baseball caps for me, but I'd never dressed myself before. The summer before first grade my mommy bought me ten identical teal cotton sweat suits, and I wore one every day of that school year because, according to her, they "worked." She would dress me in one the night before, and I'd sleep in it—it also worked for sleeping—and then getting me ready in the morning took just no time at all. I'd dread my classmates' daily observation: That's what you wore yesterday!

And then: *Why* do you wear that every day? Like, honestly. Tell! Us!

I couldn't say, "Because it works." I said I didn't know. The kids weren't ever mean about it, but I was sensitive and I felt different. Like I *was* this neon and ugly sweat suit. Like I'd never grow out of it, have to wear the ten sets of it forever.

Luckily—perhaps because of Jacob—I never got teased badly. Our relationship granted me amnesty. But when I went to summer camp for the first time, I didn't have my brother to protect me.

Alone at camp, the task of picking out my clothes seemed daunting, I felt incapable, and I tried to assemble an outfit that would "work." I made it: tall white socks and high-waisted pink jeans-shorts and a purple Harry Potter T-shirt. No underpants. No one could see underpants, so I didn't need those. I'd check everything in the cabin's tall bathroom mirror before I left each morning: the shirt didn't cling tight to my soft belly; my stiff shorts hid my thighs. I wore the same thing each day for the entire month.

Each day a new grass stain or marker-line or spill of paint or juice.

Each day I felt worse about my reflection in the cabin mirror, uglier.

The girls would ask me if I "touched myself," and no matter if I said yes or no, they'd glance at one another and giggle. I felt horrible. One night in the cabin, when they all thought I was sleeping, I lay in my bunk bed and listened to the girls as they—all of them—and our on-duty twenty-three-year-old counselor talked about the too-high white socks I wore, my "grandpa shorts," how hideous I looked. They decided together that I must have no friends.

Through that night I replayed their voices' contempt of me, their high tight tone, quiet high pitches, harmonizing in their disdain for me. I felt betrayed by the counselor—a grown-up. I wanted to die— or to become queen.

On the final day of my month away at camp, sun high, grass still damp from overnight rain, my mother finally came to retrieve me. I was relieved, but I also felt embarrassed for her to see me. She would see that I couldn't care for myself. I hid from her in the dining hall bathroom; I held my hairbrush bristle-up under the faucet, peeled off my Harry Potter shirt before the sink-mirror, prepared to brush my hair. My hair was matted—I had taken all my showers but never brushed— and my old purple shirt, a tiny pile on the bathroom floor, was stained and smelled a little. I pressed the brush-head against my rat's-nest dread and pulled. Strained my little neck. The brush didn't budge.

Back home my mother resumed dressing me.

There was no full-length mirror in my childhood house, no mirror in my parents' room at all. I once pointed out that we had no long mirror, and my mother said with pride that we weren't people who would ever notice that, it wouldn't occur to us to miss it. She was speaking for us both.

She told me that women who wore makeup had bad values. Putting on makeup would have been a statement—a rebellion. I didn't try it. I grew to feel guilty for wanting to feel attractive.

Through middle school, I didn't shave my legs or use deodorant. Girls began to ask about my hairy legs. One day in eighth grade, I found deodorant in my locker, with a note written in girlish handwriting, unsigned. It told me I smelled. It was true. I was hurt. But after that I still didn't simply commit to wearing deodorant daily, instead passively subjecting myself to adolescent years of whispered disdain. Basic hygiene was a terrible struggle. Anything my mother didn't do for me, I didn't do for myself.

I was blushing—panicked. In my mind in months holed up in the Cinder-block Palace alone, Kickoff had become a place I could flee to and be myself—and be liked. But at last at Kickoff's golden field, I feared I looked slapdashly dressed in my pink shorts; they were ancient. I thought I must look terrible—awkward and tactless, embarrassingly flushed and frumpy. I felt the full presence of all my amassed problems with me.

Mounting anxiety paralyzed me.

I wandered to the concrete bathrooms: Men, Women. Then I saw others: an old man and gaunt boy by the water fountain, a woman in a sports bra stretching her arms.

I walked in the open women's doorway, the space felt cold and hollow. It was blindingly dark. My eyes adjusted to the lack of light. I had already tried to reinvent myself on this trip, but all I had done was avoid my real life. I had told Left Field that I was going back to school. It no longer felt true. I'd left my freshman year with four weeks left. I was now only a girl, a dropout, walking away from life into a desert. I wanted to cry, to once and for all purge my endless self-loathing—to change.

Looking into my reflection above the sink, I dreaded what I already understood to be true: I wouldn't reinvent myself at Kickoff. Just being someplace new couldn't just suddenly imbue me with new confidence. Fleeing to the desert didn't transform me into the poised and lovely woman I wished I were. I was here—on the PCT *at last*—

and I was suddenly aware of how uncomfortable I still was in my body. I was awkward in Newton and at college, and here on the trail I remained just as uncool. This place wouldn't change me. Nowhere could.

Through my darkly tinted prescription sunglasses, I saw myself: a chunky dirty girl. I was ugly, had bad posture and thick glasses. I was chubby, my curly hair a mess. I felt unattractive, I always had. I had been mocked for my too-big-for-my-face lips, for wearing the wrong socks; I'd never had clothes I felt good in, not beautiful or even comfortable within my skin. I hadn't gotten attention from the boys at my high school or my father either. I was unseen. I had always been unseen.

Tomorrow a crowd of mystery faces would filter in, and the pressure to reinvent myself among my new people, my very tiny new community, felt momentous, and I remembered camp, and I remembered Colorado College, my many failed beginnings, and so soon people could find out I was uncool, long-rejected, damaged—unlovable—and I decided, my heart revving, *No.* I never wanted to go back to summer camp, or to Colorado College. Now, finally actually standing on Kickoff's grounds, I saw a big vacant space, the stakes for me felt so impossibly huge, the pressure felt tremendous, and anything could happen—the greatest night of my life or an immediate terrible fall.

Again away from my mother, I'd begun to wish for beauty newly. I wished to be a girl who possessed it. I wanted to occupy my body in the way that dancers do—fully, and with grace and intention. I wanted to be able to touch my fingertip swiftly to my eye, one-two, the way people do, the way *everybody could.* The way I couldn't. It was useless. *I couldn't.* I stalled in the campground bathroom, squinting, seeing only that I was unseen, uncool, unattractive—raped—profoundly defeated, and alone. It was a little hard to see crisply in the dim bathroom through my sunglasses. In my effort to redefine myself, I realized I'd condemned myself to see my whole walk through dark lenses. In the mirror I could detect only a fat girl destined to be forever hidden behind glasses so thick no one could see that she was beautiful.

Jacob had told me I could put on makeup, do my hair—and I agreed, but I never had. I felt helpless to make myself feel attractive.

It would be months and more than a thousand miles of wild independence before I would begin to truly see how my face and my body were transforming—my wide hips and little waist, C-cup breasts; my eyes: honey brown and as big on my face as they were when I was two. Huge, kept beneath dark shades. My skin olive. Warm and smooth.

My self without my mother.

Myself as I was seen.

I wish I could have known that my lips would soon transform in my vision of myself from too large and awkward into my most alluring feature.

To my reflection I said, "I am the girl who wears glasses." I turned the faucet off and tried to straighten. Blushing, hands still wet, I walked back outside and into the sun, and saw the man and the boy, speaking to each other, muted in infinite relentless brightness.

It happened quickly. I saw that the boy was smiling at me. I stepped over to them. "Hey," I said loudly. Closer, I saw that the boy wasn't a boy, really, anymore, any more than I was a girl. He was probably twenty, just very thin. He had high cheekbones, his features masculine but also delicate; he was handsome. "Where you guys from?" I asked them; my face flushed. I couldn't place them.

"I come to here from Switzerland," the young one said. He was still smiling, so big, watching my face. "I like to be here for hiking. Yes."

"From outside L.A., just here for Kickoff," the older man answered. So they were not together. I made a note then to myself: people together on the PCT are probably not together; they just only happen to be walking the same pace.

"And you come to here, too? For the hike?" the young one asked me back. His cheeks were hollow like a hungry teen's. I watched his exposed arms, their graceful gestures. This boy was athletic, poised and confident—asking me. He was also here to begin walking the trail north.

"Oh, yeah," I said. I looked away, to his running shoes. "Thru-hiking." I pressed my lips together, trying to thin them.

The young one smiled, I nodded and walked back toward where I'd left my pack, fleeing, and without my asking, he followed me, all the way back to my picnic table.

He told me that his name was Daniel.

I said cool, ha. I watched him. His effortless posture; he was so beautifully at ease in his body. "Wild Child," I said—tentatively breaking the naming rule. I was trying on a fresh identity, a brave new name for what I was, still not liking who I was in truth. We were supposed to be given our trail names, but I trusted no one with my identity. I didn't want to keep being Debby Parker.

Daniel said that he wanted to hike on, not stop and wait for Kick-off. It would be hectic. He just wanted to walk. The older man was gone, the boy was talking to me alone now. He was looking at me intently. I felt his stare and shifted in discomfort; I felt terribly exposed. I looked down, away, at the dead quivering grass.

His accent was thick and strange, though, and I liked it. I liked his boyish grin, those sure, toned arms. His posture—that beautiful ease I terribly envied. His smile was undeniable.

When he finally looked away, hopped up to sit on the picnic table, I realized the statement that he was going to skip Kickoff was really a question to me, and, coming from him, the invitation didn't seem aggressive or frightening. I trusted his smile.

And so somehow in only that sweet moment he had entirely convinced me that his intent eyes weren't scanning me for reasons to dislike me or ways to hurt me. That his grin's curl wasn't predatory. Instead it seemed he was looking at me unapologetically because he liked the girl he saw. He simply wanted to walk with me. He'd only just met me and already he was interested. I felt a small thrill in my anxious chest. He was cute, magnetic—and, amazingly—he seemed to believe that I was those things, too. It was crazy. He was staring, stirring my core; I was shifting. I wanted him to look at me longer, wanted to hold this feeling longer.

This boy, his interest in me, was the god-sent exact best antidote to my social fears. His easiness soothed me.

I reminded myself that I'd come to Kickoff to make friends, to find someone good to walk with, and here was someone who was trying to befriend me, to walk with me. And I was here to hike. Not to arrive and immediately start waiting. And Kickoff might be raucous—dangerous.

And I believed these things.

But the truest reason I was compelled to leave with this handsome Swiss boy I didn't know at all was not my need for a hiking partner, or desire to walk more miles immediately, or fear of getting gang-raped by rowdy men. It was simply that leaving with Daniel would mean that I'd miss Kickoff—and thus defer the massive pressure I felt. I felt the hurt of my first day of camp, Day 1 of college. The next day. How I'd fallen. How, arriving to new green lawns, new places populated with people who'd never known me, I was forced to confront the truth I really already knew: being here was not enough to make me different.

I feared I'd wreck this new beginning, too.

Leaving with Daniel would mean skipping the risk of falling tomorrow again.

I looked squarely at him. I said okay.

I walked first, Daniel tight behind, to the edge of the field, into the shallow hills and openness. Pale sage and creosote bushes lined the trail, and I felt vacant, a little scared. We exchanged questions, better questions than answers. Daniel, what'd you do in Switzerland? I raced the mountain bikes for the cycling competition. What did you to do when in Colorado? I studied writing. I was a college student.

How old are you?

Twenty. But he'd be twenty-one in three months.

How old are you?

Nineteen.

Yes. He thought I was nineteen.

I didn't yet know what I wanted from him, a companion or some-body to be nice to me, to redeem men, or just a friend to walk with. I didn't know why I was talking to him; he was another college-age stranger.

Tomorrow nearly a thousand people—gear vendors, hikers, as-piring thru-hikers, trail angels—would populate this mute space. Since winter I'd daydreamt of the big bonfire consuming wood, the joy, the starlit barbecue and pre-journey camaraderie. They would grill hot dogs and burgers, laugh in the light of fires, in the darken-ing chilling evening desert air. Meeting, talking, finding their future closest friends, their future selves.

And I would be gone with Daniel.

I walked with Daniel out into the open desert, low shrubs and dirt in all directions, my heart knocking against my breast. I no-ticed Daniel also was not ultralight, his tall pack stuffed-taut, dense. I guessed his base weight was thirty pounds, though his feet still sprang quicker, lighter than my own.

The plants along the trail grew taller, greener; the trail climbed up in elevation. We were hiking to the base of the Laguna Moun-tains, six-thousand-foot peaks that actually get snow. These new big plants were bushy, abrasive looking, like steel sponges. I breathed deep in, out, in, out, trying not to sound too winded. We were hiking fast. I was striding quick, jog-stepping in determined spurts to stay with him, feeling good about my impressive pace so far.

His arms swung gracefully as we walked on. My pulse was bumping in my thumb pad, I was grinning and also sad, excited, ter-rified, walking out into open desert, impossibly vulnerable, exposed to Daniel's goodness or his bad, wishing on every puff of dust spray-ing behind his heels that he was good.

After about four miles, four hundred feet of elevation gain, we took a rest at Cottonwood Creek, a weak little streamlet. The brush grew taller, fuller here, one of those little water-made oases thru-hikers walk into and then out of in a moment. Back out to desert.

That's where another man, Edison, caught us. Edison told us he'd seen us leave Lake Morena together and had been tailing us all morning. We looked "less gay" than everyone else. "Yo," he said as he tossed his pack down and sat. "'Sup tards."

"Hi," Daniel said. That big smile again. "The water is good."

Edison raised both eyebrows at me and licked his chapped lips. "'Sup." He unzipped his pack and pulled out a paper can of Betty Crocker chocolate frosting, started eating it with a spoon. "This shit's ridic for calories," he said. "Best thing to carry."

We talked as we walked. Edison was twenty, from some small town in Tennessee. He'd been working at a cannery in Alaska, but had lived in Colorado before, working as a ski lift operator and liked that better. More fun and hot girls.

I said I went to school in Colorado. Or, *go* to school.

Daniel said he skis, too.

"Man, no," Edison said. He ignored me, talked toward Daniel. "I'm a boarder." His limp straight hair flap-flapped against his shoulders with each step; his head poked forward, forward, forward like a prehistoric bird. Primitive.

They talked for hours. I remained quiet. Edison had a joke—Why aren't little niggers allowed to jump on the bed?—and I felt suddenly awake. Scared.

"Why?" I said. Daniel hadn't said it, I'm not sure he knew he was supposed to.

"'Cause they'd get Velcroed to the ceiling." He giggled.

Daniel laughed, though I don't think he understood, or I hoped he didn't.

Daniel had a joke, too. "There is two gay men, and one man says to the other man: I have to break up with you. The other man asks why this is. The original gay man says: because when we started anal fucking your asshole was the size of a dime, but now it is the size of a quarter."

Neither Edison nor I laughed. "Um," I said.

Daniel was first in our single-file line, and he turned back and grinned at us and nodded.

"Kinda think something was lost in translation," I said.

We walked along the edge of a long canyon, Daniel in front and Edison last. A black-speck chopper flew low, descended out of view, still loud, near here, and Edison talked about snowboarding out in Colorado, about what makes girls hot and hot names versus not hot names. Kaley is a hot name. Emily is not. Tara is hot. Rebecca no.

I didn't ask for judgment on my name.

The sky was dark with clouds now, and for the first time since Mexico we lost the sun. It shined through a bright cloud. The helicopters were loud, those double-bladed choppers. They flew low. We walked fast, all three of us; Daniel stepped high over a rattlesnake and said, "Snake is here." I stepped over it. A moment later we heard a hard rattle. Edison skip-jumped over the snake and jogged to us. Thirty feet up the trail, Daniel and I waited.

"What did happen?" Daniel asked.

"I kicked that fucker," Edison said.

I looked at Daniel, prayed he hated Edison's stupidity, the absolute idiocy of creating such a massive and senseless risk. He'd just risked his life for nothing. He was entirely unpredictable—and, therefore, unsafe—and I was horrified, finished with him. I was done.

The sky hung over us like a shadow, and I opened my mouth and a silent word came out and then I tried again: "Idiot. You're an idiot."

"And you're a dumb fucking cunt," he said. He grinned.

I didn't respond to Edison and planned to camp that night somewhere where he was not.

One month later to the day a marine AH-1W Super Cobra helicopter would crash on that exact spot of desert, and two men would die. The debris would scatter, strike the canyon like shrapnel and leave in the white sage and yucca packs of unexploded rockets. The United States government would close this section of the trail, ten hazardous miles.

Under a field of clouds we followed the canyon's rim, walked in and out of canyons, deep drainages, most of them dry. Brown, parched ridges sloped down to green cleavages; the green was poison oak. The trail was good, flat. We hiked in deep Us, just level, never climbing to the dried ridge or descending into the bushes threaded with poison. I thanked the trail for its kind route.

Daniel talked specifically to me. He asked me about my college. He wanted to know if I was "a happy girl." His questions were generic, he wasn't entirely fluent, but I could sense what he was trying to gauge was: can this girl be mine?

Which absolutely shocked me. Daniel was an athlete, he seemed popular and graceful, yet when I spoke he listened and he smiled. He was trying to make me like him. I wondered why he couldn't see I was a weird fat dirty mess, maybe his limited language blocked him from noticing. Maybe he was just happy and friendly to everyone. But I saw how he disregarded Edison, stiffening a shoulder, gracefully muting him, leaning toward me. It seemed crazy, but I sensed that he liked me.

We talked about Texas. He had lived there as an exchange student for one year. I'd never been there. He'd never liked it. He wanted to know names of United States places I liked. I told him, "Yellowstone." I told him, "Boston's nice." I parted my lips to say "Colorado" but quickly closed them, pressed them against each other tight.

"That is right," he said, to all the things I said.

Sometime during those green poisonous miles, Daniel had become sweet to me. There was something that he saw in me that he wanted. He wanted to walk with me, spend time with me, maybe he even wanted to kiss me.

And I felt happy. And as the miles unfolded, even my hate and fear of Edison subsided. He tried to engage me with friendly questions; what food did I most crave? What candy was I craving the *worst*? I ignored him. I discounted him, and though he had been reckless, eventually he only seemed pathetic. The less I looked his way, the more he wanted my approval.

I thought maybe it'd be okay to camp where he camped, after all.

That night we three stopped at PCT mile thirty-eight—I'd hiked twenty-two miles, that day. I wasn't tired. I was absolutely wired. We set up our separate tents under that shadow-sky and I climbed into mine—"Night, guys."

DAY 3, THE DESERT, CALIFORNIA, MILES 38–53

I awoke that next morning to Daniel's voice, low and tender, his silhouette against my tent wall, speaking. "Wild Child, this is the morning. Hey? You are awake for hiking?"

My hand lay on my stomach and I pressed it there firm, eyes still shut. "Yup, thanks," I said back, my morning voice gravelly like a teenager's. "Getting up."

Outside my tent the sky was blue, the sun already distant from the horizon. It was eight o'clock.

We walked in silence that morning—I could think of nothing to say—and I wondered what Daniel and Edison thought of me, if they liked me. If they could sense my anger, blankness. Or not.

The terrain that morning was abnormal, strange for this southern latitude. We crossed a creek, entered the trail's first forest: fir and pine. We walked through the forest—good shade and new dark soil—and then out of it. At mile 42, we emerged onto a paved road, the first we'd seen, to a long wooden building: Laguna Mountain Lodge.

We left our packs on the steps. Inside, the general store had coke and ice cream. I bought a pint of vanilla and a can of whipped cream to eat out on the porch's precious shade. Paying the cashier for my sugar, I noticed a thick book with the seductive title *Mountaineering: The Freedom of the Hills.*

The ancient, tweed-suited Hispanic man working the tiny store's register saw I was looking at it, and he told me, "That should be the bible for you kids." It was a battered hardcover book, worn soft and rounded at its corners. I flipped through it, spooning my ice cream thoughtlessly, reading, stopping at a list that seemed important. Clearly, calmly and with authority, it named the "big ten" items no hiker can do without:

1. Map
2. Compass
3. Sunglasses and sunscreen
4. Extra food
5. Extra water
6. Extra clothes
7. Headlamp/flashlight
8. First-aid kit
9. Fire starter
10. Knife

This list seemed reasonable, and it made my chest tighten, and I swallowed, ice cream chilling my throat. The cashier told me something else, but I didn't quite make it out.

"What?" I asked.

"You didn't look like most hikers who come through."

Rather than ask him to tell me why not, I felt a hot jolt of fear, shut the book and walked out, fleeing the list and the man, unfinished.

He called after me to say I should be carrying a gun.

For the rest of our first full day together, we discussed girls, past relationships. Sex. Somehow it seemed necessary, pressing, even, to know where we'd all been. Where we were at.

Daniel said he "had had love;" he even told her "love you." He didn't have much to say about her, though. "She has a big heart." "Her sisters they have many kids."

Edison'd never had a girlfriend, but he'd hooked up shitloads.

"Like sex?" I asked.

I don't remember what his answer was, but I remember I doubted he'd done much. I guessed he was a virgin.

When we took a break a few hours later, Daniel pulled out a wallet photo. "Zis is her," he said. He handed Edison the picture.

It was a mocha-skinned black girl, maybe seventeen. Lovely.

"She has a big heart," Daniel said.

Edison tapped her butt with his finger, tossed it back at him. "Big booty, you mean. Boo-tay-*licious*."

I picked it up from the dirt where it'd landed, looked at the girl's dark eyes and perfect teeth. It was a high school picture-day photo, awkwardly posed. Her skin was flawless, glowed like clear sky.

"You fuck her?" Edison asked. His voice was quiet, almost reverent, a tone I hadn't heard from him.

"I never did that," Daniel said.

North of the Mount Laguna store-diner-post office, the trail stays high, follows the Lagunas' uneven ridge. A vertical mile below, the Anza-Borrego Desert lies, a beige wasteland, waterless and baking. The air five thousand feet down over the desert floor shimmers, distorted by heat. Shallow badlands erode, slope down to flat, shrubless dirt too hot to touch. Dust haze hangs like smog, softens the dunes, rippling to the horizon. Beige against blue. On and on. We would not, today, descend into the Anza-Borrego's beige inferno; for another thirty-two miles we'd stay high, skirt the mountain spine's sharp edge, view the desert's lunar beauty from above. I was relieved that for now we'd remain cooler, high and safer. At this elevation oaks and incense cedars grow in clusters, and we walked in and out of the harsh sun, loved the gaps of cool. Endured the flashes of bright heat. I saw a ladybug in flight, that tiny red vibration in the air by my swinging arm. You can wish on ladybugs; I made a wish: I'd not get hurt.

We got water 0.1 mile off the trail to the east at Oasis Spring; the water was cold and delicious; I wished all water could taste that good. I chugged and chugged. I felt revived. I drank two liters and filled them back up to carry. We walked past sugar pines, Jeffrey pines' great red trunks. They smelled like butterscotch. Brown clouds like exhaust puffs polluted the sky, blotted out the sun. One puff glowed, backlit. Pure gold. I listened to my iPod as we strode—the Red Hot

Chili Peppers, eight songs replaying. I felt tranquil. Yet energized. Off on an adventure with a team.

We camped a little early that night—only hiked about 14.4 miles that day—because we were, all three of us, inexplicably tired. We all wanted to stop. This night would be the first night of Kickoff, and we were officially missing it, 32.7 trail-miles too far north. I felt a pang of regret. We set up our separate tents that brown-sky evening on the dead grass at Pioneer Mail Trailhead and filled our Gatorade bottles from a concrete water tank beside an oak tree. It had no lid, was open to rain and rodents. A metal sign stuck to it read: Non-Potable Water for Horses Only.

I leaned over the top and saw in the water a dead mouse floating. I didn't say anything. We had to drink it. The next reliable water would be 24.9 miles north.

My mother overstated the dangers of the world—invented threats. And so I saw: Starbursts' hoof-made gelatin never gave me mad cow. Mad cow was not a threat to me. And so I thought: most risks weren't truly real.

It wasn't that my mother's fears were outlandish. People do die of infection, of cancerous moles left to mutate, and of pneumonia (it starts as a common flu) and mad cow disease. Children on bikes get hit by cars. She did not fear wild boar attacks or an alien invasion. The things she feared were theoretically possible. Horrible. But statistically as improbable as a flipped coin landing standing on its slim rim.

Ten thousand times less probable than rape.

I took a swig of the contaminated water. We sat down with a few thru-hikers we'd just met at a picnic table, talking, sipping our water slowly, as if small sips would combat the chance of disease, when suddenly it began to rain. It was abrupt and shocking, the smell of desert dust rising. Daniel looked at the gray-blue sky, to me, asked: "To my tent, yes?"

Wordlessly Edison and I followed him to his well-built tent's taut rainfly.

We pulled off our smelly running shoes and slipped them into the tent's tiny vestibule. I climbed inside. "It's nice in here."

We sat there dry under the deafening rain, making bad jokes, asking each other too-private things. But what did we really know about each other? Did I really know Daniel's plans, his path to the southern tip of the Pacific Crest Trail? There was so much I still didn't know.

And I gave the men half-truths. "Jacob and I are super close. My other brother Robert's like the mayor of Newton," I told them. It was true only that Robert was running in the election, and Jacob had once been my closest friend.

I can say I did know by then that Daniel was an athlete, one of the top downhill mountain bike racers in Switzerland until he got injured, he hadn't said how. I knew he'd lived a year in Anaheim, Texas, as an exchange student in high school. That's where he'd met that girl in the picture. I knew he hated fat people.

"I'm fat," I'd said, back at the picnic table.

"No." I could see the muscle harden in his cheeks. "No. You are not."

I had been joking kind of, and his hard response surprised me. But then it made me feel good. He was certain of what I was and what I wasn't. I wasn't fat. I felt that he liked me.

Now in his orange-lit tent, my folded body only inches from pressing into his, I felt him looking at me again in exactly the intent way he had back on the golden field—determined. Unapologetically, happily watching. It was strange to suddenly be so close to him in the small shelter of a tent; in the wide wilderness of these days our forms had endless space, but bent over together in the little tent our arms and legs made heat. I could smell his sweat and sunscreen. I felt his eyes on me, even as he talked to Edison. Edison had no face, his name didn't matter. I felt only Daniel's eyes.

I kept my eyes ahead, pretending to study his vestibule's fine mesh, a little giddy, willing myself not to flush fiercely.

Then I felt his skin. It was sudden, he skimmed my arm carelessly, easily. He was chatting with Edison, stirring me, I was burning. Edison had entirely vaporized. His hip shifted closer to mine; now we were subtly and fully touching. I looked at him finally, and I could feel the electricity between our limp arms.

I boldly called him Icecap instead of his name.

He looked solemn.

"You're Icecap. Like?" I needed to be the one to give him his trail name.

He looked so serious. "For me, yes," he finally said. He nodded slowly.

"Okay yes," I said too.

Outside parched desert plants were dark, erased by night and quivering in rain getting soaked. I listened to the drops fall on the tent, feeling the patter's small vibrations, Icecap's warm breath, body heat, the hard hip of the boy beside me, stirring me.

I would call him Icecap thereafter always—it fit him because he wore a white cap, and because he was from the snow-capped mountains in Switzerland, and because he seemed quiet and intense and lovely. The boy who raced until he got too hurt. Icecap. It would become his trail name, the person he'd be to me.

Wind pressed against the tent—we heard a tree crack and, through the gap between the rainfly and the ground, saw a snapped branch swaying—and we said good-night, and I climbed out, ran to my tent.

In my tent I lay still. I was damp from my sprint back and cold and inexplicably wet—turned on. My nipples were chilled and stiff. My palm against my hip bone, fingers tucked under the elastic waistband of my shorts. Thinking of Daniel's eyes on me on Kickoff's golden field. His hand brushing over my wrist lightly back in his tent. How the touch had thrilled me. I replayed the quick slip of his fingers. The adrenaline flood of an imagined kiss. Lying there dry under the deafening rain, I imagined Daniel—Icecap—on his bike flying downhill, the flooding adrenaline and swell of joy.

I saw him crashing.

I felt an ache of compassion and wondered if he had had to crash before he walked this trail. I thought about the risks we were sharing; all the hostile things we would survive together.

In the middle of the night Icecap's voice woke me. The rain had stopped. I could feel the wind chill through the tent wall; he told me everyone was up, awake. In a hiker named Chopper's tent. Chopper and Savior. They were brothers.

We were all going to smoke weed.

I twisted my feet into my shoes and clicked my headlamp on and followed Icecap's light into the blackness.

I smelled the weed at least a hundred yards from the lit tent. I thought to myself: I should do this. I should smoke this weed to get over a low feeling, to create a new association. I would do it; nothing bad would happen. No harm would befall me, not out here. I tried to fully believe it. The air was clear and cold. I hadn't smoked since the night I was raped. I felt that memory heavy like an uncomfortable sweater against me. White smoke hung around the tent like a ring of dissipated ghosts, unbound but pausing.

I climbed in; the smoke inside drifted slowly, each curl fading into the lamp-lit haze. It took a minute to see through the lit white air people's faces. Someone passed me the joint. I put it to my lips, inhaled.

"Quit nigger-lipping it." That was Edison. I smiled. I held it out and a large guy took it.

I watched his masculine jaw, his hulking chest-silhouette expand and drop as he sucked in, breathed out smoke. His hair was cut short, a flat crew cut, and he looked half American Indian. And military. This would be Chopper.

I said hi to him, to Chopper, to the other faces in the tent that I could hardly see. "Thanks for waking me up, assholes," I said.

"Can you see anything with those sunglasses on?" a voice asked—I couldn't tell whose.

"Of course," I answered quickly. "I wear my sunglasses at night, like from the eighties." I was trying to seem cool about it, not wanting to confess I couldn't put in contacts. I didn't want to be known as the girl who wore glasses. But the song was obscure, and I couldn't sing it. It was awkward.

Someone laughed. "It's mad humid in here," the voice said. It was from a thin face, very young.

I felt the uneven giddiness of weed, bright heat, hanging white lanterns buzzing like fireflies in night's still infinite black pool. The tingled joy of *drug* surging. Inked night heating.

Edison and Chopper talked softly—I listened, dizzy—and I learned Chopper and his nineteen-year-old brother were hiking to honor their mother's memory, to spread her ashes along the trail. Ten years before, their mother had died attempting to thru-hike the PCT. She'd frozen to death in the High Sierra.

"So why're you Chopper?" Edison asked. Insensitive, I wanted to apologize for him. He was still an asshole, I decided, but *oh well.* He was an asshole on my team.

"We got airlifted out," Chopper said, "me and Savior. We ran outta water a few miles 'fore Lake Morena and had to push our SPOT." The SPOT is a GPS-synced emergency device that, when you push SOS, sends your GPS coordinates to the local wilderness rescue people, whoever that may be. Wherever you are.

I didn't carry one.

His little brother said, "Got to ride in a chopper. Was mad fun."

Chopper took a long drag, coughed a deep cough. It didn't sound good. "Got two more free evacs too," he said.

I asked what he meant.

"We've got emergency evac insurance, so we can get lifted out two more times free."

I laughed.

Icecap's eyes got big.

"I'm sorry," I said. I was laughing, couldn't stop. "I'm just," I said, "I'm high."

It had, at some point I hadn't noticed, started to rain again, but now I felt the tent lean, lean with the wind's push. Someone passed me the joint again. Looking down at it, I saw the red of my lipstick just along the edge. I tried slowly thinking, pushing myself to pay attention to the men, but all I could think of was that last time—the night I'd lost control.

I'd saved the too-short-to-smoke stub of the joint Junior had rolled us before he raped me. I had kept it safe in the right-front corner of my underwear drawer, just right next to the plastic button that had broken off my shorts that night. The underpants, which I no longer wore, were pushed against the back-left corner to create space for the evidence. I needed to create space separating these things from *my* things. I opened the drawer to check the evidence too often.

Five weeks after Junior raped me, I removed the cold still joint stub; a burgundy lipstick stain glared on the lumpy end. I couldn't throw it away or burn it to smoke and ash. I crushed it in my fingers over a bowl of brownie batter and poured the batter into a pan and brought those not-really-pot brownies to a small party in the on-campus apartments to which a friendly boy with curly hair had invited me. He'd liked me. I acted like a drunk idiot at that party, though I was sober. I ate a brownie. You could hardly taste the ash or trace of weed.

CHAPTER 7

MIRAGES

APRIL 22, THE ANZA-BORREGO DESERT, CALIFORNIA, MILES 38–77.8

The morning sky was still empty and pale. The wind was loud and cold; I yawned. I shivered. I was overcome by disorienting melancholy. The night before had not been a bad night; I was okay; I was fine. But taking down my tent, I realized I didn't want to have to see Edison or Icecap. I didn't feel like talking, I just needed time away from boys. Tears dripped out of my eyes, they were wind tears. The wind tripped me one way, another. I quickly packed my things, boys still asleep.

Through Icecap's tent wall I mumble-spoke: "'Bye. I'm leaving now. You'll catch me later." He'd catch me soon, I thought.

I left the two boys sleeping. And then I ran.

The mesas were windswept, colorless and endless, and I was a small speck of a girl darting across them. The trail north from Pioneer Mail campground grips an ancient eroding mesa edge—hugs the sharp dirt cliff for six exposed miles. I'd found my tribe, I fled it. I was alone again, and soon I would descend to the desert floor—

the chalky waterless Anza-Borrego Desert. I noticed the ground was already fully dry again. Amazingly, last night's rain had entirely vanished.

I felt the urge to sprint, my body felt freer striding faster. I was terribly shaken, though nothing bad had happened. Intellectually it seemed that I should want to stay with Icecap and Edison. We had all smoked, I had decided to make myself vulnerable to new men, to trust them, and these boys had proven themselves to be worthy of my trust. They hadn't touched me, nothing bad had happened; I had proven my mother wrong. I had weighed the situation, I'd felt safe, and this had been my chance to remind myself that rape wasn't normal.

It seemed that smoking weed with men had confirmed just exactly that which I hoped it would confirm for me. That men could behave better—that strangers could be safe; that hanging out in new places with new boys isn't inherently stupid or extreme or risky in nature. That girls do this, especially when they're also with a boy they know, and such girls are not tempting rape. Nothing bad had happened, I'd proven my mother wrong, but I was sad to see how I was wasting this walk already.

I realized what I was doing out here in this foreign landscape was only a continuation of what I'd been doing when I was inside the Colorado College Inn; I was smoking weed, returning to that place; I'd wanted Icecap's affirmation just as I'd wanted an unknown man who existed on the Internet, safely far away, to desire me.

I was disappointed in myself. Weed was an escape path I already knew was fraught. I didn't come out here to smoke. Obliteration was not what I'd come to wilderness to find. I was on a grand walk hoping to discover my best path forward, my strength, my place in a frightening world. The weed distracted me. I was wasting my own time.

I was seeking answers in things that weren't the answer. I'd tried the whole getting annihilated thing in the months after the rape—I'd even woken once in the campus hospital sick from vodka, desolate—and it got me no place good. I didn't feel good smoking, slipping away from myself. The Pacific Crest Trail was my place to try something different.

The cells in my forehead were tingling, I was thirsty, I was wanting to be quenched awakened and fulfilled. Weed left me wanting. I no longer wanted boys and weed.

Walking alone felt better. It felt right.

I leaned over to the mesa edge, stared down three thousand feet, and my prescription sunglasses lifted like wings, and I gasped; my arm reached out almost before I registered what had happened, a violent jolt, clutched quick at what it knew I absolutely needed. I caught them; I *got* them. My god. If they had actually blown away I'd be both blind and blinded in the desert sun—stranded. Below me thin canyons undulated like magnified combs of sand, the vast drab desert's bloodless veins.

Squinting down at the waterless valley, I remembered something terrible. I had forgotten to top off my Gatorade bottles in the tank of mouse water. I was in a waterless quandary, the oak tree beside the Pioneer Mail campground's contaminated water was hours out of view now, there was no going back the way I'd come. The next reliable water was supposed to be beside a paved road on the desert floor, about twenty miles along the trail to the north.

I tried to calm myself. There would be someone who had water. I spun it for myself. Now I'd have to drink less of the dead-mouse water, so this was probably even for the best, I rationalized. I didn't have to drink that contaminated water. All I'd need to do was become bold enough to ask someone for help. And I could do that. That's all. It would be easy, something would come.

I ran north, down. I tried to think. The endless wind pressed me, pushed me, back onto my old footprints.

I forced myself forward through air that seemed to want to hold me back.

The mesa I slowly skirted sprawled across the sky, 5,260 feet above the desert valley's hot mirages, its gold mine ruins and mining-poisoned springs. The air was hot, restless; wind tripped me gracelessly forward, downhill. The valley I approached had been a hideaway for human traffickers back in the 1930s, and in the dirt hills below me, many slaves were slain. In the next seventeen miles I would drop three thousand feet, dramatically descend. The monochrome bio-zone lay at my feet, lifeless. Scanning the expanse below me, I could see no one.

I drifted down, off the mesa's cliff edge, into a narrow canyon—shelter from the blasting wind—and out of that canyon, down, into another and another, continuing toward the soundless valley floor. The slope so gradual I hardly noticed I was losing elevation. In silent unison, the plants withered and shrank. I strode long steps, quick even around turns. Mindless momentum. Like when you're running downhill, striding, striding bigger, bigger *bigger*—praying you don't trip. The Anza-Borrego was the true desert, all baked mud, sun drenched and waterless. Something would come. Nineteen-year-olds do not die.

And soon I saw: I was impossibly lucky. Just ahead on the trail an old man was hobbling forward, bent under the weight of a massive external-frame backpack, staring down at a dust-colored square of paper. He didn't look like he had the energy to speak. I nodded at him—I knew I needed to ask him for a little water.

Close, I saw he was frail and had no teeth. Looked like he could snap at the waist. I said, "Hey? How's it going? Hey, what's that?"

He asked, "Dear. Do you have *The Water Report*?"

The Water Report? I wasn't sure what he meant. I asked him carefully, "Do you need water?"

"No," he said. "I have it." I saw his pack was strapped with three full sloshing bottles. "You need *The Water Report* or you're going to die, I think." He unfolded fully the dirty paper, smoothed it with slow hands against his thigh. Extended it out to me. "It's always accurate," he said. He sneezed. "It reports just how the water is. Where to drink."

I said, "Oh." I stared at it. "Where's it from?" I asked. "It's always right, really?" I felt unsure if he was crazy or a god-sent savior. I straightened, preparing to ask him the embarrassing favor.

He explained how a trail angel had been handing them out outside the Mount Laguna general store; he didn't know where I could get one, now. But he was shocked I didn't have it; it was important. I should copy it down with a pen so I'd have it, so I'd know which water was safe to drink, which was lead contaminated, motor oil contaminated, ripe with E. coli or even *Naegleria fowleri*. I'd die without it. I needed it, he was absolutely sure. Then, extending his bony arm, he handed it to me.

I gripped it, read it quickly; I was joyous! The next water source listed was a long thin natural stream—only a few hours up the trail. It was called San Felipe Creek, and I would make it tonight, although barely. *The Water Report* promised: the water would flow alongside Banner Grade—a State Route a mile to the north. It would be 250 yards off-trail, north by northwest, trickling beneath a tangle of large, healthy-looking cottonwood trees. At last I knew where I would get to drink.

I pulled from my pack my Moleskine journal and copied into it the next several water sources—most not listed in *The Pacific Crest Trail Data Book* at all.

And then I thanked this kind old feeble man. Newly armed with *The Water Report*, I felt invincible—charmed, so lucky, and safe again. Again I parted my lips to ask him for a drink of water—and quickly closed them. I felt he'd already given me so much. I felt embarrassed by my lack of planning, my atrocious neglect of myself, and I dreaded revealing to him how absolutely incompetent I was. He'd question me further, like any concerned person would, and of course I would fall short—I'd swiftly wreck his trust in me. He would clearly see I was incapable. I didn't want to fall in his esteem. I didn't want him to think so lowly of me. I wanted to act like I was taking care of myself by myself smoothly. I didn't want this kind old man to see me for what I still was.

And so, wordlessly, I picked my pack back up. Without asking for a drink, despite his three full sloshing bottles—certainly more than he would need before he reached the trail's next water source. I said goodbye without ever revealing to him that I was dry. I was very

thirsty, disoriented and dizzy, but I walked silently away from the
man without taking even a sip.

By six o'clock my tongue was dry as toast. I had walked twenty-two
miles. By seven I'd walked 25.5. The air still weighted with heat. Me:
tired. I was stepping over rattlesnakes now as if over shadows; in my
thirst-silenced mind they became only bones. Through the hours,
the sun and moon shared the flat cobalt sky, both pale in the big
beige, quiet and solid. Dusk is persistent in the Anza-Borrego Desert
in late April. The moon refuses to set. Moonrise to sunset is as long
and bright as an entire northern winter day. Then slate-stone gray,
night light, shadow-world. No vision is absolutely clear.

I strode, numb as a ghost.

I was hiking through blue dusk, bright with particle haze, when
I thought I saw something glowing in the hills. I squinted, and the
small light brightened. It looked like a steady sphere of clementine-
golden light, drifting with intention over the low and distant hills. I
watched it drift; it vanished. The blue air was shimmering, infinite as
open water; I watched for the light. I stood there for a while, breathing, the world was silent, leaning in the thick dusk, heart knocking,
hoping. But soon enough time had passed that I was no longer sure if
I'd imagined the light to begin with. Disappointed, I started walking
again.

And then, soon as I looked back out to the east, I saw something again. Across a low brown mountain as unassuming as a
collapsed balloon, a light was floating low over the land, drifting
steady and brilliant bright white. It seemed unlikely there was a
road out there, there was no place for one to lead to, but I thought
that maybe the light was car headlights. It was a pure burning
white. Then there was a second light, visible at the same time,
this one bigger and bluer, like a star that had fallen and was caught
hovering, independent of the smaller whiter light. The white light
glided and slipped someplace out of sight. It didn't fade; it simply

was no longer there; the blue star-light remained, slowly growing. I was suddenly scared.

I wasn't ever good at intuiting how things worked. I was awful with technology and mechanics, I often encountered things that simply didn't make clear sense to me, and I resigned myself to the unexplainable and strange. There had always been mysteries in my life—how all the other girls knew the right style to wear; how build-ings were built and highways—infinite and everywhere—were so smoothly always there, impressive things I couldn't comprehend, and so now I simply decided: what I'd seen were only car lights on an old dark road.

I couldn't yet piece together the disconnected clues to understand the origin of these lights. To explain away strange magic, I'd con-vinced myself there was an unseen road cutting across the boundless desert floor like a scar. I imagined its different possible courses. The mystery intrigued me. I couldn't think of the real destination this road would have been built to lead to, but I accepted that I couldn't see, and I accepted that it was there, strange but—from where I stood—a beautiful vision.

One flattish light was shining. I looked away, west. I had ex-plained away what I was seeing, because my secret fear was that the strange lights were a trick of my own tired vision. I feared that my eyes might be changing strangely. I feared I needed water—now.

I hoped water would banish the phantom things.

And when the air became again purely empty, I envisioned a dis-tant bend in the aimless snaking desert road.

I persisted north thinking, "Where was that team of lights going?" speculating about the destination of a desert route that didn't exist. I'd been afraid, and so I'd named the phenomenon "car lights"—banal things—which killed my fear. I wasn't afraid because the unknown force was now explained, and so I was again free to bypass, thoughtless. We aren't afraid of what we can ex-plain.

But the truth was stranger than an aimless road, it always was.

The world was full of blinding mysteries, and I was blind to the truth of what they were.

There were things about the world I couldn't understand.

It was nearly eight, the sky newly cool, gleaming. The moon a brightening yellow bulb. I saw the desert though a curtain of glittering stones, objects had become shadows. I had noticed a long ink thorn, a horn of darker ground. As I got closer I noticed the shadow-casting thing was smaller than I'd thought; it was hand size, alive and still. Looked like a rock. Some creature.

In dusk's permissiveness I wasn't thinking; I knelt down, picked up the thing, and suddenly, painlessly, my hand was glistening, covered in thick liquid. I blinked. Thought: venom. Thought: do something. Why can't you ever? Drop it. Run.

After a milky moment I flung the thing off, its smooth stomach slip-slid like a naked body against steep ice, down, down, maybe to crash, frighteningly soft, like a man's stomach, sweaty and tender. Like Junior's sweaty gut. I couldn't believe I touched it. Its spiky back caught the sand-gold light. I wished I'd brought a first-aid kit, wiped my hand on my dirty bandana and felt dread.

But, looking at my hand, I saw that I wasn't actually cut; I wasn't harmed. The fluid wasn't mine. The creature had squirted me with two strong streams of its own blood.

I'd soon learn in my first trail-town that I'd had in my palm a horned lizard, an ancient animal, its surface a shield of raised scales, its resources so primitive that, to defend itself, it increases its own blood pressure enough to rupture the vessels at the corner of its eyes, scaring bad animals away by shooting them with blood. I was the bad animal.

I had no water left to use to wash the blood from my skin. I was striped with blood, I was thirsty. I couldn't focus to complete a thought, my thoughts were primitive desperate fragments that led me nowhere.

I thought: the colored lights had been sweetly dancing. Those drifting lights I'd seen weren't all the same. Each looked distinct—carrot, bright white, and bluish—independent and unrelated, their movements quick, then slow. I couldn't make sense of my vision. It could have been a symptom of dehydration—it could have been anything. It was frightening. I had turned away from the east's vastness, where I suspected the lights still hovered over dusty hills of dry pebbles and silicon dust, violent blue and orange, maddening.

Sand smog hung like morning vapor over the blackening hills, and I kept walking, trying not to be frightened by the strange magic I had seen in my thirst.

I didn't have any water, I needed water, and I had no plan to follow forward, no path out. I was in the middle of a desert, dry and desperate. I'd left myself dehydrated, hot and overtired, endangered, and I thought I could very well die—and *why*? What had led me to here? Into the Anza Borrego, alone. What the hell was I—little Debby—trying to do? Crossing a desert alone on foot, what did I expect to happen? I couldn't remember.

I was losing sense of my remaining space, and time. I didn't know the distance to the creek.

I wished for a tall glass of frothy chocolate milk, made by my mommy. I wished for one of her egg creams, which was chocolate syrup and cold milk plus seltzer and vanilla ice cream scoops. I wished for her to appear here to take care of me, to carry me, in her hands. I wished. On twirls of pallid stars in moonlit air, on the cream moon.

I persisted past a blood-red cactus flower, another bloom the innocuous color of cream. Somehow these spiny plants had found enough water to blossom, and for a moment I wondered if I could extract water from their flesh, but they were fiercely needled. I wished I could. My vision was blackening.

Two moonlit cars flashed by—light, gone—and I shivered. At last I saw the actual road. I was too exhausted to feel joy. I passed a strange, shiny wood-and-plastic contraption I could barely distinguish from night's dark pooling air—an abandoned hermit's shack, or a mirage. Down the straightaway—the patch of scrawny cottonwoods; *The Water Report* had very specifically instructed me to "Walk right side of streambed until near these trees." I jogged to them. But when I arrived at the roadside place where San Felipe Creek was supposed to trickle, precisely where it should have been, I heard no water. Instead, damp dirt gleamed, slicked with a dark rainbow of oil.

I walked up the slick, back down, pacing it smelling for the coolness of clean water. I didn't find it. I gripped my hand-scrawled new copy of *The Water Report,* squinted in the darkness to reread it, furious at it. I skimmed the very top listing: "San Felipe Creek." And there it was. I was an idiot. I had written at the top of my journal page a long entry that described how the San Felipe Creek was most likely dry by late April—now. The source, I'd further noted, was often tainted by trash and oil. *The Water Report* suggested that hikers boil any water they do manage to draw from San Felipe Creek. But I didn't even carry a camping stove. I had written these words: *rarely drinkable.*

In eagerness I'd transcribed all these things, read them, scrawled them, and hadn't absorbed any of them.

My taste buds were raised, abrading my mouth. My arms felt limp, too weak to lift my backpack on. I felt despair ringing in every sunburnt cell. I was dying of thirst, this water was not drinkable, it would not magically become drinkable, and I needed to—swiftly—change my course to solve this problem.

I'd been such an idiot for not asking the kind man for some water.

Shell Oil lists motor oil as a carcinogen, even to the touch. Mechanics should wear latex gloves to handle it. The legal maximum of motor oil in United States drinking water is one part per billion. Or, worse than motor oil, benzene, a gasoline additive, attacks bone marrow. Consuming it can cause anemia or, even, leukemia—cancer of the blood. I feared drinking a slick of it would blacken my vision, still my mind. Yet my tongue felt dry and coarse. I spit up saliva in my mouth and tried to spread it with my stiff tongue. I saw pale copper blotches from thirst.

I panicked. I had tried to mask that I was incapable, passive and in need of others' care without doing anything to care for myself better—hiding seemed easier than changing. I still wasn't self-sufficient. I wasn't even brave enough to ask for what I so desperately needed. And now I'd bypassed my one chance.

All I could think was to pray for another car to appear on the highway and notice me. I would wave; the kind driver would glide over, give me a liter of Gatorade, and save me.

I imagined grapefruit juice, cold, plump pulp that pops into juice in your mouth. On ice. A tall cup of ice. Cold Glacier Freeze Gatorade.

I decided that that this oil-slicked water *must* be drinkable, I willed it.

I said aloud, "Good water, good water." I would have to drink it. The road was rocket straight.

I waited facing the still moon but another car never came.

I stood over the purple, green, and yellow shining film of truck-leaked motor oil that slicked the feeble trickle of a wild creek, imagining lemonade.

I made a decision to use all my energy to fight, to live.

I stood up straighter on the road—straightened my posture—and went back the way I came. Briskly, back down the lonely highway, back onto the trail I'd needlessly left. My skin was throbbing, my pulse beating beneath my salty skin. I passed the shack again. But this time it didn't look like a hermit's old shack. And then I saw a bookcase full of huge water jugs. It stood right on the western edge of the widened trail.

I blinked, knew this couldn't be real. I remembered seeing strange lights at the base of Oriflamme, fearing my thirst was warping my heating mind. Maybe I hadn't been paranoid to fear it. This was impossible. I walked closer to the hut—and its image didn't waver, only grew closer, clearer. Water. I examined it with my hands. It was a three-tiered rough-wood bookshelf, approximate in its construction. I'd dismissed it as a shadow mirage and passed it, but here it was, undeniably solid. It was real.

Someone had just sawed a bunch of two-by-fours and eyeballed it. The shelves were thin plywood, warped under the gallon jugs' weight, and across the top its builders had seared:

RELAX-ENJOY
TRAIL RATZ
DAVE-DAVE-JOHN

And "PCT," the acronym, burned inside an equilateral triangle with beveled edges: the trail's crest. It was incredible, I stared at it in disbelief. The mirage had sustained its presence. I felt it was a miracle with me.

I'd discovered trail magic, placed here for hikers. My first trail magic.

Off the eastern edge of the Pacific Crest Trail, a low brown mountain rests, unassuming. It lies like a collapsed balloon, and by day it appears drab as dust and forgettable. But it isn't what it seems.

Imagine blue night. Imagine yucca shadows, long and spiny, black on moonlit ground. Imagine you are walking, alone, and a sliver of low-distant mountain in an orange flash is spotlit.

Thirst isn't blinding you. This is Oriflamme Mountain, and it is real, and, in night's flat blue, it does spark. In darkness, it makes its own light. Come nightfall, orange spheres of light drift from this mountain's still surface like corpse-size sparks. The light is strong enough to be mistaken frequently for an automobile headlight, and, when seen from a short distance, seems to produce a directional beam.

On approaching it, the experience is again that of walking into the "eye" of a headlight, but when one reaches the supposed point of origin, the light disappears. It may appear at any hour of the night, may come several nights in succession or be absent for weeks at a time, and there is nothing purposeful in its movements; it goes here and there as a bird or a wandering animal might do or perhaps like a person out for an idle stroll.

The mountain's sparks have ignited legends. They were said to lead to gold. The restless lights were originally noticed by the Indians of the area; they believed it was "a spirit light . . . the ghost of a chief who died." The spirit light might appear as an orange spherical shifting shape with a light in its center, or as highly reflective metallic-looking spherical configurations. As blobs of orange, red, green, white, light. Blue huge stars, resting in brush. A drifting spark. A flock of sparks. It was known to the smugglers and gold miners in the area, too, "a strange light that appears from time to time in a remote valley of Southern California. . . . A curious light." Every culture to observe it has developed myths to explain it.

The *Journal of the American Society for Psychical Research* reported in February 1940, "It is known, too, that Malakia [Oriflamme Mountain] was once a 'hide-out' for smugglers of Chinese (from Mexico) and *supposedly* the scene of various acts of violence." As if violence could make light. Maybe violence could make light.

What I'd really seen that night was the magic that would save me.

In the aftermath of destruction, a silence settles—the stillness of fresh loss. People's cheerful chatter is fainter, the blue color of sky dimmer; now that horror is undeniable and feels inescapable, the value of life seems lessened.

Rape had shocked me like white electricity and left me hurting. All men after looked three shades darker. Small tasks became too exhausting to attempt, all good efforts seemed futile. The wound, flushed with the heat of blood, pulsing, was all that I could feel. I was swallowed inside the mute darkness that follows loss, I was fading in it. I could have passed my life staying in it.

But some slim nameless cord inside tugged me. The harsh dimness that follows loss isn't static, but charged with the energy of immanent change. Hurt, I was left with a choice: wallow and stay in the dark, or seek light and fight to reach it. These two paths emerged. I had this choice to make.

Loss is the shocking catalyst of transformation. I saw that this mountain valley, haunted by senseless murders, darker, had absorbed unthinkable violence and turned it into mesmerizing light. My rape became my catalyst. Rape gave me cause to flee the muteness—forced me into making a bold and forceful change. I chose to fight to find a way to leave to seek my own strength and beauty.

I was searching to find the way to make light.

There's no scientific understanding of why, at night, Oriflamme Mountain sparks, but there are people who wish they could know for sure. The general term for the phenomenon of nighttime mountain-fire is *earthlights*. The International Earthlights Alliance seeks a scientific explanation. It's fringe science. They go to the sites with cameras, magnetic detectors; they'll stay on-site for weeks. They still don't have an answer.

There are things about the world that I miss, can't understand and cannot see. I had long ago accepted this. But here was something I remembered that was not what I'd thought it was—a dry mountain that made light—and I never would have known it.

And the idea of light unexplainably produced out of nothing was haunting, it shook me. A flat drab mountain could produce its own light, no one in this whole world knows why, and if that was possible then of course there must be other things that seemed impossible but weren't, and so anything—great and terrible—felt possible to me now.

I wondered what else there was out in the world that I had never seen through my lenses. I had speculated about the destination of a nonexistent desert road, I'd kept going. What other magic had I wrongly explained away? I felt like I'd lost something I hadn't ever had.

A thousand things I didn't even know existed *had* to exist.

I wish now that I had stayed. I wished I'd made camp and watched the strange lights dance and let myself wonder.

This light was not something everyone will get to see. People tend not to see what they're not looking for. The truth is, if you're not looking for it, it is invisible.

That was the blackest night of my life and I saw nothing.

CHAPTER 8

Hollow Words

I had nothing to offer anybody except my own confusion.
—Jack Kerouac, On the Road

APRIL 23, SCISSORS CROSSING, DESERT, MILE 77.4

As I drank the bookshelf water, my mind switched back on like power after a storm. Black holes I saw were swallowed by light blue sky. Cactus needles glinted, and I saw I was sitting in pooling daylight. I looked down at my body, dusty from dry earth. I was unsure if I'd passed through night lying in dirt, or if the blackness I'd taken to be night had only been my own vision made dim and colorless by thirst. My heart was galloping, I had no sense of how long I had been lying there. Maybe really it had been daytime all along.

I needed to remember precisely what had happened. It was April 23. An empty late spring day at Scissors Crossing. I looked out at the desert around me, from pale rock to pale rock, from pebble of sand into the glare of sun calm and still. Wind and sunlight dried the water on my upper lip, and from the low eastward place of the sun, I discerned that it must be a new early morning.

The lost hours scared me. They were opaque like a vodka blackout. I didn't know where the boys were, and I wondered if they were near me.

I had just nearly ended my life through my neglect. I was freshly—so massively luckily—alive and here in the sunlight, out of death's light-less nightshadows, and all I could seem to feel was a relaxing mounting drowsiness. The only thought I could conjure was *stillness*. The word *death* was empty of weight. I could feel no fear—and no gratitude.

I imagined how my body would be aching to be sated with bright water if this bookshelf of water hadn't been placed here. I would have slowed, then laid down to rest. My hands would unclench passively, relax into sleep. Nineteen years old and alone. Twenty feet from a paved road that no one seemed to travel. I pictured my dying skin, turning copper in hard sunshine. The warm wind lifting dust onto my resting body. In my sleep I would be singed into a soft endless bed of dust. And that'd be it.

I shivered a deep shudder. I hadn't seen the boys, they would likely discover me. The loveliness of my daydream of death disturbed me. I romanticized death, I was unfeeling. I was learning for the first time that I wasn't invincible. The risk was unpredictable and real and I didn't always pass it by unnoticed. Sometimes, I was discovering, it bites.

Death was not a drifting spark in the night I could simply turn away from.

I had left the boys, sure that solitude was safest. I'd rather be alone—other people were not the answer. I was proving my mother wrong, systematically—I could care for myself. This was all very true. But it was also true that if I were still with Icecap, he would have helped me. My wild aloneness had led to this desperation. If I was going to put myself into a situation wherein I had no one to depend on, I needed to step up and be the one to actually take good care of myself. The universe wouldn't simply do it for me.

My mind slowly explored what might have happened if the book-case weighted with water had been a mirage—the terror. I tried to conjure death.

The sunlight heated my face, the air tasted brassy, and sun-swallowed hills glared like intent eyes blankly colored. I looked at the dusty one-gallon plastic milk jugs of water. They were tied loosely to one another with an orange nylon rope, bright and solid. I saw an image of my mother this Sunday morning lunging from table to sink to dishwasher, cooking, feeding and swiftly cleaning. Moving through the old house, organizing but in truth pacing, in the evening circling from kitchen phone to bedroom phone, waiting for me to call and say I was safely going to sleep.

My god, what would my mother feel when she didn't get a call?

I felt sick with myself, my thoughtlessness.

Every cell of my living body felt at once sunburnt—enflamed— and absent. I wished to be back safe at home cupping my mother's Sleepy Time tea, watching the world pass from safety.

What was I doing out here all alone and un-fucking-prepared, as I'd known for so long, *seen* in that list of Necessary Things back in the post office-general store—*fearful*—but passed over like some naive and blind child. I kept walking anyways.

I wanted myself to remember in my body what I only very abstractly intellectually knew: that death is not a pretty flower that had almost pricked me. It was not a small annoyance I could simply bypass and quickly disregard. It was really The End.

Water was liquid silver, water was gold. It was clarity—a sacred thing. Drinking was no longer something to take for granted. I'd never needed to consider water before. Go to the sink and pour a glass of water, it's the easiest thing in the world, but it had become what my new world revolved around.

Children believe they are immortal, *death* is an empty word like the name of a country they've never been to on a time-faded map. I wasn't a child anymore.

I felt a fierce and sudden need to protect my parents. I didn't want them to know that I had felt death's presence; I didn't want them to know the daughter they loved could die.

I was a damn lucky girl, but I knew that I might not be so lucky next time.

I got up from the hard dirt, the air shadowy, the sun full and white. I unscrewed another gallon jug and filled back up all of my dented, dusty Gatorade bottles, arm shaking, trying to hold the gallon steady. I chugged and drained each bottle empty again, drinking the whole gallon's worth—eight pounds of water. I let my head cool, feeling full and chilled and *fed.*

Slipped between two sandy jugs on the top warped shelf of the bookcase leaned a thin black binder. Inside I found computer-printed copies of *The Water Report*—that list of places along the trail to find drinking water—for hikers to Take One. I did. It was my vivid map to water, the treasure, charting the best way and I would read it carefully from now on, rely on it. It would lead me to a clear puddle thirty feet down a faint trail; to a well; out to a spigot in the shade behind a vacant and rotting house. It would prove to be reliable, and soon it would save my life.

The other item in the binder was a composition notebook sealed from sandstorms and rain by a Ziploc bag. I pulled the bag open, opened it. Yogi Beer, Miss Information, Silverfox, Strider, Boomer, Prison Jim, the Stumbling Norwegian. They and dozens of others wrote "thank you," made dumb jokes and told stories, and signed the notebook with new trail names. Each person had just walked through what I had just survived.

In one entry, a hiker named Jack Rabbit described the earthlights phenomenon—it mesmerized me. It also seemed he had actually met the Trail Ratz at Kickoff. Someone else wrote about meeting the famed Hendersons, a husband-wife team of trail angels who live alongside the trail to the north up in Green Valley and run the oasis known as the Casa de Luna. People who'd celebrated at Kickoff seemed to have inside jokes, and I was jealous. I wished then that I hadn't skipped it. I read the book of names, each entry marked with the date and time the writer had passed by—the last was April twenty-third, this morning's date—and I felt newly alone. I wished I had met a woman on Kickoff's grounds that day, not Icecap.

I skimmed the list of hikers, up and down, looking for a girl I'd like who would like me back. I scanned the trail names. None of them were familiar to me. It was tough for me to discern gender, most people could go either way. Silverfox as a girl could be sweet and pretty; as a guy, the name seemed predatory, like a silver-haired professor who slept with students. I didn't want that. I wanted someone cool to hike with, a lovely girl, funny, who could make a joke of anything. She'd be light as a bird; her name would be Sky Blue. She'd have a pixie cut, perfect even out here, and a compass tattooed to her foot, and she'd ask me, "What's to worry? What to wear today?" and look down at her one pair of shorts and shirt, clinging to her, sweat stained and dusty. She and I both would have only one set of clothes. "Oh! Good choice," she'd say at it, making me smile. She could make me laugh at the heat, the deergrass, the absurdity of our quest, the endlessness of our pain. Together we could sneak rocks into the packs of mean hikers.

I would find a partner to walk with, I decided, and she needed to be another girl.

I was feeling better, drunk on water—high on the huge kindness of faceless people. Generous strangers were somewhere out there, loving, plotting to help. I was in awe: real trail magic exists. I hadn't been imagining things at all. Euphoria struck me. My aloneness led to this desperation, and it was people who had saved me.

The notebook filled with names and notes was called a trail register—my first of many. I'd find them along the walk, some in coolers full of warm cans of soda, some just on a flat rock or at crossings. In this endless desert where cell reception was rare—dead spots can span long days—registers would tell me who was ahead, who was close. Whom I could catch up with and by when and where he'd be. These baggie-sleeved notebooks would become the hikers' telephones. I'd soon learn that, unfortunately, registers were also men's best tool for smart Pink Blazing—the act of following female hikers they wanted—tracking.

I walked away from the magic water that morning rested and awakened. The trail that led into the sallow gravel was two feet wide—unusually constricted—and rimmed with thorny plants. I walked an hour over dirt like powdered bone, the desert sky seemed to brighten, and I felt calm and intensely grateful. That fourth day on the trail I walked just under thirty sun-whitened miles. My footprints distinct, south forever, behind me.

The first star blinked on, a weak white speck in immense clear blackness. I ran northward, evening's air tasting cold and good. Hard night fell. I pitched my tent on a flattish strip of sand, a gap in the thick tangle of scrub oak. The air had cooled to a rich pooling black, and the cacti were colorless as wax. The sand felt harmless, very soft and flat. I built my tent—clip-clip-zip-*done*. It only took me about two minutes by now. Lying contented in my fluffy sleeping bag, I noticed a distant light in silky desert blackness, bobbing. My heart rate fluttered, fearful. In dreamy half sleep I wondered if it was an earthlight. The light drifted unsteadily. As it came closer, I saw it was somebody's flashlight. I hoped that it might be Icecap and Edison's. But the nearing light was singular. It was a lone headlamp.

It hadn't occurred to me that someone might be directly behind me. The idea of camping alone with a stranger frightened me. I lay exposed, in the night, with no one in the desert I could summon to come join and protect me. I quickly clicked off my headlamp and slipped soundlessly inside of my sleeping bag, hoping I wasn't visible from the trail. I hoped to God that the light wasn't a man.

The shadowed figure grew. It leaned its weight forward onto its trekking poles with each step forward as if it had a broken rib.

It was a limping man.

His headlamp blinded me even through my olive-walled tent's mesh. Then he stopped. He was not hiking on past me. He was going no farther. It would be just me and him. This strange man was a snake at dusk: maybe a Mojave Green, maybe harmless; it was impossible for me to see.

Alone and scared, I wished I could talk with my mother. I wanted to call her to tell her that I was okay. I found my cell phone—it had two bars of reception out of four—and I touched MOM. The digital ringing faltered, the signal not strong enough. I touched her again, but I couldn't get through to her. This was my fourth night on the trail, and each night but the last I had tried to call her, but so far I'd never once actually reached her. I imagined my mom had been unable to sleep these past few nights, knowing her baby was out in the desert, not knowing anything more. The satellite phone waited for me in a post office in Warner Springs. I curled up small in my tent. I imagined her back in Newton, trying to fall asleep.

I spent that night clutching myself, tensing my neck, praying to night's flat blackness that, if my zipper unzipped, I'd fight for the first time.

I had planned to wake early yet somehow I slept and slept. In mid-morning's bright heat I awoke and climbed out of my tent to find the night man's boots. He'd camped two feet from me.

I left him there and walked, through a field of twiggy deergrass, scraping pale lines across my shins and knees, past Snake Cholla—plants tall and whimsical, like Joshua trees, but emaciated. After last night's scare, the reasons I'd left the boys behind seemed misguided. I'd believed I needed to be steady in myself before I could function with others—but surviving alone no longer felt like a good way either. Now I tried not to hike too fast because I wanted Icecap to catch up with me. He'd scare off this guy and other men I'd meet. I didn't want to have to camp alone again with a man I didn't know.

At a turn in the trail I ripped a page out of my journal and wrote: *Icecap and Edison, Please catch up with me so I can enjoy your company!—Wild Child. (Take note with you.)* Beside my name I drew a heart. *My* name, a choice now. I left the note right on the path, held down by three jagged fist-size rocks.

I passed through the low San Felipe Hills, one of those forgotten ranges like any other ridge of mounds one sees when flying over the country and then can't conjure back at all. On top of one, only a child could feel atop the world. They go up for ten miles and then they go down. Their soil doesn't absorb water; rain flows over the hills' sur-faces, funnels through the deepest folds, forms steep rivers that rage for a breath—evaporate. Dry. Noticeably wider. Each flash flood cuts the drainage deeper, carries a little more ground away.

The Pacific Crest Trail is horse-graded—a horse could, theoretically, clomp the whole great length—and so the trail can never be steeper than ten vertical degrees. Mellow inclines, mellow declines. Loose dry soil poured through my shoe mesh, and I had to empty, empty, empty out my running shoes; they'd fill like magic bowls. Spiny balls, pea size and brown, stuck to my socks. Hitchhiking seeds. At mile 88.3 I emerged onto the ridge crest; I could see Oriflamme Mountain from here to the southwest, lightless now. The ridged hills to the north. More of the same. The trail followed the ridge despite its inefficient course, and the crest S-turned east, west, east, west, stayed high. Barrel cacti lined the trail like spiky melons, clumps of plump green balls. Grapevine Mountain, just dust over stone. Hedgehog cacti, otherwise ugly stubs covered with thick porcupine-type needles, flowered soft and delicate magenta blossoms, the brightest, loveliest thing in all directions for a hundred miles.

I picked a bloom and immediatley felt terrible. Carried it for seventeen miles in my sweaty palm. By the time I dropped it to the dusty bedrock five hours of walking north it was the color and shape of fox scat.

Beige dust-dirt unfolding before me, beneath me. The chaparral below like tufts of drab weeds. Fishhook cacti. More small balls stuck on my dusty socks. Blue hills in the distance, low and pale like soft blue corpses. Motionless. Lovely.

"That cunt," someone called out. I looked behind me. It was Edison. My boys appeared like lanky goats atop a grassy hump and lunged down to me, as if I'd willed them back. Their backpacks thumped as they jogged down to catch me, panting, their presence fitting this landscape naturally, shifting it around me into a familiar dry field that suddenly felt safe.

"We have felt worried for you," Icecap said, his Swiss-German accent strikingly foreign.

"I have felt worry for *you*," I said, mocking him.

Edison's face was wet-dirt brown and shiny. *Filthy.* Happy.

"I feel at this time glad, now," Icecap said. "It is a good day. Yes."

And I was glad, too. I wouldn't have to camp alone with last night's man—or a worse unknown man—tonight.

We three walked north, together again, and I wanted to stay with them, to move north with them for always.

"Miss me very much?" I asked Icecap. I pinched his arm. My face heated.

"Aw, look. An insecure girl," Edison said. "How awesome."

I shoved his pack, laughed.

"We missed you so much because we're in love with you and we cried and jerked each other off to sleep," Edison said. His back faced me, walking, but I heard in his voice a grin.

"Fuck you both," I said. "And thanks."

Icecap was looking at me, his eyes were smiling, I could feel them on my cheek, but I didn't look back at him.

Another half dozen miles of walking later, we emerged from a sandy canyon onto an arid grassland, expansive as the African savannah. Rolling hills carpeted with brown grass, whipping like a flag in the twisting wind. I glanced behind us time to time, looking out for the limping man, half-hoping I'd see him as a speck across the sea of grass and he'd see me with my two young, rowdy guys and be let down and embarrassed. Clumps of pale rocks dotted shallow brown-grass hills, and the sunlight tinted the whole field golden, like fairy-tale straw. In my high-strung joy I couldn't think how the limping man might not know he had even slept next to a girl last night. I might easily have been another man. To him, I was just a faceless fellow hiker who had already made camp. Really, I had probably made him feel safer.

The wind firm on my back, pushing me forward. The sky a bright blank vacant hole. Me, tripping forward, into it. These plains felt foreign, African; lions might pace here, hide in packs behind a white rock. This open grassland was vast, easy to get lost in if I wandered from the trail. Three or so more miles of walking and we saw Eagle Rock, rising from the horizon like a live bird. In its blue shadow we rested.

Icecap said again that he'd worried about me.

Edison said again that I was annoying, "the third wheel." "You smell weird, too," he said. "Like blood."

"Like blood?" I said. I was startled. I no longer felt so marked by rape, tagged by my terrible seeds of blood. But at Edison's remark, I felt suddenly guilty, like I had been lying to my new family. Like it was time to tell them of my rape, after all. I suddenly wanted to share the secret burden I'd been carrying so that they might actually help me to bear it. I didn't know if this new family would offer me more compassion than my real one had, but I felt hopeful. I hoped they'd care for me and validate me—tell me, "Fuck them! Fuck them all!" and we three would be my wild tribe in the middle of the desert, warriors, invincible together, bonded against the world. They made me safer. I thought I wanted to stay with them forever.

Then before I could remember that my words could strip me naked, I told my two tribe mates, "I'm not—I was. I was raped at school."

Edison threw a rock at nothing. He told me, "Tons of girls say that."

My ears felt hot. Tears hit my thighs, streaked inward to dusty bedrock. Edison was talking, but I didn't want to hear it. I tried to not hear it. He was so close to me, my knee an inch from his knee. I didn't move away. He was telling a story. He was saying he needed to teach me how things worked. "Simple," he was saying. "Try to learn."

He was talking about his town and the trouble there. "If you're white, dum' niggas say you rape them all the time." It happened in his Tennessee town constantly. He said they lied for money, for attention, because they regret "fucking nasty men" and like to make believe that they have some self-respect. Because rape is better than when it's your own fucked choice.

"They should know nobody wants to get with their black ass so bad."

The word *ignorant* was on my tongue, I was ready to spit it at him, but I found my dry mouth unable to propel it out.

Every group of new people who knew me would make me feel ashamed. My history was shameful. I would always need to explain it, or mitigate it, apologize for it, hide it, or bury it. I fucking hated it.

I finally looked at Icecap but saw in his distant eyes the thickness of the barrier of the languages of our lives. He was indifferently eating a cracker.

I supposed this was the way it would be. Forever after. This family also didn't understand. I was taken aback all over again to find that after all this time of chanting Rape Is Not My Fault, I still believed somehow it was.

Tons of girls say "rape," I'm sure. I didn't say anything about it after that.

My shame was unearthed, alive. That tightening in my chest, the wish to fade away like a shadow in diffused light. We passed a desert school—a plot of pale dirt enclosed by a chain-link fence, a cinder-block building the dirt's same color. Five- and eight- and thirteen-year-olds played. One cute redheaded child waved, his hair huntsman's orange, the brightest thing around, and a group of the youngest kids ran up to the chain-link fence, tiny noses and eyes patterned with green metal crisscrosses, small fingers gripping the fence, one kid shaking it. They watched us walk by with our bright backpacks. They knew we were the hikers—we walked through their tiny town each April, year after year—but I can't imagine they understood why. Even I didn't fully understand why back then. None of us spoke as we crossed into Warner Springs.

It was an old-fashioned western-type resort town built around a handful of clear, natural hot springs, a tourist attraction for people of a bygone generation. No seaweed wraps, no masseuse or skybar. Not one stoplight either: just an old faded gas station, and a temporary-turned-permanent modular post office, shoe box shaped and creaking, where hikers picked up their food resupply boxes. We came up on, the post office and outside in its empty parking lot, in the small shade of an oak, we noticed a half-dozen men sprawled out drinking beers. They were thru-hikers.

We joined them—Spicy Mustard, Jack Rabbit, Dale, Blake, Twig, and gigantically tall White Rhino. Spicy Mustard had been lounging by the hot springs, drinking, venturing over to the gas station to buy a pint of Ben & Jerry's and then some hot taquitos, first a day, then two, then a week.

"Time fliiies in the Vortex," he said handing me a can of beer. I held it, between cupped hands, unsure about what to do. Spicy reached over and popped it open in my hands. "Take your pack off. Stay awhile." He said this town was the place, the spot, the mark.

"But," I said. "But I have to go in the post office, actually." I had to pick up my resupply package from my mother.

He wasn't listening. He was talking to Edison, who was now also holding an open beer.

"Isn't it illegal to drink in a post office?" I asked, then repeated, standing with my warm beer, no one listening to me. I waited, still and awkward for a minute, and then stretched out the elastic waistband of my shorts and placed my beer against my stomach and released it, my waistband holding it in place, and carefully walked inside.

A man was behind the counter. Before him, a notebook register lay open for thru-hikers to sign, just the same as the one by the bookshelf of water. Postal workers provided this one; I nodded to the clerk—thank you—and skimmed it. It listed Freedumb, Miss Information, Yogi Beer—many of the same names I'd seen before. Also many real names: Jack, Andrew; Blake outside had signed "Blake." The people who didn't have trail names, yet. I found Belle!—a girl—but saw that she was three days ahead of me, probably eighty or a hundred miles to the north. Most people had scrawled gleeful, one-hundred-miles-and-onward!-type notes—and the clerk asked me, as I signed, where I was from.

"Massachusetts," I said. I almost added, But I go to school in Colorado—but I didn't.

The clerk had colorless eyes. He leaned toward me, his forearms pressing down onto the counter, bulging. His voice was croaky, low, as if he had a secret to tell me. "You's too pretty to be a vag-bond."

I looked down at my box from my mother—an overstuffed fifteen-pound package of food. "Oh," I said. And then I thanked him, and left. I walked out, just as Icecap and Edison came in. I avoided their eyes, though I sensed no memory of Eagle Rock in them, only light boyish forgetfulness. I badly wanted to forget, too.

Out on a patch of yellowed grass by the lot, I sipped the beer Mustard had given me. I surveyed my goods. My mom had mailed me fifteen pounds of Werther's Originals and parmesan and cute little chocolates and Kashi TLC crackers—just what I'd asked for— plus some freeze-dried green beans and berries and some calcium supplements I hadn't asked for but probably needed. The men also unpacked their resupply boxes, and I felt watched. My food, mostly from Whole Foods, was the nicest, by far.

Edison's box was bizarre, filled with paper cans of Betty Crocker chocolate frosting and beef jerky and Gushers fruit candies. What didn't fit in our overstuffed backpacks we ate right there, trading sugar for salt, bartering like schoolkids. At the bottom of my box, protected inside two Ziploc freezer bags, was—as promised—the big satellite telephone. It lay beside an innocuous little silver-gray device I hadn't asked for. I didn't know what it was, I just slipped it in with my things, packing it also. My beer was empty, I cracked a second.

"That's some shit," Edison said, mouth bright red from cherry Pez. He was holding Icecap's foil-sealed tuna. "Eight Pez is worth one fish."

Icecap let him have the tuna, didn't want some of Edison's "pills."

We wandered, canned beers gleaming in daylight in our hands, across the tiny town and got Creamsicles from the gas station. Late dusty sun slashed through the shop's old lace curtain, heated my sun-kissed cheeks. Then, dehydrated, heavy with our packs and drunk, we stumbled to the "resort" and three-way-split the $90 cost of a night in a wooden cabin. The cabin had two twin-size beds. The clean room made me feel filthy. I needed a shower. I was nervous, trying to have fun, trying to relax. It was uncomfortable, imagining sleeping in a bedroom with them, still mortified and hating myself. I watched as Edison laid down his sleeping bag on the floor without discussion.

Right in front of the boys, I called my mother. I hadn't ever gotten through to her from the trail. But now my cell phone rang steadily;

I was pacing, conscious of my body. I was nervous to hear her voice out here. I feared the old tension it carried would somehow swiftly sweep me backward. Icecap and Edison were on the rug drinking from a clear plastic bottle of tawny alcohol.

She answered. "Hello?" my mother said quickly. She sounded at once very eager and surprised. "Hello, *Debby*?" At the familiar breathless upturn of her voice my stomach tightened, my neck curled my head downward, and then quickly I made an effort to try to straighten back up, embarrassed. I hoped the boys hadn't sensed the shifting adolescent stature.

I apologized for never having called her from the trail yet. "I never had reception. I tried."

Without hesitation she offered, "You can still come home."

I was quiet through our connection.

Then with no pause she asked if the satellite phone had arrived. I should keep it on me, she told me, waterproofed and padded. Now she'd be waiting for my phone call nightly. I absolutely had to call before I went to sleep, or she couldn't sleep. I understood the implication; she hadn't been sleeping. "Now you can reach home from anywhere." In the Mojave, from the Sierra—everywhere—I would now call my parents.

Abruptly she asked me if I'd gotten the food she'd sent me, if I liked it, when I'd need my next food package sent, and where? Was I taking a multivitamin? How was I getting enough calcium? How were my running shoes holding up after all these miles I'd walked through the desert's gravelly sand?

I asked her what the small silver device she'd mailed me was.

"Oh good!" she answered. She explained that it was a portable GPS from R.E.I. She'd already unboxed it, put lithium batteries in for me, and had Daddy upload into it all the maps I would need. "Now you can know where you are," she said. She told me that, now on, when I called every night, I had to read her my latitude and longitude coordinates. My exact global place.

I examined the device, its silvery plastic. Even its small bulk felt excessive. I didn't need the extra weight. I pushed the black rubber button on its side, watching the slate black screen flash to green. It played a twinkling tune, like a carnival game, a dozen black plus signs appearing, swirling, multiplying to form the black, block-letter words LOCATING SATELLITES.

I told her, "I don't want it." I asked her if she wanted me to give it away or mail it back.

"Wherever you camp," she said, as if she didn't hear me. "Look at the latitude and longitude. Read the numbers off and I'll write them down and read them back."

Nightly I would call to report to her my GPS coordinates. All I had to do was call and read to them where I was. No matter what. It was her and Daddy's only requirement. If I wanted them to support this walk, I had to.

The boys were drinking. Edison tossed his sweat-grayed shirt off and lay back on the carpet, took a swig. His ribs showed like a greyhound's. My mother was still talking, I said "Uh-huh" to her and slipped out into the cabin's bathroom. In the frosted mirror my face and arms were darkened by dirt and too much sun. I could see that I was somewhat thinner. I dragged my hand over my abdomen, up and down the inside of my thigh—I felt the pulse—my body already slimming—and felt pride. I stepped up on the beige plastic scale to see my weight.

The scale's hand swung and stopped abruptly, surprisingly shortly. The number it hovered on struck me. It was what I'd weighed at the start of college. Before Junior. I had made a choice and had in just six days lost all my post-rape pounds. Look at me. My body was just what it had been. This change felt impossibly quick. It felt amazing. Standing in late-day's light, looking in the bathroom mirror, my mother on the line with me, I realized in a sweet rush that I'd already finished walking one hundred miles.

My mother repeated her statement in my ear. Finally, I said, "Okay." A GPS and a satellite phone, making my pack heavy, connecting me to the outside world. Things I now needed to keep on me, safe. I had to bear the burden of her love.

Back in the bedroom Edison lay, pink lips parted, a smear of liquor glistening on his chubby cheek. On the whole slim longness of him, only his cheeks carried pudge. He passed me the big bottle of yellow-brown alcohol, I didn't know what kind it was. I took a full gulp. It tasted dizzyingly synthetic. My mother was saying, "I love you Doll Girl." She told me to enjoy sleeping in a bed tonight.

I was drunk already.

I feared sleeping. I looked at the tidy bed. I felt angry, drunken hatred burned me. I was wrong for this world; the world wanted me to be purer—a virgin—to hate the body I was given and be thinner, and also be at ease in my body, I couldn't—*fuck* them. I'd fled to wilderness to hide, but even here I was made to feel unlovable, to question the integrity of my body after my rape. Even on the faraway Pacific Crest I had to confront ignorant men's judgments of me. It was fucking Edison. I would show him.

Edison and Icecap changed. I kept my clothes on. We stepped out into electric blue dusk to go find the resort's thermal swimming pool. Evening's air was chilled. Soon it would darken. The pool was a glassy ground of black ripples. Sodium lamps lit the wet asphalt in gold Os, like fallen suns. I swayed, unsteady. I grasped at a shining ring of yellowed light. The pool was surrounded in every direction by waterless desert floor.

Pure fantastic hatred possessed me. Edison was not seeing me, he was trapping me. I was trying to find a way to shed the skin I was enveloped in—that obscured me. It was men's vision that was ensnaring me. I was exhausted of having to negotiate myself around people's judgment, hated it, had had enough. I wanted to strip these boys of the power they tried to claim with smug eyes watching, assessing, deciding. Deciding rape was my fault, my shame.

Dizzy with liquor, I decided to shock their eyes, smash flat wrong-boxes Edison and other men had placed on me—retaliate. I pulled off my salt-stiff brown T-shirt, unhooked my sweat-stained bra, letting it fall to the rough wet gleaming concrete, shedding everything. The boys stood on the pale concrete, watching. It was not a clothing optional pool.

I closed my eyes, inhaled through my nose, and felt high and wonderfully wild. The rings of sodium lights illuminated my dry body, lighting my form before Icecap and Edison, and anybody else who happened to be there. Icecap and Edison stood in their shorts, not getting in, not sure what I was doing. I couldn't remember the last time I'd been naked in front of strangers. It was uncomfortable, but in my passionate frustration felt somehow necessary.

I shivered and slid into the pool, joining the black water. The strangers around me shifted. Silky water struck me like an awakening. I'd become lucid again, sobered, as if I'd just awoken in the middle of a dream to find I was, in fact, exposed in public. I didn't feel powerful now. I felt panicked. I was in water with strangers, and my vulnerability frightened me.

A fat man spun and drifted slowly, like a redirected ship, and stared at my nude body. I was hugging my breasts with my forearms, covering them—mortified. The big man had no hair. He floated over to me.

"You the lifeguard?" he asked. He had a buoyant Southern drawl and no eyebrows. I shivered in the hot water. "No," I whispered. "No. I—sorry. I'm not."

He nodded.

In hindsight, the big bald man had been making a joke. His hairlessness was likely from chemotherapy, and he was passing his final time in these desert hot springs.

I floated in a trancelike state. I felt wrong in my nudity, no longer secure or powerful, or even stable—or safe.

I wanted Edison and Icecap to finally see how very exposed I was, even with my thin skin of dirty girl's clothing. How unformed. I was terrified. My sexuality made me uncomfortable, and I'd lost control of it, and I flailed to reclaim it.

The boys had to see.

They slipped into the pool but stayed in the far corner, shadowed, away from me.

CHAPTER 9

WILD DREAMS

"You wanted cock up you *bad* last night," Edison said, and I stiffened, my body rigid under a threadbare sheet. He was lying on the floor, his eyes rock gray and lifeless. He detailed how I'd stripped down naked at the swimming pool for no reason. He told me I'd acted like a slut and like a fool. His eyes were unflinching. "You're a slutty drunk."

I winced, stared blank at Icecap's feet. They hung huge and white over the edge of his bed. I watched them shift, he rolled over to face me.

"You drink too much," he said. "You should learn your limits by now, actually."

I let my eyes close again. His words seared my entire chest like a splash of acidic paint marking me—they betrayed me. In the redness of my dark vision I relived what I had done the night before. I had stripped naked in front of men. Drunk. In morning's somber brightness I tried to remember why I had done it. Total exposure had seemed like the only way to be seen more clearly, heard, but now it seemed the opposite: a wild act that would define me.

I didn't want Edison near me anymore. I was sick, nauseated with shame. I had awoken in a bed and there they were, spitting wrong words at me, they hurt, and I had to get away. I hated Edison purely.

In that sun-hot new day's hostile shut-eyed darkness, I wished I could hit him right there, make him feel what I was feeling.

But I had been looking for respect from someone I myself didn't respect. Edison was not worthy of it. On the floor, he was sprawled out like a spill of water, the left side of his face and his left arm were intestine pink, imprinted with the shag texture of the carpet. He panted softly, even in his stillness. So terribly snug in bed, sober once again, I saw for the first time that I could stop giving people the power to make me feel disrespected. In my anger I began to see the absurdity of allowing this boy to shame me.

I tried to meet Icecap's eyes, pleading—needing to have a better interaction—but his pupils were glassy, lightless. I felt let down by Icecap, just as I had back at Eagle Rock, when I'd revealed that I'd been raped, and Edison was cruel and backward and Icecap had done nothing. Again he wasn't sticking up for me. I wondered if I'd feel differently about nakedness if these boys weren't here to tell me to feel ashamed.

I couldn't continue walking with them.

That afternoon, Icecap, Edison, and I hiked out of Warner Springs. Yet we were not together anymore, not in the same innocent, intense new-best-friends way. Climbing the steep hill out of town with Icecap and Edison, melancholy and breathing hard, I replayed in my head how on the night we missed Kickoff I had leaned toward Icecap, my folded body only inches from pressing into his. I had felt his eyes holding me again exactly as intently as they had back at Lake Morena—determined. Bent with me in the little tent, our arms and legs made heat. I could smell his sweat and sunscreen, feel his breathing, the hard hip of the boy beside me, stirring me. I remembered tingling air between our arms. I'd felt seen by a boy who believed that I was worth noticing. I'd wanted him to memorize my face and not ever forget it. I wanted him to touch my cheek and tell me I was lovely.

His hip shifted into mine, we had been subtly and fully touching, and I'd looked at him finally. In the line of his eyes, I had believed—I was beautiful.

I had wanted him to love me.

I sadly knew now he didn't see me the way I wished he would.

He hadn't treated me with the love and compassion I wanted, but I was worthy of that love, and someday some boy would have it for me. I hadn't found it yet, but I would find it soon.

I was beginning to feel compassion for myself.

Ascending up relentless switchbacks out of town, I felt awkward in my skin when Icecap stepped too close, restless; his body now repelled me. My eyes bounced quickly from his when they accidentally met. Icecap hadn't talked to me all morning.

In the first ten miles out of town we gained fifteen hundred feet of elevation and entered a deep forest. I was wounded but climbing hard, ascending toward the high ridge above the desert. The guys were trailing me, jogging to keep my pace; Edison stopped to retie his shoelace; Icecap stopped and waited. I kept hiking, faster. We crossed Agua Caliente Creek—dry—the boys were like black commas far below me—and then, four miles north, crossed another fork of the creek, burbling sweetly, silver in the sun. Icecap and Edison caught up and collapsed to the ground to drink. I filled my bottles, standing, slipped them in my slung-on pack, and ran. With no goodbye.

I crossed Lost Valley Road—a note written in the dirt read: Not Our Trail—and another old dirt road—no sign but I knew better. I ran, upset and hurt and wishing I hadn't told these boys about why I was walking. Icecap and Edison being a mile behind me was the same as them not existing. On this trail, you can walk and persist and remain a mile from someone moving north at the identical rate you are, and never see him again. I was on my own here. Coulter pines closed in, thick trunks that smelled of vanilla cream, football-size cones like stones littering the trail, hard and dense and five pounds each, the largest "seed" of any tree in the world. I kicked one and hurt my toe.

I was making miles. I was making progress. But after some hours I thoughtlessly slowed my pace to watch the buttercream sky flare rose pink, and fade. From somewhere behind me, Icecap yelled out, "Wild Child!"—I sped up to get away. I didn't want him anymore; he'd ruined it. But then he sped up too and I was absolutely exhausted and let up, and he caught me. He wasn't with Edison.

"You have a good pace," Icecap said. He was being very nice. "You're a good hiker." His face looked lean and sculpted, slick with sweat. He smelled like silty water, like wet sediment. Not like a frat boy, sweating liquor, sharp with Axe. He stood close to me, though out here we had infinite space.

"I have to run to catch up with you." He patted my shoulder too hard, like I was his teammate. He knew he'd done something wrong.

I wanted to be angry but instead I felt touched that he had run to reach me. Already I'd forgotten what I wanted. My rage and shame from the past few days lessened. Nothing he'd failed to say or do in my defense outweighed my attraction to him. I turned away and started walking so he wouldn't see me smile.

He followed me silently. I knew he knew he'd hurt me. I kept on walking, my back to him, not saying anything to reveal my joy. I noticed the pain—my toe was still throbbing from the cone I'd kicked.

"Let's run away from Edison," I proposed, surprising myself.

He said nothing back to that, but we walked together. He tried to walk beside me rather than out front or behind me, though the trail was narrow. He asked if I had been a high school cheerleader, his intonation was hopeful. I told him no, but I'd been athletic. I had raced cross-country and had been diligent and good, but then the summer between my freshman and sophomore years I'd sprouted hips and breasts—gained fifteen pounds—and my times slowed. I was kicked down to the junior varsity team. I feigned injury and then altogether stopped showing up.

Icecap told me stories from the years when he'd professionally raced bicycles down mountains. It sounded cool to me. It sounded terrifying. He'd been second fastest in the seventeen-to-nineteen-year-old age class in Switzerland until he crashed badly and had a concussion and was never as fast after. He was no longer fearless. He was skittish now—an imperceptible hesitation when the bike jumped and he felt out of control. He said he didn't feel it; he wasn't any different. He insisted. But he couldn't ease off the brakes. One by one he lost his sponsors. After a dozen disappointing races, he chose to retire.

I couldn't imagine the heartbreak. Icecap had found his passion—as Jacob had—decided what it was he wanted, worked so hard to get it—to have it slip out of his grip. We talked about racing and how good it felt to be fit, to be your fittest, to beat your fastest time, to win. Walking with Icecap in the silence that followed sunset that chilling evening, I made mental lists of things I wanted to accomplish.

I started to imagine what it was I wanted to find in my life beyond the Pacific Crest Trail's dimming horizon. I imagined myself elected Colorado College Class of 2012 President, being loved there. But in truth, in August the new fall semester would begin, and I wasn't even signed up for classes. I was no longer even enrolled.

My dreams grew wild. I saw myself on *The Daily Show with Jon Stewart,* discussing my new book about women and achievement. I saw myself having tea with Salman Rushdie at a sun-worn café table in New York. I saw my face on the cover of *Interview Magazine*—a gorgeous head shot of me in contact lenses and professional makeup, looking beautiful, like no one but Jacob could see me. My book release party would be on the Pacific Coast of San Francisco, with big glass walls and a dizzying cliff-top view. I would publish a "Personal History" essay in *The New Yorker.* Everyone from Newton South High School would hear about it. I saw myself as a woman with beauty and poise, an acclaimed writer known for potent tales that did good in the world. I saw: I had always wanted to be a writer.

But the vast terrain before those destinations still seemed pathless and tremendously wild. Through all my confusion and needless walking to an arbitrary signpost among pines—there was nothing waiting for me in the woodlands of southernmost British Columbia—all I knew was that I wanted to write stories. I wanted to speak without interruption. I wanted to be heard.

Inwardly I smiled. Finally, instead of making lists of Things I Couldn't Do and didn't believe I was capable of, I was describing paths I hoped to follow towards a life I wished for after I reached the place in the forest where the Pacific Crest Trail would inevitably end.

I looked into Icecap's distant eyes and saw him newly. It was heartbreaking not to be as fast as he had been, to lose his chance to improve—and win—so young. I understood. I told Icecap about my brother, how proud I was of Jacob for defying chance and making it to the Mets. How Icecap reminded me of him a little bit. Then I realized the difference and said, "I'm sorry." I pinched his swinging forearm. "But maybe you'll get better?"

His gait sped a little, and I had to jog to stay with him. He didn't seem angry, but I sensed his thoughts had shifted. His pupils were pinpoints—competitive.

We walked into a patch of copper evergreens, dead and dried. Icecap passed me and sped, faster. I called after him, trying to tease him, "Are we racing?"

Night fell over us. We didn't slow. We walked arms out first, like zombies, through the spiderwebs that appear across the trail with astonishing quickness after the sun's set. They were sticky and annoying, nothing frightening. I found my headlamp in my knapsack and clicked it on, stumbled forward over the rocks and roots. The webs shimmered in my light. Then we heard something—a stick snap?—and a shrill voice. We both stopped short.

Edison stepped into our lights, squinting, breathing loud. "Shit," he said. He'd confided in us early on that he'd never slept outside alone, and now he declared that he wasn't about to start "out in this shithole." Desert people are creeps, he said, you never know.

It was obvious he was absolutely terrified.

I looked at him. I'd assumed Icecap had finally spoken and explained that he was leaving him to walk with me now—but maybe he hadn't. I was done with Edison, finally I'd escaped, and fuck—I just couldn't cleanly ditch him. Some other woman might have yelled, told him in rage to leave, that she never wanted to see him ever again, but I felt no energy for that kind of anger, I felt almost nothing for him at all. And so I looked blankly at him. I was fed up and I was ready. Prepared to talk back, to tell him what an idiot I thought he was, to show him I'd had enough and so to him I was untouchable. I hoped he would cower and realize my strength—how he was wrong about me. Steely, I was finally ready to fight.

"No one's out here," I told him. "Seriously relax." Then I turned my hips away, open toward Icecap. I was looking to Icecap for permission to escape.

Edison's reply was only a mumble. "Ass cunt."

I'd hoped he'd say something horrible like that back to me. "Why's that?" I said. I could have been all done. Instead my eyes spit venom. I finally challenged him.

"I ain't *fuck*ing night hiking," Edison said, so loud the *fuck* echoed. And that was that.

I resumed walking. Icecap stalled, rearranged his awkward limbs, eyes on my back. This was his moment to show alliance. But he didn't follow. I was leaving Edison, and Icecap was staying. So I left them together.

I built my camp late that night alone. I wasn't scared. Snug in my tent I wasn't thinking about how I'd lost them both. I listened to my dad's music, feeling I was going to be beautiful and triumphant and rebellious. Then, I wrote. In the dark, in my hardback journal, I lay down fragments of old poems and storybooks made new by my forgetfulness, memories, *walking through woods in dreams of waking/made by an ancient season/summoning spring newly.* I penned: *Writing is a way to make a living dreaming wild dreams.*

It was to me the truest—most hopeful—thing I'd written on the trail yet.

I woke that next morning late, unsure if the guys were behind me or ahead. The night before I'd written in moon's shadow-light for hours. The new morning felt colder, and frost glittered on the fine dust and yellow grass. I shivered and grinned. "Helllooooo!" I called, expecting an echo, hearing none. "Iiiiiim free."

In cool daylight I passed Combs Peak, Tule Canyon, and Tule Canyon Creek, approaching a notable road called Pines to Palms highway. The sky shone lollipop blue. I reached the road that midaft-ernoon, hungry, tranquil but also feeling charged and happy. The highway was wide and quiet, and I slipped through a gap in a fat cow grate to finally reach it.

In the distance, I saw a dark clump of people sitting. Six thru-hikers were huddled below a brown tarp fastened like a drooped roof to three stunted manzanitas and a backpack, and—closer—I noticed that one was a girl. I jogged over and ducked down to join them in the block of gold-tinted shade. But the pack didn't acknowledge me. One looked up, through me, out to the silent arid hills.

"Hey? Hey." I nodded at the only girl I'd seen in a long time. She was baby blond and thin as a dancer, folded up onto herself, deli-cate legs neatly crossed. Her eyes were blocked from me by a huge floppy straw hat. "I'm Wild Child." She was humming a tune, sewing a patch on an emptied backpack. She looked up at a young, olive-skinned guy, Turkish looking, and said, "Here, Squirrel. 'S done." She broke the thread off with her teeth, elegant even as she bit.

She was the only woman of their crew, and older—about twenty-seven or even thirty.

The olive-skinned man leaned in, took the patched-up backpack from her. He thanked and thanked her again, perhaps ten times. They were ignoring me.

"I'm Wild Child," I said, wanting to be acknowledged. I leaned closer to the woman. "What's your name?"

She answered without looking at me. "Silverfox."

"Oh, Silverfox!" Hers was a name I'd wondered about since the very first register! I wanted to ask her every question. "Where did you come here from?" She answered curtly. She'd lived in Hawaii. She was a yogi and a dancer. She'd worked on ships in the Pacific. This was her new crew. They'd all met on the first day on the trail, so it was fate.

"Lots of people meet on the first day," I said.

"Hey, Squirrel," she said, her voice quiet, melodic. "You need some water."

"Thank you," he said.

Silverfox passed him a Nalgene bottle. "You should hydrate before you're thirsty," she said, as he chugged. This group was a pack, but I didn't actually feel the closeness among these men; they felt it was fated that they had met each other, and I observed their little cluster's closeness, but right now all I felt was Silverfox. This cult was one that revolved around this girl. She looked at me, finally. Her eyes were glacier turquoise—gorgeous—striking out here. "What was that, hon?"

"Oh, nothing," I said, happy to finally get her direct attention. I should say something smart, I thought, her eyes so huge and marine, two lit globes. She looked to me like the ideal woman on the trail. She seemed to be what I wanted to become. "Can I hike with you guys?" I said. I hadn't meant to ask like that.

"Sure honey," she said without a pause. Someone handed me a quarter of a big, delicious cheeseburger, still hot, the orange cheese melted. It smelled like Johnny's Luncheonette in Newton Centre. "You're burnt." She passed me her sunscreen, the Banana Boat kind that smelled like summer camp.

I smeared it on my cheeks, my neck, my breasts and thighs, feeling at once welcome and excluded, like a girl joining a cult for the purpose of research. Silverfox was all any of us saw. I felt the eyes of the others on her, how they looked at her, spoke to her, and I felt the heat of envy. Silverfox became in my eyes the vision of the powerful woman I wished to be.

"Your mother should teach you to use sunscreen before you're crispy," Silverfox said, her voice a soft hum.

"Sorry," I said, too loud, squinting at her.

That evening I built my camp with Silverfox, Squirrel, and the four other guys whose names all smudged together. I couldn't get them straight. We made a campfire, told stories about other hikers we'd met, made fun. No one talked so much about life before the trail. I confused the men's names, offending them, but I couldn't care less about learning anything about these smudgy men. It was only when Silverfox squinted at me, disapproving of my repeated mistake, that I felt embarrassed. I asked Silverfox about Hawaii, "Are you from there, originally?" and all she said was, "No." We slept on spongy pine needles at the spot Silverfox had apparently already decided everyone would camp—we'd all stopped with her when she stopped without question.

That night, snug-warm in my sleeping bag, my tent only feet from Squirrel's and Strider's, I called my mom. I placed the GPS on my tent's cool nylon floor and waited for it to "locate satellites" and my coordinates to appear. I whispered them to my mother through the phone, her yelling to me, "Talk *louder*. I can't. Hear! You," me whisper-talking at her, "Shh Mom! You're hurting my ear." I gave her my coordinates and she repeated them back, I knew she was transcribing them, saying she loved me, saying "pleasant dreams."

I slept deeply that night, feeling safe even beside all those men, their tents snug against mine, our tarp and tent cords crossing in an intricate web. I felt Silverfox had them under control. And yet I sensed, I knew in my palms, that Silverfox didn't want me with them, there. This pack of men was her entourage, not mine. She was my mirror image, slightly distorted, flipped, older, larger, more able to coexist with a pack of men. I'd be their pawn. She was their queen.

These men hiked the trail with hope of sexual freedom—a wilderness with wild girls, no rules. But girls were rare. Empty space was vast. A man could hike for weeks not seeing a woman. Condoms would freeze at night and, jostled in overstuffed knapsacks, actually shatter. Undamaged ones would prove just as useless. Months into this long hike, up in the volcano lands of Northern California, *take-what-you-need, leave-what-you-don't* "Hiker Boxes" would begin to fill with old beat-up condoms, carried a thousand miles before being abandoned, purposeless.

Because here is the math. There is one girl for every five guys on the trail. Half of these women hike with a significant other. So the ratio of single girls to single guys is one to ten. This was the nature of the trail. Be a girl. Be surrounded by men who are longing.

I'd left college to get away from young reckless men, yet I'd run away from them, directly into herds of them. I'd found the odd place on earth where men multiply and women divide: ten guys to one girl. If anything, I'd magnified the risks of college.

That next morning, before anyone else had gotten out and broken down their tents, I left them all. I didn't need Silverfox and her crew of sheepish losers. I ran from them, as had become my pattern. I wasn't scared of them. I simply felt unwelcome. And I didn't need them, so I didn't have to stay and feel that way.

The day was blue and beige, like a desert beach. Wide open. I wondered where Icecap and Edison were, if Icecap was still with Edison, if Icecap would have left Edison to be with me if I were more like Silverfox. If I could ever someday find the way to be so powerful.

Alone, I hiked without stopping. Into a green oasis and out of it: flat desert. Into a sanctuary of pines. Up to a shadeless ridge, narrow and exposed. There was no water up here. I was glossy with sweat, my arms looking polished and lean. I was on top of Southern California. I felt sexy out here, skinnier, a girl striding herself northward. I could be an actress. I could be on *The Daily Show*, talking about my heartsick character. I felt ready to walk alone for a very long time.

I was high on a narrow ridge. To the east, Palm Springs's green sunny fields. That's where the Pines to Palms highway takes you now: Palm Springs's golf courses: the resort. Los Angeles's richer residents come to desert, to a valley below snowy mountains, and whack golf balls. To the west, vast foothills. The San Jacinto's icy, periwinkle peaks to the north, smack before me. The trail bloomed. Blossoms the color of sunsets, pink with orange centers, yellow blade-thin rims. The ridge widened, no longer a fine crest, now a hump, lower, a persistent snaking hill. I passed over a patch of drooping blooms like orange Chinese lanterns, elegant, suspended above the desert of beige. Even out in this swell of dust and silt, desert flowers look clean. I saw deep red stains in sky that should be blue.

I felt around in my hip-belt pocket's mesh pouch for a candy, only to realize I had just one left. My very last watermelon Jolly Rancher. I didn't see how that could be—there had been so many. Back in the hotel with my father, I'd separated the watermelon Jolly Ranchers from the others, spilled them all carefully into my knapsack. Now, I unzipped the pocket fully and peered in. "No no no," I said aloud; how had this happened. Cherry was the only other kind I liked enough to carry, but it wasn't comforting. It didn't taste like wandering the green fields beyond the baseball game, to the woods, while Jacob played.

My face felt very hot. My legs felt cold. I was shocked to see that I was squatting on gleaming feather-white snow. Frost glittered on the white fir needles, the ponderosa pine cones at my feet. Ice crystals grew in curls from under dry cold rocks. I'd been walking on endless glistening packed snow. I had been climbing, gaining elevation, and the trail was not a trail any longer, only a wide band of footprints.

I studied the tracks. Icecap's swoosh-dot-dot—I knew it well by now—wasn't among them. I had climbed three thousand feet, but the mounting had been mindless, and it felt I'd just appeared here in the San Jacinto Mountains, a snowy world above Southern California.

The hillside I was walking along steepened, my right foot awkwardly lower than my left. For stretches, the trail was one-foot narrow, almost gone. I feared it would disappear altogether. Without the trail I was just on a steep and frost-slick hillside in a vast wilderness. This place on the trail felt more dangerous than all of the others. I wasn't scared that I'd be lost here; I thought I could always backtrack. It was that I had committed myself to following this specific path and without the trail to lead me, I felt I would somehow be more vulnerable. I felt unsure of my footing. The evergreen tops three feet below my shoes looked pointy and abrasive. Then they were fifteen feet below, then fifty, a deadly four-story fall down to them. Something could go wrong, and I'd have no chance of getting help.

At last I stopped. I stared at the blank snow slope, frantic, vexed. Snow holds tracks well, yet there wasn't a footprint here. I glanced down, up, down, desperate for a sign of the tread way, for the route forward. But I was lost.

I kept hiking. Out onto a death-slide, ice-slicked and sheer. If I were a mountaineer, armed with everything *Mountaineering: The*

Freedom of the Hills recommended—much less the ten "necessities"—
my backpack would be heavy with thick climbing rope and carabi-
neers and steel-spiked crampons to strap to plastic boots for better
traction; I'd set up a belay system with knotted ropes and, with each
footstep, stab my ice ax's shaft through the ice crust to prevent a fall.
But I was an ultralight thru-hiker. I had only my running-shoe-clad
feet and my own recklessness and skill.

The snow chute gleamed like a blade's edge, and I trudged. Kick
toe-toe-in, and step; I inched, higher. My legs shook, tired. I felt dread
tighten in my chest. I wanted this to be the way, because I could do
it—I was scared to try to cross the chute, but I could climb here—
though it was wrong, and it wouldn't ever get me to where I needed
to go.

And now I'd stranded myself. I pivoted, feet stuck-safe, legs pulsing with warm blood through numb skin. Adrenaline drugged me.
Below, the city of Palm Springs looked close, reachable, a giant yellow
gem gleaming through my fright's haze. I could go glissade down
and call it the Amber City. It'd be like the Emerald City, Dorothy
Gale's first destination, only this one was real. Maybe I'd stride down
and down this slope, through snow then shrubs, to there, to finally
have a shower. I was filthy, calves splattered with slush-mud, my hair
matted. A grocery store would have huge bags of Jolly Ranchers, but
I'd just have the watermelon kind. Then I'd slip back to Newton, to
my house, to bed, into sugared sleep.

I daydreamed short-cuts to comfort not knowing that Palm
Springs is the classic trap. Hikers actually die in pursuit of those gold
lights. It happens, I would soon learn, nearly every year.

They are lost or cold or shocked from a tall fall; they see the lights
of Palm Springs and wander toward them. This is their first, irreversible mistake: after falling, abandoning the trail and heading not back
up toward the crest, but downhill. Into the bush. Toward the magic-
trap city that kills fallen hikers. They must navigate ten thousand feet
of elevation loss through scrub oaks, down rock-ledge cliffs. There is
water, but not much, and they may never stumble upon it. There is

no cached water, no trail magic. The town always looks closer than it is. The hiker, even in good health, with good maps, gallons of water on him, will take three or four days, arrive scraped up. More hikers, though, will lack something they need. They'll get lost in trees, on cliff tops, hungry, mad. They'll cramp with thirst or hunger, lost. Fatigued, they'll trip. Over a cliff.

On the day he retired, April 19, 2005, John "Sea Breeze" Donovan left for California's border with Mexico. In San Diego, his final stop before the Border Monument, he lit two candles, one to honor Saint Christopher, patron saint of travelers, and one to Saint Anthony, patron saint of the lost. Then he joined the trail. He hiked steadily until—in a freak snowstorm on May 6—snow dumped down on the San Jacinto Mountains. In a desert snowstorm, he scrambled up the ridge, missed Saddle Junction, and became lost—where I now stood. Disappeared.

The thru-hiking community is small, and when someone in it dies, his loss is felt deeply. Sea Breeze was a thru-hiker—vanished. Four years later, trail angels and trailblazers still spoke of his strange sad disappearance. I heard his name in Warner Springs, in woods, in trail-town bars. In a register five miles south of Idyllwild, his legend was a warning:

> *The Riverside County Sheriff clearly did not comprehend the gravity of the situation. They literally said, "Maybe he wants to be missing." Missing day hikers and weekend backpackers were understandable to them, but they did not understand thru-hiking the PCT, someone not having a specific arrival date at a trailhead, or the depth of meaning of a hiker not picking up their box.*
>
> *Everyone who arrived here at Hiker Heaven was asked if they'd seen John, aka Sea Breeze. . . . There was an intense juxtaposition of oblivious NoBo hikers having the time of their lives, and the unfolding tragedy. . . .*

The night before he vanished, Mr. Donovan had camped with a group, but was not a "regular member" of that group . . . as the hikers studied their maps and got out their compasses to choose their route for the next day, Mr. Donovan did not pay attention or come over. . . . When they broke camp and took off hiking the next morning, Mr. Donovan was slower than those he had camped with. Those who saw him last thought that he was behind them, and were completely unaware that he had become lost. . . . In fact, no one was aware that he was missing for many days. . . .

The San Jacintos have claimed many victims, the area is vast and extremely rugged and steep with breathtaking vertical exposure and long runouts. It's famous for being icy in early season. Some missing are simply never found. You probably know that while they were searching for John, they found the skull of a missing hiker from years before.

We would later learn he had died before his absence was noticed, and certainly before the Search and Rescue was called into action.

I see so many hikers every year heading out similarly ill-prepared: inadequate food, water, maps, clothing, and shelter, paired with a cavalier or over-confident attitudes. If only my angel wings could stretch as far as I wish they would.

The note was signed "L-Rod," also known as Dana Figment, the Pacific Crest Trail's most beloved trail angel, the matron of Hiker Heaven.

Reading the page, I was struck by Sea Breeze's lack of tact, his defiance and isolation. I carried no maps and often declined to look at Icecap's; I felt alone, had wanted to be alone, had wanted "to be missing." I was struck by how much I—a girl, nineteen—was like this lost, dead man. Now I was stranded, trying to discern for myself the right path toward the promise of lights that flicker through the distance: imagined paradise.

A year to the day after Sea Breeze vanished, on May 6, 2006, Brandon Day and Gina Allen decided to ride the Palm Springs Aerial Tramway up into the San Jacinto Mountains. They were both from Texas and on their second date, having met at Coachella. Down by their Palm Springs hotel, they could lounge at swimming pools shaded with palm trees and play golf on dewy green courses with Los Angeles escapists. Just ten minutes in a tram, though, and they stood high in snowy mountains, Chino Canyon vast below them. In these mountains, just east of Saddle Junction, Brandon and Gina looked around, stunned and grinning. They ambled around the mountain plateau in a five-hundred-meter radius, stuck to wide, flat trails. They hadn't planned to wander too far from the top. They'd expected to take a day hike, had no food or water, and no shelter—nothing. But then they heard a waterfall down below and walked off path, down-hill, to snap a picture of it.

According to the article in *Backpacker* magazine, they "followed voices for a while, only to discover that, in fact, they were chasing echoes." Then they tried to head north, toward the tram, but ended up farther downhill. "The mountain forces you downward," Brandon told *Backpacker* reporter Bill Donohue. "It was like Chinese finger cuffs: the more we tried to get out, the tighter and steeper it got."

Four days and nights passed. Gina Allen, a Catholic, prayed. Like Sea Breeze, she pled to Saint Christopher and Saint Anthony: save me. Then she and Brandon saw downhill, through the trees, a yellow backpack. Inside was a journal; an entry was dated May 6—just days before they thought. They thought someone must be nearby. They thought they were saved. But they soon realized the entry was dated one year back. The journal was signed, *John Donovan.*

The couple panicked. They found inside the yellow backpack a plastic baggie full of matches, and Brandon gathered dried vines and leaves and branches and logs and attempted to light a signal fire. Everything ignited. Smoke poured in a skyward river, white and thick. It swallowed the backpack, the land, the ground and high tree branches. The trees were on fire. The sky was again feather gray.

Yet the fire didn't destroy John Donovan. His body lay fifty yards from the desperate lovers, downstream, in a quiet pool contained by mossy rocks, at the base of a tall, hidden waterfall.

A helicopter emerged, low, faded in smoke. Gina blew kisses; it circled. It lowered a rope and winched them up inside, to carry them out, to save them.

This was trail magic. Sea Breeze's fire, his light, his heat, his life, remained, their salvation.

It is a fact that all drainages, if followed downhill, lead to the same lowland water body. Lost and fallen hikers follow drainages down because walking ridges is harder. And so, despite the complex web of paths, waterfalls, cliffs, as a hiker wanders downhill, drainages merge, faint, abstract paths coalesce, thicken, until there is one path—the one, natural, trodden way. It isn't a coincidence that Sea Breeze, Brandon Day and Gina Allen, and countless other hikers all wandered, lost, down the same steep slope to nowhere.

Here I was, the same time of year, and the same place—a snowy silent May mountain day—as when Sea Breeze had first disappeared. I remembered the story. I looked ahead for the first time, really looked. Before I stepped one more step off the trail, before the promise of the Amber City had time to magnify my hope and concentrate hot light into my mind and burn my brains, I noticed something: the sourceless shadow snaking through distant trees. I breathed.

I knew suddenly and without a doubt that the trail was not gone; all along it had been there, across the death chute, faint but clear. My path, beyond doubt or denial. I just hadn't looked toward it. I wasn't lost. I'd always known the way. If I'd only allowed myself to look. I had never been lost, only scared.

I craved safety now, someone supportive and protective—Icecap, maybe. I didn't want to be alone in this danger.

But there was just one way to go. I had to cross the snow chute.

And so I tried to go on; I stepped lightly. My foot slipped. I gasped, swayed back upright, looked down to the treetops and white rocks. The snow here was crusted with glossy ice. The trail was buried,

but now its course was clear: it contoured straight across the slope—
over the tall chute. The chute I'd been so vigorously climbing beside,
hoping to bypass.

I thought: fall here, you die.

I thought: that's his story, not mine. I would not be him, lost, alone
forever. I needed to return to the world, to find my way back into it, to
find someone whom I could trust and love. I sure as dirt wasn't going
to die here alone. I was going to find my place, safe ground.

"You got this, Debby, *you* got *this*," I said aloud.

I took one lunge-step out to the glossy slope. My running shoe toe
punched a notch into the ice. I stood on it. My downhill leg was shaking. I could not take another step, no way. Okay, okay, I told myself:
okay. I held my eyes on my forward foot, half planted, half balanced,
whole leg quaking violently. I did not look down the fifty-plus-foot fall,
but I could see the void. My whole right side could feel the open air.

Ten steps across, and you're done, I told myself. You're one-tenth
done. That's good. Ten little steps. I lunged again. Step two!—and
with momentum kick-kicked in step three with two hard strikes.
"You *got* this, Wild," I said, heart hammering. Just seven steps more,
maybe only six. Then I glanced down. Then I leaned forward,
swayed—hands left low toward the snow—and slipped, slid fast,
cried out, kicked hard, stopped.

I was halfway down the slope. I was all right. My feet and knees
had lodged into the snow, through the ice sheet. My thigh was bleeding, cut in a thin slash. My blood like scarlet lichen on the ice. I was
okay. My thighs were baby pink and throbbing, my shins hot and
shocked.

If I hadn't stopped myself, if I'd picked up a little more speed,
bounced off a bump, I'd have slammed into the rock beds below and
I would be dead.

I cross-stepped up, up the stripe of virgin snow my falling body
had left in its wake, up the twelve or fifteen feet I'd slipped, the ice
shattered away, no longer in my path. I made it back to the top of
the chute—the middle—sawed flat ledge after flat spot with my shoe

toe, trusted the palm-small ledge I'd made, stepped, straightened my shaking knee, stood upright, crossed back to trees, blood surging, still bleeding, safer, now.

"Lucky *girl*, Child." Thank the lucky stars.

Shaken, I walked along the dry trail, slower. Then I stopped, sat down. I decided I'd wait for someone, whoever caught me. It only took a dozen minutes before two men emerged out of the trees. Icecap. And Edison, thank *goodness*. They'd never been all that far away. I'd been so fed up with them, yet somewhere on the steep snowfield what I felt had shifted. My anger toward Edison had softened since I'd last seen him—forgotten—muted by my harsh fear and solitude. I no longer hated the thought of walking with Edison; I didn't even want to lose him, now. The trail with them felt so much safer than walking lost, alone until the end.

Edison shoved me. "I hiked with the same two guys the whole way on the AT," he said. "Fucking Georgia to Maine we stuck together. That's how you get her done." He poked my upper back with his elbow. "We're Musketeers. For the long haul," Edison said, now holding my elbow. I wiggled it from his grip. "*In it.*"

I wondered if this meant that he'd be nice to me now.

We walked down, down, along the Pacific Crest Trail, grateful to be back on dry-dirt ground, grateful for each other's bodies, now, down into the trail town of Idyllwild.

In town we all three again split a cabin, but this time one with a living room that had a pull-out bed and also a separate bedroom with a door that locked. It was spacious. Icecap seemed unsure in the roominess; he didn't look at me but got down on his knees in the kitchenette and separated the trash out of his clean blue and yellow gear. Granola bar wrappers, the folded-up foil of his European cheese, an old plastic baggie stuffed fat with graham cracker waxy wrapper and Wasa paper. He looked intently focused, yet he was blushing. I was blushing, too. Edison had pulled his shirt off, thrown it on the couch, claiming it.

We all knew where that left us. Icecap and I would share the bed.

CHAPTER 10

Trail Magic

Between every two pine trees there is a door leading to a new way of life.
— John Muir

Icecap showered. I brushed my tangled hair. I bathed as he shaved. Though we'd been sipping red wine—I felt the happy warmth of it—I remained clear eyed. Icecap had tied a bath towel around his waist, and, through the gap between the shower curtain and the white tiled wall, I could see him leaning toward the mirror. I bent over and rubbed my hands up and down my shins, scrubbing off dirt, brown puffs in the bathwater. In a deft move I knocked the curtain so it was slightly open. I shaved my legs smooth and soaked in the bath, felt warm and safe. I waited for him to glance through the curtain-gap I'd made, but Icecap looked at the mirror, the floor—everything except my naked body.

Edison was gone from the cabin. I didn't remember him leaving. Icecap was finished shaving now and back out in the bedroom unpacking. The light was gone outside—dark small-town night—and alone inside the brightly lit bathroom I wrapped myself in a towel. I was nervous, suddenly, as if I was supposed to give a speech I'd forgotten. "I'm so drunk," I said through the bathroom door, though it wasn't true. I'd declared it to him in my anxiety to take pressure and responsibility off myself for what I wanted to do next. I had already decided I at least wanted to kiss him, be held. Yet my desire surprised me. I felt the weight of shame not only on rape now, but on sex, too. I was confused by it. I felt unready to hold myself responsible for the decision if I slept with him.

I stepped into the bedroom. Icecap's dark blue nylon shirt was a small mound on the rug. His beige nylon pants were tidily draped over a chair. My little pink shorts and shirt lay on the bathroom floor, soaked in the puddle I'd thoughtlessly created. "You should want to hang those up, ya?" he'd said before, but I'd ignored him. I flicked off the bathroom light and we were together in the dark.

Icecap was in the bed.

"Come to me," he said, and I wanted to, and I did. I thought I'd lost trust after the rape, questioning men always, fearing they would be kind and gentle now, if I gave them what they wanted, but that they might respond badly if I said no later. But I trusted Icecap. He had been respectful again and again, for two hundred miles now, and I finally felt safe. For the first time since I was raped, I wanted to trust a man again, maybe even have sex.

I kissed him. He kissed me, his tongue pressing itself against mine. I'd only French-kissed three times in my life. I liked it, but I worried I wasn't good.

"I'm bad at kissing," I apologized at his mouth.

He was sweetly smiling, saying, "Don't talk. Have fun at this, okay?"

I said okay. Okay, okay, okay, this is okay.

I felt the charged warmth between our bodies from those first kisses. He progressed downward, toward my neck, my knocking chest; I breathed, unclenched.

When he tugged at my hip gently, asking, I smiled. "Yes, okay," I told him, my eyes lit. This was the first time I would be with someone since the rape nine months earlier. I wondered how long after you're raped you're supposed to start having sex. I felt it was somehow wrong of me to want to be touched after I'd been raped—I thought it should feel sickening—but this felt warm and exciting.

I felt wet. I felt his eyes, his desire heating me. I felt beautiful. He was fingering me and holding me tightly at the same time. I had never been touched like this by someone I knew so well. It felt exciting to trust. I felt safer with Icecap, like he saw me differently than other boys, better—respected me. I decided to see how far I felt comfortable going.

His fingers were confident, playing, it felt amazing. I was safe in a bed with a boy, it was wild. Yet in that euphoric moment I knew that I wanted him to kiss me and kiss me and touch me this way, graze my waist and belly and clit so everything felt wonderful—but not to have sex with me. I was going to say stop and he was going to respect my word. I smiled, I *knew* it.

At a small squeeze I pulled away. It would seem arbitrary to him, it could upset him. Yet I said: "Icecap, shh. Let's stop."

He stopped instantly, and we both slept like little kids. We didn't have sex.

I thought I might want to do it with him someday, someday soon. It seemed incredible. I knew with certainty now—I could say no, and he would stop. Above all, I felt the fierce beauty of the choice. I knew now what it was that had held me from falling into my desire to be with him fully: I first needed to make sure he was a man who would respect my "No."

I woke. I'd been slowly drifting from an airy dream. My cheek was imprinted with the texture of his chest hair. I fit so nicely under his bent leg. I remembered I was in a cabin in a mountain town on a long trail with a boy. The clock said that it was nearly noon. Normally I'd be sorry I'd wasted so much of the day, but not today. Time sped. I lay there beaming—heartened by last night's magic, feeling securely bonded with a lover.

I sat up and pulled my shirt on, still bare below the covers. Icecap was packing.

"You look more skinny," he said, tying his huge shoes. They stunk.

I felt uncomfortably warm, glad, he'd noticed. "I weigh like 108," I lied, shedding pounds.

"No, I think," he said. He frowned at me. "You weigh at more than this."

He would never lie to me, ever. Unfortunately.

Outside in midday light, Edison was sitting on the porch beside a pile of stones. He had gathered them and had been chucking them at trees. He didn't say hey to us or acknowledge us, and we were still and silent, shy with him now. Edison felt it. "We" was now Icecap and me.

Yet Edison remained. He didn't hike away, and we didn't ask him to. And so all three of us began to walk the trail's most hazardous stretch yet, a steep 9,500-foot decline along the face of Mount San Jacinto, the first cliffed peak we northbound thru-hikers meet. The highest mountain drop-off in the lower forty-eight. It rests above the desert like a petrified shadow, permanent and hard. Our trail traversed that face. This was Fuller Ridge, our notorious descent.

We would climb right where John Donovan had died.

Edison and Icecap and I hiked up the steep hill. We approached the merge with Saddle Junction, sweating, tense. I tripped and fell and caught myself, palms on damp rocks.

"Dumb bitch," Edison said. He laughed. "She's a prissy little bitch this morning, look."

I stood, wobbly, squinting. Then I actually smiled. After my night with Icecap, sharing the same bed, knowing I was audible, knowing I could say no, nothing Edison could say mattered to me. He was a weak joke. I didn't feel anger, wounded—nothing. I hardly heard him.

But from higher on the hill, Icecap twisted. He'd been out ahead, hiking fast, but now he stopped. "You can't talk to her like that," he called down in perfect English, his accent inaudible from the distance. He jogged back down, a fluid dash and hop, and took my hand in a fierce grip.

My palm's pulse sped, my body straightening. I was consumed with Icecap. My first time giddy kissing a boy since the rape, since ever, his hand on mine again, protecting me. Icecap's hand was smooth and dry, and hot—and I was wet again. I didn't look to see Edison's slack smirk.

The mountain rose above us, silver-blue and pocked with shadows like a near moon. Edison had curled his lip and said nothing; we all hiked on. The wind pressed us. I tripped and gripped at Icecap, steadied myself. My breath was fast and shallow, and I felt dizzy. I felt bonded. Icecap hiked close to me now, with Edison way down below. Shrinking, a speck.

That evening Icecap and I pitched our tents up north of Saddle Junction, on a long flat whited-out with drifts of snow. Edison showed up, glossy with sweat, gleaming in the falling sun's gold light.

"Pitch it out zair," Icecap said to him, pointing far out to the other side of the flat. He was telling Edison to pitch his tent somewhere else, protecting me. He was claiming me.

I felt safe and adored. Edison walked away. He pitched his tent far away, out of sight, blocked by far trees. We both knew he'd never camped alone before. He was terrified; we could see in his stiff gait. That walk pleaded with us to call out, "No! Wait." We didn't, though. That was the last time we ever saw him. I knew it would be. Here Icecap's tent touched mine. Our p-cords crisscrossed. We whispered stories to each other through our thin tent walls long after we turned our headlamps off.

The last thing Icecap told me that night, in the dim air, had "not a good ending." Through the black space between our tents he told me a true story. He was whispering, and his voice cracked mute at the words after "the last race." The inaudible gaps were bygone moments lost. It was the story of the premature end of his racing career. He wasn't crying, but the words came to me in soft, short exhales:

A month after his crash and concussion, against the neurologist's orders, Icecap had resumed his cycling training. He was desperate to regain his speed, his muscle tone and fearlessness; after an hour on the bike, he developed a knocking headache. He needed to stop. It passed, but then that evening when he sat down to do his homework, it returned. He took a nap. It didn't help. He could not concentrate. That night he couldn't sleep.

He returned to the neurologist, who informed him that premature exertion had damaged his brain. In his impatience, he had caused himself further brain trauma. Now, because of that irreversible mistake, he'd have headaches and trouble focusing on school, on words, on anything at all. He'd been desperate to regain his fearlessness, but instead he'd only damaged his mind. He could never get better. "But so is what?" he asked me. "I'd fuck school anyway."

"You can still go back to school," I told him. I asked him what he wanted to study.

"Maps," he said. "Rocks."

I fell asleep picturing Icecap at a scratched-up carved-up wood desk, drawing topographic curves, breathing through his relentless headache.

That night I dreamed John Donovan wasn't dead. He had been living with just his yellow backpack all this time. He lived off big acorns and sap. John. John of candles, of wild hope and loneliness.

MAY 2, 2009, DEER SPRINGS, CALIFORNIA, MILE 184.3

My first full day alone with Icecap.

New day brightened. Sun flooded through our little fabric homes as we packed; a wind slid through the gap between the two mounds of pine needle–crisscrossed snow, the snow chilling the wind, white sunshine warming our torsos and our arms, everything hot and amplified. Icecap was packed first, all ready, waiting to flee with me. Edison would be furious. It felt evil and wonderful to ditch him up high on Fuller Ridge. He'd be kicking rocks and shivering, pissing himself with fear. Maybe he'd learn. He'd be sorry he'd been such an ass to me. Icecap had cast Edison away, we left him to traverse Fuller Ridge on his own, in danger.

Icecap had freed us. I felt he took care of me in ways I couldn't yet care for myself. I strode downhill. Icecap followed me close, matching my gait though his natural pace was faster, gliding with me through the thawing world. The trail's stones glittered, flecked with mica, and the dirt path switched back and back under itself, slashing down Fuller Ridge through snow then scrub oak forest, then back down to desert and in 105-degree air. We descended together, gaining oxygen and miles, losing 7,000 feet of elevation.

The muted desert turned loud with birds and wind. Icecap's ears popped, and he lowered his voice. From the desert floor, yesterday's ice-chilled wind and cold granite felt like a dream we'd shared. Now we were down, where we could breathe, just us and the trail through vastness.

With Icecap the desert no longer felt like a severe and lonely world. It felt pristine and grand, like an ocean we could walk on, bright open water. This was our world, population: two. Whatever we did here would be the culture. The language was English, though words like "rape" and "racing" would fade out of use. I spun and grabbed Icecap's swinging hand, we kissed. We were solemn, both amazed this was where we were at, that we were here, together. John Muir—my trusted guide—once declared this face of the San Jacinto Mountains we now walked across "the most sublime spectacle to be found anywhere on this earth." But I could hardly see it.

I hoped Icecap was my boyfriend. I wasn't sure. If he was, he was my first. When my high school classmates were at prom, dancing, making out for the first time, I was in New Hampshire's Appalachian Mountains, building a trail with the Appalachian Mountain Club trail crew. Nobody had asked me to come.

I wondered if Icecap liked me as much as he liked the beautiful mocha-skinned girl in the school picture he carried. I wondered if he still carried it.

We walked another twenty miles into a marigold sunset and silk blue night, playing R-rated twenty questions that devolved into what-have-you-done-naughty talk, just talking.

"Have you ever—had sex?" I asked him, finally. We were walking side by side now, not our usual single file.

"I did," he answered me. He grinned. "Did you ever had an orgasm?"

I hadn't. I hadn't felt this at ease with a boy, as happy, since before the rape. I had never been in love. I answered, "No."

He was looking at me, smile lines deep. "We'll fix that."

MAY 3, THE DESERT, CALIFORNIA, MILE 209.6

We traversed vast fields of hills like swells of ocean frozen in their turbulence. Tall white windmills dotted the horizon, and we climbed then descended, then climbed then descended the sea of sand's smooth waves, infinite waves, the windmills growing, rising higher. We were two dark specks in a metropolis of windmills, shrunken, the great blades rising and turning slowly, each white arm swooshing up to a thousand feet, sweeping blank sky.

"I hate windmills," Icecap said as we passed the massive steel base of one, it humming and rattling, wide as a house and tall as a skyscraper.

I smiled. "Why?"

He looked upward. "They are loud machines for us," he declared. "I hate the wind." His mouth pouted, but when he looked back to me it cracked open into a grin. I thought maybe he was being silly. Windmills seemed a thing too blank and approachable to hate.

Each windmill's shadow was a wide stripe of shade. The shadows patterned the hills, dim twigs of cool. Our stomachs growled, our hunger stopped us, and we took a short break by a windmill's shady base. A scorpion scampered out from beneath a sandstone rock, down the stripe of shade, away, and I ate a granola bar. I ate another. I ate an entire box of crackers and a half a pound of cheese. I craved Creamsicle milkshakes. I craved citrus fruits. I was always hungry. I thought maybe I was starving. I was sick of dry trail food, and I needed to work to eat the 5,000 daily calories my body required to maintain its weight.

I pulled out my notebook and began a list—"all the things you hate"—making fun of him: THINGS DANIEL HATES.

Number ONE: windmills,
TWO: the wind.

The next day the sky was matte periwinkle, cloudy. The sun was hidden, the air bright and electric, poised to flash. We walked to a wide backroad, faded as in a dream, dirt soft as dust, puffing up in clouds behind me.

"Sorry," I said to Icecap, who remained close, dust in his air. "Give me some space, yeah?"

I glanced back at him, and he was dark with dirt. It stuck to his sweat like the sheen of black tar. He wasn't looking at me. He was staring. He looked hypnotized. He looked crazed.

"Keeping going to the tiger," he said, pointing, ignoring me, apparently not bothered by the metallic taste of dust. Now he seemed happy. "Look zis!" He shook his pointing arm.

I turned and looked and gasped—he was right! A tiger like a sleek sports car stood before us, large and shrewd. It was beautiful. I was frozen. I pressed my eyes closed and opened them, unable to respond. I saw that it was in a long cage, goodness—I unfroze. Then I saw a Saharan lion with a mane like a shock of golden grass. And then, of course, a bear: a humped grizzly. They were wild, fierce and shocking, but they were captive.

"What is this?" I called out. The tiger, lion, and grizzly all twitched—looked at me. No voice called back an answer.

"Don't bother at them," Icecap whispered, unnerved. "You are too loud here. Sit to watch," he said.

I did sit. He sat down, too, and we watched them pace and stretch and sprawl out on concrete ground. The lion sneezed.

I tried to imagine what all this was, what it was for. The cages sat right beside our winding trail. The first bear I'd seen on this long walk through wilderness was in a cage. Beside a tiger. Beside a lion the size of a horse, shockingly sneezing.

"For movies," Icecap said.

"What?" I said.

He handed me his open guidebook, pointed. This was a training camp for wild animals in Hollywood movies.

"Thiz tiger's famous," Icecap said again.

This was a vision of wildness contained—caged. Huge, powerful animals whose wild dignity was stripped from them.

Panic jolted me. These animals had had their freedom seized by people who put their own desires first. In the glint of the silver cage bars I saw the same steely repression, the same cold entitlement that allows people to feel it is okay to steal bodies and lives as I glimpsed while frozen beneath Junior. The boy who had put his few minutes of pleasure before my entire life.

Great as these creatures were, they had no power to free themselves and reclaim their bodies. I'd finally begun finding my strength and happiness in the wild, I had the power to move out of the cage he'd put me in, to escape the trap. I saw I was lucky, released in woods, finally no longer caged by my rape, free.

"I feel like Dorothy Gale," I whispered to myself out loud, at last. I wasn't powerless now.

MAY 6, THE DESERT, CALIFORNIA, MILE 250

Slipping through oak and yellow pine woods, we came to a clearing in which a La-Z-Boy chair sat. We were no longer disbelieving of such strangeness. The chair's tan fabric was sun-faded and impossibly clean. Beside it sat a big bucket full of fresh grapefruits, pink and huge, small bright oranges and bulbous mangos.

I flopped into the plush chair, grinning. "Welcome," I said. "Step into my office."

"How does these fruits get here?" Icecap asked, amazed. He lifted a grapefruit slowly, with two hands. "It is real, actually," he said. He broke its thick skin with his thumbnail and sweet juice sprayed like silver. It smelled like candy.

We each ate a grapefruit; it was gone too fast. We then opened two sweet oranges, savored each segment, how the juice sprayed the roofs of our mouths like water balloons bursting. We split a mango. I sat there in my cushioned chair, half reclined, elated and full of just the fruit I'd craved.

"Best trail magic yet," I said.

"Yes, actually. But yes, how does these fruits get to here?"

The kindness of the trail magic overwhelmed me. The planning and strain the creation of this little oasis required must have been tremendous.

Someone local must have found the nearest Jeep road and trudged from the place where it ended or switchbacked away, hiked with heavy fruits—and furniture—to the PCT, just to help morale. We couldn't stop smiling; it was all so unexpected. When we finally left, we were still giddy, high on the kindness and absurdity of the gifts.

We talked about tomorrow, how we'd reach the trail town of Big Bear, about next summer, how we'd climb frozen waterfalls together somewhere snowy. He hated windmills and the wind, he loved climbing cold mountains. I found his stitch of harshness alluring, his judgments making him more appealing to me. It seemed he knew what he liked and didn't—he liked me, and he was going somewhere. It was incredibly important that we get there. He took it for granted that I would come with him.

After just twenty more minutes walking together down the straight, tree-shaded trail, we saw a mustard seed yellow treasure chest—still more magic. I was growing spoiled. I felt high, really, and feared for a moment that I was sleeping, dreaming all I wanted vividly.

The chest was golden, weighted with candy bars and beers. Inside the chest, along with gold and silver cans of bubbly Coors, a register lay. One note read, "On behalf of mice, thanks much. Nice place you've built." I laughed. I popped a can of beer. Another note was signed with a name I recognized—Never-Never. He wrote, "Cruising at four-and-a-half beers per hour. About to drink and walk. Living dangerously."

I felt warm lightness, I felt nothing.

We were in a clump of trees in a measureless desert, a cool pool of shade and Milky Ways and Coors. Behind the treasure chest of treats a dozen or so gallon milk jugs full of water sat below a sign: For Every Beer, Drink As Much Water. I noticed that on the one swollen three-gallon jug a tiny ladder made of chicken wire and string led up to a cut-out doorway hole the size of a playing card. It was mouse house water, so small critters could drink safely. The teeny ladder was adorable and kind, a contraption straight from Wes Anderson's *Fantastic Mr. Fox*. It tripped my heart. I tipped my beer at it. I proudly signed the register, "Lions and tigers and magic, oh my! Wild Child seeks home." I lay down with the lugged jugs of mouse house water. The dirt was comfortable and fine.

Icecap curled up beside me, dry soil sticking to his sweaty skinny legs. He dragged his fingers up and down my hip. I shifted closer to him finally, so close our bodies touched. His fingertips mingled with this strange wonderful magic, leading me deeper into daydreams. Trail magic was filling me with new hope, changing the temperature of my mindset—warming it a hue. I felt lighter, like I'd dropped some needless weight from my backpack.

I watched Icecap, lost Swiss boy, a wonderful trail gift of his own kind. He belonged with the magic of this forest. Just as the grapefruits made me feel cared for and important, validated, so was he beginning to. They unified in my mind, tugging me forward, past my rape and my despair. Lying in that moment, on dirt, with Icecap, inches from the forests' most compassionate mouse house—within abundant magic—for the first time since I was raped, I felt lovable.

I hoped *that* magic was a shift in my life at large, a reflection of a better place I was reaching.

In the center of a silent, beige-white desert, a pyramid of hundreds of gallons of water stood at the end of a long, cherry red carpet. Crossing the desert, Icecap and I would periodically find a hundred or so milk jugs full of water, sometimes tied to one another with twine with no note or nametag at all, some displayed creatively, but this place was a vision. Chugging water there, lying on the red carpet, I felt taken care of—and worthy and important—in a way I'd never before and haven't since.

MAY 7, BIG BEAR CITY, CALIFORNIA, MILE 274

After ninety miles together without Edison, Icecap and I emerged into the desert mountain town of Big Bear City. We both needed a break from sleeping on sand and stones. We looked at motel rooms together.

Audrey, the "motel resort" owner, led us along a wooden plank past the Mountain Lion Room and the Lizard Room to the Bear Room. Inside was spacious, wood-walled: a dark-wood king-size bed and a Jacuzzi beside it, awkwardly close. It was funny. Two dozen stuffed teddy bears, tiny and large, covered the bedside table, the dresser, the wide square rim of the hot tub.

I used my parents' card to pay for the Bear Room. "It's adorable," I said.

"Key's in the door."

We left our packs out on the wood boardwalk, shoes out, even our hard sweat-and-grit-crusted socks outside. We wanted to keep our little bedroom nice. Icecap pulled off his shirt and put it in a plastic laundry bag. Then his pants.

I undressed, too. I slipped off my T-shirt and rolled down my filthy shorts. I unhooked my bra and put it in his hands.

Icecap glanced at my naked body. He said that he would go do our laundry. He tied a threadbare bleached bath towel around his waist and zipped his rain jacket on. He told me to "get clean," and walked out into the bright daylight, naked underneath the skimpy towel, just a gust of wind away from indecent. I thought he was bold to go out into the world like that.

I tiptoed to the bathroom mirror, my feet brown with dirt. I didn't want to spread my filth over the white plastic-tiled floor. In the scuffed mirror my waist was narrow, but not as small as I wanted it to be. My shoulders and upper arms were marked with a hundred pale half-moons—scars from when I'd pinched myself in the Cinderblock Palace, hating my own body after the rape. Now the scars embarrassed me. I thought I'd have to wear long sleeves for the rest of my life to hide them.

In the shower I scrubbed; warm water washed off caked dust. More dirt, more dirt. Endless red dirt. I shaved my armpits and legs, and scrubbed them again. Icecap didn't know, but I think I already knew: I wanted to have sex with him tonight.

I stepped out wearing no clothes and felt a twinge of dread. I didn't know what I wanted to happen next. *I decide what happens next*, I thought. I was nervous—but I wasn't doubting my desire to sleep with Icecap, it was what I wanted. I wasn't questioning my reasons, or the timing suddenly—I felt ready. My dread bloomed from a more cerebral fear. It was the question of whether he would still like me as much after, if he'd still want to be as sweet and gentle with me, if he'd stay with me. Or if our shared dreams of distant summers in South America and southern France and on remote frozen waterfalls would abruptly fade.

I wanted them to last.

I breathed, stepped out and wrapped myself in an old white towel and hugged myself dry. The towel, I saw, was streaked with reddish brown. There was dirt on me I couldn't see. I was still dirty. I slipped into the full hot tub and drained it and filled it again over me—the water went tan—and drained it again. My filth's persistence stunned me. I wondered where Icecap was. I went back into the shower.

I was struck by the impossibility of getting clean.

Icecap was still gone and I was missing him. I draped myself across the bed and waited. I rearranged my legs, crossed one ankle over the other, pointed my toes. I waited, got cold, slipped under the covers, the worn sheets cool and smooth against my nude body, and just as I was sinking into soft sleep, the door opened and daylight kissed me awake. Icecap was back, bright with sweat. He stood above two taped-up cardboard boxes: his resupply and—he lifted it to show me—mine, too. He was wearing only a thin small towel, and he had walked not only to the laundry machines out back of the motel—but inside a United States post office.

"I said I am your boyfriend, and they give it to me," he said. His lips broadened in a sly smirk. Then he said, "We have to buy groceries to supplement. The Big Bear City's supermarket will close."

I felt at once confused by the leniency of the postal system—that apparently anyone could pick up anyone's mail here—and delighted. "Boyfriend?" I said, rising up to my knees on the bed, the covers falling off me. I walked on my knees across the bed toward him.

"Would you like to have sex with me, boyfriend?"

My chest heated. My entire body pulsed and I gulped the room's warm air and I choked on nothing and quietly gasped, heart thrashing like a half-drowned bird in me remembering to breathe. I was flushed. He brushed my bare breast with his fingertips and quickly murmured that he'd shower.

I had a boyfriend. A boy who knew I'd been raped, and yet he didn't treat me any differently than any other girl, except perhaps that he was careful. He always stopped the moment I whispered, "Stop." In five minutes, soaked, somewhat less filthy, he returned.

I leaned into him, pressing my breasts against his chest.

"Sexy girl," he whispered. "On your back. Good girl." He cradled me in his arms and kissed my neck.

A boyfriend seemed to me the opposite of a rapist. A boyfriend took care of you. A rapist cared less about your entire life than only minutes of his own. A boyfriend gives you affection. A rapist takes you.

I lay there, limp, unsure of what to say or do.

"You want to?" he asked softly. "You're sure? For sex?"

"Yes," I said, my voice too loud. "I am."

"Good," he whispered, his lips brushing my ear.

I had to think out each movement before I made it. He kissed me. Kiss him back, I thought, and I did. I thought of something to say, "Do you like role-playing?" I didn't know what I'd do if he said yes. "I could be a nurse, or your student?" I asked, hoping it seemed sexy.

He smiled and pulled back, and said no. "I want to have sex with you," he said. "No nurse."

I smiled and exhaled, relieved. He kissed my forehead and nose and chin, and down. He was so gentle with my breasts that I giggled. Then his face hovered, inches from my shoulder. He said he would be easy. He told me I was sexy, and pretty, and for the first time with a boy, I believed it.

It truly didn't hurt.

I told him that I loved him.

He turned, faced me completely. "Really?" he said. He seemed incredulous but also very happy.

"Yes," I whispered. I laid my head against his rising-falling-rising chest and tried to breathe.

He held me more firmly then.

After the rape I wanted to flee; now I felt like staying in that motel bed forever.

PART II
The Range of Light

CHAPTER 11

Love in the Woods

Morning was a honeyed spill of light, the Bear Room lit by a small skylight. Every cell of my body was buzzing—I'd had sex. I had told him I loved him. A maddening excitedness consumed me. I floated through the morning.

I read aloud one of the motel guest book's sweetest notes to Icecap, but he walked away as I was speaking. I followed him out without finishing the note under my name. He told me he didn't want to "waste" any more time; we had to get back to the trail quickly to "make miles." After the comfort of the night before—my first good sex ever—the word *waste* hurt me. I hardened my posture.

On the way back to the trail we passed Big Bear City's small post office. Outside stood a man I recognized, but just barely. After a moment, I knew. Never-Never. This was the first time I'd ever seen Never-Never in the flesh, but it was undeniably him—I recognized him from Facebook photos, and also photos he had sent.

And now here we were, six months later, in California. He was another faint echo from my college past, haunting me here. In person Never-Never was stumpy, short and balding, shockingly chunky given his active life. His pictures must have been shot from the best possible angles.

I didn't know what to say to him. I didn't even want to say hi.

"I guess we should hug," I said, or maybe he said it. He seemed gregarious and goofy, physically a little unsure and awkward. He glanced at Icecap, shifting his weight to stoop inward, and quickly hugged me. Then I said I remembered I needed something and jogged over to the post office with Icecap, though I had nothing to pick up there.

When Icecap and I emerged from the post office, I saw Never-Never with a group and walked away without another look. I already suspected that when he saw I was Icecap's girlfriend now, he would begin to hate me.

MAY 10, DEEP CREEK, CALIFORNIA, MILE 306

Icecap felt the pull of Canada intensely. We couldn't possibly reach it soon enough. I didn't understand his rush, but I'd joined myself with him, and so I pushed my body. Together we moved briskly. The day after we made love, Icecap and I walked nineteen miles. The next day, nineteen miles, again. The day after that we walked twenty-six.

Beneath our quick feet, the path flowed, that river of pale gravel, of snakes, of butterflies and inchworms and dead leaves. Each day's miles were easier.

Each night Icecap would ask me if I wanted to have sex again. Each night I'd pause and think—and I would find I really didn't want to. I thought it was strange—I was very happy walking with him, euphoric sleeping beside him, so lucky. He would lean into me, hoping, but I no longer felt turned on.

To me, sex now felt irrelevant. Doing it hadn't actually felt amazing, physically. Making out in Idyllwild had been much more exciting. Sex with him had been beautifully safe and good, but lying beside him sexless did the same thing.

Each night when he asked me, "To have sex?" I would finally say no.

And then he'd nod. He never pushed me. He'd never ask me to explain why.

After each night's no, he'd hold me, we'd kiss and cuddle, and melt, into dreams.

We went on like that. Day after day: big miles. Each night: do you want to? No. Okay, hug, kiss, and warm sleeping beside him.

We strode along the desert trail, the dirt pale orange, and approached a wooden sign. I read aloud: PCT McDonald's 0.4. Icecap read it, smiling. I was laughing. The word *McDonald's* was so strange to see seared into sun-faded wood. After seven more minutes of walking, I emerged beside an interstate, at a rest stop. The golden *M* branded the big blue sky. I glanced behind, but didn't see Icecap. I faltered, considered staying, waiting here, but he knew where I'd be.

I crossed the concrete parking lot to the McDonald's, feeling self-conscious, nervous my trail smell would offend the people inside. A man dressed in a beige polo shirt and ill-fitting Walmart jeans limped past the row of cars straight toward me. I felt scared until he got closer, nearly at me; he looked kind, his fat cheeks rimmed with deep smile lines. I stopped short and he shuffled right up, eyes widened at the smell of me, and handed me a twenty-dollar bill.

I blinked.

"I know how it is," he said. "I know. After my father died, I lived in a rickee old shack south'a Mojave. I know it." His eyes were small and blue. "But look at me now, 'kay? You'll get back on yer feet. 'Kay?"

I was holding on to his money, my arm still outreached, as if I'd just taken it. As if I was handing it back. "I'm not," I said, hoping I'd understood, "I have a home. I'm not homeless, really." I kept my arm outstretched, waiting for him to snatch the money back. When he only looked at me, directly at my eyes, I thought maybe I should explain that lack of money was not my problem. I'd grown up well off. He needed his twenty dollars more than I did.

"I know," he said, "that's right. I wasn't either." He told me I'd want to get something to eat, anyhow. "In case you return and home is gone. You know?"

Then he shuffled back toward his car. I didn't know, not really. I felt a little guilty and confused and grateful, too.

I stood, disoriented, holding the man who was now gone's twenty dollars. But I wasn't homeless. I had a home. My parents' colonial in Newton. My dorm room. Good places to sleep, but maybe not true home. Wrong places. This homelessness he feared on my behalf was actually me on my feet; this homelessness was my safest place now.

Icecap emerged from the manzanitas—he'd been "cleaning up," he said. To me he looked the same. I took his hand and we entered the McDonald's.

A dozen thru-hikers—what must have looked to normal rest stoppers like a happy gang of bums—overtook the place, their cell phones charging in every available outlet, a hot stink polluting the restaurant air.

"Is this a homeless retreat?" I heard an older lady with big fake breasts ask the cashier.

A young, handsome man with silvery hair and emerald eyes, and trim—I imagined he was a Vegas magician—said to the chunky blond cashier, "You can kick hitchhikers out. They don't pay tolls."

"They ain't," she replied. "They walk here."

The young man with hair like white silk took his coffee. "To McDonald's?" He pinched his nose, and strutted back outside to a purple convertible, not staying to hear the true, absurd answer.

Most hikers didn't even notice the scene, or didn't care. One, with a huge blond beard, nodded at me. He was cute. I could hear a girl at his loud table call him Surf. I smiled, ordered a parfait, but sat down at a booth sheer across the restaurant from the boisterous group. I wasn't feeling social. I was too hot and exhausted.

Icecap tried to order three Big Macs, but they didn't have hamburgers so early in the morning. Instead he'd gotten the Big Breakfast with Hotcakes Bigger Biscuit breakfast, "the most calories of anything on the menu," he said, and a chocolate-dipped ice-cream cone. Apparently so many hikers had asked for cones and shakes that the

McDonald's manager had turned the ice-cream machine on early.

"A Big Mac," Icecap said, picking up the savory sausage patty, which was flat and round, smushed between two hotcakes. He was confused about why they were serving breakfast sandwiches but not hamburgers; they seemed the same—both a "meat sandwich." He insisted the beef burger patty looked the same as the flat sausage he now held.

I smiled at his point.

I deepened my voice, moved my mouth in exaggerated shapes to create twang. "But how's these bums get here?"

He laughed. Then he feigned seriousness. "But how do they do it? It is crazy. They're walking to here?"

"Yes." I said, as if I were teaching him. "They are crazy."

At the big booth across the McDonald's, a hiker was completing the twenty-buck challenge: eat twenty dollars' of McDonald's food. Icecap had eaten eleven dollars' worth of food. "Twenty-buck eating competition isn't so much. It's easy, actually."

"You gonna do it?" I asked him, hoping he'd say no.

"If I'm hungry for it."

For Icecap it was not a competition; it was a possibility.

But then—again—Icacap was eager to get back to the trail. The day heated, and outside the sand-white air was 95 degrees. I said I wanted to stay and wait out the midday dry heat in the McDonald's air-conditioning, but he wouldn't have it. While other hikers were back at the McDonald's, licking their soft serves, waiting for the high sun to slip behind the mountains, we left the air-conditioned restaurant in midafternoon.

I hadn't noticed the trail's descent down to the McDonald's, but the climb back up from it, into the mountains, was relentless. The trail zigzagged up toward blue sky, up. My belly was full of sugary yogurt parfait and ice cream and apple juice and a carton of chocolate milk, sloshing in my stomach; my waist cramped, throbbing. Icecap walked fast, faster than usual, unslowed by the unstopping climb, not noticing my pain. We climbed five hundred feet.

We climbed five hundred more. I ran to stay with him and didn't complain, though the pain in my waist now looked bluish, like a bruise. Icecap didn't slow a beat.

We camped that night on a dusty flat high on the mountain. I was exhausted and didn't pitch my tent. Instead, I crawled into Icecap's shelter, curled myself small. My right side was bruised like a snowstorm cloud, shapeless and dark. Icecap pressed his palm against my lower back. "Wild Child," he whispered. "Wild Child?"

I didn't answer. I curled smaller, into myself, into the warmth and rest of necessary sleep.

"Wild Child," I heard as I faded from him. He was whispering. He was asking me if I wanted to make love. He was asking me why I never wanted to.

I curled tighter, ignoring him.

One blue night Icecap woke me with a pat. I had been dreaming. I'd slept beside him in his tent for the past week. In puppy love, we'd moved in together.

He patted my back again.

"Time to hike," he said.

I opened my eyes, but it was dark. "It's nighttime," I mumbled, rolling over, snuggling down deeper into my sleeping bag.

This time he shook me. "Time for *hiking*," he said. "We can do a thirty today."

I didn't want to hike thirty or more miles that day. "A thirty" was a challenge, a competition without a prize. Hikers who'd done it bragged about it in the registers. That was the only point.

But I felt no need to accomplish such a thing. I was exhausted. I wanted to rest. Lately, we'd been hiking twenty to twenty-six miles a day; I'd stumble into camp, spent completely, my knees throbbing. Twenty-six miles felt like my limit, a literal daily marathon with a backpack on. I'd been beating myself up to keep up with Icecap's pace, but now, at whatever damned black morning-night hour it was, all I wanted to do was sink back into my soft sleep.

So I did. Icecap did, too, it seemed, and the next time he woke me the sky was grapefruit pink. The sun hadn't yet floated over the far mountains, but Icecap said, "Get *up* now. We waste time."

I rocked upright, lurched onto my hands and knees, and moaned. I mumbled, "Ah. Fine." I rose and broke camp and walked and tripped my body forward, my legs aflame with lactic acid, heavy and trembling, the early morning world still cool mute blue.

That morning, my knees both ached. I feared I'd hurt myself. I knew I should listen to my body, tell Icecap I *must* rest more, but I couldn't. I hated to debate. He'd say something like, "You can accomplish what you work hard for. If you cannot do it, this is because you can't work hard."

I was passive by nature. I had always been. Arguing felt unnatural and uncomfortable. I was always agreeing even when I didn't really, instinctively looking for ways to forfeit power, to become more dependent, to be taken care of. I realized how intensely Icecap reminded me of Jacob. They were similar, both diligent and harsh in their judgments—and my big brother's sureness had always comforted me.

But as I ran on sore legs to keep up with Icecap, my tendency toward silence stressed me. I knew that if I ignored my knees and inflamed shins, the pain could become chronic. I could develop tendonitis and shin splints, both were common. The only cure for either was a month of rest without hiking and then I'd miss the narrow thru-hiking window. I would effectively end my hike. That would be death. That would be the end for me.

Still I walked behind him. Beneath hot sun, desert roses bloomed. Under cold moon, I still refused to.

And every morning after that, Icecap would rise with the first light. Packed, ready to hike, in twenty minutes, tops. Often he would time himself. Sometimes he timed me, but he was consistently disappointed. "Forty-seven minutes!" he reported one morning, stressed. "Too slow for this." I wondered—maybe he was mad that I wouldn't have sex with him again and, in his rush, he was beginning to run from me.

MAY 13, WRIGHTWOOD, CALIFORNIA, MILE 370

At last Icecap and I came to a wide paved road, and I stuck out my thumb. Down the road was the tiny mountain town of Wrightwood, California, where we planned to eat a hot meal of fajitas or big cheese-burgers and milk shakes at a home-style restaurant. We were starved. We'd get a room for one night and then hitchhike back to that same spot where the trail crossed this road and keep on north from there, resuming our wiggled line of continuous footsteps.

After a dozen minutes an old mint green truck pulled over and we hopped in the back and it sped off to town. The paved road snaked along the bases of blue and white mountains, through San Bernardino County, down to a pine-shadowed valley. Watching the soft blue peaks recede, the dark trees streak past, I felt so different than whom I'd been down at California's border with Mexico. I occupied my body. I'd walked 370 miles. I'd stepped over rattlesnake after rattlesnake—they didn't scare me one twig, anymore—and hitchhiked with strangers and found water and shelter, too, pitching my tent each night, sleeping like a babe regardless of it all. I had finally truly had sex with a boy. I had wanted to. Here I was in the bed of a stranger's truck, holding Icecap's arm, swaying gently with the road's wide bends, against him. The old truck let us out outside a red cottage inn. It was idyllic. Yellow marigolds lined the patchwork-stone walkway to the front door.

We thanked our ride and offered him gas money, but he encouraged us to keep it. "You'll be wanting that," he said. "Have steak and fries."

Then I blinked at the inn and he was rolling down the clean gray road, silently drifting around a bend, and gone. So this was Wrightwood. It was beautiful, but I felt disoriented here, off our trail—felt lost. I saw no hikers on the cottage's tidy lawn. We took our packs off and left them on the red-and-white-painted porch—they stunk and suddenly felt ridiculous—and stepped inside.

No one was there. There was no bell at the tidy front desk. I called, "Hello," but then saw beside the old ticking clock a handwritten, taped-up sign, addressed to thru-hikers:

Please know we are a small staff and have white towels. PCT folks
turn our towels black. There are trail angels in town who
all would love to host you.
Our apologies!
The Innkeeper
White Fence Inn

My stomach tightened, and I felt embarrassed. I walked out the front door. Hikers were outsiders here. We were two ghosts within a very pretty ghost town. "Let's find the trail angels," I said to Icecap. He seemed confused. "We can't stay here," I said. I picked up my knapsack and kept walking down the road, kept going until we came to the town's small hardware store. In the shop's window, a browned handwritten note said: "Welcome hikers! Come in for hiker box with free stuff to swap and register and book of trail angels."

Inside it smelled like glue and dust and wood. On the dirty cream-gold carpet, a beat-up cardboard box with Hiker Box written on a flap in Sharpie sat full of crinkly old ramen packets and paper packages of white-creased Lipton Sides and duct tape and grommets—free food and knickknacks hikers who didn't need them had left for people who might want them. Only a thru-hiker would ever want them. On the linoleum front counter, once red but now so old it appeared pink, a binder lay open—a register. We signed in, lost.

We read through, hoping to see names we knew, a clue. No one. I was just about to leave and wander farther down the gray-paved road when the front door's bells jingled and a man walked in and welcomed us. His hands were huge as beavers' flat tails and filthy. This was his hardware store. He took the binder from Icecap and flipped to the final page, a scratched-up, sleeve-protected sheet that listed Wrightwood's many trail angels.

"For a spot to stay," he said. "For free, you know?"

The page listed more than twenty names and phone numbers. Some listings were couples, some only men. I picked a couple, Maria and John Moore, and called the number. Maria answered, told us to do our grocery shopping two doors down from the hardware store, and then she'd pick us up out front there in an hour. She'd have dinner ready. Her voice was fast, her accent slight but audible. "I'll see you two for taco dinner," she said and then hung up.

She appeared as promised. Maria's house was small and white, and inside it smelled like roasted corn and pork, absolutely delicious. The walls showcased several gorgeous wedding photos, blown up to three and even five feet tall. The bride was childlike, tanned and very pretty. The groom was older, pale, but handsome still. The woman in the pictures must have been a young Maria.

Her husband wasn't home, she apologized. He was away, "bothering hikers" for the weekend.

"Doing trail magic?" I asked.

"Yes, he really loves it."

Maria had made tacos for us from scratch, dozens of them, and laid out delicate crimped-edge porcelain bowls of minced green peppers, tomato and onion salsa, a dozen pretty little dishes on her small round table. She told us to go run and shower. We did, though we were hungry and would rather just eat filthy. We changed into oversize "loaner clothes"—huge faded T-shirts and shorts with elastic waistbands—and then, at last, she pulled corn taco shells out of the oven and carried over ceramic pots of spicy ground beef and pulled pork.

Soon we had devoured a dozen tacos' worth of fixings each. Maria brought out more of everything. "Keep going," she kept saying, "you are starving."

I asked about the wedding pictures. "They're so beautiful," I said. "Is that you, the bride?"

"Me, yes," she said, it was. It was "a story."

She told us that once, when she was young, she went to a church retreat in the forest. One night, the minister told her that she should take a walk. "When, out in the woods, you turn around," he told her, "whoever is looking at you will be the man God wants you to marry."

She walked a ways, into dim woods, terrified, thinking how her timing could change her life, wondering if she had any power over her fate. That—she said—remains the mystery. She walked slowly through the moonlit trees, the night a velvet sea. She turned around. She found her widowed boss behind her, an "old, white man." He was twenty years her senior, pale and very thin. She was not attracted to him. She could not imagine ever loving him. "I was like, oh *please* Papi Lord, not him. I was like, anybody out here now but him." But she resigned to it. She knew that God had done it.

Six weeks later, she married the man she met in the shadowed woods that night.

That was fifteen years ago. Now she loves her husband terribly. Now when he leaves on summer weekends to do trail magic, she misses him so much she cannot sleep. Her eyes were bright with tears as she told the story. Here she was feeding strangers in her little cottage, missing him, nostalgic; she seemed divine, and wonderfully happy. She held in her eyes pure and total faith in love.

What magic.

In the photos she looked twenty—near my age. She had big eyes, full lips, a messy bun of curly hair, like me. She was pretty. In my closed eyes I saw shadowed forests and imagined my future love among trees, also seeking: walking blind into the woods with such faith in love.

It seemed such a perfect blip of storied hope. There was something romantic about the notion of walking blind into the woods and finding love, building a home in which Mexican spices mixed with the scent of sweet pines and endless mountain wind.

I had never worn a diamond, but I suddenly wanted one, or a bright ruby like a talisman that told me I was loved and would be safe for always.

And I saw with clarity that my relationship with Icecap was not what I had hoped it was. Icecap gave me hope for change—his confidence inspiring mine, his adoration lighting me up like a moon—but my bond to him felt delicate. In truth it felt temporary, fire sparks flaring in a strong wind, the wind pressing me forward toward its light faster. The trail would end in Canada. We were reserved for the trail. He would fly back to Switzerland. I would go somewhere else. I didn't actually think we would get to travel together before the light we chased burned out.

I knew that my relationship with him was ending. My affection for Icecap was beautiful, but it was not really love. What I felt with him was trust. But my hope was fiercer now. I was seduced by the idea of walking blind into the woods, and from darkness finding love.

As days went by, Icecap became less amenable to resting. He had to finish the trail by September third because he had a Phish concert to get to in Portland on the fifth. Also, his United States traveler's visa was going to expire in September, so he had to finish the trail before then. Also he was starting school on September seventh, so he wanted to finish the trail in August. Whenever I suggested taking a break he'd fiddle and fidget, uneasy, as if I had proposed snorting cocaine or driving drunk. He'd say words like *willpower* and *commitment* and *drive*. One bright open day after we'd traversed a desert ridge for seven unstopping hours, I collapsed onto my pack and found in it my crumpled, scrawled list, THINGS DANIEL HATES, and added in dark ink: THREE.

> Number ONE: windmills,
> TWO: the wind.
> THREE: breaks.

I smoothed it flat, heart shaken. This time it didn't seem sweet. It didn't seem funny. Icecap hates windmills; Icecap hates wind. Soon he would announce he hated sand, and also beaches. He would list things he despised.

For the sake of speed, we bypassed a cardboard sign that said Meadow Mary's Magic, and then later a paper beneath a stone right in the blond dirt of the trail that read Free Hiker Foot Massages by Hector. At a wide junction, where a quiet Jeep road crossed our trail, we stood, arguing about which way to go, whether to go or not. A poster-board sign at the junction said Thru-hiker Bananas and Beer 1,000 Yards above an arrow that pointed down the Jeep road. I told Icecap I *needed* to go see. It would be *fun*. An echoing *hoot!* resounded from down the road. I widened my eyes at him to say *see*, to use my feminine power to sway him. He kept walking up our trail without me. "'Bye then," he called back as he hiked onward, north.

I jogged behind him, going too fast for myself, furious at myself and him. I decided this was the last time I would bypass a trail angel so Icecap could make this pilgrimage a race. There was no competition. The first to reach Canada would only be in Canada, no trophy in hand, likely all alone. Dana "L-Rod" Figment, the Pacific Crest Trail's most famed and beloved trail angel, lay only sixty miles ahead, on the southern edge of the Mojave Desert, at a shady oasis she'd built known along the trail as Hiker Heaven. I couldn't miss that. I absolutely wouldn't.

I caught Icecap and kissed him, though I didn't feel affection. I kissed him to soothe him, to calm him down, if I could.

"Why do you call at me this? Ass-cap?" he asked me then.

"*Icecap?*"

"You want to name me?"

I didn't understand. Icecap was his name. I'd already named him. He knew about trail names, everyone had one. "Icecap" was how he'd signed the registers. I hadn't known he was unhappy with "Icecap." It was true, though, that no one else called him by it—but then nobody else talked to us at all. We were isolated, outsiders within the trail community around us. Suddenly I wanted other people to know me—Wild Child. Not just him. He'd become a coach to me, like a dad. A prison. I didn't need that. I needed to make my own rules.

"You want to be something else?" I asked. "What do you want to be?"

He thought for a moment, solemn, and then said he had the most comfortable inflatable sleeping pad on the whole trail, and said, "It is ze best, most comfy. Call me Pad Man."

I laughed. "I'm not calling you that, sorry," I said. Really, though, he didn't seem like Icecap to me anymore. Out loud, I was still calling him Icecap, but privately I'd reverted back to Daniel. I noticed I'd titled the list THINGS DANIEL HATES.

"Pad Man," he said, his voice slow and tight. "That's who I am."

"I don't think so," I said. "I think you're Daniel. You don't get to choose whatever random thing you want to be."

But when the next day we met a hiker named Chuck Norris, a big potbellied guy with long copper blond hair who was from the Florida panhandle, Daniel introduced himself as "Icecap." At Icecap's name, Chuck Norris stopped walking. "What was that?" He was grinning big. He was huge and goofy and warm and seemed unrepressed, farting loudly as he walked the road north with us, ignoring his gas.

"*Ass*-cap," Icecap said, more slowly this time, annoyed.

"Okay Ass-cap," Chuck Norris howled. He cracked up. "No beans now or you'll pop!"

Chuck Norris quaked with laughter, his whole body shaking. I was laughing, too, I couldn't help it. Icecap paled, mad and embarrassed, having no clue what the joke was.

Chuck Norris recomposed himself and got back to telling his life story. His daughter had just gotten married in the most beautiful dress. His lovely wife was a woman named Tigger, but she was doing trail magic at the moment, wasn't on-trail now. He loved her "much as cherry ice-cream pie." He'd met her in the woods, on the 2,180-mile-long Appalachian Trail. He'd been thru-hiking it. She'd been thru-hiking it, too, by good God's luck.

"I am Pad Man, actually," Icecap said to Chuck Norris, apropos of nothing, in a lull.

I would watch diligently now for the trail angel signs, and, when I saw the next portal into that world, I'd take it. I'd turn off the PCT and onto it. I'd slip in—without Icecap.

CHAPTER 12

Distance to Paradise

There are pioneer souls that blaze their paths
Where highways never ran;—
But let me live by the side of the road
And be a friend to man.
—From the poem taped to the concrete wall above
Hiker Heaven's washer and dryer

MAY 15, PINYON FLATS, THE CALIFORNIA DESERT NEAR SULFUR SPRINGS, MILE 400

The desert had become beautiful. Radiant evening light bleached the hills of low scrub oaks white-gold. A long desert jackrabbit, the ghostly color of dust, bounded across the open desert floor, spraying silver sand. Indian Ricegrass curled like wild animal hair, tracing both sides of the trail in two thick lines to the horizon. My path was singular and clear. I no longer wanted the desert to end. I had become strong, walking here. I was happy.

Icecap and I walked without talking and camped somewhere on a high ridge, between golden dust and soft pink sky, empty of things to say to each other. He pitched his tent and I climbed into it, as I'd done the night before, and the night before that, too. I no longer had to build my own shelter each night. It was nice. I crawled inside and sat behind the tent's small arched doorway, removing my running shoes.

From outside, Icecap flatly told me, "Get out of there."

"What?" I said, annoyed, not looking at him.

"Get out!" he repeated with such intensity that I feared he'd seen a rattlesnake nesting on my sleeping bag.

I pulled my feet under myself and ducked back out of his tent, heart speeding, carefully stood up, too scared to take one barefoot step. But he was off beside a pale rock, peeing, not looking at me. "What?" I asked again. "Icecap. What?"

He said he didn't like how I kicked my shoes off from the inside of his tent. It was "a mess." I should take them off outside. I always got dirt inside.

I was barefoot. I was exasperated and out of pace with myself, working my knees until they ached to stay with a guy who would rather race to Canada than have any fun at all, whom I'd told I loved but no longer even liked. I said nothing back to him. I stepped slowly back to his tent, knelt, and wiggled my feet back into my stinky, dusty shoes. Kicked them back off. Ducked and crawled back inside and shook deep into my sleeping bag.

A minute later, he came in, too. We'd stopped putting our rain-flies on and I stared up through Icecap's tent's low mesh roof, didn't look at him. *Our* hike. I didn't start out with Icecap. I didn't ever intend to hike with him. Yet I'd camped with Icecap all but just three nights. My first night on the trail, the night in the flood wadi with a stranger, and the night I hiked alone through spider webs, the moon high and pale, the sky dry-blood red-black, walking through the night to get away from Edison and Icecap.

Now, inside Icecap's tent, I felt melancholy. My knees were bruised. I felt Icecap lying next to me, not touching me, neither of us sleeping as the air above his tent's mesh roof darkened to blood spattered with stars, to velvet black. In that darkness beside him, I

was remembering what I was walking across this desert to shed, remembering that no one could do it for me. It was time to begin again
the work I'd come out here to do.

It was time to stop compromising. I should have stopped compromising long ago, before I let Junior overstay his welcome, before
I lost myself to 66-tattooed Tyler. Before two red-black seeds at once
dropped from me and grew in me, my limbs its limbs, my face its
terrible face.

I felt every mile I'd walked with Icecap was wasted. I needed, for
once, to walk alone. It occurred to me that I was in a relationship. This
was my first relationship; Icecap actually was my boyfriend. I was a
girlfriend. We were a couple. I didn't know how to end a relationship.
It took time to break up a relationship, it seemed to me. The next day as
I walked out front, he following, I plotted how I'd leave him.

It was daunting—not the thought of being alone, but of telling
him I was going. I opened my mouth, then closed it, entirely unprepared to say something final. We walked along like that, me in front,
my back to him, imagining he wasn't there, wishing he would leave
me, but still unable to flee, myself.

The trail cut across the side of a steep mountain ridge, paral-
leling Pacifico Mountain Road, which snaked along the high crest
above us. We were in the tan shade the ridge cast, on a thin trail
that did not ascend to the ridge or descend to the valley, but hovered
between five and six thousand feet. The mountain's shadow darkened, and desert scrub oak gave way to thicker, grand oak trees,
their canopies broad, their shadows over shadows. Miner's lettuce
grew bright green in that cool shade. Icecap stooped down and
plucked a tuft, passed it to me, stooped in his stride and picked another for himself. The leaves were flat green, bright as stained glass
glowing in golden noon light, almost yellow in their luminescence.
I ate the crisp flat leaves and stems, listening to the snap of stems
still alive. We walked faster. California junipers rustled in the warm
wind, smelling sad, of roses and of gin. I picked two juniper berries,
tiny hard frosted blue, and opened my palm to Icecap. He took one.
At last we shared a moment's rest, put them on our tongues like

after-dinner mints. His delicate hands looked sad. I realized we had walked in silence all day.

Near the light's end that evening, the sun low and red, air chilled as if blown off invisible ice, we approached what looked like a distant pendulum, thick and dark, hanging from a tree. It looked like a small body. Closer, we saw it was a black plastic garbage bag swinging on a rust-red-brown manzanita limb. I peered in and sugar kissed me. The bag was full of plums. A paper note taped to the bag said "Thru-hikers enjoy" with no signed name. Gifts simply came. I broke one's skin with my teeth, heard the fresh snap. It was sweet as honey. It swept me back to the grapefruits, pink and huge, that Icecap and I had found our first day alone together, back when I'd first felt safe.

That night I built my own shelter again, at last. It had been a week since I'd slept in my own tent but felt like so much longer. I missed its smell: desert sage and dusty nylon. That smell was right. Like shelter—a room of my own. Yet when I stood back to look at my work, I saw that my good old tent wasn't standing. It was drooped, flopped into itself like a sheet draped limp over a scrawny bush. In my weak lamplight, I examined it. To my horror, the most important tent pole joint had snapped. My tent was now dead weight. I no longer had a place to go, a *home*.

Icecap was nearby, a floating headlamp on an adjacent gravel tent pit. He was eating the hot dinner that he cooked himself each night. I approached him and asked to please borrow his duct tape.

"Why is this?" he asked. I didn't want to have to explain; I was exhausted. "You want to take my tape that I carry?"

I mumbled to him that my tent collapsed.

He inhaled, exhaled dramatically. "Because you break it!" He said that I should take better care of my things. He threw his duct tape at me and I caught it. I taped the joint together. It sagged apart. Duct tape was not strong enough to hold the three metal poles in place. My house was now hopelessly collapsed.

That night, I took my shoes off outside, trembling with exhaustion and with rage. I had to sleep with Icecap in his tent. I lay beside him and closed my eyes to the rhythmic *woooh woooh wooh* of him blowing up his inflatable sleeping pad, as he always did, fell asleep to it. Plotted in my half-dream how at the Figments' Hiker Heaven, I'd leave him. I'd walk into the High Sierra alone.

Right beside him, I called my mother. I still called her every night. When she asked how my day was, I told her my tent had broken. She asked did I need her to send another overnight? She reminded me I could use her credit card if I could get to town. I told her I could stay with someone, Icecap, in his tent that night.

"That's good," she said, not asking anything more. Then she paused. "Do you need me to mail you out some vitamins?" Then, "I love you, Debby. We love you and we miss you. Pleasant dreams."

I hung up feeling empty and far away. Our nightly conversation on this satellite phone she made me carry was bland and repetitive. I was beginning to resent it. I hated my inability to explain my life on the trail to her and my mother's inability to comprehend. I hated her consistent need to know the list of different foods I'd eaten that day. I remembered how she'd asked me if I'd had a good dinner in the same phone call when I'd told her I'd been raped.

I considered, tomorrow night, not calling her.

MAY 17, VASQUEZ ROCKS, THE CALIFORNIA DESERT, MILE 451

Icecap and I crossed the tracks of the Southern Pacific Railroad, unending in both directions, descended a gradual half-dozen miles, into Escondido Canyon, down to where Antelope Valley Freeway 14 crosses the PCT, traffic flashing over a wide concrete bridge. The trail passed through a tunnel under the freeway, and then in just ten more flattish, easy miles, we'd emerge in the small town of Agua Dulce—wherein existed the famous Hiker Heaven. Just ten more miles to paradise.

A trickle of water gleamed on the curved mint green concrete wall, and little green and white wildflowers blossomed where the gravelly sand was dark and damp beneath it, their petals serrated, at once delicate and rough, like torn up lace. I swooped down and picked one as I passed, feeling wicked, still happily believing that I was nearly done with Icecap.

We emerged on the other side of Freeway 14, ready to walk fast and hard the rest of the way to Hiker Heaven, the sweet home stretch. The desert was open, treeless and signless, and the path divided from itself, splitting into two, two distinct trails to follow, without a sign. The two dusty footpaths were both about three feet wide, both shooting out both approximately northward, but only one of them could be the Pacific Crest Trail.

I leaned in toward the dirt. I saw a sign. Not a wood and metal sign, but faint footprints, all pointed in the direction we were going. One arm of the split held far more north-pointing feet than the other. I leaned down, closer. Flat and large in the middle of that same arm, drawn thin and shaky with a hiker's trekking pole, was an arrow and the faint letters P C T.

Without a word of explanation to Icecap, I went that way. Without a word, he followed.

The trail I'd chosen soon proved right when we passed a rock painted in white letters: PCT. Hikers' footprints and an arrow drawn in dirt with a trekking pole tip had shown me the correct way to go.

Then it happened again. The trail split; I followed the denser footprints.

Searching for Hiker Heaven became fun. Just when the footprints would fade out, and just when I'd begin to fear I was following a foolish band of tracks to nowhere, I'd see the next clue marking the invisible PCT. Only the knowledge I gained out here in this desert could help me discern the correct way to go.

Walking beneath Vasquez Rocks, in and out of the shadows of tilted red stone pinnacles like wind-pressed spires of rock, as tall as towers, I never once saw the Pacific Crest Trail. Thru-hiker-made clues are what led me through. People got me through, not the trail itself. At last we emerged onto a pale gray asphalt road.

A telephone pole bore a white paper-plate sign that told us in scrawled letters Hiker Heaven → 1 Mile! Hanging on that same telephone pole was a trash bag—full of plums. Swinging slightly, like the one before. So they had been from Hiker Heaven. I was euphoric, excited all over for this crazy hiker fort, this hideaway, high from all the little trail-magical clues and signs and treats that made me feel this trail was made just for me, for people like me who needed it.

Icecap and I each took our dark sweet plum. We were exhausted, hot and glittering with sweat-salt, but we sped our gait, and followed the main road past Agua Dulce Hardware and the Sweetwater Café to Big Mouth Pizza, outside of which flapped a twelve-foot-long white vinyl banner: Welcome to Agua Dulce, Pacific Crest Trail Hikers!

Just as we began to realize that we didn't in fact know how to get to the Figments' Hiker Heaven, a rickety Jeep pulled up and the young woman driving called to us, "Jump in!"; she'd take us there. She'd known from our filth and our packs that we were hikers. In her creaking Jeep we rode to a long property enclosed in a white picket fence. "Here it is!" the young woman sang. She waited long enough for us to gather our knapsacks and then drove away.

We were in a shady residential neighborhood, had arrived at last outside Hiker Heaven's big white gate. I beamed at it; Hiker Heaven *would* have a big white gate with tall wide wooden double doors. And we'd made it. We rang the gate's dinner bell, heard dogs barking, a melodic laugh and a shriek over muffled voices, and a metal latch *click-ping*. The gate swung open and there Chuck Norris stood before us. "Welcome," he said. "Ass-cap! A pleasure. Good gas." I already knew: I would leave Icecap here.

Inside was not a hideaway but a sprawling, sunlit tent city. Dozens of hikers swung in colorful cloth hammocks and reclined in beach chairs, sat eating sweet-smelling barbecue while crystal wind chimes tinkled their music. The lawn was impossibly green, the greenest thing I'd seen since before Mexico. Pale green desert plants grew from terra-cotta pots, quivering in warm and farm-sweet breeze. A spot-shag band of mutts sprang to me, back to the beige ranch-house where crystal wind-chimes tinkled their ceaseless music, out to the shimmering gravel beneath a wide pine tree, their tails wagging wildly. They rested at last in the shade beneath the pine's soft shaggy arms, all flat-limp in its shade. Horses neighed from across a field, spraying golden dust with each high, graceful step.

Chuck Norris led us up the driveway, pointing out an open-walled tent stacked high with crates of clothes we could borrow. Then he brought us to "the garage," a post-office-meets-home-style-laundromat, tidy and more organized than most small towns' official ones. Hikers' resupply packages filled the concrete room's high shelves, alphabetized by whatever name or trail name was written on them. There were hundreds of them. Washers and driers spun by the concrete back wall. Before them kneeled a middle-aged woman, loading a new mound of filthy hiker laundry into an open washer: Dana "L-Rod" Figment herself. She was fit and lovely, her brown hair trimmed short, exposing suntanned skin and smiling eyes. She instructed us to go behind the house, out to the hiker trailer, and take off our dirty clothes and give her all our laundry. Inside the trailer, we should put our names on the dry-erase board on the hiker-bathroom door to sign up for a nice warm soapy shower. She had soap, Q-tips, and shampoo for us to use.

In the space of a minute, she explained that (1) she would do our laundry while we showered; (2) we were welcome to any of the food inside the hiker trailer; (3) if we wanted pizza, we were welcome to borrow a bicycle or her car to ride to the pizza place back in town so we wouldn't have to walk; (4) to claim a bed for the night, we should throw our packs on any open cot under the big white tents, or on a sofa or bed in the hiker trailer, or we could pitch our tents anywhere on the lawn; and (5) most astonishing and impossible of all, everything she did for us was entirely free. She hosted a maximum of fifty hikers a night and had a maximum-stay length of two nights and three days. I didn't understand how she could do it. I asked about the fortune it must all have cost her.

She said only, "Cast your bread upon the waters today, and God will give back tenfold tonight." Then, "Geez, it takes so little to make you guys happy."

We stripped and gave our filthy clothes to Dana, went over to the loaner clothes tent and chose new outfits—there were navy blue

nt yard. Childhood in Newton,
ssachusetts. Newton is the Garden City

Walking in the woods on a path with my
un-pictured family. Seven years old (1997)

ome with books

A watercolor from my first "book," published by my family

On a hike with my mother, presenting: water
Eight years old (1998) New Hampshire

irch Hill Sleep Away Camp,
leven years old (2001)

paintings made in private lessons that my parents generously gifted me

A Newton South High School cross-country race, Newton. Fifteen years old (2005)

Nordic Ski Race, Weston, Massachusetts

Day 1—a trail sign warning of the dangers of the desert

The Sonoran Desert, California. A selfie in desert solitude

I was here at 12:20. I couldn't stop at water because I w FREEZING.

I'll be walking slow from here because I'm tired and cold. Please catch up with me so I can enjoy your company!

♡ wild child

Scissors Crossing, the California desert. The bookshelf full of water that saved my life

LEFT: Icecap's tarp-shelter
RIGHT: My Seedhouse tent

The PCT's crest, marking the way

Hiker Heaven, a free thru-hiker hostel in
Agua Dulce, run by trail angels

A field of suncups in the Northern High Sierra

My hand, picking huckleberries

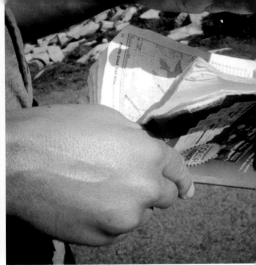

The PCT Atlas, as if the trail were a world,
in Dash's hand

The Cascade Range, Washington
Dash, high on the crest

A selfie at the gap in the woods, where the Pacific Crest Trail ends

The first time I saw my face without glasses, with makeup (my wedding day)

With Dash, back in the Cascade mountains on our wedding night

*Back at Colorado College, speaking about my rape
and the long walk I took in its aftermath*

shirts that said in white lettering Figments Electric (in real life Dana and her husband, Mitt, were electricians), all sorts of corduroy and elastic and jean shorts and sundresses and flip-flop sandals. I chose a lavender sundress, worn but clean and smelling of baby powder.

We waited our turns to shower in the hiker trailer, the list of names on the mini whiteboard on the bathroom door expanded below ours, the names above mine—Thump, Rambo, Sketch—one by one erased. While we waited, another hiker explained that the place runs on a donation basis, pointing to a glazed maroon vase in which hikers could drop cash. It looked like any other vase on the vast premises, not advertised or marked. Dana herself never mentioned it. I slipped in forty bucks. Icecap put bills in, too.

When it was my turn, I hung up my towel and showered, shaved with a fresh new disposable loaner razor. I scrubbed my filthy matted hair with coconut shampoo, with Georgia Peach conditioner, grinning. I ran my hands over my smooth legs, my hips and stomach, and stepped onto the scale. I stared at the number. My five-foot-four frame had lost eleven pounds. I had lost my post-rape weight, then a few pounds more. I was *hungry*, beautiful-slim. For the first time I felt beautiful. I felt sexy. I was happy to feel pretty, if only for myself.

I dressed myself in the lovely low-cut dress I'd chosen and emerged seeing more clearly, as if I'd cleaned my eyes off, too. I was still wearing the same scratched-up prescription sunglasses, but no matter. The pork and pineapple on the grill, sweet-smelling, a new batch ready. Thru-hikers I'd never seen before were eating and sleeping, laying on the big lawn beneath big blue sky. My heart like a caught bird, fluttering wildly.

That evening I went to Big Mouth Pizza with Icecap and a dozen new hikers, all the men other than Icecap bearded, the only other woman named Magic. Her eyes were sweet and dark, milk chocolate brown. Through the meal, she and I exchanged sly smiles; our lives as we lived them on the trail were nearly exactly identical. We walked the same terrain, girls among men; we shared a certain power. The beards all leaned ever so slightly toward us.

That night, I sat on Hiker Heaven's sweet-smelling lawn and, in the light of the amber porch lights and stars and moon and flickering bonfire nearby, I opened the box my mother had sent me. It held gallon Ziploc bags full of Trader Joe's dried blueberries, dark chocolate calcium supplements, milk chocolate calcium supplements, a bottle of Flintstones chewable vitamins. It also contained every single item I'd asked her for: sour cream and onion potato chips; three kinds of cheese; a one-pound bag of Jolly Ranchers, out of which I would pick the watermelon ones and leave the others in Hiker Heaven's massive hiker box.

I joined the hikers by the fire pit, each man a bearded silhouette. Never-Never was on the stump beside me, a hiker I didn't recognize on a long low log at my other side; Never-Never was loud, talking in short, quick bursts. He was telling a story. The hikers were all listening, grinning, laughing, but I couldn't hear it. Something was happening, I could feel it, but I couldn't grasp it. I watched the fire; I felt someone watching me. I glanced around but was blinded by the shapes of flames like stamps of light on my vision, jumping from place to place to place my blind eyes looked.

Never-Never was charismatic. He was the focus of the hikers' attention. He made deadpan joke after joke, his words so short and few it sometimes took a beat to understand. When I did hear him, I laughed, though each crack was at someone's expense. He mocked one middle-aged lady hiker who was thru-hiking with her small dog for her adoration of it. He made his voice squeaky and giddy like a teenage girl's, his hands flapping, "Darling was a champ today. Whooo's my champ? Ooh *there*'s my little Bernie-boo-champ-chum." Never-Never flutter-flapped, "*There* he is." Then he went deadpan and said in his own voice, "Funniest part is she's killing it. Doggie's gonna die," and the lit bearded faces laughed and gasped.

I could see each face better now—my eyes had adjusted to the light's strange redness—and Magic was not around, it was only men, and I felt exhilarated, and then a little scared. The strangest thing is I wasn't entirely sure if Icecap was there. There was a face across the fire that was thin, it looked like his, but then it didn't. I wasn't sure. I said aloud, "Icecap?" but I'd spoken too softly, and no one responded at all.

Then suddenly there were marshmallows, a pillowy bag of them, passed from man to man to man to me. I smelled them toasting before I could see the bag of them moving from lap to lap. I took one and passed it on, to Never-Never. Another hiker—Salty Butt—was talking, now, about the High Sierra, about girls. I was talking to the man at my side whom I didn't yet know; his name was Jimbo 6,000 because he was so tall, so hungry, that he needed to eat six thousand calories each day or he would starve. I understood his hunger, I told him. I was always hungry. I was probably eating about four thousand calories a day.

While I was watching the fire silently, Never-Never would look at my legs. But when I said anything, he would scrunch up his eyebrows, frown, and squint dramatically, as if he not only hated me but wanted everyone to know that he did. A few men were talking about girls and who was hottest on the trail. One voice declared that Magic from Santa Fe was the hottest, and a chorus of voices hooted and murmured, huge tits, they agreed. She was beautiful, I thought so too, amazing glowing copper skin, elegant posture. But someone murmured, "Vulture Death"—her boyfriend. She was unavailable. Rambo, a petite little blond girl, was pretty hot, too. And Silverfox, not bad. Not bad. I was sitting right there.

I looked into the fire. No one yelled out my name. I feared that I looked ugly, but then, of course, I knew: the thin face blocked by the big fire *was* Icecap's. Wild Child and Icecap. Wild Child was unavailable, the bearded men knew.

The talk had lulled and I tried to participate, to fit in better—said the first related thing that popped into my mind: *Surf.* He was the boy who'd smiled at me, way back at McDonald's. Surf was the hottest *guy* on the trail; what do they think? He's pretty handsome, isn't he? Right?

Salty Butt blushed, I could see even in the firelight. No one said anything.

Icecap and I stood on Hiker Heaven's lawn, beside his pitched tent; the night was coal black. "Surf?" He was furious. "I was also there! You had embarrassed yourself. No one likes you now." By saying Surf was the hottest guy on the trail, he said, I had insulted every guy there. I'd implied all the guys sitting there weren't hot.

No one liked me now. It was my fault, I'd mortified myself. His words cut back to that feeling of my mother assuming I couldn't dress myself and make it to school on time, of being underassessed, shut down and shut up. Of being appraised as a concerningly helpless inept child. I had to hear the opinion of my mom, my big brother, know their judgment, feel how it muted me, smothered me out, see the limitations they saw for me—there was no escaping that. My mother was my mother, but the Pacific Crest Trail was supposed to be my refuge. I hadn't come here to be silenced by strangers. I didn't need to know what Icecap and Salty Butt thought. I really didn't care. So I'd bruised Icecap's tender ego. So fucking what. I'd embarrassed him and myself; no one liked me now. Absurd.

I felt betrayed. I was finished. These men were insecure, building identities on spreading judgment, pressing down all things weaker to gain power. I was done letting Icecap decide what behavior was appropriate, done giving him the power to make me feel little.

I told him I had claimed the TV-couch in the hiker trailer with my knapsack, I had, and "I will be sleeping there." In fact, I said, I'd never sleep with him in his tent again. I was breaking up with him. This was it.

Icecap said, "Fine is good!" He walked back out across the dark lawn to the fire party, and I went to the hiker trailer couch to try to sleep. His tent was now the only tent I had; in the morning I would have to get a ride to L.A. and get a new one. I would sleep in it without him. I would.

But then, not an hour later, me still lying there awake, Icecap appeared in the dim trailer and knelt beside my couch. He apologized to me. He was very sorry he'd gotten so angry. He leaned down to my ear and whispered that I had been right. He wanted me to come back to his tent.

My face felt taut from dried tears, from crying too much. He told me, "You are beautiful. The most pretty." He wrapped his hands around my face; I took his hands in mine and let him pull me upright. I followed him across the lawn to his glowing orange tent. I said nothing. I climbed inside.

He went down on me, trying to make me come, knowing that I'd never had an orgasm, sure he could be the person to change that. I faked pleasure, faked it loud, thinking I'd said all of the right words to break up. Thinking how then he said he was sorry. He said I was right, hardly anything, but everything I wanted to hear, and now, his mouth tickling me, I didn't know what I wanted anymore.

After, thinking he was done, he pressed his cheek against my stomach and said that tomorrow we would get a ride to the R.E.I. in L.A. and I should get a two-person tent there. I should mail my old broken tent home.

I awoke beside Icecap. He was already awake, but lying still and waiting for me to rouse naturally.

"Good morning Wild Child," he said and kissed my lips. "You were a sleepy girl."

Icecap spent the morning trying and trying to get my tent to stand—the pole slipped out and out and out from the metal joint. He then made it known that my tent was broken. We needed a ride to L.A. Was anyone going there? To R.E.I.?

As he asked around, I slipped to the big desktop computer and—for the first time in a hundred and twenty miles—logged into my e-mail. My mom had sent me a story about a hiker becoming ill in the High Sierra with pulmonary edema, a high-altitude disease. His lungs had filled with fluid, and he'd drowned. I closed the page, I didn't want to think of the danger in Muir's mountains. No harm would befall me, there; none could. I logged off and ran out across the gravel, to Icecap.

We hitched a ride the twenty-eight miles west with Chuck Norris's wife, Tigger, and a few other hikers who also needed new gear. The thought of such a distance—fifty-six miles round-trip as a day trip!—astonished me; for a moment it seemed impossible. Their van was covered with at least a hundred trail names written in every color of Sharpie, a mobile register; it was ridiculous and charming. Icecap and I shared the mattress in the back where Chuck Norris and Tigger slept together when they weren't sleeping on the trail. We lay into the old couple's bed, rocking along the road, to sleep, down to L.A. where I'd flown to meet my father before I'd taken a single step. All my progress erased. I felt the bed, Icecap pressing against me. I felt sad in my half sleep. My mind was caught on that boy from my mother's e-mail—the dangers of the mountains. I felt very small.

Icecap had confidence and competence I lacked and desperately needed. I trusted him to keep me safe. Maybe my trust of Icecap could blossom into love. At a gas stop I woke with a jolt and Icecap and I signed Chuck and Tigger's van: Icecap + Wild Child. I was becoming afraid.

At R.E.I. I chose a two-person tent, the bigger model of my broken tent, the same green color. The salesclerk who showed me it was sure I needed a ground tarp to lay under it, too, and Icecap agreed, but I said no. A ground tarp was unnecessary weight. Icecap still didn't understand my ultralightness. I paid $269.95 for our new home with my parents' money and wandered out into the strip mall's lot, the sun hot and pallid, the sky flat rich L.A. blue. I walked toward Skinny Chick Smoothie to get a frozen yogurt, passed an old man hobbling, his body pressing down into his cane, passed two teenaged lovers, swinging hands. I ordered a large mango smoothie, famished and feeling catastrophically out of place. Icecap would mail his own tent back home at the next post office. Maybe moving in together would change things between us.

I left with Icecap, returned to the van mattress melancholy, aching for something I couldn't name.

I would walk with Icecap. We had just one shelter. We had to stay together, now.

CHAPTER 13

NO HARM WILL BEFALL YOU

MAY 20, GREEN VALLEY, CALIFORNIA, MILE 478.2

We emerged at a Pacific Crest Trail trailhead to find a parked mini-van with a man inside it, smoking weed from a glass pipe. The man was Boo Henderson. A dozen people at the Figments' had told us about him. He was a trail angel, patron of the Casa de Luna. He had been waiting there for hikers.

"There anybody close behind ya?" he asked.

We didn't think there was.

"Then hop in kids!" he said. He said he'd give us a ride to his place, the Casa de Luna. He'd feed us good with some beers and taco salad, homemade.

Boo's minivan was pungent with weed. The road hugged the edge of a canyon, switchbacking down into a green valley called Green Valley. He drove slowly, telling us about Green Valley's essential desert water cache; there was no reliable water for twelve miles north or south without it. Dana Figment used to drive an hour each way several times a week to refill its jugs, until Boo, who lived just down the road from it, convinced her to pass the job off to him. "You gotta make sure it's filled," Boo said Dana had told him. "You can *never* let it go dry."

Boo said he'd acted nonchalant, but in truth, he was vigilant. Several years later, someone else offered to take over, but Boo was reluctant. "In the end I was a real uppity dude," he said and laughed. "But ya got to be dependable." He packed and lit another bowl, steering with his elbows.

Boo shuttled us to his house, then turned back to the trailhead to wait for more hikers. "No sir-ee," he said as we hopped out. "Can't keep the hikers waiting!" he called, driving back the way he'd come. He did this a handful of times a day for two months of each summer.

It was late afternoon. A dozen beach chairs dotted Boo's driveway, hikers lying in all of them. Someone handed us beers and Hawaiian shirts. "Unload. Put your shirt on," he said. He had straight greasy black hair down to his shoulders, and his breath reeked of liquor. He said his name was Doug. "I'll be your tour guide of the Magical Manzanita Forest," he slurred.

We took our packs off and put our Hawaiian shirts on, maneuvering gracelessly, beer cans in hand. A squat, middle-aged woman named Gracie pulled us over to a banner made from a bedsheet with Casa de Luna 2009 stenciled in bright blue spray paint. She was Boo's wife, matron of the Casa de Luna.

"Now we've got to get you two's picture," Gracie said. "Stand at the banner."

Doug counted one, two*oo*—and Gracie mooned us, her huge butt like a splash of white paint. We gasped, our faces bright and shocked, and the camera flashed.

"The Casa de Luna," Gracie said. "You kids are too easy. The house of my moon."

"The picture's good," Doug said, his eyes amused. "You should see your faces."

No hiker around had reacted to the scene at all.

"It's always a smile," Gracie said. "Every damn time!"

I looked at the display in Doug's hands. To my surprise, we looked delighted.

Each year, Gracie Henderson moons a thousand strangers, collects their shocked faces in an annual photo album.

If Hiker Heaven was a homeless shelter, Casa de Luna was a homeless encampment. "Boo calls it Hiker Daycare," Doug said, his words slow and indistinct, as Icecap and I followed him out past hammocks strung under the tangled arms of trees, weighted with bodies. It seemed everyone was recovering. Doug led us to where the manzanita woods thickened until we could no longer see the sky, the thick canopy of branches like a woodland fairy's roof.

"Welcome," Doug said. "You are in the Magical Manzanita Forest," he said, his smile lines deep ruts. Doug deadpanned his words like welcoming people to the manzanita forest was his boring job. The rust orange nest of branches was so low where he stood that he couldn't straighten his back. "Ya can pitch your tent or put yer backpack into a hammock. Find a spot to sleep. There is more to the tour."

He led us to the shower, its floor slick with grease from "the oil wrestling"—it happened nightly—to the basement packed with broken yard chairs and cracked plywood. Amid the stacked junk, Doug pointed at a wide, low figure I couldn't make out. "The wash-er and the *dry*-er," Doug pronounced as if they were foreign words, and then giggled. "Nobody uses them, but it's parta the tour." He slipped back out onto the grass. "Spooky in there! I don't like it." This was not a place of productivity, only celebrating the endless flow of trailblazers, every day's light and starlight, too. There was oil wrestling. There was day drinking and wildness and sleep. There was no order.

That night I paid Gracie to buy me wine, and a hiker named Tattoo Al, a middle-aged retired pro-surfer, went on the booze run and came back with a pink bottle of rosé, for me. "Thanks?" I said. I asked him if he wanted to share it. He didn't answer but instead unscrewed the cork and poured a big red Solo cup of it, full to the rim, and closed my hands around it. "Thank you," I said again and he ignored me, strutted over to Billy Goat to talk.

Icecap stared from across the lawn. Ever since I'd stripped at the hot springs in Warner Springs, Icecap had felt I should stop drinking. He said it muted me. He didn't like me when I lost myself that way.

I hated him for telling me how I should behave as well as how fast I should walk. I looked right at Icecap and took a long drink.

I turned back into the darkness of the Magical Manzanita Forest, the canopy of branches thickening. I sipped my wine as I walked, thinking about how Tattoo Al had pressed his palms against my fingers. I thought about how he had filled my cup to the brim. I thought about why he might have done that.

Alarm bells rang. Through the thick buzz of pink wine, I could still hear them. I should be wary. Here was a man singling me out and without even a word beginning to funnel alcohol into me with specific intent. I knew I should be concerned about that. I knew the words, but I couldn't feel them. Yet I was also giddy at his attention, and at wickedly, gleefully upsetting Icecap.

In the darkness, I saw that Icecap had already built our tent. I hadn't helped. I stumbled, tripping and falling onto my palms. I landed on decaying leaves. I didn't spill my wine. I'd already finished it.

When I returned it was nearly dinnertime. Gracie Henderson had set up a huge spread of tortilla chips and shredded lettuce, diced tomato and ground beef and yellow nacho cheese from a half-gallon can. "Taco time!" she called out, and we all sprang.

A mass of hikers swarmed the buffet in an instant. They stood around the driveway, talking, gulping food, their paper plates piled high, limp as tortillas. Everyone was ravenous. I made a plate, moved slowly, feeling drunk.

Gracie was a gregarious woman, social and loud. She talked to everyone, asking inappropriate questions, giving men sexual compliments. She wore lots of makeup and now sported a furry baby blue costume halo. "I have a devil one, too," I heard her say to Never-Never when he asked about it. He'd been right behind us on the trail today, apparently. My stomach tightened. After the fire at Hiker Heaven, he'd shrunk in my perception into a man who built his small self up with cruel and cutting jokes made at the expense of others. I didn't trust him.

Tattoo Al touched my shoulder—I froze—and filled my wine. The cup still had dirt and leaves in it from when I'd fallen. I swallowed them along with the rosé. It was all so mindless, so easy to slip into passively accepting it. It was given to me, and I took it. I was weak, and I hated myself for my weakness.

I slipped inside the house to get a cup of water, to try to sober up and maybe find Icecap. No one was in the kitchen. On the fridge, I spotted an old newspaper clipping from the local paper about Gracie and Boo. The story was about how Gracie and Boo got clean from meth and became trail angels. Also stuck on the fridge was a picture of Gracie from the '80s, before meth, when she was young. Her eyes had been embers, her cheeks defined by high, delicate bones.

Back outside, I stepped through the bodies—standing and eating, talking and drinking and doing goofy dances and making funny faces—looking for Gracie. I had to ask her about what happened. I wanted to know why she'd tried meth and if she had been addicted and if it had ruined her face and transformed her into a trail angel and why she made taco salad every night instead of something different. Finally, I found her holding a beer, talking to Tattoo Al and Billy Goat, still sporting her fuzzy, glittery halo. I walked right into the group and interrupted. I touched her arm. "'Scuse me," I said. My questions felt urgent. "How did you become a trail angel? Is that taco salad your favorite food?" suggested, "We could make spaghetti? I actually know how."

She grabbed my butt. I was so shocked I didn't move. "No," she answered, making eye contact with me, her eyes stretched too open, comically intense. "I love the *smell*," she said and released my butt cheek, which now hurt.

I could understand stopping here and eating taco salad—of course you would—listening to the story of Casa de Luna's creation once, and moving on. What I couldn't understand was making the same dinner every night, and then oil wrestling again. The repetition sounded maddening.

I stumbled to my backpack, found my satellite phone, and called my mother. As I waited for the call to go through, I saw that Tattoo Al had followed me. I was frightened. Icecap was still back at the party. I didn't know where he had gone. But now I wanted him here.

He asked me if I was calling my boyfriend.

"No," I said as the phone searched for satellites. I thought of saying, "My boyfriend's Icecap," but I didn't. The satellite phone was ringing.

"Calling my mom," I said just as she answered, "Doll!"

"Hi Mom," I said.

"Hi Mommy," Tattoo Al mocked. He squeezed my shoulder and I looked at the dark ground.

I told her about Casa de Luna as he looked at me. I couldn't describe what went on here to her, and yet I tried. I said, "They make the same thing for dinner every night 'cause the hikers like it." I said, "Taco salad. And then there's oil wrestling after."

Tattoo Al leaned and whispered on my neck, "Look at you. I wouldn't let my daughter do this trail alone." He said he had a daughter who was seventeen, said he saw how the degenerates looked at me. Older men, he said. Guys in their thirties and forties. I tried to hear my mother. His mouth hung in the darkness behind my ear.

"I love you," my mom said. I wondered if she'd heard Tattoo Al's low voice. "Have pleasant dreams," she said, and we hung up.

Tattoo Al's face had softened, as if he were concerned. He wasn't teasing me anymore. Without my mom on the line, I felt less safe. I wanted him to leave.

I straightened my posture. "I don't want to oil wrestle," I said to him though he hadn't asked. "I'm so sleepy. I'm going to go to bed."

"Look at you," Tattoo Al said. He slipped his fingers behind my hair and cupped my neck. My whole body felt cold. "You are a child," he said and pressed my neck away. He walked away, through the dark trees.

I fell asleep that night on a wicker couch out front of the house, not in my new, immaculate two-person tent; I passed out. I was too drunk to feel healthy fear. The party around me twirled, and I could hear in my dreams a hoot and a string of curse words, cheering and a thud. In my drunk stillness I could feel heat against my leg. I opened my eyes. Tattoo Al was sitting on the couch's edge beside my leg, looking at me. His butt against my shin. Waking me up. Asking if he could have a "sexual favor."

"What?" I said. I was shivering.

His eyes were smiling, as if he were amused. As if he'd told a joke. "Wild Child," he said, leaning down, over me, down toward my ear, his voice a whisper. "Can I get a sexual favor?"

I laughed a silent laugh, which was a shudder. I said, "I can't." He was sitting on the couch, leaning hard against my legs.

Tattoo Al suddenly looked disgusted.

I sat up as if doing a crunch. "I'm sorry," was all I could say, my face inches from his cheek. Then I stood. I stumbled through the dark trees until I found my tent and ducked inside, relieved to find Icecap there, careful not to wake him.

The next morning, Icecap and I left Casa de Luna barely speaking. It was clear we weren't the same anymore. We walked north, into the Mojave Desert, both a little sadder. Icecap continued to push me, refusing to take breaks, but I didn't bother fighting with him. I was tired. The desert was no longer our own world, only an empty plane of nothingness. It had lost its thrill. The thought of walking the snowy crest of the High Sierra with him had become bleak. We were numb to each other's pain. He needed to race, wanted to be fearless again. I couldn't help him. Yet we stayed together.

MAY 31, KENNEDY MEADOWS, THE GATEWAY TO THE HIGH SIERRA, MILE 702

We had at last reached the northern edge of the desert. Kennedy Meadows was the last resupply stop before the High Sierra, a clump of wood buildings on dry hills of sand and pine, desolate. The air smelled cold, of snow. The High Sierra would be more beautiful than anything we'd yet walked through, with white lakes glimmering in granite, cold and wild. We were at the gateway to John Muir's Sierras, the Range of Light "like the wall of some celestial city." I had expected the mood of the place to be festive, but the hikers here seemed solemn. Thin, bearded men crouched on the general store's porch, huddled in circles. They smoothed out their fresh maps.

We went inside to pick up our resupply boxes. He had one, from Anaheim, Texas, sent from his high school host mother, who still told him she loved him, and was logistically supporting his whole hike. I had three, all from my mom. Out on the porch we began to organize our things. It was crowded, everyone packing their fresh sausage and crackers, their guidebooks for navigating 150 miles of signless snow.

The dozen or so hikers with us here were new to me. We were now at the front of the thru-hiker pack, among the very fittest and fastest.

Icecap and I spoke softly about the upcoming miles, thrilled and scared as if we were embarking on an older kind of Great American Expedition. I felt like a pioneer. I overheard two older thru-hikers discuss in quiet voices the snow levels in the mountains to the north.

The High Sierra snow is deepest each year in mid-April—right when we all set out at the Mexican border—and the hope was that, in the two months it usually took to traverse the seven-hundred-mile desert, it would have melted away. But Icecap and I had crossed the desert in just thirty-nine days. Most years the High Sierra "opens" on June fifteenth. Dana Figment warns hikers that to enter before then is stubborn and foolish. She tells John Donovan's story. But it was the last day of May, and here we were.

And worse—this was not a normal year. Spring in the California desert had been cooler than usual, in the eighties instead of the low hundreds. This had been a blessing for us earlier—the cooler weather had allowed us to walk faster—but now we'd arrived to mountains that were frozen and white. The safe, familiar path I'd hiked my past two summers was still buried under fifteen to fifty feet of snow. We would need to rely on maps and a compass, neither of which I had. But even with a map and compass, I didn't trust my navigation skills. I didn't know how to triangulate. I could never remember how to discern uphill from downhill from the topographic lines, their cryptic, pretty patterns of unfurling blue and white circles. I couldn't even depend on my GPS, because all I'd learned to do with it was push the button that told me exactly where I already was.

Icecap and I needed to commit to staying together. We'd have to promise. We'd have to swear on stars. Trying to do this alone would be suicide. The High Sierra Mountains were steep and cliffed, and the rivers that carve their valleys were swift and frigid, deeper than I was tall. They'd be impossible to ford. We'd have to make our own safe routes around them. The snow on the high passes melted in the spring sun and refroze in the night, sheeted with ice. The dangers were real. We were the front of the thru-hiker pack, proud to be the very fastest and strongest hikers, yet we were trapped.

Of course this was an old American story. Ethan Rarick, who documented the Donner Party's perilous journey west, told how "Pioneer families left Independence as soon as the warmth of spring gave them dry ground to travel over . . . and—they hoped—reached the temperate climates of the Pacific before the first snows of winter closed the mountain passes." He wrote that there was "little room for error. The journey was a race against time."

A slight middle-aged man named Warner Springs Monty was rallying a group of hikers to skip the snowy High Sierra. His voice was squeaky, like something unhinged. Monty said the Sierra was "deadly" in these conditions, but up north beyond the Sierra, elevations were lower; the snow up there was gone. Monty himself was not a thru-hiker, but he was from the desert town of Warner Springs and had "been hiking for years." The group of thru-hikers he was organizing would take a ride with Chuck Norris and Tigger up to Donner Pass, land where presumably there would be no snow, and walk back down south. By the time they arrived back at the High Sierra, all this snow would also be melted away.

Monty preached to the store porch like a glad convert. He'd figured it out; all we need do was follow. Yet I didn't trust him. He seemed too frantic to be honest, and I didn't want to stray. My way through was the PCT, buried or not.

When he asked me directly if I was coming, I said no. He ignored Icecap, who was squatting, packing his food. "No, we're going to try to hike it through," I answered him.

He said I would need an ice ax and mountaineering crampons and snowshoes to attempt "such a foolish thing," and, even then, there was no guarantee. "Probably freeze," he said to me. "Probably worse."

I noticed Chuck and Tigger's white van-home parked out on the dirt road. Hikers tossed their backpacks into the back. Was I making the right choice going into the High Sierra so early? I tried to drop the thought that I could be walking toward my death. My third package contained gloves, a fleece, a windbreaker, and an ice ax—I did at least have one necessary tool. I lifted it. It was smooth matte steel, yet light, with a beaked head. Icecap held his own, stoic. I could tell he was listening to the men deciding to go with Monty. He was scared, too.

The other hikers loaded up into Chuck Norris and Tigger's van. They were actually doing it: skipping the High Sierra. As much as I knew I had to fear those mountains that rose against the sky, I still couldn't understand it. After enduring seven hundred miles of desert, how could they finally arrive at the gateway to the High Sierra and bail, not even try to go on?

Icecap and I said goodbye to BoJo, a computer programmer, to Trout Lily, the only girl in Monty's pack. Mystic, a sweet stoner from New Hampshire. Goodbye, very best luck. Hikers I'd just met, leaving. In jest, they called themselves the Donner Party.

The van rolled up the high desert road. The dust puffed, a long drab cloud.

I stood there with Icecap. I felt scared, nervous and excited, as if I were about to jump off a bridge either into water or onto rock, no way to know.

There were 239.6 trail-miles from Kennedy Meadows to my next resupply point, Tuolumne Meadows. Not one road transects that expanse of wilderness, the longest uninterrupted stretch of wilderness left in the lower forty-eight. I was about to cross it on foot with my boyfriend and our one shared tent, using our one shared map.

"Ready for it?" Icecap asked me.

"Yes," I said. "Just let me just buy some Jolly Ranchers at the store."

"Waste time for this, for candy?" Icecap asked, annoyed. "We don't waste time for this. It will be dark."

The sun glared high in wide sky. Pale clouds, brown at their edges, lay flat and low, storm clouds, maybe. On my whole walk through the desert, it had rained just once. I tried to press away the threats the bearded men had whispered. I'd subtracted my options down to just this one. The only way through was to stay together.

We left Kennedy Meadows and walked over the hills of sand until they became a sparse pine forest. With time, the trees grew stout and the footpath became granite slabs. Where we were going there would be no trail magic, only a two-hundred-mile expanse of snowy peaks.

We trudged into the high, white mountains, tense, hardly talking. It was June first. I thought again of that single month that makes the difference in these high peaks between skinny dipping and napping by a creek in evergreens' inky shade and getting lost in a whiteout blizzard. We were bundled up in all our clothes, bracing our slim, tired bodies for relentless cold.

By late afternoon, the light had vanished. The sky was the silver color of fur, dim as shadow. More immediate than the snow, there was another threat we'd ignored. My hair was light with static electricity. We were walking up into a lightning storm.

We decided to stop and make camp. I pitched our tent while Icecap built a fire. The air was charged. The sky had not yet broken. In the chalky light, Icecap sat, lit from below by the orange flicker of fire. He was emaciated. A gust of wind swelled the fire, illuminating the bottom of Icecap's nose and the bones above the hollow of his cheeks. I thought: Icecap hates the wind. I smirked. The air was frozen; I could see it, my breath like smoke.

That night in our new tent, when I again told him no, he rolled over, his spine arched at me. His delicate backbones were more hostile than the stony ridge of peaks spread black on the electric northern sky. Through his thin goose down sleeping bag, I counted his vertebrae: bone, bone, bone, bone, into sleep.

JUNE 4, THE SOUTHERN SIERRA, MILE 731

The early sun lit the morning fog and backlit the twisted trees. Their silhouettes intertwined against the pale sky. Icecap trailed me. I walked through the gray-white morning, the ice-crusted soil crunching under my running shoes.

My ears rang; absence of sound made my forehead ache. Snow began to accumulate on the ground. Against the white air, I hadn't noticed it was falling. With each mile the trees thinned. Everything was scraped with frost, the glittering snow piling higher. Soon we smelled pinewood burning. Fifty yards off-trail we noticed a campfire glowing, amber through the willow-gray, with three bundled male hikers crouching around it. We climbed the hill to join them.

I hadn't met any of these hikers before, yet I recognized each name when I heard it. One man, Slim, was not a thru-hiker; he had skipped the first five hundred miles of desert and hopped on-trail in the Mojave. He was hefty and very loud. The other two men, Buckwheat and Puck, were quiet and slight. Buckwheat was shivering; his lips were pale as wax.

I told him he looked freezing.

He grinned and nodded, *"Yes,"* he said, "we might die."

I leaned closer to him. I thought I'd misheard. "We'll die?"

"Yes, might. The snow's going to keep on coming," he said. His voice was so quiet, it annoyed me, and I was still unsure if I'd heard him correctly. "Supposed to snow five feet tonight, I think." He described me walking through a field of snow up to my nose. "You'll burn every calorie you're carrying and only go ten miles."

I ignored him. I asked Icecap if he was warm enough.

Icecap mumbled something I couldn't make out.

I felt very cold and agitated, anxious to leave this new strange crew. Yet we couldn't keep walking to stay awake and warm in this snowfall; we could hardly see through the downy flakes. We'd walk off the route and get lost. Searching for our way back we might eat too much, run out of food, and fulfill Buckwheat's prophecy. We agreed we needed to stay. Icecap and I excused ourselves, shivering, our hands shaking, stumbled fifteen feet though gleaming powder, and built our tent. We made camp early, after only nine miles.

I bundled in my sleeping bag in the tent, looking at Icecap; he looked different. He told me I was very pretty when I was cold.

"You look older," I said. With his face chilled stiff, he did.

He pulled his arms out of his bag and wrapped them around me. He peeled my bag down. He pressed his two cold hands against my bare hips and squeezed. I was freezing. I knew he wanted to have sex.

I stared up at the tent's olive green rainfly, listened to the frozen flakes clicking against it. I leaned against him and stroked his cold soft hair, his neck. It was too cold. I was not feeling turned on. I looked at his pale eyes and told him, "Hey, there. Let's just kiss tonight."

He pulled away and pulled his sleeping bag up, zipped it up from the inside, all the way up, swaddling himself. He rolled so his spine was arched at me, like a mad cat, just like the night before. He said, "I don't actually like kissing. I hate it. I just only do it because you always want to."

"You hate kissing," I said. It wasn't a question. I wasn't even shocked. He was cold and I was numb. It wasn't tolerable, seemed impossible to me. I thought about all of the things that Icecap hated—beaches and wind, trains and resting, kissing. So many of the things I loved. I pictured: kissing on trains, windswept mountains, white-sand beaches. I imagined a beautiful world composed of things Icecap hated. I loved more than he did.

I felt maddeningly lost. I thought about my brother Jacob, maybe he would understand. As a kid, five years younger, insecure and unsure, I would often ask myself, What would Jacob do? What would he say? How would Jacob act? I wanted to talk with him. His advice was always good.

I bundled up in all of the clothes I carried, zipped zipper over zipper, and crawled out into snow-furred light. I had talked to Jacob only once since I'd begun my walk. He had no way of calling me on the trail. And I hadn't called him. But I needed him now more than ever.

I dialed my brother's number, shivering, and he picked up.

"Jacob? How have you been?" I wanted Jacob to tell me the game-plan, the answer, to tell me the thing to do so that I would be okay. I didn't see a safe way through without Icecap. But I couldn't see a way through with him now, either.

My brother answered, "Debby?" and I immediately started crying. I was scared. I had gotten myself stuck. Jacob's familiar husky voice made me feel catastrophically alone.

I wanted to tell him about how I had been hiking with a guy, how we were out of pace and I'd stupidly bought a two-person tent and let him move in, and now I was stuck with him. For at least another 240 rugged snowy miles. Miles through which I'd wanted to walk alone. How I'd finally arrived here, in the Range of Light, in the land of Muir, and I couldn't be alone with it. I couldn't even enjoy it.

I thought all this, and yet I couldn't speak it. He was silent through my sobs.

"Hello?" I said. "You there?"

Tears had frozen slick on my cheeks. When he spoke at last, his voice was gravelly, low and stiff. "You're nineteen. You shouldn't be alone this much."

"I—" I told him, "What? I'm not alone. I'm with a boy."

Jacob explained that normal nineteen-year-olds don't go off alone for six months. They have fun with other college kids. They're *kids*. "It's one thing to forsake people and decide you hate everybody and you're all fed up with it when you're seventy. But you're nineteen. Now's the time to live your life."

Snowflakes spilled down in thick white sweeps, intricate flakes. They caught on my black fleece gloves, delicate stars shiny as metal. Clinging, not melting. I didn't know what to say. His concerns were irrelevant. I was with people; of course I was. I was one in a tight community of nomads. Trail angels were supporting me. I was one in a pack, surviving, migrating north. This was me living *my* life—it was back at school that I'd felt lonely. Here at least I had hope.

"No, I mean," I said, "I am." I didn't know how to explain that I'd made closer friendships out in this wilderness than I'd ever made in Newton. "I hike with people," I said. "They're really nice."

He cut me off. "This whole thing is self-indulgent." He explained that walking alone in the middle of nowhere serves no purpose. "It doesn't help anyone. What Dad does as a lawyer helps people. Playing ball is entertainment for people, and I'm part of something larger than me. Baseball gives fans a good time. I'm on a team with people, interacting, learning how to be a team player. Being alone all the time in the woods doesn't contribute anything."

I said nothing. I could see Icecap's headlamp click on inside the tent.

Frost burned my lungs. New tears froze over the cold trails of the last. "Indulgent," I repeated back to him. "Alone," I said. "You think I'm too alone?"

I'd actually only been alone three nights of this whole hike. Only just three. All other nights, I'd slept by Icecap. In fact, I hadn't been alone nearly enough.

I had needed his sound advice—should I go on with Icecap, unhappy, or should I go on, mapless and alone? I had needed his faithful big-brotherly wisdom. But instead he'd ignored everything I said about my problems hiking with Icecap and insulted the value of this walk. He'd insulted me. He could not understand, and I couldn't make him.

He was silent for a long cold moment, and so was I, and then he suggested I go to India with his girlfriend. She'd be doing some important community-service-type stuff there. It would give my summer purpose.

I told him I had to go back to my boyfriend—*my boyfriend*—"I'm *never* alone"—and clicked off the phone and crawled back into our tent. I wanted to say, *This is important work, This is important work, This is important*—but I couldn't find the words to explain how.

Back in the tent that night Icecap didn't kiss me. We didn't cuddle. I tried to explain to myself that I'd already known that we were over. I had to end it. Regardless of snow's danger. Because of it. I had to do this alone. Tomorrow I would.

But tomorrow came and went. I remained with him.

JUNE 6, UPPER CRABTREE MEADOW, MOUNT WHITNEY SUMMIT ATTEMPT, THE HIGH SIERRA, MILE 766

One cold dawn, my running shoes frozen stiff as wood, Icecap and I packed, painfully cold. Wind bit my chapped fingers, my throat burned. We were to climb Mount Whitney today, the highest peak in the lower forty-eight, a seventeen-mile round-trip detour off the PCT but worth it, everybody had said. Icecap was confident we would summit. I wasn't. I was losing faith in myself. I still hadn't left him.

We were in a rush. We pounded our tent stakes deeper into the frozen ground, pulled tighter our rainfly's cords, retied the knots, and then slipped all our belongings inside of our tent to keep them safe. He and I dusted frost off our knapsacks with gloved hands, packed granola bars and cheddar cheese, and filled all of our water bottles in the snow-rimmed creek. Ice rested like delicate fingers spread open on the water. We double-checked everything. We had secured our basecamp. Our tent would stand firm in snow or wind. With our ice axes strapped to our limp packs, we abandoned our shelter and food, hopeful we'd be able to reach the summit and find our way back through the mountains before dark.

I trudged through the foot-deep powder, dry snow sifting through my shoes' mesh, Icecap behind me. Mount Whitney did not, from here, look attainable; it looked like a tall mountain, far away. I tried to wiggle my toes but couldn't. They'd gone numb. The blanket of snow that draped the mountains' contours gleamed. With clear blue sky over us, it seemed like a good day to summit. Icecap strode fast, passing me, and the gap between us widened. Two, three, five switchbacks above me, he became a dot fading away.

I thought about everything but the danger of my situation. I forced my mind toward pioneer stories and *Blood on the Tracks* songs. In running shoes and spandex, I traversed ice-crusted snowfields, some so steep that a slip would be fatal—three thousand feet of elevation lost in a moment, ending on jagged rock. My ice ax was still strapped to the back of my pack. I wasn't using it precisely because Icecap wanted me to.

"Use your ice ax!" Icecap called down to me, again, again, a weak echo of a voice. I didn't answer. "Use. Your. ICE. AX." He must have thought I couldn't hear him.

"I don't need it," I whispered back to him, to no one. "I'm in balance. I'm in balance. Go fuck off."

He screamed something unintelligible, loud, and I didn't respond. I just trudged on, kicking steps through the ice crust, into snow like biscuit crumbs, and breathed. The air was empty, thin. The valleys of the High Sierra receded and the lakes became petals the pale color of sky. The Range of Light expanded, outward, bright and boundless, a low blue sunlit snow-draped garden of trees. I kick-stepped across snow slopes, over chutes to abysses. Not stopping. Not using my ice ax.

The summit hut poked out from low clouds. I ran up, through snow as deep as my knees, kicking my feet free. The world opened to me, glittery white and vast. I collapsed on the rock of the wind-scraped summit, next to Icecap. He stared straight outward.

He was furious. I hadn't used my ice ax. I was irresponsible, reckless, idiotic. He spat these words. He sounded fluent. He said it was horrifying to watch me. "If someone slipped down a slope and broke a leg, and she had an ice ax but did not use it, I would have to think twice," he said to me, not looking at me, "about risking my life to save her."

I hadn't asked him to risk his life. I didn't want him to save me. "I was in balance," I said. I folded my legs beneath me and stood back up. I looked at the grand view, our deep footprints down the mountain, two distinct trails, and slung my pack on, ice ax still strapped to it. Fuck it, *fuck* him. I began to descend.

I descended the way I'd climbed, plunging my heels into the hard snow, run-slipping down the mountain. Icecap behind me always. He was patronizing. Who was he to tell me I would fall? He was not my father. I was out ahead, down below, when Icecap called down to me, "Wild Child, wait!"

He caught up and told me he had somehow lost a glove. He yelled it at me, as if it were my fault. He had lost one of his gloves somewhere on this big white mountain. I thought we'd freeze trying to find it. In three hours it'd be death dark. "Look for it," he said to me, looking back up the mountain. "My hand will freeze off."

I was annoyed. He'd been acting like he knew what to do to make me safe, but staying on the peak to look for his glove was foolish and dangerous. I told him I'd help him look for it for a minute, but then we needed to get down; we needed to get back to our tent before dark or we'd freeze.

"You're a bitch," he said. He said it loud; his voice echoed.

I was a bitch, I was a bitch. I was so done. I left him there, looking for his glove, and trudged down the snow to our camp, fuming and sad. I strode at last back into the openness of Upper Crabtree Meadow; in the dusk I saw that a tent city had sprung up. The next day's wave of hikers had caught us. I hadn't known so many hikers were so close behind us. The registers tell you who's ahead, but who is behind you is always a mystery. Our seventeen-mile day-long detour had stalled us just long enough to crash us with a new wave of hikers, mostly new faces, and I was ready. Ready to get to know who was who. To make new friends. To leave Icecap. Today. Right fucking now.

I was enraged by him. Mad, so mad, and why? I was in a quandary of my own making, created by my passivity. I'd purchased a two-person tent for me and Icecap. I'd done it after I already knew I didn't want to be trapped with him, night after night. Day after precious day. I'd been unable to speak up, to say what I'd wanted, and that inability had once again trapped me. I was incapable of escaping my infuriating silence. Despite my new muscle tone, my tanner body, this new big tent was proof I hadn't purged one cell of my old psyche. Since Mexico, since fucking Colorado, I hadn't changed one molecule.

He was still gone, up on the mountain, searching for the glove he'd lost, looking for something to keep five fingers warm while the rest of his body chilled and evening blackened. That idiot. That dumb fanatical nonsensical boy. I crawled into our tent. Our tent? It was *my* tent, really, wasn't it? I'd bought it. My parents had paid for it. I wondered if I could keep it, if it would be a fight. If he'd insist on staying with me because of it, despite us. And what would happen if I told him to go. If I kicked him out in the High Sierra. That would be cruel. He'd have nowhere to sleep. I imagined him at night alone, cold, homeless in snow, lying down, dying; I'd feel guilty. No, I couldn't do that to him.

He arrived back at Upper Crabtree Meadow only fifteen minutes after me, still without his glove.

"Goodbye, Wild Child," he said before I could speak. "I am done with it. You are alone."

Tears welled in my eyes and broke and dropped, silent. "'Bye," I said back, and wandered over to the fire pit and the ring of new hikers huddled around.

Never-Never was there. He seemed to come with fire—I always saw him by it—as well as an entourage. He was telling jokes, and he was funny, deadpan, making everyone laugh, tonight at Gracie Henderson's expense. Silverfox was also sitting there with her new trailboy, Boomer. He was cute and slim and looked Italian. She seemed so different from when I met her in the desert, more girlish, younger—happy with him. She'd commanded his attention yet still ignored me. She hardly even looked. I envied how gentle and loving Boomer seemed with her, his hand wrapping the small of her back. It had been three hundred miles since Icecap had been gentle like that with me.

I walked back to our tent and saw that Icecap had left without a last hug or a word. He'd left the tent for me, but taken our one set of maps. He'd set off into the frigid and vast High Sierra with no shelter. And I had no guide. We'd both need to fight to survive the 150 miles of snow-covered wilderness before us.

Terror struck me. I dropped down to my knees, to the dark frozen ground that smelled of pine, so cold against me. Where would he sleep, where would he sleep, where would he sleep? How would I find my way?

I felt the smack of something, a brutal blow that cracked through my numbness, my ears *ringing*. This was fear. It was fear that I would die.

I called Jacob. It was irrational—every attempt to reconnect with him had failed—and still, I wanted badly to hear my brother's voice. I paced at the meadow's edge. I was deep into the High Sierra, alone and mapless and confused to find myself feeling hurt, heartbroken.

Icecap had been my first boyfriend. I had never thought I'd been in love before. I was already crying. After just two rings, Jacob answered.

I told him everything. He listened, said softly, "Sorry." Then he said, "It sucks. It's going to suck, but it gets better." He told me the story of his breakup with Amanda, a girl he'd been in love with for two years in college. I remembered Amanda, how tender they'd seemed, how they'd taken a cross-country road trip and how at the end, in Newton, Amanda had given Jacob a scrapbook filled with photos from their trip together. The cover said in script, *And let us marry our souls together*, and I had never seen my brother so cheery. He probably would have married her if she hadn't left him.

At the end of the story he paused. He said, "But I'm in love again. It feels like you'll never have that with someone else again, but of course you will." This was not the end for me, he guaranteed. It seemed impossible that he could know for sure, but I trusted him, and so his promise consoled me.

Until my brother answered, it had seemed that I was the first person ever to feel heartbreak, that no one before me had felt the sadness I felt now. I sniffled into the phone, wiped my nose. "There's someone else I'll meet who will love me?" I asked him back. I asked it because I knew he would say yes, and I needed to hear yes from him.

He answered, "Absolutely." Absolutely I would be loved.

"Love you, Jacob," I told him, as I squinted back at our tent through the blurring dusk. I wasn't crying anymore. He understood. In lovesickness we had found a common language.

I went to our tent and slept alone as Icecap hiked alone and without shelter, north by moonlight. I passed the entire next day at Upper Crabtree Meadow, sitting, watching fire consume wood. I didn't want to risk running into him again. It felt easier to let him go, to give him time to get away. The morning after, I woke inside the Range of Light, in Muir's wild cathedral, silent and still.

My wish to be alone in the mountains would come true. I would traverse the High Sierra, and until I reached the dreamy town of Bend up in central Oregon, I'd hike almost exclusively in solitude.

CHAPTER 14

THE RANGE OF LIGHT

Every man has the right to risk his own life in order to preserve it. Has it ever been said that a man who throws himself out the window to escape from a fire is guilty of suicide?
—JEAN-JACQUES ROUSSEAU

Beauty is an ecstasy; it is as simple as hunger. There is really nothing to be said about it. It is like the perfume of a rose: you can smell it and that is all.
—W. SOMERSET MAUGHAM

The sky broke like an egg into full sunset and the water caught fire.
—PAMELA HANSFORD JOHNSON

Go quietly, alone; no harm will befall you.
—JOHN MUIR

JUNE 10, THE HIGH SIERRA, MILE 838

Fire, shelter—and then the hunt.

In all directions: snow; sun: white. Silent snow swallowed the world, burying every rock and twig. The snowfields terminated in smooth humps. I feared I'd wandered off the trail; the PCT hadn't ever been this steep. I looked down, five hundred feet below, at slick and glossy cliffs of ice. I was scared.

I hoped I was on-course. I needed to find my way through Muir Pass, somewhere 11,955 feet up in thin sky-air. I wasn't sure which low point between peaks it was. I looked down, forever far, at the bluish ice-cliffs, skyward at the swells of snow, infinite trackless moon-white mounds and edges.

My toes tingled, cold in my running shoes. I needed to keep them warm. Hypothermia kills more thru-hikers than do bears or wolves, hot springs ripe with deadly *Naegleria fowleri* or rattlesnakes. When it sets in, basic motor skills and judgment turn off. Our movements become clunky and imprecise. We cannot zip a zipper, move our tongue, speak, think. No pain or burning, just a mounting incompetence. Hiking through the High Sierra, the single most deadly threat is losing enough heat to lose your judgment.

I climbed higher. The angle of the snow slope increased and its surface slickened, coated at this elevation by a glossy ice crust. I kicked my feet through the crust, punched into powder. I should have been using my ice ax, again willfully underestimating risk.

Despite the cold I panted and sweat. Two hundred feet above me the vertical appeared to top-off and, kick-step after kick-step, I climbed toward the plateau. But then false top unfolded to false top. Dark clouds sunk and smothered the sun. Pellets of hail, first small, then marble-size, struck my shoulders and bare legs.

I took a break, sat on the snow, in fog, so high the air itself dizzied me drunk. The snow burned through my spandex. The world turned. I pulled out my shrinking food bag to find I was nearly out of food. I could feel myself slowing and knew I needed fuel to continue forward. I had heard of people pausing too long at this altitude and getting pulmonary edema. These hikers needed to be airlifted out by helicopter, or they'd quickly die.

I felt an insatiable growl. For hundreds of miles now, I'd been growing smaller, disappearing beneath my clothes; now, that new lightness made me feel vulnerable, precarious. The air blew through me. I was ribs and fading muscle, a desperate body. I shook the food bag. All that fell out were crushed-up cashews and a half-sandwich-size Ziploc of dry oatmeal that I'd found in the Kennedy Meadows hiker box and taken. I tasted it; it was so salty that it was inedible. Someone had mistakenly filled the bag with salt instead of sugar. The only food I had left was useless.

I gasped; cold thin air burned. *How* could I have not planned for this? Stalling by the fire at Upper Crabtree, just hanging out and eating my rationed food in the cold, had been so unbelievably stupid—I still had sixty-four High Sierra miles to walk to the still-warm ski resort town where there'd be pizza and hot cocoa and Ben & Jerry's. That town could take me up to five days to reach. It was only my third day alone in the Sierra and already I had eaten all my good food. Yet I was so *hungry*. I could eat all the food I carried, and still starve. And now, because of my irresponsible incompetence, I didn't even have enough to let my body function. *I could really starve.*

What had I been thinking? Why hadn't I been thinking? I learned this lesson in the desert, had almost died of thirst, promised to do better for myself—how did I walk into this wilderness unprepared, blinding myself again?

This time, there would be no trail angel miracles to save me, no treasure chests harboring hot meals high in winter-dead mountains. This was a silent white desert of another sort entirely, its version of Hiker Heaven not one you walk back out of.

I was now 131 miles from the last resupply point, I knew I couldn't make it back there in time. My only option was to move forward.

I was nineteen. I repeated my age to myself aloud, as if it were protection against death. *I was nineteen*, nothing could be so serious. I couldn't die.

I continued on, trekking through icy hail that stung my skin. I couldn't see anything, only white. I had at last reached Muir Pass, but I was too exposed to camp, and I didn't know which way to go. I plunged downhill toward tree line, hoping the trees would provide warm cover. Every few minutes my heel would punch through the ice and send me into waist-deep powdery snow, heart pounding.

In frigid time I couldn't measure, the hail subsided and I broke through the cloud's lower barrier, out, into afternoon's pale rose-bud light. The snow shimmered, washed golden by the sun. Muir Pass sprawled above me like a grand castle. I stood, cold and disoriented, on level ground at the edge of a long lake. Lake McDermand, I thought it must have been. The snow here was patchy, clumped on rocks' north faces; damp ground shone black, smelled sweet, safer, but I didn't see the trail. I couldn't find it.

I trudged along the lake's eastern rim. I breathed, thought: just follow the lake. At some point it had to end—hopefully back on the PCT, if this lake was in fact Lake McDermand, which I needed it to be. Finally I noticed a shadow, pencil-thin and constant, skirting the lake's western edge: beyond a doubt, the Pacific Crest Trail. I followed the lake's rim, running, hopping from wet rock to wet rock, relieved and happy.

But then the lake's eastern side became a cliff, not high, but if I tried to down-climb and slipped, I'd snap something. I stared down the wet rock ledge, to the bottom. Just twenty feet, if that. I stepped to do it, to down-climb, but then pulled back my foot. I didn't want to fall. I couldn't chance it.

I thought I should go back the way I'd come and descend on the correct side of the lake. But reentering the blinding, freezing cloud seemed like suicide. The sun was falling fast, it was nearly tucked away behind the mountains, and I needed to break into the trees before nightfall to camp.

The lake was here, near-frozen, rimmed with snow.

I stepped into the lake.

I had made a reckless decision. I'd been cold, my body temperature too low, and in my state of hypothermia, I believed that submerging my shivering body in snowmelt to shortcut back to the PCT was a reasonable plan. It was not. I stood in that water, cold as knives, my teeth rattling against each other, biting my tongue, my tongue bleeding. I hadn't even put on my gloves. *Move*, I thought, *walk through the water. It will be easy.* The water was soft and thick, like bedsheets beneath a heavy comforter. I wanted to lie down, float and sleep. *No, walk*, I thought.

My heart pounded quickly, faintly, struggling to keep me warm. My bottom half was numb. I felt nothing, no fear of the fact that I was close to freezing. My whole chest throbbed. I stepped through the water. I didn't stop stepping. I knew how to walk.

At the western shore I stepped out onto the snow. The trail lay at my feet. I said *Thank you, thank you, trail*. I tried to run, but tripped. My legs were stiff. I kept pushing. My legs tingled, hot life returning to them.

The trail was mellow, gradual downhill and well-marked, and I thought I'd beat the sun into the forest. I was going to be all right. The trail neared the edge of Lake McDermand—and then it did something terrible; arching along a stone footbridge, the path crossed back over to the frigid lake's dry eastern side. I hadn't needed to cross through the freezing lake. I kicked a rock, devastated by my stupidity, the futility of my pain. I crossed back over the stones, fingernails milk pale. I ran down into the trees.

Downhill, in pines, day faded to shade, night. Snow twirled and stuck on branches like white fur. I was hungry and cold, and tired of my hunger, of the mental stress of searching for the trail, the constant exhausting attentiveness required to stay on course. The slope's decline was steep, and I kept slipping, squinting, hoping for a flat spot in the inky pines to pitch my tent. I clicked my headlamp on. My vision became a tunnel of light, of swirling white snowflakes, all trees and rock ground outside of it: blackness.

I walked through night's woods, my legs shaking, stomach rumbling like a rock slide, for three miles, more than an hour, before I finally saw a flat clearing. I fell onto it, down on hard ground, pitched my tent kneeling. I crawled inside and took my clothes off. The mountain night air burned me. My sleeping bag and fleece were still damp from the lake-crossing, half-stiff with frost.

I lay down naked, shivering, rubbing my hands up and down my ribs, starving, remembering my crushed cashews, chewing them gone. My shoulders ached with exhaustion and with stress. I was tired, worn out, too cold and hungry to sleep. Wasting an extra day at Upper Crabtree Meadow had been a mistake. I'd made many mistakes, but this one was irreparable. My mismeasurement was catastrophic. I was alone in vast cold mountains with no food. I had to walk to the next town— sixty-point-five snowy and steep miles north—with nothing to eat.

I didn't know what I would do. There was no way I could survive. I stared at my damp tent ceiling, feeling the frigid air against me, the frozen ground against my bottom, so cold my bare skin burned. I needed to get to the next trail-town, Mammoth Lakes. There was no one here to save me now.

I rose at first light to snow falling. I'd been too cold to sleep. I couldn't stay. I needed to find food somewhere out here, somehow. I was violent with desire to eat red meat.

That day I walked ten, twelve, fifteen miles. In total, I'd covered eighty-two miles—the distance from Philadelphia to New York—on nothing but Clif Bars and cashews. I trudged through snow, each step sinking, then over frost-slick rocks, slipping, catching myself without grace, the cold trees glittering. I was spending the very last of my body's energy on miles that seemed to take me no closer to salvation.

The trail became buried. Its rutted outline was visible and then very faint beneath new snow, then gone. I ran through trees, down- hill to some unnamed place I assumed the path might lead, not think- ing about losing it. I ran the way that felt easiest, angry at the trail for being so exhaustingly unreliable when I needed it most.

Time passed—I couldn't find the trail again. I was lost and utterly alone.

I slowed, blinking out cold tears to see the leafless trees, aspens stripped of their gold—at the absolute limit of where this life could take me. I looked at their pale skins like ghosts of what they would become if they lived into spring. They'd blossom, green and gold beauty, if they could only endure this awful winter.

My stomach growled, a subterranean rumble like a quake. I was desperate not to confront the fact that this really could be it—that "nineteen" didn't matter, that there really was a point at which even young bodies fail. I was not immortal. In a quiet wind, last night's flakes sifted like fine sugar from a pale tree's weedlike branches. I'd walked all this way and now it seemed this very well could be the end of the trail for me, in all senses.

There had been so many hikers at Upper Crabtree Meadow after we'd finished Whitney; I should have asked Silverfox or Boomer or even Never-Never for extra food. I could have begged. But I didn't, and now there was no one out here with me. I was now hoping some other hiker would appear with extra food and save me. But I was off the trail. And no one ever came. No trail angels lived here. No boyfriend, no mother.

Still I walked into the snow, moving to keep warm, burning precious energy searching for an answer I couldn't think of. I didn't turn back, compelled to continue without the trail. I didn't want to risk futilely backtracking. If I couldn't find the trail before dark, I could wake tomorrow disoriented and desperate, without having even made any new miles; my loss of the PCT should have distressed me, but a new instinct led me forward. In this moment of despair I was refusing to stop fighting. I asked the mountains for some guidance, the strength to get myself out of here, and pulled wild power from within myself I'd never known I'd had.

I was no longer following a trail.

I was learning to follow myself.

I emerged from the aspen forest into a clearing bordered by peaks: a snowfield—and a distant bridge. Weak and quivering, I stood in snow, within this unrelenting High Sierra dreamscape. I began to sense that I'd been here before. It was a vague ghost of a memory: beneath the pristine snow, this meadow was cut by a side trail I'd once followed.

I ran across the field, tripping, scanning for clues to confirm I knew this place. I crossed the bridge and, recognizing it, began to remember with impossible elation—I'd crossed this meadow two summers before at seventeen, when I'd lied to my mother about being on an organized trip and hiked these mountains alone. It had been clear of snow then, green and budding. Those were the most liberated weeks of all my teenage years. In a swell of joy I remembered with certainty— this clearing in the woods was called Aspen Meadow. I was not lost.

I finally reached the bridge, my temples pulsing with adrenaline, my memory extending further—this meadow led to a side-trail I'd once followed down to a sanctuary that could rescue me again. My breath caught, my eyes searching between trees—miraculously falling on the wooden sign I was seeking. It pointed down a steep hill to the right, read: Muir Trail Ranch.

After all this time questioning whether I could trust myself, my instinct had proven right—I'd found a path in pathless woods. When I was lost and without hope, I'd found again the man who first taught me to trust my own will. When I needed him most, here appeared John Muir.

But my gut dropped—this was not summer. I was here too early in the season. Muir Trail Ranch was likely closed. I knew that if it was and there was no food at the bottom, I'd never have the strength to climb back up the steep hillside. It would be a long way back, uphill miles.

My options seemed dismal. The Ranch would be a dangerous gamble. But Muir was a miracle. He was hope in hopeless wild.

I began to walk down Muir Trail Ranch's path.

I strode for an hour down, downhill, letting gravity take me. I thought of thick noodles with garlic cream sauce, marinara sauce, red meat sauce tangy and fatty. I thought of Junior and how if he hadn't touched me, I wouldn't be here, a girl in the woods, in trouble. I felt thin and weak yet quick, like a gliding bird. I was overheating, had lost seventeen hundred feet of elevation, so low that the snow had disappeared. I reached a level flat of soil, then a wooden pen—the ranch.

It seemed no one was there. I stumbled across a flat of damp dirt, muddy, suddenly energized. I was going to give this place every last calorie of hope; there must be food here. Three small naked wood buildings stood. I ran to one, the next, banging and calling at the doors. I screamed loud as my body could, "Please help me!" and fell to my knees in the mud. I was crying. I wasn't going anywhere. I took my knapsack off right in the muddy grass, let it become damp with filth.

I heard a motor and smelled gasoline. I thought conjured motor oil must have been the beginnings of my final unhinging. Reality was fading. I saw a tractor, green, with paint chipped like flecks of bark.

"Miss," I heard a voice. "Miss, hey-lo. Girlie?"

I looked up, and the tractor held a man. He'd driven up to me. "I need food," I said. I had no other words. I began to sob. "I don't have anything to eat." I then whispered, "Help me. Take care of me."

He looked down at me from his tractor. "You have no food?"

"No food," I repeated.

"Young lady," he said, climbing down, "I'll ask inside."

I nodded, trembling, squatting in the muddy grass. I pushed myself up to stand, legs wobbling.

I looked at his cracked hands. "Hungry. I'm very hungry."

He was walking, away, saying "I know," patting the air for me to follow as I stayed standing.

"C'mon inside," I heard him say.

I'd have followed him anywhere. I had been reduced to the mindless slave to what I wanted: food.

It was dark inside. Before my eyes had adjusted, I smelled onions browning, carrots. "Cooking," I said slowly. Colors came into view and I saw I was in a cavernous dining room with a woodstove, linen yellow curtains bright with light. In a tall mirror beside the woodstove I saw my hair had grown impossibly long. It curled down to my bottom, overtaking me. The air was warm. I hadn't felt warm air since the desert south of Kennedy Meadows.

He was looking at the dark wood wall. He said, "Hey-lo Bonnie! Girl here needs some supper."

"Hey-lo Bonnie," I repeated, and then giggled, dizzy, and a woman appeared. I hadn't seen her there. She was old and small, pinning cloths up on a clothesline beside the stove. She asked me if I was thru-hiking, said, "You're early."

Yes, I was, I knew. I told her, "It's pretty here." I asked if she'd seen Icecap, "Swiss-German boy."

She hadn't. I was the first. "Did you go to Kickoff?" she asked me. "No."

"Should have." She explained that if I'd gone I would know not to be in the High Sierra now. "Should be mandatory. They give seminars and you'd learn not to hike alone. You pick a partner. And not until there's no snow below ten thousand feet."

She asked if I had money. The ranch was opening the next day, it was a guest ranch, and the cheapest cabin went for three hundred a night. "Yes," I said, though I had only fifty dollars cash. I had my parents' credit card, but I doubted she took cards.

She asked if I knew how to work. "Can you wash windows?" It seemed a strange question. Of course I could.

"Windows," I said.

"You'll wash these windows." She pointed to the dining hall's long row of them. "And keep your money."

The unheated cabin bedroom Bonnie gave me in exchange for this small labor was charming. I ran my fingers up and down the porcelain candlestick cup, smooth, a relic from another kind of life.

Dinner that night was smashed sweet potatoes and glazed pork, root salad with milky cheese and fresh fennel. Loaf after loaf of fresh dense bread. The meal was served family style: me, seven wind-worn ranch hands, and Bonnie. I never stopped eating. They were all kind to me.

That night I lit my bedside candle, the porcelain glowed orange, and I swaddled myself inside my sleeping bag, under down covers, alone, in a beautiful bed.

In the morning the ranchers fed me a big breakfast of fried eggs and fried potatoes, and I devoured everything at the table nearest the woodstove. Bonnie brought me fifteen giant PayDay candy bars to fuel me during the forty-nine remaining miles to the town of Mammoth Springs. Then she walked me out, back into the bright cold, the light blinding and described to me how to get back to the PCT.

Bonnie had saved my life.

"Send me a postcard from Canada," she said. She told me not to forget.

I hugged her and told her I'd remember.

I was alone again, in an enchanting expanse of frozen ground bright with sunlight, comfortable. I ate one king-size PayDay bar each time my stomach cramped up. They tasted wonderful, each with 440 calories. I was too starved to ration. I emerged back up above timberline, rock-strewn peaks exposed to wind and sky. The High Sierra glittered, virgin. The trail was buried in ice-sheeted snow. Again, nothing marked my way.

I saw the saddle, the low-point on a distant ridge against sky, and hiked toward it, ascending. Soon the mountainside became a cliff of ice, milky mesmerizing blue, impossible to climb. I hiked along its base to the east. I could no longer see the pass on the skyline.

I found my GPS and clicked on a topographic map with a small arrow like a V on it, representing my location and orientation, but I didn't know how to read it. My fingers were windburned and numbing. I needed to keep moving, but I didn't know which way.

I found my satellite phone, called my dad.

He picked up, "Debby?" It was the middle of the day on June 12, the sun high in California. I tried to picture what the day was like in New England's quiet suburbs, how the light looked, if the sky was gray or sapphire blue. I thought of my old lavender comforter, the clean bright matching curtains with their twirling baby pink and cream-white ballerinas. My bed would be nicely made for me. Hearing Dad's voice, I missed the comfort of my Newton home.

I asked if he was at a computer. "Have a minute?" I asked, trying to sound warmer, hoping I seemed calm.

"I am, yeah," he said. "At my computer. How's it going?" I usually didn't call until past dark, past midnight at the house, but he didn't sound alarmed to hear from me so early. He sounded tired.

"Going good," I said as I clicked through the GPS's screens: a compass, waypoint spreadsheet, and topographic map, cryptic as ever. I didn't know if I should tell him I couldn't read it. I didn't want to alarm him. I wanted him to think that I was capable, resourceful and able on my own. But I didn't know which way to go. Northward was a mountainside of icicles as large as tree trunks. It was a waterfall, months of compounded icicles. I took a deep breath of freezing air and quietly said, "But I'm a little lost, I think. It's icy."

I heard papers moving, probably work he had to do. It was a Friday. I knew because my GPS told me so, uselessly. My father's chair creaked. He asked me where I was, "Your coordinates?"

It hadn't occurred to me to look at them. To me they were only decimals, long and complicated. I pushed the protruding round black button as I did every night when it was time to tell my parents where I was in the world; my latitude and longitude appeared faintly in green. I read them to him. He told me that I was actually literally on the trail. He read me the high pass's coordinates, Selden Pass, and described how to program them into my GPS as a destination.

I followed his instructions. The *V* arrow ticked slowly, settled on a direction. It pointed straight through the wall of blue ice, but if I walked off-course the *V* would adjust, float to constantly point at the pass. It wouldn't let me get lost.

My dad asked me, "Got it? How's it looking?"

"Looks good. Thanks," I said. I didn't mention Muir Trail Ranch's Bonnie, the cabin bed and fried eggs, that my mad will had taken me to generous people. That I had mad will. I said only goodbye, hiked; the arrow floated.

I maneuvered along the base of the frozen cascade of icicles. I felt protected, stronger, like I was on a team, like Bonnie and my father and this GPS I suddenly sort of knew how to use would not allow me to be harmed. For so long, I'd felt only burdened by my satellite phone and the GPS, extra weight I hadn't wanted. But now I could call my dad and give him the coordinates of my precise global placement, he'd tell me the way I needed to go. I would love him for telling me, for knowing.

These tools were my parents' way of saying: What you're doing is important. We support it. We want to help you find your way.

I meandered up Selden Pass, never needing to stop and wonder which way was right. I mounted it; I stood high in sunlit clouds. The north side of the pass was a perfect sheet of untouched snow, steep and glossed with ice, its runoff long and safe, like a thousand-foot-high natural wild slide. It would take hours to hike down this slope tall as a skyscraper, straining my thighs so as not to slip. The effort seemed tedious. This pass was a straight slide, a thrilling shortcut. I tightened my knapsack's hip-belt, sat down, pushed off against the ice-glazed snow, quick, hard. I glissaded down Selden Pass, the mountain my own gigantic slide, to the flat bottom, shrieking, exhilarated, fine.

I stumbled to my feet, programmed the next destination into my GPS, Silver Pass, and saved the waypoint. I grinned at my new competence. The sun was falling, blocked by glowing pink clouds, and I walked down into a forest of foxtail pines.

In the trees, I found a stripe of snow compacted by new footprints. Each print pointed north. I had stumbled back onto the PCT. I turned my GPS off and followed the band of footprints through the snow.

The trail was clear for a while, scarred with fallen pine needles, but soon the footprints disappeared. But I didn't retrace my own prints or pull my GPS back out. Instead I kept walking. In that pink light, in those woods, on snow, I felt new confidence. The position of the sun, at my left cheek, told me I was going north. The smooth fold of the foothill told me this was the natural way to walk, the logical place to build a trail. And then as fast as they had disappeared I saw across a field of open white the footprints, a whole crowd of them together, the same band I'd seen before. I jogged down to them, followed their course. The path of tracks thinned to a few, then two, then again none.

The sun was low. I saw its place. I kept hiking, gliding, fit and light, descending, calm. Again, again, again I found one print or mark or sign and ran to join the team of feet once more. Again the marks of our way would vanish, and I would look for the team of feet again.

I navigated the Range of Light's virgin snow, a new mountaineer, hearing John Muir's words—go quietly, alone—feeling his awe. Ascending Silver Pass I saw no human footprints, only the tracks of a lone bear. They were deep and large, the snow packed beneath the lumbering creature's weight. I paused and looked around, but didn't see their maker. I relaxed and fed myself a giant PayDay, my last. I had seventeen miles left to get to food in Mammoth Lakes. I would hike without food but also without fear. I knew I'd make it. My pain was temporary. I could walk through hunger. I thought: Muir survived on stale bread and spring water. I hoped Muir would have been impressed by me—a wild girl traversing the Range of Light.

I camped that night at the PCT's junction with Goodale Pass trail, above ten thousand feet, on trackless moon-blue snow. Bright bands of stars twinkled; they were far and kind. That final night before Mammoth Lakes I drank and drank water, filling up my stomach, trying to trick it.

I woke to the music of my rumbling stomach, powerful as a wildcat's growl. I had slept in. Sunlight poured through twisted foxtail pines and danced corkscrew shadows, spinning, on my two-person tent's walls, on my face. I was exhausted, determined, puny and nearly to a mecca of cake and meat.

Approaching Mammoth Lakes, in the town's outskirts, I collapsed on the gravel outside of a white and blue Chevron gas station and ate pint after pint of Ben & Jerry's. I stank of sweat. Tourist families wandered in and out and in, their little girls in Uggs and Juicy sweatpants, pink, candy blue, all similar. They smelled of baby powder and strawberry perfume. They stared. I was shameless.

I had swagger, now. I had navigated deadly passes, mounted them. I'd faced sixty-four snowy miles without food. I had persisted on faith. And then food came. Because of good people. The world no longer seemed violent and unkind.

In town I attended restaurants in the order that I saw them. I consumed everything. I devoured pad thai, hot chocolate and wine, French fries and a rare, bloody hamburger. At a diner, eating alone, seated apart from the families, I noticed in the booth's sliver of mirror that my forehead was marked with something; it looked like a gash, blood dried on it. I saw that my neck had a dark streak, too. I leaned in, examined the dark marks. I grinned, embarrassed. It was dried chocolate ice cream. I not only smelled filthy but looked it, too. I pulled a pine needle from my hair. I had been walking about town, looking feral, Wild Child.

SEAVEY PASS, THE NORTHERN HIGH SIERRA, MILE 976

I went back on the trail the next day, happy in the cold once again. I navigated icy passes, quads hot, stabilizing me, ice ax heavy in my uphill arm. I sung in clean air.

Each night, freezing and lightless, I pitched my tent, one-two, boom-boom, voilà!, delayed getting inside, feeling the cold, blinking at the boundless star-sprayed sky. The stars were specks. I was a speck, too. I shrieked into the charcoal-still and listened to my sound, raw and carnal, echoing through the inky Range of Light.

I sensed my place. I could feel the presence of the mountains through the blackness.

Each morning, I woke to light. Silver flakes of mica shimmered, stardust on the pale rock beneath me. I saw the intricate black lace shadow pearl-green lichen cast on stone. Mountain sunlight exposed beauty within beauty. I was high and light with it.

I slipped up mountains, Muir's cathedrals, now my home, the mecca that almost took my fragile life. I'd entered his mountains so early, so unprepared. In rock masked by clean snow I should have died. In this daylight I saw: I was the luckiest girl.

"Between every two pine trees there is a door leading to a new way of life," Muir wrote. I wondered which trees Icecap had slipped through, without me.

Then I stepped over a wood bridge in the forest, out of Muir's fabled chosen homeland. I had passed finally through the entire Range of Light.

NONDESCRIPT MEADOW, THE NORTHERN HIGH SIERRA, MILE 1,000

I was striding through a clearing, a gap in white-bark pines, in sunshine. I felt stronger and faster than I ever had walking with Icecap. If I were with him now I would keep up.

On the yellow grass I saw white stones placed in a loose pattern, a formation as large as a reclined body. I stilled for a moment, looked more closely. They were in the wobbly shape of a 1-0-0-0. One thousand. Stones telling me I had walked one thousand miles.

CLIMBING SONORA PASS, THE NORTHERN HIGH SIERRA, MILE 1,013

Ascending Sonora Pass, the Sierra's final steep and icy climb, I heard someone shriek my trail name. "Wild Child!" It was a woman's voice, thin and desperate, calling to me. "Wiiild Chiiild, heyyy!"

I was startled, nearly at the top of the ascent, heart knocking. Sun bounced off the slick slope; I squinted down, saw Silverfox, below me, bounding up the steep snow toward me. Queen bee, queen bee, big bitch, I thought, but I waited for her.

She was so slender now. So tall. When we'd first met down in the desert, I'd sensed she didn't want me near her, but now she hunched toward me and grabbed my forearm, held it tight. She was leaning on me. She seemed weaker now, nicer.

"What's up?" I asked.

"Saw your footprints," she said to me, her breath streams of silver hot air. "I had to catch you." She confessed she didn't even care whom the footprints belonged to. "Any other hiker," she said.

She had left her trail-boy Boomer and had no maps, just like me. The guys had made fun of her for her dependence on guidebooks and paper, how she was always double-checking. So she'd given her maps up. But without them these past few days she'd been lost more often than not. She needed someone to hike with who knew where they were going.

"Why'd you get rid of them if you wanted them?" I asked. She ignored me. She was looking right at me. "I haven't got maps either," I told her then, because it was true, and because I didn't want to hike with her.

"Where's Icecap?" she asked. "You're hiking alone now?"

I was getting cold, the sweat from the climb chilling. "Alone, yes," I said. I turned and started climbing again. She followed me to the top of the pass, stopped there, the whole pale glittering Sierra beneath us.

"Just fuck all of them," she said. "*Fuck* them. Men are animals." She told me Boomer and Never-Never and a hiker named Shell and a few other guys had been joking around, teasing a marmot. It was getting dark and everyone set up his shelter. "There was this marmot, hanging around, and Boomer chased it away. But it came back. The guys were rowdy."

They started to harass the animal, circle around it, close in. Boomer threw pebbles, then stones. With a makeshift slingshot, Shell shot sticks. They struck it until it was crippled. It hobbled and squeaked, terrified, and it trailed blood.

She leaned against me. I was freezing by now, shivering convulsively. "I left," she said, "but I know they killed it."

Silverfox and I hiked down Sonora Pass together. The pass's northern side was even steeper, cragged and cliffed in places, frosty slick granite sheeted with black ice. We descended in small steps, quiet, focused. This was my scariest descent yet. I stepped with precision, tentative now, gripping and planting my ice ax, thinking of Icecap to distract my frantic heart. Far more frightened here than I'd been on Whitney with him. Letting myself miss him, the safety he gave me.

But I also saw he wasn't what I needed now. To have stayed with him any longer would have been a forfeit, a shortcut that bypassed the intention of my whole hike. I'd needed to walk on my own. I hoped my solitude would help me reclaim my innocence, remember who I'd been, to find who I wanted to be. To become her. To love her, Deborah, Debby, Doll Girl, Wild Child, *me*, despite the irreversible truth that I'd been raped. I was learning again that I could trust myself and, also, I was seeing, other people. I was brave enough now to go out alone toward what I wanted, to trust that I was strong enough for it, to know that help would come when I needed it. It always came.

Silverfox and I made it down. Safe now, we descended the gentle slope of a wooded foothill, along a loud stream.

"Fuck them *all*," she yelled. "Icecap was a total dick to you. Jesus Christ, Icecap too."

I blinked at her. The sky behind her white-blond hair was bright deep blue. Her split ends glowed, lit by sun, a thousand tiny frayed golden strands of light, wild and lovely. "Not really," I told her. "He actually isn't."

Speaking this, I realized that he really wasn't. He had been good to me. Night after night after night, alone with him in wilderness, I had trusted him. Lying beside him, naked sometimes. He had held me through forty-three nights and nine hundred miles as I said *No, No, No, No, No.* He had never pushed. He'd never asked me why.

I gave him forty-three tests to see if a man could listen and not take what I hadn't offered. Forty-three whispers praying he would erase the man who didn't stop.

I didn't get hurt. I had shown him my power. I had shown myself, and together we had obliterated my fear and dread.

At last I knew what I'd been doing with Icecap-Daniel. He had shown me not all guys are Junior Mason. He had shown me that some men can be kind.

I was grateful to him. He left me better off than he'd found me.

I looked at Silverfox, into her ice blue eyes. "No," I told her, "Icecap was good."

She leaned away. We walked the rest of the evening without talking. I didn't like her. Her squint and lean showed that she again despised me.

That last night, my final night in the High Sierra, we camped together, but didn't huddle or chat. Silverfox and I went our separate ways after refueling in Bridgeport, California the next day. I entered the Northern Sierra alone again.

My thrilling solitude had begun deep inside John Muir's exalted Range of Light, in beauty, at Upper Crabtree Meadow three hundred miles behind me. I couldn't know then, but my isolation would extend from the Sierra to shadowed pine forests, up through southern Oregon's Volcano Lands: a thousand consecutive miles of walking the wilderness alone.

The next month I would find a note left in a register that said "I miss Wild Child," signed "Icecap," but I never saw him again.

PART III
The Way Through

CHAPTER 15

A Thousand Miles of Solitude

Solvitur ambulando
—A Latin term that means
"It is solved by walking"

All great and precious things are lonely.
—John Steinbeck, *East of Eden*

you say it was lonely only sometimes
what was the rest of the time
—Corrina Gramma

JUNE 18, UNKNOWN PLACE, THE NORTHERN HIGH SIERRA

The mountains of the Northern Sierra rise and fracture like the shards of a dropped ceramic, impaling the uneven ground, erect. Sun-poured and slashed by shadows black and long. Deadly, lovely, angular faces thrilling to witness: frightening; they morph you. You're merely a blackened speck. Long ridges cut the sky, drop down into fog-washed forest, hemlocks with arms like soft walls, sweep back up again to sharp summits, gray.

I stepped carefully, walking along a slick and rocky ridge, down toward timberline, down down into woods that smelled of black soil and sage. In the forest, on my own, I felt like a dandelion seed, caught circling in gusting wind: lonely, but also sometimes gleeful, riding on my own safe current.

One day I came upon a register in the forest. Trail registers had become my only link to other hikers, my way of communicating with my north-drifting community. I always liked to read the registers' notes—but in this particular Ziploc-protected notebook I saw something that startled me. It was an entry by a hiker named Vic, telling that Monty's Donner Party from Warner Springs had failed. Up north they had encountered just as much snow. Not one of the group's members made it through. Each one abandoned the trail. BoJo—I remembered him from Kennedy Meadows; he'd been a computer programmer and the PCT had long been his retirement dream—had fallen in the snow and broken his foot. I hoped this was only a rumor.

I remembered BoJo, how insecure and sweet he'd seemed. He'd told me that ever since he'd learned of the long footpath from Eric Ryback's old boyhood travel memoir, he'd wanted to hike the trail. He'd saved up to quit his programming job for seventeen years, since long before he'd begun to lose his hair and balance. I found his fall so sad. He had followed Monty and in a blink derailed his wild dreams.

I wondered where he was now, if he was back in Cleveland, if he was happier than he'd been before walking. I signed "Wild Child" without a note, shut the book, and sealed it safely back into its Ziploc bag. I kept walking north, thinking about where the trail was taking me.

My beauty and independence were new for me. They brought me pride and satisfaction; they changed my sense of possibility. I felt awake in my body. Living in the woods, building my little shelter each night, a silent shadow, drifting in and out of mountain towns, a ghost, I was entirely self-reliant. On the trail I had persisted despite fear, and walking the Pacific Crest had led me deeply into happiness. I felt amazing now. In this body that brought me twelve hundred miles, I felt I could do anything.

But I also began to fear the place where the trail ended. I wondered what I'd do after the walk, where I would land, if I should go back to college, if I could even face it. The image of the gap in the forest invaded me—the trail abruptly stopping. After all this hard work walking, strong in motion, the hike would leave me in Canada, myself still. What if the PCT's essential lessons were only ephemeral? I feared I could simply lose the trail's grand gifts—regress. The PCT would end, and I felt panicked.

I felt truly homeless, directionless. I hadn't been making my own path; I'd been walking an old established trail, only mindlessly following it. And it would end. And Junior was still at Colorado College. I couldn't go back there.

Maybe I could move back home to Newton and live with my parents, get a job waitressing at Johnny's Luncheonette. Other girls I knew did that on their summer breaks. And lots of young writers supported themselves with mindless jobs. I'd again live with my folks. I would waitress and also write. I would be safe. My mother loved me madly. Yes, there were certainly worse things in the world.

Home in Newton my mother would resume blocking me from harm. She'd drive me to appointments. She would feed me well. I would be taken care of. She'd make sure that I was proactively protected against sicknesses, as she'd insisted on doing since I was a child.

But I also knew that she wouldn't see me, didn't get me, couldn't see what I was or what I am. Back home, my mother would still impulsively choose my clothes as she'd chosen my name. But all the identities she'd chosen for me felt wrong, now. I could not return to the person she'd picked for me to be. My relationship with my mother trapped me in the identity of a child.

I was here, alone in the Northern High Sierra, learning I could survive on my own. I was not fragile and weak; I'd have to learn to face adversities. My mother couldn't protect me from Junior. She couldn't protect me from life, yet she had never taught or trusted me to go and live it well. She didn't recognize how capable I was, respect my autonomous capabilities. She taught me only how to need to be taken care of.

I was here because I needed to learn to take responsibility for making my own decisions—to earn my own trust.

And now, finally taking the chance to make the mistakes that would allow me to learn, I felt stronger. I found, within my solitude, my competence. I was learning to take care of myself—to feel powerful.

My strong body pushed me across the peaks of the High Sierra, I could survive violent hunger—find my way through, against all odds. Debby Parker couldn't.

Now the idea of returning home, to my pastel wooden childhood bedroom, made me feel just as weak and claustrophobic as imagining going back to my cinder-block dorm. I feared returning to Newton would mean the loss of all the progress away from Debby I'd been making as I hiked. Just as I'd known I needed to cross the Range of Light without Icecap in order to get what I needed—to grow—I sensed that I couldn't go home and go forward. At home, I would be trapped as helpless Debby Parker.

But the trail would end, that was inevitable.

I walked down the blond sand trail, the sun was white, the foxtail pines brick corkscrews, the sky China-silk blue. I was placeless. I carried everything on my back, exactly what I needed to survive. I didn't know how I'd survive without this structure, silent bears and vista highs, the infinite beauty.

A thick sheet of water cascaded off a smooth granite ledge like a glass curtain. Soaked moss gleamed. The far edge of the waterfall ended in a rock, and there the glossed sheet shattered, sprayed violently. My heart fluttered, frantic.

I pulled off my shirt, unhooked my bra, exposed my body. I was slim and strong now. I stepped into the frigid pulse of the waterfall, braced and goose-bumped, struck by thrill. I was on my own. I had passed two bearded thru-hikers several hours before, but I didn't care. I'd seen others nude on the trail, though not so often; timing-wise, it just didn't happen a lot. And I loved my body now.

I was shivering, euphoric. The granite smelled fresh, of roots and sand, and the freezing water pounded the rock-slab floor, the spray golden, pure light. I wouldn't be embarrassed—or even endangered—to be seen naked out here in these woods. I had the body of Wild Child. I knew that if anyone saw me, they'd sense my strength. They wouldn't touch me.

A warm spring wind shook the pines, I watched them quiver. I felt heated from within, as if by an internal fire flickering. I had never felt so strong—so defiant. I was so far from my mother, from my coddled, suburban self, from the sad-mute raped girl who stood at Mexico's edge. A thousand miles past that girl. Getting clean.

I knew fiercely that I couldn't move back home.

The next register I came upon again had a note that struck me. It read, "Thirty miles yesterday, twenty-eight already today. It's been a little extra fun. Wild Children are gettin wild. Hand massages, foot massages . . . other massages." It was signed by a hiker named Panther, whom I'd briefly met back near the town of Bridgeport, who'd been quite sweet to me. He was olive skinned and blue-eyed, a striking combination to me, soft-spoken and intent in his eye contact. His voice low and gravelly and quiet. I remembered I'd needed to lean toward him to hear him. We'd spoken for a minute; he'd passed me.

I hoped maybe his wording was only an unfortunate coincidence.

Day after day I trudged north, through snow, alone, pitching my tent in darkness, waking each new morning in the fetal position, disoriented. Mornings were terribly cold. Often I'd emerge from my shelter to find the forest dusted with snow, shimmering. Sometimes the mound of old snow I'd slept atop was fifty feet deep, which, if it weren't for the treetops poking through the white ground at my feet, I wouldn't have known.

The landscape opened. I emerged from low woods to a field of boundless snow. I entered it, feeling exposed, stepping carefully into an uneven ocean of sun-cups, the bowls' bottoms weightless snow, melting in daylight. Step in one, and I might fall through. I tried to walk the whole way across the field only balancing on the pockmarks' glossy rims. Focused, I nearly stepped on a pika, the cutest little mountain creature, a puff of fur like a crossbred bunny-chipmunk. My foot fell toward it; it squeaked and flashed, gone. My heart sped; I flushed hot, shaken by what I'd almost done. I thought about Never-Never and Shell and Boomer, slaughtering a marmot for no reason. It was inconceivable. Barbaric. They were savage. I pictured the scene, the pelting stones, hot momentary madness obliterating compassion as they took a life, what their cruelty had required. I wondered if killing required very much at all, or if anyone could be a brute if angry enough, hungry enough for love. Blind enough to suffering.

The snowfield sloped downhill. My gait was wild now, floppy, my steps careless, heels punching the crust of glassy ice, shattering it. My hard steps shot cracks through virgin ground, I was the hammer to windshields; my impact shattered and shattered the world. I was loving the jolt of breaking through—

Then I fell through—up to my neck.

My body stopped. Adrenaline struck my heart; I wriggled. I freed my arms, tried to push out, free. But my legs were stuck. I couldn't shift my feet, not an inch; my heels were numbing. I thrashed; my ribs felt bruised. I couldn't even move my toes. Nothing. I pressed my hip left, into the sea of snow; it burned me, I held my core against it until the hole melted wider, harder, dripping. I tried to contort myself out, breathe, pressed my bare snow-burned palms against the snow, pushed, pushed—determined. Still I was trapped. Fighting still—

And I broke out. In one slick thrust I popped my body free. I was euphoric—success!—I breathed, okay. But my right shoe was gone. It remained in snow, five feet deep down, stuck there. I didn't think. I didn't stop. I pulled off my fleece shirt, tied it around my exposed foot, and violently, maniacally dug.

I was wearing only thin black running spandex and a polypro shirt. I hadn't planned for this long delay on the snow. As the hole widened, my body heated; my right foot cooled, freezing and then burning. I thought I'd lose my foot. I was desperate to live, digging. At last I produced my icy shoe. Shoved my numb foot into it. Limped north.

I placed my feet down on the holes' glassy ridges, tried to follow the shade where snow was more compact, not melted by the sun into soft bowls like death traps—but I couldn't always tell. I was alert constantly, meticulous. I was scared.

I heard frantic squeaking—a tiny fluffed pika resting in a snow hole. June was still winter in the High Sierra. At long last back in the forest, trees were dripping, everything melting, the sound of budding spring. I'd thought I'd gotten out of the cold without harm, lucky, but as my foot regained feeling, I realized I couldn't step comfortably. I saw that there was damage from the fall. My left shoe was torn open, its silver mesh now a flap clinging to a gaping hole.

I immediately used the satellite phone to call my mother and asked her to mail me new running shoes to Sierra City, the mountain-resort town with the next post office the trail would meander by. She said she'd overnight them. She said she'd already sent that post office dried strawberries and freeze-dried green beans and also a plastic baggie of children's Flintstone multivitamins I could chew, so I wouldn't need to try to swallow a grown-up pill. She'd picked out the purple "grape" ones, leaving me with the oranges and the reds, as she knew I liked those flavors better, and she didn't want me to have to carry any needless weight.

There was no need to overnight the shoes, as I wouldn't reach Sierra City for another six or seven days, but I knew that didn't matter. She wanted to help me quickly; I wouldn't dissuade her. I felt grateful for her devotion. I simply thanked her.

I slipped past a father and daughter out for the weekend, and then, several days later, a bearded thru-hiker hanging out with a troop of raucous adolescent Scouts. Though I was starved for contact, I didn't stop to talk to any of these strangers. I had forgotten how to convincingly speak the polite things strangers say to each other. When I was alone in the woods and a robust troop leader spoke to me now, I responded only with an aloof and chilly, "Oh." I'd hardly glanced at him. I didn't need another Edison, or even another Icecap. It was difficult, but it felt good to walk this path alone. The trail became low snowless spring pine forests, and for three days walking in my broken shoe, I encountered nearly no one.

The trees were friendly, they gave me rest and shadowed refuge. Slipping through them, I felt safe and competent. My whole body was occupied. I had little energy to think or worry.

The thoughts I did have were very simple. I repeated the same lyric a thousand uninterrupted times in a row. I replayed: *I forsake these men who kill, I forsake these men who kill.* I pitched my own tent every night. It took me only a minute and a half to pitch my tent, lay down my sleeping bag, take off my clothes, swaddle myself, use my unpacked knapsack as a pillow and fall asleep. My body pulsed softly into feral dreams. I became efficient, mechanical. I was walking about thirty miles each day. I expected it would be lonesome and it was, but sometimes it was good.

I saw soft brown bears. A huge one the shadowy color of soil lumbered through dewy fog toward me, the green pines muted, everything quiet, until at last it nodded my way, noticed me, and hurtled back into the silent woods. I was a little sad it had gone so fast. I saw others but none quite as mammoth and beautiful.

I wanted to come close to fierce wild things. They seemed prehistoric, rare and sacred. The survivors of ancient America's desert battles. The grizzly is the state bear of California, yet there were none left here. We'd long killed them off.

In those quiet miles, something disconcerting began happening. I began to hear stories about my name—Wild Child—and felt a nameable danger. Threatening men. One day the granite peaks and alpine

lakes suddenly gave way to pumice fields in the shadow of Mount
Shasta—the beginning of the Volcano Lands, a hardened lava landscape, stark and shadeless—and I saw something horrifying. It was
written in a remote trail register in blue ink. I read it, read it through
again. It said that I had tried to seduce Shell at the Motel 6 in Mammoth Lakes.

It was an anonymous blue note. Beneath it, unknown men called
me a slut. One declared me the Paris Hilton of the trail. Someone else
said I was young, dumb, and full of cum. I read about Wild Child in
this public trail register, and so did men I knew, and so would men I
didn't know, but who believed they knew me now—whom I would
meet. Man after man would read these notes, and I would feel it in
the way they'd look at me.

I felt panic, the notes shoved me back to the helplessness of
my rape. That same nauseating shame, gutting me again. As if I
somehow felt I deserved to have whispered lies obscure me, even
though—clearly—I did not. These rumors cut to my older strug-
gles and fears—to camp girls whispering about me, believing I was
sleeping: *Debby wears grandpa shorts.* They brought back memories of
being bullied and deemed an outcast when I was small and without
my brother. I felt humiliated.

Dust twirled from my heels as I resumed hiking in the day's thick
smoggy sun. I passed through Northern California, in early autumn's
woods; it was August now. There was a frigid bite in the wind. It was
as if I'd slipped from winter into autumn, entirely skipping the span
of summer. Fall was sudden. Cold came fast like that.

I kept walking in this crest of northern desert, the volcanic
rock like a husk of dead earth beneath my broken running shoes. I
screamed to hear my echo, and with each footfall heard the crunch
of gravel. I crossed a field of stones—volcanic rubble. A sunset struck,
its curled rim red as lips, and the sky was pursed, smirking down at
me, the clouds unclean smears.

I retraced my path, my steps and my choices, trying to locate
where these stories about me had come from, trying to believe that

I could finally walk away from them for good, that they wouldn't be able to follow me forever. Men were telling stories that were untrue. The rumors made me feel dirty as I walked this very trail I'd fiercely hoped would distance me from shame.

I badly wanted to feel anger—people who would write such things were disgusting, pitiful scumbags. I wished I felt immune to sexual shaming, knowing these were lies that had no bearing—I wanted to see this, but instead these notes about me made me dread meeting other hikers. They caused anxiety and fear and the desire for isolation. The words these strangers had written stung something that I feared was true in me—that I was forever an outcast seen as someone to shame and to change, not to love and accept as I was.

No hiker had said anything crude like those notes to me yet. I told myself that if somebody did, I would correct him. I would boldly tell him *no*.

I promised myself I would.

One afternoon in a patch of woods where the trees were tall and thin, I came to a homemade wood sign: OLD STATION HIKER HIDE-AWAY. FIREFLY AND FIREWALKER WELCOME HIKERS. I followed the post down a dirt road, through an open painted gate, to a sprawling mowed lawn, to somebody's house, a trail angel homestead. It was whimsical, overgrown with twisted trees, dozens of big faded luxurious carnival-type tents set up, some with giant air mattresses or cots inside, one with a waterbed, for hikers to claim so we could sleep easy.

A dozen hikers were lounging, sipping Shasta sodas and tossing a beaten-up Frisbee. I felt guarded. I wished I didn't need to feel so wary. For dinner we devoured sloppy joes and buttery corn on the cob, and Firefly was very sweet to me, everybody was.

Firefly set me up away from the men, high in a bunk bed in a stained-glass tree house that her husband, Firewalker, a retired firefighter, built. I feared she must have heard something about me. Or maybe she sensed the low hum of threat I felt. But she was lovely, she'd fed me and let me bathe in her old classic claw-foot tub, perched gracefully on metal feet like tiptoes. That night I slept soundly in the stained-glass tree house, in woods, under stars, above boys and men.

Nothing bad happened.

In the morning I packed up and slipped inside Hiker Hideaway's little whimsical kitchen in the small house Firewalker had also built. I helped make breakfast and felt nourished, clean and feral, strong, happy.

Until two young Mormon brothers I'd seen but didn't really know told me softly that they felt sorry for me.

I didn't ask why. Instead, defiant, I made a pancake for my breakfast in the shape of a penis.

I ate it without sitting, feeling the brothers blushing. They squinted at me, believing they hated me. They didn't know me. I thanked Firefly and Firewalker and quickly walked away from the boys I didn't want to explain myself to. I tried to, but I couldn't forget the way they'd said they felt sorry, as if I were truly damned.

Within a mile all the trees had vanished. This was Hat Creek Rim, Northern California's crest of desert: dusty pebbles, stones sifting into the hole in my shoe's mesh, torn when I'd fallen. The ground became unstable.

When, the next day, I found myself again unhappily alone with a male thru-hiker, a teenage boy with a dirty nose named Pig Pen who hardly knew me, but who asked me, quickly, only part-joking, if I'd ever given head for ice cream, I didn't dignify him with an answer, but I asked back, "Where are you hearing this?"

I wished I could be clear and cutting as a shard of glass, but the question of the source—the violator—was all that filled my mind.

He answered me without hesitation. The answer was Never-Never.

All the rumors, the lies that trapped me, had leaked from just one faulty source: the man I had, in my fading innocence, seduced and then in the reality of meeting, rejected. Our relationship had existed exclusively in e-mails, in our minds, online in the air and in pixels in the cloud. He'd never even touched my hand. The first time I'd ever really seen him, after the single time I had made love to Icecap, we had hugged each other, it was a terrible hug, and that was the only time he'd ever touched me.

That night in the cluster of woods just south of Burney Falls State Park, sitting beside my tent on a soft bed of pine needles, a field mouse chewing at my shoelaces, I cradled my Moleskine notebook over my crossed legs and wrote a letter to Never-Never. I told him that at college I'd been raped. I told him I assumed he hadn't known this. But now he did. So he could stop. Because his stories about me were hurtful; he was lying, calling me all the things I felt about myself after the violation.

His lies stung, I really wasn't shocked. I had secretly expected it was him. And for the first time in my young life, I saw how someone I once believed I'd known could be so different from who I thought he was—and the huge magnitude to which a relationship could change. Relationships aren't static, they're fluid; poorly rooted ones are as unretainable as water in bare hands. I was stunned by this old half-friend's unkind intentions. It was my first lesson in the fragility of attraction.

I wrote madly. I was trying to discover what I truly thought about him and what he'd done. His accusations and words locked me into a shame I hadn't asked for, an imposed shame I was here to grow from; the accusations themselves were unfair because I hadn't earned them—but I saw now these truths were only the beginning of the light I was grasping. Somewhere in the sun-washed space between Southern California's hills of sand and the present desolate volcanic sprawl I was crossing, my legs had strengthened, but—invisibly—so had my will. The wisdom of my body had cultivated vibrantly since those sadness-drunken months after the rape when I'd felt so numbed by the hurt and shame that I didn't move further. No longer. The way I felt about being sexually shamed had changed. Now I was angry that others were trying to shame my sexuality in the first place.

I flushed—this time not in shame—but in rage. Even in my incredible assertion of my power, I was being reduced. It was maddening. But I was stronger than it, now.

Never-Never had intended to shame me, but now these accusations angered me instead.

I scrawled to him, again communicating in writing, the form in which we'd bonded, and I felt better having written out all the anger, the shock, I'd been unable to speak. I was pointedly showing him where his wrongness lay; showing myself. I felt better seeing that I reacted this way, this time. I was beginning to see the importance of my words. I felt my strength.

Then I slept soundly in my tent, away from the men and boys eager to believe I was available for them to take, happy to be entirely alone again, feeling madder, smarter than I'd been at college.

I was still in shock Never-Never would do that to me.

I thought this would make him see how blind he was.

But in morning it felt wrong to give him the letter. I thought: I wouldn't waste it on him. I needed to do something good, for myself, but more than that—something bigger. To say something, to make a statement—make a change. Silence had the rusty taste of shame. Jacob had told me how this walk was self-indulgent. My post-rape shame and pain endured, and I finally needed to do something productive with it.

I had a plan. Instead of giving Never-Never the letter, I recopied it, altering it slightly here and there, boldly directly addressing it not to a man whom I now hated but the people I most loved: my family.

This letter was for my mother and my father, Jacob, my oldest brother Robert, and Grandma Belle; Grandma Dorothy, Grandpa Mel, my cousins, in-laws and uncles and aunts, everyone who mattered, the people who loved me and could finally help. The letter explained that I'd been raped at college; I needed everyone to finally know. I was sorry I hadn't called them. I asked them to donate to the Rape, Abuse & Incest National Network on my behalf, in honor of my walk. A penny a mile would be $26.50. A dollar a mile would be $2,650.00, a value that astonished me. It would be such a relief to know they finally knew.

I didn't mention that my parents and brothers already knew, or that they'd already disappointed me.

I carried that letter in my journal, stepping faster, feeling stronger, despite my broken shoe's flapping, the pumice-pebbles sanding my feet raw, abrading me, blistering me—veered onto the road that guided me to Sierra City, to the new running shoes my mother had mailed.

In town, a local trail angel named Slueth had paid for the upstairs of the Buckhorn Motel for ten days, so hikers passing through could stay for free. The place was Spartan but festive, wooden floorboards and rafters, a communal fridge stocked with gallons of vanilla ice cream, and hot dogs, a huge plastic jar of sauerkraut, and potatoes baked in foil, all free. Slueth's generosity made me giddy. But then I saw the faces of the people who were eating: On a worn corduroy couch, Shell and Never-Never, and Silverfox, again together with Boomer. They were all staying the night. I breathed, I said hi.

No one acknowledged me. Everyone was cold, and I felt uncomfortable and unwanted. I walked back down the wood stairs, into the cooling evening.

My shoe was desperately broken, but I hiked back the way I'd come, out of Sierra City. Past the post office that held my new shoes, now closed. I left without confronting Never-Never—and without waiting for the post office to reopen so I could mail my letter to my family.

That night I called my mother to ask her to have the running shoes and food forwarded to the next town to the north. I still carried both letters in my knapsack, my shoe was practically disintegrating; everything felt half-finished. I felt unsettled.

I walked without breaks, slept through nights without waking, inhumanly smooth—a small machine—until I reached a highway and caught a quick hitch down into the next blip of civilization, descended, the highway snaking, slashing the rock mountainside.

We glided into a microscopic town in north-central California surrounded by pine woods called Etna.

I hopped out of the car and walked into it.

The pine trees at the town's edge were dark. I was in a shadowed valley in the mountains. The Masonic Hall loomed. The churches loomed. I walked past an overgrown cemetery, past the old Alderbrook Manor, past the Etna city limits sign, crossing into the town of Etna, proper. I followed Main Street down. There was something sinister about this trail-town, although I couldn't name it yet.

The soda fountain/pharmacy was marble with high ceilings and worn wood counters, lovely, airy and vacant. This town was too silent. If I closed my eyes, I could forget where I was. It was strange. Already I missed the unbound beauty of the High Sierra, unredeemed, unneeding of redemption. A cold wind pressed. I should have known that something bad would happen.

I passed the Scott Valley Drug and the library, the museum and the hardware store, found a place called the CCTG—described as a "hostel," though there was neither a check-in nor a fee. It was a complex built within an elementary school that had been repurposed. The place was funded entirely by donations.

Inside the odd young hippie lounged—people about my age, everyone from Germany and Korea, the Netherlands, and Prague. They were convening, planning something. The "trainees" were all young, in their early twenties, and they all wore hemp bracelets and wooden beads. There were dildos everywhere, a big black one prominent on a purple-and-gold-painted bookshelf, a smaller rubber green one on an old fake-wood particle board folding table for education purposes. There were condoms and also lube, left in old cubbies, placed between kids' picture books. The thru-hikers stole these "free" sexual things. The CCTG had no telephone to use, and weirdly it was a cell-service dead spot.

It also had no beds, but hikers were welcome to sleep on the couches, on the floor or on the porch, and the deck had some couches out back, faded and sunken. Everything felt a little bit sticky.

The complex hosted hikers, but it was really a training and education center for volunteers who were going to Africa to distribute birth control and spread the dark word about AIDS.

I dropped my bag on an ancient concave couch and walked to the post office, my shoe-side flapping open with each step, the sole of my foot raw and reddened, burning. I'd walked way farther than I should have wearing these broken shoes, wrecking my left foot, but this was the end of it. I couldn't keep going. If my mother had failed to send the new shoes I needed now, I would be stuck here in Etna.

Entering the post office, I realized I was limping.

I asked the mail clerk if there were any packages for Wild Child. She produced them; they were sealed and tidy, miraculously here for me. Seeing them, my trail name drawn in my mom's familiar handwriting in the same cheap blotted blue ballpoint she'd always used, I felt relieved. My mother's support of me touched me in this eerie town's post office, which felt as removed from Newton as a Norman Rockwell drawing. The smaller of the two boxes contained running shoes. They were brand-new and smelled of clean carpet. The shoes on my feet were blackened with soil and six hundred miles of dirt, my right toe poking a hole through the reinforced silver mesh, entirely exposed. I looked like a little feral hobo-child. My mother had sent the shoes from a running store in pristine suburbia, the same one she'd shopped for me at back in high school. I exhaled deeply. Right there in the little post office, the only patron present, I put on my new shoes and dropped my blackened wrecked ones in the trash.

Before I threw it out and left, I checked the empty shoe box's top-flaps. I saw she'd had it overnighted from Sierra City, just as she'd told me she would, though she could have saved the money and just had it forwarded priority mail, and they'd still have arrived here days before I did. Her rush to help me was unnecessary, but it made me smile. I felt loved.

I slept that night on the rug at the CCTG, surrounded by hikers and also trainees, uneasy. The next day my body was still exhausted, but my feet were beginning to heal. I decided to stay in town just one more night and got a room of my own at Motel Etna.

I had a plan, I had a plan.

I paid for the room with the card my mom had given me, knowing she would understand—that she'd actually want me to get some rest somewhere I felt comfortable and safe. I showered, put on Sublime, then Dylan, sat on the carpet to sort the food and vitamins she'd sent me. The best food of any thru-hiker I knew. She took good care of me. This was her way of showing she supported what I was doing. I could count on her. At last I sat on the bed. I dialed my mother. I was doing something good, finally, I knew it.

She answered quickly. She was very happy and relieved to hear from me. I was calling on my cell phone, not the sat phone, and it occurred to me I'd forgotten to call the night before, from the CCTG's floor, the AIDS education center that was strangely off the grid.

"Did I forget?" I asked her, knowing I had.

"It's okay, sweetheart," she told me, though I was sure she'd waited up, she probably hadn't slept, and I felt guilty.

I sat at the very edge of the bed, my bare feet against the carpet, which was old faded golden. My big toes were swollen. My left foot's left side was a massive blotch of blisters. I felt very close to her, fully and wonderfully loved, but I also felt the risk of wrecking it. I felt nervous to speak. I didn't want to chill our warmth.

I took a big breath, consciously released it. I told her, speaking slowly, that I would like to send a letter out. I told her I had composed it from the forest and that it was for everyone we loved. It told them about my rape. It asked them for their support in the form of donations to RAINN. I would feel better no longer carrying my shameful burden: the secret.

She listened to me in silence without interrupting. Then we were both silent. I waited, shaking. She spoke and told me, flatly, "No."

She said that I could not tell our entire family that. I couldn't ask my uncles and aunts and cousins and grandmothers for money for that. It would kill them to know. If I didn't tell them, she said, she'd donate $1,000 herself: "More than you could possibly raise."

My mother was a tireless public defense attorney who represented abused and neglected children. She financially logistically literally and *completely* supported me—her defiant nineteen-year-old daughter—her baby—on this insane pilgrimage through wilderness. I had believed that her tremendous assistance was meant to show me that she supported me not only in shoes and money, but in her solidarity too. That she still loved me, just as fully.

Sitting on the bed that her money had bought me, in a room filled with the expensive healthy foods and running shoes Mommy had lovingly sent to fuel and carry me, I couldn't reconcile her support of my walk with this awful offer.

She told me to read a legal article she'd written about blame-the-victim mentality, told me she could send it to me if I wanted to understand.

"Are you still there?" she said loudly, after I'd been wordless. "There's a blame-the-victim culture in this country," she repeated. My left foot looked pink and bloated. My shoulders were sore, aching, and I could feel my pulse knock-knocking in my palm. My mom wanted to donate money to help raped girls on the condition that my family—the people I most trusted and most loved—not find out that her own daughter was raped. She was afraid my secret shame would shame our family.

Through the dirt-framed window of my motel bedroom, I saw a little girl scramble up to the top of a mound of rocks. Her face was sun-lit, and church bells bonged the hour. My phone felt hot. I closed it without saying okay.

I couldn't sleep that night, though the bed my mother bought me was comfortable.

In the morning I was ready to leave Etna and disappear into wilderness.

It was hot, a cloudless Sunday morning. I stood outside the empty ice-cream parlor, stuck my thumb out. There was not a car on the road, though this was Main Street, and it was ten o'clock in the morning, a very reasonable time to be driving. I let my arm fall, gave it rest. No point aching for no one.

After a long time of silence, a huge commercial truck screamed down the road, into town—past me. It didn't stop. And then another rattled through, deafeningly loud; minutes later, another. Thirty minutes passed, another thirty, the sun was high now. The ice-cream parlor was open. Three kids with their mom wandered inside, out with huge white and pink glistening scoops dripping.

I got myself one. It was creamy and sweet and cold, just what I wanted, just what I needed here alone in the sun in Etna, California, where no one was picking me up, where there was nobody here for me at all.

Tears dripped into my ice cream; I licked them. I could taste the salt.

An hour passed, then three, the sun was high, hot, I was gleaming with sweat, only about six cars had come through, and no one wanted to pick me up. In the three months I'd been walking this trail, hitching into and out of little towns, I'd never had this much trouble.

But time passed on. It was a Sunday morning; it was an early Sunday afternoon. Etna was a damned town, I decided; it was tiny, terribly backwardly religious. And then it occurred to me, after all those hours in sunlight: it was a Sunday. Almost nobody was driving; they were praying. Etna's residents were filed inside the town's row of white and pale buttercup and brick churches.

I was about to give up, call it quits and finally after four hot hours of standing on the sidewalk of this sad town, being ignored and passed by, begin walking the ten miles up the highway back to the place the PCT crossed Etna Pass myself, when suddenly there was a white speck. It was a Ford pickup truck, and I stuck out my thumb and it slowed and glided to a stop on the street beside me. A man was driving, alone, about thirty, and he was handsome, though his eyes were blocked by shades.

It all happened so quickly. He asked if I was hiking. I'd been waiting four and a half hours, and I was tired of it, maddened by it, hot and dehydrated and feeling terribly slighted, and I told him Yes, he said Get in, and I did, thoughtlessly breaking the single hitching rule I'd made in an effort to keep myself a little safer. For three months it had been my policy never to hitchhike with a single man, only to get into cars with couples and families and, occasionally, groups of friends. But he'd seemed so nice, letting me in, and I had been waiting so long.

As soon as I got in I heard the truck doors click—lock—and he pulled a U-turn and began accelerating away from where I was going, where I wanted to go, the Pacific Crest Trail shockingly receding.

I was scared, frantic; I acted confident. "I'm going up the pass, back to the PCT," I said.

"I'll take you there."

"You will?"

"I will."

I thought: what should I do, what should I do. Should I call him on the fact he'd turned around? He knew he had, so no, I decided. He'd lied to me already. He might be capable of worse things. I shouldn't offend him. I calmly twisted and pointed back the way we'd come and asked him, "Hey? I think the trail's that way?"

He seemed distracted, gazed straight at the road ahead and slowly rhythmically nodded, chin down, chin down, chin down. He said, "Yeah, we're just gonna run a couple errands first." It was a statement; he wasn't asking. We were getting farther and farther away from the trail, and I was scared.

I said, speaking slowly, matching his cadence, that he could let me out and leave me here on the side of the byway, and, after his chores, pick me back up and drive me back the way we'd come, up Etna Pass, back to the PCT.

He removed his sunglasses. He glanced directly at me. "It's okay," he said, "we're just picking up some clean laundry from the Laundromat out this way. It'll take ten minutes."

He was not letting me go.

I studied my captor's face. Dark shades removed, his face unblocked, he was uncommonly handsome, I could see. His hair was thick, chocolate brown and neatly combed, and his eyes were sage-green, squinting, very light. His goatee was trimmed neatly, and he was older than he'd first seemed, middle-thirties maybe, maybe older than that. What he was doing scared me, but he didn't look like a bad man.

But now we were on the highway, coasting in the opposite direction of the way I should be going. I didn't know where we were going, and I didn't know what I should do, or if I should do anything at all.

After ten minutes of silence driving in the car with him, he pulled off the highway and onto a gravel side road, I stiffened, I reminded myself to breathe, and we stopped short. I couldn't move or see clearly, I was so scared.

Then he hopped out. "You can wait here, or come in if you want," he said.

I looked up. I laughed, relieved. We were in the gravel parking lot of a Laundromat. He wasn't lying. He hadn't lied at all.

"I'm running in getting my laundry," he called back and jogged inside.

I was sitting in the truck at a juncture. He had left me alone, the truck doors unlocked, my escape easy. I had the choice: I could wait for him to come back and trust that he would take me back to the trail, or I could get out of his truck here, twice as far from the trail as I'd begun, outside of town, on a gravel road through pine trees, in the woods, literally, and start hitching all over again, though there were even fewer people out here, and in some hours it would be dark.

I thought about it. I was afraid if I got out, he'd see me and get mad.

And he had not lied, it was true. He hadn't lied.

But I was scared of him, he had driven me away without asking, and I shouldn't stay with someone who'd done that.

I sat there. I did something purely irrational. Rather than making a decision, thinking or leaving, I pulled out my cell phone and called my father.

And he picked up. "Hello?" he answered. His voice sounded surprised to hear from me. I realized it was the middle of the day, and they usually didn't hear from me until nighttime.

"Hi Dad," I said. "Just want to say I love you." It came out sounding stilted, though I meant it truly.

He was quiet for some seconds. It was a strange thing to call to say. I imagined it was worrisome to hear. He told me that he loved me, too, but his voice drifted high at the end, and it sounded like a question. Then he asked me, "How's the hike going?"

"Fine," I quickly lied.

He waited while I breathed. He said, "That's good Debby."

Then I said 'bye, and he said 'bye, and I closed my phone, and I wished I'd said something different, I wished I'd said more; I could have hopped out and taken a picture of the white truck's license plate, even if I ran the risk of the man catching me and getting angry. I could have not taken this minute to senselessly call my father as I waited in a stranger's truck for him to come back and to find out if he'd hurt me.

Even then I knew I was in a really bad situation. I wished I were a fighter, but I wasn't; I was paralyzed.

I wished I weren't the same girl who'd been raped.

What I should have done was run.

The man came back with laundry. We started driving down the highway, in the correct direction. I thought maybe I'd been being paranoid. He asked me a few questions about the trail, and I answered them, and everything I said was super interesting to him, and I was wary. He told me about himself, that he was recently divorced. His eyes were watery. He seemed legitimately and earnestly bereft.

He told me that he had built his own lake. He had dug it himself out of the stony ground.

I said, "Wow." All I could think as he was speaking was that, if he touched me at all, all the miles I'd walked, the pain I'd felt, the beauty I'd drunken like milk, like good wine making me happy, the four million steps I'd taken, would all add up to nothing. They'd be stolen. They'd vanish like the teeth children lose when they get hit. Only after the blood was washed away would I see that they were gone.

Then it happened. We crossed out of sleepy Etna. I saw the lot at the top of the pass where the road meets the PCT—and we drove past it. The pass—my trail—was gone, we sped, I had no motion, and then he turned hard, jolted, onto a dirt road that quickly became a snaking gravel road. Dark pine trees smudged. He told me he was going to show me the lake he'd made on his ranch.

My vision blurred, trees blurred, seconds minutes, my hands, body and years. I was back to my new room at college, the smell of dank red clay mud, the smell of rust, back to Grandma's and Grandpa's mint leaves and afternoon thunderstorms braved safely huddled inside the ranch house among old clocks.

The man was talking. I was hollow, elsewhere—hurt: rejected by my mother, bloodied and ruined, wounded and acting out. Entirely worthless, listless, distant and isolated, numb numb numb to the wind, the sun, the wilderness I was entering, the man who was taking me deeper into a forest I didn't ever want to know.

"Okay," I heard my voice saying, my mind waking, not knowing what I was answering, realizing we were parked. "Sorry," I said, "what did you say?"

He repeated that his daughter was inside.

"You have a daughter?" I asked. For a moment I relaxed.

"Sixteen years old."

"Oh wow."

"She's inside the house. You two will hang out."

I looked around. There was a house and also a lake, dark blue and perfectly round like a velvet hole. We were on his land, at his ranch house. He had driven me miles and miles into a forest on a gravel road I hadn't wanted to go down, he had lied to me again, and now this time we were on his property and I couldn't merely just get out, away. I was still sitting in the pickup, it seemed like the safest place left, trembling. But there was no place left to hide there. I climbed down.

I didn't know where to go.

The man led me toward the house.

I thought clearly as I could. I was a girl in this man's woods. Taken. He had told me he had a daughter; she was sixteen. He looked middle-thirties, there was a small chance he was forty; the math was easy. It was biologically possible, but he was a liar. This was his vehicle, his town, his home, I didn't know anything; I felt completely vulnerable—stupid. Weak and exhausted. I had stuck my thumb out on Main Street at ten o'clock in the morning, and now it was almost four in the evening, and I didn't know how to get back, away from him, I was terribly dehydrated, I would be losing light soon.

We were inside. His place was nice, a tidy one-level ranch house with tall windows and sliding glass doors. The wood was real, fresh-cut and painted white. The TV was on in the other room, I could hear it, see its light's color changing, changing on white walls. He told me he was going to go check on his daughter. "Sit," he said, and I did, up on a high kitchen stool.

He went into the room with the television, came out almost immediately. I could see through the door's gap. I could see no girl was in there.

"She's sleeping," he told me, as if I were blind. He sat next to me, up on a high stool, too. He leaned slightly toward me with his shoulder. "But you can ask about her."

He was suggesting the girl he'd taken ask him questions about his almost certainly hypothetical daughter. It was an insane game, but I tried to play. I asked the first thing I thought of: "Where is her mother?"

He looked at my face. He said flatly, "She's dead."

I blinked back at him. My lap was getting wet. Something was dripping. I had to think to realize I was crying.

I walked out his kitchen door, outside. I grabbed my knapsack, which was on his porch. He jogged after me. I faced him squarely and demanded, "Take me back now."

I watched him as he bent to pick a weed that was growing in a thin gap between the porch's wood planks. He controlled what happened. I stood steadily, inhale; now exhale.

"How comfortable are you on the back of a motorcycle?" he asked me.

This was ridiculous. "Not very!" I said. I had never been on the back of a motorcycle, and we were standing within view of his pickup truck.

"I want to take you to the trail," he said, "on my motorcycle."

"Jesus fucking Christ!"

"It will be the greatest experience of your life," he said.

I reached into my pack and held something small in the fist I made. "It's a pocketknife," I said, enunciating each letter. I was asserting myself, I'd snapped out of something; he visibly snapped out of something too. I saw it acutely in his dropping posture: *doubt* in his movement. I said, "The truck works."

And so it did. He shuffled to the truck and got in, and I got in, and we drove wordlessly up the dirt road until it became gravel, which became the highway in the right direction. Finally up at the top of Etna Pass, where the PCT crosses the byway, he slid to a stop.

I hopped out, pack slung over my shoulder, and walked the fuck away.

He called after me, "Hey wait!"

I didn't.

"Wait!" he yelled.

I spun. From a distance I called at him, "What is it."

He yelled that I'd forgotten my cell phone. It was true. I'd left my phone in the truck's cup holder.

The man whose name I'd never asked, who'd never asked my name, came down onto the ground and handed my flip phone back to me. I zipped it into my bag and walked away up to the trailhead, up the dirt trail. Away from him. I hadn't unclenched my fist. My knuckles had gone white. In my fist I had a dead GPS battery. I hadn't ever carried the pocketknife my father long ago gave me for when I was in the woods.

I wouldn't open my hand until his white truck was a black speck in the blue mountain dusk.

I slipped quickly through darkness. A thousand unseen frogs were ribbetting and croaking, a symphony of primal night. I felt like an animal; I ran through the Marble Mountains to my home in the dark woods. The rocks were abrasive pumice, rough and hard like sandpaper, perilous, and yet I felt euphoric, much safer navigating them without light than I had in Etna, in the daylight. I was safe in this world. This was a place for creatures—I felt I had become more of a creature than a girl. I could handle myself in the wild.

The path hit a black pool of water with rocks that were furry with moss, pumice wet and gleaming, breaking the water's surface; I felt the desire to step into it. This was not a pool that a day hiker would swim in. I was braver. I submerged myself, waded—the dark water was fairly shallow, warm even at dusk. The water gleamed like an eye, cradling the moon.

From the black pool I looked up to the starry sky, a million blinking specks. For all my life, I had been passive when faced with dangers. I was stunned as I swam to find that I had, for the first time in my history, asserted myself and been truly heard—respected. It felt monumental, I was buzzing with adrenaline. It was as if I'd become someone else entirely.

I had escaped a kidnapper. It finally felt real. My body unclenched tension in the balmy pool.

I was proud of the strength I'd found. *I* was the one who asserted he take me back; I caused him to listen. I was no longer a passive Doll Girl, trapped. *This* was me *learning* I could trust my voice—I'd used it, and it finally worked! I was triumphant. This escape showed me: I *had* grown, and grown vividly.

I hadn't asserted myself with Junior the way I asserted myself with that kidnapper.

In glinting water I replayed the most fateful moment of the kidnapping, where the way things almost went had sharply turned: it was the moment I had told him, "The truck works." My tone had shifted, I'd felt it happen; he had felt it, too. And in that moment, our positions flipped; he had become obedient to me.

I saw now that bad men existed who would take advantage of any weakness and insecurity they found when violating a victim. I saw it was not my fault; I did not choose to be raped or kidnapped. But now I was learning how to protect myself from predators, to trust my No and my instinct and my strength. I was learning I was not to blame, I couldn't prevent men from trying to hurt me, but I could definitely fight back. And sometimes fighting back worked.

The woods were alive—frogs humming, my cells ringing—I stuck my tongue out and felt the power of adrenaline. I was so much more powerful than anyone knew. I was an animal learning to fight back, instinctively, fiercely. I was a brave girl. I was a fit fox.

I realized that the most empowering important thing was actually simply taking care of myself. It felt wonderful to protect myself—to feel growing. To feel how I *had* changed.

In the black pool, black night, black forest an inky spill enveloping my small brave wading body—a spot of light—I finally cried.

I would not be a passive girl.

I traveled five or six miles, walking then running until I disappeared in night.

That night when I pitched my tent in dark chilled air, I didn't put the rainfly on; I was too thoroughly exhausted. I just slept under the mesh and blinking stars, alone again. In the middle of the night it began to rain, and instead of getting out of the tent and clipping the fly on to shelter myself, I only softly smiled and slipped back into sleep, dreamed deeply through it.

Where the trail ended, I wouldn't still be a helpless doll girl. I wasn't trapped within her limitations.

High in the Marble Mountains; I was only beginning.

The rain was euphoric for me.

I awakened in the night shivering; rainfall had stopped. The sky cleared and stars gleamed through thin mist like buttery stains of light diffused by water, it was beautiful, and I decided I'd never let myself be manipulated into danger ever again.

My walk along the PCT had led me to the place where I could finally see that it was my responsibility to trust myself enough to fight back against dangers I could clearly see. To love myself enough to know I didn't deserve harm, and to stop blaming myself for it.

I could see the man with the white truck was dangerous.

I needed only to allow myself to know what I already knew.

I was able to pitch a tent and carry a backpack twenty-five miles a day through mountains—I'd mastered a thousand amazing physical feats—physically I'd become undeniably confident and capable—but physical weakness had never been the problem that I had. My true problem had been passivity, the lifelong-conditioned submission that became my nature.

Solvitur ambulando, "it is solved by walking"; the Latin proverb only seemed half-true. I could walk the height of a country, summit a hundred mountains, cross rivers and borders, and none of it would fix anything real. It doesn't matter where you're going. Canada. Colorado College's green campus. Around Newton Centre. Hiking the PCT was merely a pause button. The trail wasn't a destination. It was no answer. Walking in solitude fixes nothing, but it leads you to the place where you can identify the malady—see the wound's true form and nature—and then discern the proper medicine.

My malady was submission.

The symptom: my compliance.

The antidote was loud clear boundaries.

It took me almost two thousand miles in the woods to see I had to do some hard work that wasn't simply walking—that I needed to begin respecting my own body's boundaries. I had to draw clear lines. Ones that were sound in my mind and therefore impermeable, and would always, no matter where I walked, protect me.

Moving forward, I wanted rules.

First—when I felt unsafe I'd leave, immediately. The first time, not the tenth time. Not after a hundred red flags smacked in wind violently, clear as trail signs pointing the way to SNAKES. Not after I'd been bitten—the violation. If I wasn't interested, I would reject the man blatantly.

Eighty-five percent of the people who hike the Pacific Crest Trail are male; I'd always known this. I was surrounded by stranger-men. I had believed that immersion in a wilderness of men would heal me. Passively and completely. That I needed only to show up—their omnipresence would desensitize me and cure me of fear. But I saw now it didn't work that way.

It worked only one way. If I could mark clearly, convincingly and consistently what was good for me and also what was bad—if I could say yes and also no, as if it were the law—it would become my law.

It finally had to.

I understood that it wouldn't be easy, it would be very hard; I'd need to resist the habit I had developed long ago—with conviction. I'd have to be impolite, an inconvenience, and sometimes awkward. But if I could commit, all that discomfort would add up to zap predatory threats like a Taser gun. I'd stun them. They'd bow to me. I'd let my no echo against the mountains.

And better to feel bad for a moment saying no—and stop it—than to get harmed.

I would take better care.

The small word, *no*. I'd see its deity.

Second—I'd take much better care of myself.

There were simple things I could do. I could start with my poor feet. These little two feet carried me each day for miles and miles, steady and flexed, tired and aching from constant daily pounding, bruised scratched and sometimes rubbed red raw, my weight pressing and pressing them. I decided now that each night in my tent I'd massage them. I would knead them with lotion because they always ached, and at the end of thirty-mile days they burned—and it would be luxurious—something I could have done the entire way because I had been carrying sun lotion but had never taken the ten sacred minutes to do for myself. I bent over myself, down into my soaked-through sleeping bag, and cradled my left foot. I felt my foot's pulse against my freezing hand's palm, and exhaled. I was going to mean what I said, to be direct and firm.

I found my Moleskine notebook and on the page behind the pages addressed to Never-Never and my family—two unsent letters—I wrote: *I am the director of my life.*

When I felt strongly I would say it strongly.

I was the director of my life, it was already true, and I would soon lead myself to my dreamed-of destinations.

It was the task of my one thousand miles of solitude.

I woke to sun, to sky so entirely blue it was blinding, half-conscious in a wonderful new dream. In sleep I'd been reading aloud a story I'd written called "A Hiker's Guide to Healing"—it was on newsprint—and kids were listening to me—rows of tiny sitting children. They were on a rough blue-gray carpet cross-legged—the light was cold. It was the Cinder-block Palace's carpet. They were bright-faced on my old motel room's filthy floor.

"I'm done," I'd told them in the dream. "Go outside now." One of them stood. She was little, with pink lips, cute. She squinted at me. She was trying to see the words.

"Go outside now," I repeated, but nobody moved. I looked at the rows of little children sitting, the standing girl, her focused squint and upturned nose. She waved a hand. I pointed at her, asked her, "Yes?"

She straightened and sprouted inches taller. "What actually are you?" she demanded.

I handed her the newsprint, grinning. I had written my story, it was an epiphany. "A writer," I answered.

I can care for myself, I can care for myself, I can care for myself. I can, I wrote in my soggy notebook. It was a new day, a beautiful one, and I was the director of my life, and I would not get raped today or ever again, and I could care for myself, I could take good care, and my hard no would stop men like a brick to the head, like lead-dead done it was the motherfucking law.

I can care for myself, I can care for myself, I can care for myself. I fucking can.

I was promising myself strength.

I had to write it, say it, make the effort and fake it before I actually believed I could *do* it.

I began with the small, constant daily things. Each morning I smeared on the sunscreen I carried, and SPF 15 ChapStick, put a hat on. It was a baby-pink baseball cap that the mobile trail angel Chuck Norris had passed on to me, and I wore it, and for the first time I was protecting myself from getting badly burned.

At each day's end, in the emerald shadow of my nylon tent, I cleaned the dirt out from under my fingernails and then drank water, however much I sensed my body needed. For sixteen hundred miles of walking I had been slightly dehydrated, depriving myself of water in my quiet self-destruction, sometimes waking up in the middle of the night parched, gasping. Finally I conscientiously drank, hydrating myself properly.

I made conscious effort to name my needs and my desires. To carefully listen to and accurately identify what I felt. *Hunger, exhaustion, cold, lower-back ache, thirst.* The ephemeral pangs: wistfulness and loneliness. Rest fixed most things. Sleep was my sweet reward. I treated bedtime as both incentive and sacrament.

If I wanted to go to bed at ten o'clock I did. If I wanted to go to bed at six P.M., I did. I woke at sunrise because the new sun lit my eyes. The sun was my clock; my body my pace-keeper. I started walking when I wanted, kept going until precisely when I wanted to stop.

When I was tired, feeling like stopping but wanting to persist, I'd listen to *Blood on the Tracks*. Dad used to listen to it when he was working out too.

I only hitched into trail-towns and back with families, couples, and other lone women. In the one-light town of Seiad Valley, a tiny unincorporated community of three hundred people living along the wide slow Klamath River just fifteen miles south of the Oregon border, I acquired luxurious Aveeno lotion. That night, camped beside the shimmering Klamath, listening to it lap, Canadian geese cry and crow, I massaged my shins, my quads and aching feet, fulfilling the tiny new goal I'd committed myself to. It felt excellent, an easy and obvious comfort I finally allowed myself. In town I ate healthier, fresh fruit and vegetables and no more Ben & Jerry's, retraining my taste buds, in preparation for life after the trail.

In northern-most California I stepped from pine forest into pine forest. It was beautiful in a gentle repetitive way, a kaleidoscope of dead red pine needles littering the trail, huckleberries the frosted color of summer plums, fields of pocked white pumice stones and clear dark azure lakes: it was virgin.

I still chose to call my mother every night, taking care of her, too.

A week later, at a library in town, I would go online and check the fund-raising Web page I'd set up through RAINN, expecting nothing, and see that she had donated $1,060 to help rape victims.

I also saw, written in bold-faced gray: the school where I'd been raped, where I'd been silenced, had donated $752.00 to RAINN in my honor. After all—they'd believed in my integrity.

I was crossing a grassy clearing in the trees, nearing the Oregon border, when I saw another hiker. I felt lonesome, and so when he grinned, flapped a hand manically and jogged to me, I took his eagerness as friendly, not threatening.

But then he perfectly wrecked it. He called me "cutie" and almost immediately called me "frisky." He was going to walk with me, and said that then that night we could "hang out." "You're liking having a fun time," this strange man told me.

I sensed he was feeling for my boundary, making a bold advance. I was stunned. I couldn't imagine I had done something to suggest that I might ever sleep with him. I hadn't had sex with anyone on this trail but Icecap, and only once. I'd believed that maybe if I ignored them, never proved them, the rumors would dissipate. They wouldn't. Instead they would spread like ink in cold water, curling, enwrapping me—staining me. It was impossible for me not to feel the power of their mark, its endurance. I couldn't clear it. I felt my value obscured by it. Men who saw it couldn't see me.

I looked at him in his dark blue eyes and told him flatly that I was a virgin, and that he was scaring me, confusing me.

I passed him without another word. He let me go, his eyes averted.

I'd lied to him, wishing it were true.

I walked alone, sometimes seeing lumbering strangers, heavy weekend campers, sometimes hiking days with myself purely.

About two weeks after I'd escaped the man with the truck, a guy who had heard rumors about me propositioned me. I said no to him immediately, urgently.

I was hiking swiftly, three months into a very long walk, taking great care of my strong body, obliterating oppressive compliance and, with it, my longstanding dread of men. Alone I'd walked one thousand miles—Upper Crabtree Meadow to this northwoods pine forest, the trees' bark the dark bluish gray shade of sharks, dry stringy lime green moss frilling them like wild mold. I was strong. I was fit and independent—able to care for myself, to handle myself. I felt powerful and elated: empowered. Truly *happy*. I was at last in control, and—just like that—hiking this trail had actually become fun.

Feeling the presence of my own power was *fun*.

Though I did keep one crutch. Rather than stating flatly, "I'm not interested," I sometimes answered by lying, telling them I was a virgin. I shielded myself with the word. In the moment of threat, I felt that the most important thing was to stop the man, and saying I was a virgin was a quick means to that end. *Virgin* had become the word to tell them: You Are Wrong About Me. I thought the lie was harmless. I hated that I lied, but felt I had no better way to regain control.

I'd feared that simply saying no without also refuting the rumors would leave some men bitter; they'd grow hateful and harm me later, as Never-Never had—or they'd persist. I feared men wouldn't respect my no alone. I had spent a lifetime having my no ignored.

It was a lie born from the fear that I was inaudible.

One by one I told each of the male hikers no. Just as I'd told Icecap. One by one they listened to me and backed off.

It felt amazing to make visible my boundaries.

The rumors dissipated, then changed. Eventually I turned down enough men that I became the girl who turned down men.

CHAPTER 16

THE DIRECTOR OF MY LIFE

I felt something hurting on the cheek of my behind, discovered a tiny scab. It was dime size, rippled and rough. I was in northern-most California, finally just miles from crossing the wooded border. It was only a tiny little raised bump. I decided it was insignificant; I should ignore it. For the next twelve hours, I did.

But the sore spread; slowly at first, then faster. I felt weak, but then I rationalized that I always kind of felt weak. But soon it was fist size. Then the raised area was palm size, wet with clear pus, rapidly growing. A doctor I met beside the trail, sitting around a midday campfire with his buddies, listened as I described it—I wasn't going to expose my rear to him—and told me that I'd developed a staph infection, "Nothing urgent." The doctor was out for a week in the woods; how lucky, I thought. It was no big deal, now I knew.

But I didn't allow myself to consider he might be wrong, that the rough raised skin was the first mark of something far more harmful, the beginnings of an infection that can grow fatal. I had walked 1,700 miles, and now all I felt was weak. The wound was devastatingly painful, becoming impossible to ignore—it wasn't healing. It was growing. It began to feel undeniably urgent; soon even the slightest contact with my shorts shot a searing pain through my entire body. I couldn't sit. And still it grew.

I couldn't keep on going this way. I was nearly to Oregon, just miles from crossing, but I couldn't manage to step another step.

I called my mother. She told me through the sat phone, "You need to come home." She was crying, her hysteria annoyed me. Her sobs were rhythmic.

The last place I wanted to go was her home. I brushed my hand over the seat of my spandex, and winced. The infection was tender and shockingly hot. It seemed to produce its own heat. "It's getting a little better, I think," I lied then hung up, cutting her shrill yelling short.

It wasn't getting better, though. Discoloration was spreading like blood on water, seeping deeper, red flesh tender and soft as fruit rot, the dried blisters flaking, falling away. That night I had to sleep on my stomach or my left side, atop instead of inside my sleeping bag, despite night's cold, as pressure on—any contact with—the blistered splotch was piercing. I shivered through my half-sleep, wishing I could wrap myself up in my fluffy sleeping bag, which lay beside me, warm, beckoning, taunting, useless. At last, shaking with cold, frost crystals glittering on my tent's arched roof, I tried to drape it over myself; it grazed my behind. My heart rate shot up, the pain a shock. I gasped. The spot burned as if pressed onto blue stove flames.

The next morning I deconstructed my tent, screaming out as my cotton shorts brushed against the rash, in so much pain, breathing deeply, swallowing. I continued along the trail north, stepping slowly, my soft pink cotton shorts suddenly hell to wear, swooshing against me, abrading the rash, dust puffing up, stinging it, each step excruciating. When I came to a junction with a side-trail marked with a sign, Trailhead → 2 Miles, I followed it, not caring where it went. I really could not go on.

I limped two dusty, rocky miles downhill to a gravel trailhead parking lot, angling myself to minimize right-tush-cheek-shorts contact, at times lifting my cotton shorts with my fingers, exposing the rash and my white rear to cool fresh wind. At the lot I waited, standing then lying on my stomach on my sleeping pad.

At last a jovial lady day-hiker returned to her van and gave me a ride to an urgent care clinic in Yreka. I thanked her. I could hardly see her, squatting in her car, hovering, my thighs and quads burning, shaking, then sitting, blinded by the pain. The clinic's doctor flicked off the lights and examined my behind under a blacklight, told me, "Terrible fluid." He gave me an antifungal ointment to rub onto the hot raised area, capsule antibiotics to swallow three times daily—I'd have to, I *would*.

I took a hitch with a young woman out toward Ashland, Oregon, the next town through which the trail would pass, hoping to rest while my hot rash got better. I'd stayed in Ashland nearly a year ago, at the end of my one-thousand-mile walk before beginning college.

The highway was narrow and without traffic, a green sign with black pine trees said in capital white letters, OREGON WELCOMES YOU. I felt a pang of regret. After all those months of approaching, all those miles dreaming, I crossed the Oregon border in a car on a highway and not on foot in the woods; I missed the crossing. I parted my lips to tell the driver, but I knew it was a tragedy she wouldn't really understand.

In Ashland I found the Shakespeare Youth Hostel and got a bunk and took the pills and used the ointment, which was glassy yellow like my pus and burned hot as red-lit steel. I didn't swallow the pills; instead I would open the translucent teal capsules and pour their grainy contents into my old Gatorade water bottle, shake it up. The flecks would float, not dissolving. I'd drink them. Each time, three times a day, the taste would make me gag. I felt a shame the source of which I could not place.

I willed this sickness to be just some weird sort of rash I could deal with without going home. I was walking to escape my rape, yes, but also my child-self. To leave the trail and return to my mother was to abandon the development of the able woman I was slowly becoming. In wilderness, I had become fit. I was overcoming the bonds of my mother, enduring situations in which my freshman-self would have collapsed. I feared that if I went home my mother might not let me return to the trail.

I tried to imagine *home*—the Newton house. My sight divided, blurred as if seen through ancient crystals strung up, tinkling and brittle, patterning whitewashed fences in an old washed-out dream from years ago, locked in the past. My father was a faint cloud in my vision.

I wondered what it would be like to see him now. My dad had been so helpful to me on the trail—I felt fortunate and grateful—I thought I should be excited to be with him again. I should want to. But I didn't, there was something wrong. Despite his support, his warmth and guidance and love, I didn't want to see him in person. We had never spoken of my rape; I'd never directly told him it had even happened. I thought my mother must have told him—at one point I'd asked her not to, but they had a very honest relationship. Yet he hadn't said anything about it to me at all. He hadn't ever asked me about it, or how I was feeling. I really wished he had. I wished he'd immediately called me after my rape, desperate to tell me, "Mom told me, honey I'm sorry." He didn't say, "I love you and I'm here."

Either it made him so uncomfortable that he could say nothing about it—or she really had never told him. I realized: I really wasn't positive that he knew that it had even happened. Both possibilities left me desolate. One meant he, my father, would rather leave me unsupported, not knowing what he thought of me now; the other: my mom was erasing my story—within our own family.

I didn't know if my mom had told him about the unsent letter, or how he felt about my desire to speak out.

The thought of seeing my father made me panicky—I just wanted to get better and stay removed.

The pills made me allergic to the sun; my skin blistered. I couldn't go outside. I took scalding showers, only hot water no cold. I held my butt-rash under them, directly in the burning spray. It was so painful my heart revved wildly, but then it felt wonderful, like I was washing everything terrible out, purging myself of a germ I had long carried.

In the hot water I ran my hand over and over the area. It was rough, raised like burn blisters, the dead bubbles of skin flaking off, my skin falling away. It looked like it should hurt but it felt wonderful.

I wrapped myself in a soft white towel and walked to my cot in the girls' bunk room, lay on my stomach, the only girl in the room at this midday hour. I lay, not moving, waterlogged and hurting, until the growing mark on me again began to burn. I walked back to the shower, through the public hall in the old house-hostel, wrapped only in my towel, not caring, turned on the hot, no cold. I showered again, held my mark under the burning steaming water. Back to my cot. Fingers dish-panned. To the shower again. As the sky dimmed, through night's darkness, as first light broke in blue dusk I showered hourly. Shower to bunk, shower to a cot that turned out to be some other girl's—I was in desperate patterns those first smudged days off the PCT, in blinding pain, hoping I could somehow break out and save myself.

I kept on paying eighteen dollars for another day and another day at the hostel, hoping for the antibiotics to kick in. They never did.

For five days and five nights I stayed in Ashland's youth hostel. Its walls and steps were painted with lines from Shakespeare poems and plays. I took a picture of the line *Journeys end in lovers meeting,* and felt gloomy. I feared my journey might be ending. I felt longing, saw no lover, wished for one. The pus-thing had grown to the size of my open hand.

I felt dread, called my mother, told her the truth.

She said, "Debby! My God." I waited as she cried, looking at the eggshell-yellow wall, the lines from Shakespeare plays I'd read and seen. The wall blurred as she told me, "Daddy's ordering your ticket. You fly from Medford, Oregon, home, direct."

I blinked; my vision cleared. The line remained. *Journeys end in lovers meeting.* Journeys end in rear-end rashes. Journeys end in Mommy's helping. Journeys end, and I have reached nowhere.

I pressed my palm firm against the rash and flushed with the pain. I said, "Thanks, Mom. I'm coming home."

When I printed my one-way ticket home at the hostel's old common-room computer, I saw that my seat cost my parents hundreds of dollars. She had found for me the soonest flight out. I felt curled rage like rising smoke in my throat. I had tried to minimize what was wrong with me, she maximized it. To her I was poised on the brink of dying, and she would save me.

I wished I could ditch, stay a final night at the Shakespeare hostel, get better on my own, but of course I couldn't. I couldn't ignore my spreading sickness anymore.

I hitchhiked from Ashland to the airport in Medford with two super-new-age religious boys who tried to convince me the evidence of God was in fire. I had no idea what they were talking about. But they bought me pizza. On the silent roads, toward home, I let myself remember the drive out of Ashland last summer, leaving the trail behind me to fly to college after having walked here all the way from Mount Whitney. I realized: The one thousand miles I'd just walked alone had been the exact same miles I'd walked alone last summer. Without thinking about what I was doing, I'd left Icecap at the exact point where I began walking when I was eighteen, and now I was being forced to end at the exact same point at which I'd had to then. It was the same one thousand miles of solitude.

The sign for Medford's airport reappeared, I felt my miles of solitude receding. I felt panic; what if this disease meant I wouldn't ever finish? My mother might dissuade me. I *had* to return. I couldn't let my mother derail my desire again this year.

At the Medford airport, a tiny flat sad lot, my plane to Boston sat, parked and waiting, and the fire-boys left me.

At Logan International Airport my mother embraced me, held me, kissed me and drove me straight from Boston to our verdant suburbia, to my childhood, home. I hadn't seen her in three months. All she could say was how much she'd missed me, how relieved she was to get to see me, how thin I looked—how good. We slipped together into the modest old Colonial, a traditional white house, and there was not much light inside, the plain white vinyl blinds were drawn, it was claustrophobic. I felt suffocated by the dim smallness, the familiar smell of the plants and cherry-stained wood. I felt ten years old. In her home office, the walls were taped floor to ceiling with the faces of baby-me. Bigger baby me. Through middle school I paced this office as I dictated to her my papers, and didn't learn to type myself, even though I wished to be a writer.

Dad was still at work. Mom demanded to see the infection. I climbed upstairs to the bedroom of my teen years, my brother's before it was mine, with baby blue walls and framed watercolor paintings I'd made as a child. My curtains just the same, lavender linen, the little pastel ballerinas dancing. My sheets, comforter, and oval throw rug matching them. The only incongruous thing in the room was a big inflated photo-collage of Jacob playing professional baseball, the central image him caught jumping high above the field's checker-mowed grass, reaching to catch the ball. It was dusk but he was lit. His baseball card was taped to the wall beside it. I pulled down my pants in front of my mother.

She cried out. "My God, my God. Sweetheart! We need to go to the emergency room."

I groaned at her. "Can't we just go to the doctor in the morning?"

"Come, we have to *go*. They close at five," she said.

I said, "Mom. No." I pushed her out of my room and slammed the door. I went to sleep.

The next morning my mother drove me to my pediatrician, Dr. Greenspan, who'd been my doctor since I was born. He was still my only doctor. My mom insisted he'd be better for me than an adult internist, as he knew my history. My history, I had argued, was nothing. But she insisted—"he already knows your low iron levels"—and finally I complied. I followed her into the colorful office's waiting area. My face was hot with shame. My mother told the receptionist, "Hi. My daughter has an emergency. Deborah Parker." It was jarring to be yanked so suddenly back into Debby. It felt foreign to me now, no longer the correct word for who I was. It was a name tied to the fragility my mother imposed. I slipped away from the check-in desk, to the bathroom, humiliated. There were no walk-ins, I knew. I felt I should disappear.

Through the waiting room bathroom's blond wood door, I could still hear them, the receptionist saying, "You need an appointment," my mother, frantic, yelling to a nurse, "Bring out a doctor." I stood in the children's bathroom before a mirror so low it cut off at my chest. It reflected sun-blistered arms. I had to hunch over to see my face. I was still wearing my prescription sunglasses.

The receptionist's muted voice, "She's nineteen. She doesn't have an internist?"

Mom much louder, yelling and crying.

"Where is she?" A man's voice. It was Dr. Greenspan.

Mommy rapping on the bathroom door, eager, me ducking out, face flushed, wanting to dissipate into the bar of silver light slashing through the window, spotlighting a blue train on the yellow rug, dust spinning in it. Mom came into the office with us.

I said, " 'Bye." I couldn't believe her. "You can go."

She ignored me, sat and put her huge purse down on the checkered linoleum floor, pale blue and green. The childish, cheery colors made me dizzy. "I need to stay to hear what's wrong," she told me.

I felt faint and angry. I had been without her and okay through desert and snow. Now that I finally was really ill, it was her chance to be my savior. I stared directly at her.

At last Dr. Greenspan spoke. "Debby's an adult." He opened the door she'd closed. "She can tell you what I say." I knew he knew how overbearing she could be, all the times she'd taken me to him when I was a kid and she used to try to convince me that I was sick. This was the office where I'd taken forty-one negative strep tests.

At last my mother walked out the open door, but left her big black leather purse. It sat on a chair beside us as he handed me an examination gown. Then he left, too. I put on the paper dress that felt more like wearing a tissue. I lay down on my stomach. I'd been sleeping on my stomach for weeks, any contact burned me.

I exposed my backside to Dr. Greenspan. He'd been my pediatrician since I was born, had always been smart and kind. But now he was uncomfortable. I was uncomfortable. I had a woman's body. Together we had just kicked my mother out into a waiting room of two-year-olds. Neither of us spoke. He put on latex gloves.

I imagined what he must have been thinking: Walking from Mexico to Canada, insane, feral girl. Crazy mother, bringing her adult daughter to come see her baby doctor.

"Oh God," he muttered. He was leaning in toward my behind, the paper dress crinkling, examining the pink raised gleaming surface, it was raw, flaking away. I was emaciated, so tired, all my ribs visible.

He pulled back and tossed his gloves and scrubbed his hands. "You got here just in time," he said. He told me the rash was MRSA, a flesh-eating bacteria, the wrestlers' disease, they call it, and if it had spread inside an orifice of my body it could have become systemic— and fatal.

"Have you recently had close contact, sweat-on-sweat, with a lot of people?" Dr. Greenspan asked slowly and carefully. "Or intercourse with strangers?"

"I haven't touched anyone in a thousand miles," I told him.

It seemed impossible that after one thousand miles of walking strong, alone, I had contracted the wrestlers' disease. The brutal bacterium spread when an infected person's sweat permeates your pores. It was filthy, and how ironic: most infected people pick up the aggressive bacterium in jail.

Dr. Greenspan told me he was going to put me on a new antibiotic, "Something strong."

"Is it a pill?" I asked.

He nodded.

I looked up at him. "I don't—because," I said. I stopped and gulped. My mouth was very dry. I knew he wouldn't understand my trepidation; he'd think I was a baby. He looked at me blankly. "I have never actually swallowed a pill," I finally said.

I had always cracked open the capsules, put them in water and drunk them. My anatomy was normal, but my psychology made it impossible to swallow even a Tic Tac. Dr. Greenspan had to Google and finally told me I could chew them. That would be fine. I felt shamefully humiliated, like a loser who had made no progress at nineteen, at my pediatrician, needing my mommy, still not able to even take a pill normally.

MRSA can go away and then return. If it becomes systemic, the way to halt its growth is to go on a crazy cocktail of antibiotics that basically kill everything else inside you. Once symptoms were at last gone, Dr. Greenspan explained, the disease would continue living, dormant, on the inside of my nose.

The antibiotic the doctor in Yreka had put me on was useless against the disease. MRSA was resistant to it. MRSA was resistant to most antibiotics, I would soon learn.

Dr. Greenspan and my mother only agreed on one thing: that I should not under any circumstances return to the PCT.

"Your hike is over," Mom said. She looked thrilled.

"I'm going back," I told her.

"You shouldn't go back," Dr. Greenspan said.

We went to the Cheesecake Factory in the Atrium Mall as a family. My dad was coming straight from work to meet us there—it would be the first time I'd see him since he'd left me at the dusty border. There I'd been so freshly hurting, 1,700 miles ago, a state ago, the last time he'd hugged me. I hoped that in the months since, in his mind, that road trip with his muted chubby daughter had faded from his vision. I hoped I wasn't locked in that image of me, weak—returned. I was nervous. I imagined he would be excited, curious, warm—at least at first.

My brother Robert and his wife, Jenny, asked me question upon question about the trail while we waited; they were excited. My little two-year-old nephew, Tom, leaned into me, curious, too. For the first time in my life, I felt like an authority. I loved it. My dad arrived, we hugged; he held me closely until I released him.

I felt wonderfully loved—but I was tense. I felt my father potently. He sat quietly across from me, his eyes evasive. I didn't know how he was feeling, or if he was feeling anything about me. I didn't want to have to ask to know. In the mountains he seemed to support me. Remotely helping me navigate snow, he was excellent, but together, feeling nothing from him, we were farther away. I longed for him to reveal his amazement at me: his daughter had come so far, she was strong and impressive, independent—she was blossoming. I craved these words.

Instead, he sat quiet and avoided looking at me. Our time together was thick with unsaid things.

My second night back home, I placed myself in the kitchen, in an old wooden chair at the wooden table, to wait for him to get home from work. The door creaked; I hopped up. "Dad." We hadn't even spoken about the rape or how I was dealing with it.

He said, "Hello." Then he went upstairs. He hadn't even looked at me, his indifference still hurt.

I went out for a walk. Yellow streetlamps cast stunted black shadows across suburban sidewalks. It was last light in Newton—the Oregon forest was shimmering in my mind, dusted with a powder of fresh snow, the air sapphire and cold. I felt expelled from Utopia. I had my earphones in, listening hard. I'd heard each song a thousand times, a forever times, through my life, when I was in Mom's womb, forever ago. I knew them by heart, every word, "You're a Big Girl Now," "Idiot Wind," playing me. How he let me off at the Mexican border and let me go, *I kissed goodbye the howling beast on the borderline which separated you from me—*

You'll never know the hurt I suffered nor the pain I rise above / And I'll never know the same about you, your holiness or your kind of love, and how I wouldn't.

The two thousand miles I'd walked did not impress him. Nothing I could ever do would be impressive to him. He'd never love me like he loved Jacob. There was nothing I could do to make him. There was nothing I could do, nothing grander, *And it makes me feel so sorry.* Idiot. Idiot wind. All this walking, all these years, and he still was not impressed, and I still felt rejected. I was hungry for his love. I was dying for it.

I imagined actually seducing a man—any man—how I could get him to take me to L.A., to anywhere, he'd want me so terribly. Tattoo Al—he had been intrigued, impressed by me. If he were here in Newton, with me now, I imagined I'd do anything with him—and he would want me terribly, he'd want my *love*.

Debby has bad judgment, my mother's words returned to me.

I wanted attention, to be seen—to be heard.

In those days, back home, I didn't see any of my friends in Newton, not once. There was no one, though it was the summer after our freshman year of college. No one knew I was back and I didn't try to contact anyone. I didn't feel like I belonged, a sun-blistered infected dropout, disgusting; didn't want to be seen. My best friend Elle still lived in the area, but she'd begun drinking heavily and had stopped talking to me. I knew she'd been raped, too, also eighteen.

Alone in my room, I lay for hours snug beneath clean sheets, melting into them. I felt how clean the comforter was, the pastel pillow case—my mom had made my bed, as she always had, and it felt heavenly now.

I explored my room. My dresser was filled with sweatpants and loose basketball pants my mother bought me at Modell's on sale, Sears bras, huge unopened packages of basic clothing, the same thing in multiple colors, blocks of white underwear and socks from Costco. I had never sought out clothing I might feel pretty in, just always wore what she brought me.

I felt a chill, cold in my body, standing in the discomfort of having to prove myself to parents who still didn't see me as a person, but rather forever as a child.

I looked at myself in the mirror I'd had when I was a child.

I was wearing a hideous powder blue pair of basketball pants with a metallic sheen, metal snap buttons along the side, though the metallic sheen embarrassed me, and I'd never played basketball. One or several of the buttons would sometimes unsnap unexpectedly, humiliating me.

I was angry at my mother. It was the truth. *I was angry at my mom.* For treating me like an idiot. For continually putting me in the position of defending my competence. For insulting my intelligence, my autonomous self and happiness. For making me feel I needed her or I wouldn't make it to school, I wouldn't make it without her helping me. For constantly creating and reinforcing the idea in my young mind that I was unable, that there was something wrong with me, that I was unwell and needed her to nurture me or I wouldn't be okay.

I was angry at my mother, yes!—and suddenly everything was clearer. I could see now for the first time that the importance of this walk wasn't only to help me move past my rape. I had wanted to hike the PCT before college, before I'd ever encountered Junior Mason. This walk was a reaction to a lifetime of having had all my needs and decisions preemptively accounted for by my mother. She'd taken care of me in all the ways my body needed, but the devastation of my rape had made me feel the weight of the essential way she had neglected me: she hadn't nurtured the potential of my strong and healthy *independence.*

It was known in our family that when she was forty-one and five months pregnant, my mother had suffered a miscarriage. The dead baby was a girl. She hadn't planned on getting pregnant again, but in her loss she found she desperately wanted a daughter. She had to have me.

She tried and tried and she turned forty-three and I was born. I was not a mistake. Kids at school would say I was an accident— they knew; they were sure—my mommy was too old. I would ask Mommy and she would say, no, "No! I tried and tried to have you," she would say. She fought for me. She wanted me. I was her success. I was her doll girl, to be protected at all costs.

Absolutely devout in her complete care of my body, she had only taught me to be weak and voiceless.

But I had unlearned that lesson. Our enmeshment no longer felt to me like proof of love. I was no longer willing to permit this silencing. Helplessness didn't have to be my identity, I wasn't condemned to it. I was willing—able—to change. Our enmeshment had been enabled by my belief that I needed her to help me, to take care of things for me—and to save me—but, back in the home where I'd learned this helplessness, I found I no longer felt that I was trapped in it.

I understood why I walked across deserts with rattlesnakes and very little water, climbed the slopes of snowy mountains and walked through soundless days in trees for hundreds of miles. I was dependent on my mom, I needed to become more independent. I had survived a thousand miles without Icecap, with no mother, mostly by my own strength and persistence, on my own. I had to show myself as strong and independent and capable of making decisions for myself, surviving. That was the task of my walk, most essentially.

I was ravenous, constantly eating. Mom cooked throughout the day: lasagna, brisket, stuffed cabbage, chicken and rice with sautéed onions in tomato-ketchup sauce. All the dishes she had made for me when I was a child. I ate it all.

My MRSA continued to produce strange heat, but the pain subsided. Soon I could sleep in any position. I was still allergic to the sun, wore long sleeves all the time. If I went outside without cover, I would get blisters all over my body. I pulled down my pants every day to show my mother that my infection was getting smaller all the time. Soon I would be able to leave again.

Mom and I fought as we took walks. "Please don't go back," she told me over and over. I ignored her. I was adamant in a way I would never have been before I started my hike.

Dad was home, but he was working; he was always working. He might as well have been in California. I still hadn't been able to do anything to tell him about Junior—I couldn't. I wanted to, my journal said *that man is NOTHING and this is your father,* I thought I *needed to* and I knew I was right, it was obvious—but I still couldn't. He didn't ask me anything.

His avoidance maddened me. I wanted him to say that he wished he'd been there for me more, after, and before that, through my childhood. I wished my dad were here for me now.

I felt belittled and reduced by him. I wanted him to feel the awkwardness and my frustration. I became cold. I was with him the way he was with me: aloof. No "I love you, I love you." I wanted my dad to tell me he loved me because he couldn't not tell me, he missed me loved me and thought about me so much. But he came home from work, went up to his home office, to write, and I wouldn't see him. I tried to avoid everyone, too.

On my third day home, I took my nephew, Tom, to the lake. We ran into two boys I'd gone to school with, Dan and Nate, smoking cigarettes. Nate was the guy in high school all the girls had a crush on. He'd sat behind me in tenth-grade Spanish class, and once when I'd worn a tight spaghetti-strap tank top he had flicked my exposed bra strap, and, weirdly, I'd been flattered. I'd twisted around to him and said, "Yeah?" but he hadn't answered. He was looking blankly at his work sheet. He'd never done it again.

Now we met eyes, assessed each other. "Nate, hey."

"Hey," said Nate, taking a drag of his cigarette, exhaling.

Little Tom said, "Smoke." I bent slightly and took his hand, though he hadn't reached for mine. I felt catastrophically out of place, seeing these kids I had never wanted to see again. I realized there was nothing I could say to explain to them exactly what I had been doing with my summer. When Nate asked, all I said was "Backpacking."

"Cool." He nodded and kept smoking.

He was doing the exact same thing he had in high school, but I had changed. I had been doing an incredibly intrepid, brave thing I had to be a bit of a maniac to do because it took so much perseverance. I was seeking something better for myself. I was trying to figure out where in the world I fit. But Nate wouldn't care. All he would care about was that I, the honor roll student he'd known, had dropped out of college. I, the spawn of stable married Harvard lawyers, had come home raped and with no job, no internship, no boyfriend or degree, nothing. Only a dangerous, leaking infection. My failure branded my ass.

I walked home holding Tom's hand, not letting it go even as he tottered across a soccer field where there was nothing that could hurt him.

I wouldn't follow my mother's plan for me. My mother wanted me to stay home in Newton to get better. Only this time, I knew that wasn't the way for me to heal. This summer was my chance to finish what I'd wanted to do before the rape had even happened, before I left my euphoric walk in the woods to begin college because I wasn't trusted to direct my own path. I had listened to her and abandoned my gap-year dream. On the trail once again, I'd found myself alone and regaining my strength, feeling invincible. But this year, it was after my entire world had crashed. I'd felt abandoned by everyone. And only because of this—because of the rape, seeing no one believed in me, needing to prove myself not only to others but more essentially to myself—I finally said what I couldn't say the summer before: *Fuck it. I'm doing what I want, proving I am capable, and walking from Mexico to fucking Canada and try to stop me.* I got to hear my mind without the clutter of what my mom thought of me, of what other people saw me as, of what I *should* be doing with myself.

I would return to walk the whole PCT, as I'd wanted to before college but hadn't trusted my gut enough to really do.

Against my mother and my doctor's wishes, I was going back.

This time, I'd become the director of my life.

Back home my mom was cooking. I told her I was going back to the trail, went online on her desktop and bought my return ticket with a credit card she'd given me for college, that my parents paid. She cried, but she didn't protest. When I'd arrived at the airport she'd seen how I glowed despite my sickness. She had seen how in only just three days home I'd turned sad, depressed, and low. She had me show her my infection one final time, already only a splotch of paler skin on my rear, smooth again. I mooned her right there in the kitchen, a new lasagna baking, its smell of acidic tomato and wet cheese melting. In a way, it was like telling her to kiss my ass. Dylan's "Mississippi" was playing upstairs, but I wasn't staying.

When my father hugged me goodbye I remained limp, not holding him back. He held me tighter, making me sad.

Mom drove me to the airport. "Every night, call me," she said. "It doesn't matter how late." She told me that nights I forgot to, she couldn't sleep. "Just your coordinates and 'I love you.'"

Only after I was airborne did I feel grateful that she'd saved me.

I don't remember having one conversation with my dad in the three days I was home, but looking back at my journal, I see I wrote about him. I scrawled about how I heard him telling my mom that I needed to go back. I was unhappy; he thought the hiking was better for me.

I wonder why he told these things to my mother, nothing to me. I wonder if overhearing his approval encouraged me to finally fly back to the trail. Maybe. Maybe my father's faith in my walk—in me—made me feel strong enough to leave. His actual words, as I wrote them in my notebook, were, "She's an adult now, she can do what she wants. It doesn't mean she's not selfish." He almost understood.

CHAPTER 17

INSIDE FIRE

AUGUST 12

I stepped back onto the trail exactly where I'd stepped off. I was so relieved, but also felt out of shape now. In Ashland and then back home, for nine days total, I'd been mostly sedentary. I feared I was starting all over again, but at the same time I knew the miles I had walked were not erased.

I was still taking the new antibiotic, still allergic to sunlight, again covered up. The mark was faint, a numb ghost of the pain it had been, pale like a birth scar. I was alone again. Tall quiet pines surrounded me. For the first time I felt lonely.

I walked slowly, listened to Dylan's ballads over and over. They never burned out. There was a lyric to explain and predict each impulse I felt. Dylan had felt it first. My father had felt it too, with Dylan, before I was born.

Long before I was born, more than forty years into my father's past, my dad bought land in the woods of central Maine, up near Mount

Katahdin, and was going to build a house and try to live there, off of the land. He'd been the age I was now, young and in love with my mother. When I was small, Mommy would tell me all about it, the house my dad and his friends began to build, the prehistoric old-growth trees rising from boundless moss the color of dark water. Bedtime stories of our forest almost-home my father had imagined for the family he knew he wanted to make.

"Maybe after that we were going to move to Alaska," my mommy once whispered, my night-light glowing faint blue, the ceiling light still on. "He looked at land there, too."

She told me often of my daddy's old wild plans. I was transfixed. I loved to think of it. I was a child. She never told me why it never happened, what woke them from the faraway woodland dream. I remember once I asked her.

"Daddy's a romantic," my mom told me as she turned off the light above me, as if that were an answer.

I walked without stopping. I had no more time to lose. Newton had slowed me enough. Going home had been strange, like a portal back, and there I was, still me. My parents still my parents.

My dad hadn't asked me one question. He had hardly looked at me. I wasn't good enough. I had to be better.

The trees' wide trunks were a blur. I noticed I was running.

"Go quietly, alone; no harm will befall you," I imagine my father once read, though he's forgotten.

But back then my daddy answered "Yes. I can, I will."

The trail was soft beneath my falling feet, cushioned, dead old pine needles over moss. The woods were soundless.

I hated Newton. I tried to feel grateful. I thought about my very best memory of home, me with my dad, playing it out in my head to the old songs again, again. Again, I was five years old and we were watching a black-and-white movie, the living room was dark, he was on the couch with my mom and brother Jacob, who was ten, I was on the floor, drawing, not really understanding the movie, but liking it. It was called *The Red House*, or maybe *Red Barn*. My mom said we needed to pause the movie for a minute so she could make some more popcorn and run to pee; we did; she stood and flicked on the light.

I had been drawing in the dark, lit only by the screen, its dim silver. I could still see. All my colors were very bright. My dad noticed the page. My drawing was of one of our Animal Ancestors, as I called them. The figure was cartoony and pastel blue, with buckteeth, a creature we'd descended from, I'd imagined. A few days before, my dad had told me about evolution, and I'd found it incredible. It astonished me. We hadn't always lived in houses. We had been wildmen. Before that we had been animals.

"Some kind of genius made that," he said. "*You* didn't make *that*."

"I did," I told him, "really." I was grinning. My dad thought my drawing was too good to possibly be made by just a kid, but I had to convince him.

"You didn't! You'd have to be some kind of genius."

I showed him my hands, they were marked by the same Magic Marker colors as in the picture, as evidence. "I am," I said, suddenly confident that I was, knowing I really had made it. But then my mom came back and the lights went off, and the movie again played, to the ending, which I think was on a field of wildflowers, very sunny, silver and white, a sad ending, and I never felt that I'd convinced him. I never got to hear him say, "God! Look, everyone! My daughter is the genius."

The next day I told my mom that I needed poster-board, and she took me to Walgreens, where she bought me a big blank white sheet as tall as I was and a new huge set of Magic Markers that had every color I'd ever wanted, even the half-shades. I was high I was so happy. I couldn't wait to draw. That night as my parents and Jacob sat in the kitchen eating dinner, I sat cross-legged on the living room's wood floor, drawing the Animal Ancestors, the Bunny Rabbit Ancestor, the Beatnik Ancestor, the Rooky Clouds, all the things I believed we'd descended from. I thought I understood something big and ancient, felt swelling pride, filled in and expanded our animal ancestors' line of grinning faces.

When I was done, I gave the huge poster-board drawing to my dad. I explained to him what it was, our animal ancestors, the things we'd evolved from, as he'd taught me, told him "My masterpiece." I was serious. It had been days since the weekend movie and yet the pride I'd felt when he'd said "genius" hadn't dissolved, and now, at last, he would know the genius *was* me.

And he did. He told me it was incredible, wonderful, and that he would teach me about anthropology.

I was passing through a woodland of gray trees the dark color of slate stone, yellowed moss hanging off them like wool; a simple wooden sign was nailed to a pine tree, just two words on it: Oregon/California. I had walked from Mexico to Oregon. I paused for a minute, feeling my quiet power, amazed. I didn't rest, I passed without ceremony into the Oregon woods.

That first night back on the trail, warm in my tent in Oregon, lonely, I studied the *Data Book* to figure out where exactly I'd made it to. I found I'd walked thirty-seven miles without once stopping.

When I called my mother to give her my global place that night, my father picked up. I read him the long decimals, "My latitude is," "longitude," and hung up. I did not tell him that this had been my biggest day. I turned on *Blood on the Tracks* as I fell asleep and heard my dad when I was five, when he was proud his little girl was an artist. When I woke, the music was quiet, my whole week's battery dead. For the next seventy-one miles, I would have to walk in silence.

I walked alone over broad wooded ridges, lonely, singing loudly, the trees all the same, pine and fir, pine and fir. I was trapped in a repetitive storybook scene on a trail to unknown places. Marching, marching north through shadowed woods, persistently blindly seeking my prophesized, long-fated final home, still marching, marching still. The sky was surreal blue, the forest dark and blurred, dappled with yellow light, the scene familiar, from an old faded dream. Green tree, green piney bush, red bark, gray trunks like elephant legs, elephant legs. Buds of yellow light playing on pale dirt trail. I choked on the cool, clean air. I'd fought my mother to get back, yet suddenly now I didn't even want to be here; I wasn't feeling wild thrill any longer. I felt hollow, still as soft dead wood, still walking all these miles.

Yet I wasn't numb, anymore. I wanted things. I felt the absence of a companion. I felt desire. I wanted badly a man's hands on my spine, my neck and cheeks, lifting me, pressing me down. I'd never pictured a man's ridge of knuckles so vividly. I wanted a man who loved me. I was tired of walking alone.

Deep in me, not leaked like black dots on cotton underpants but planted deep inside my chest, I felt a tiny sprouting seed of longing.

Then the trees parted. A lake appeared like a blue light, it was Crater Lake, glowing, two thousand feet below. Amid vast deep green and gray: a shock of turquoise, clearer than the sky and catching the sun, gleaming, blinding.

I followed Crater Lake's high rim, its yellow clay dirt trail, the pine trees' bark brick red, air sweet with sap and soil. I walked too close to the crater's edge, but I was mesmerized; I couldn't turn away, leaned toward the drop.

The water's color seemed unreal, too intense and solid, a Crayola color, one I would have picked to draw with. Misplaced in this subdued reality. I tossed a twig over the rim and watched it fall until I couldn't see it.

Down on the lake, below, a small island rested. Wizard Island, according to my book. It was a forested volcano, shadowed land on Crater Lake's expansive blue. It was the most gorgeous place I'd seen in my whole life. I imagined living down there on the island, building a life at the calm floor of a crater; this would be my island, I would be forever surrounded by vast blue like sky air, would make a wild family here. Tranquil and protected. I thought I saw a building on the island, a wooden cabin—I hoped it was—but maybe it was a mirage I'd conjured, my vision teary, wishful.

I nearly stepped on a hand. It was a man's. He was just off the trail, crouched, handling tiny mirrors, leaning one against a tree's thick root, balancing another on a rock the size of a fist, carefully setting them up so they reflected the sky and the lake water in an intricate kaleidoscoped pattern.

"Sorry," I said. I didn't want to mess him up. "That looks so cool."

He was focused, mumbled, "Thank you." He snapped a photo of his creation, another, cocked his head up and smiled. I was struck by his distinctive face. His eyes were strange, perfectly black, his cheekbones pushed outward, upward. He was handsome. "Come down here," he said to me. "You can see it better."

I squatted on the soil beside him. The woods smelled of pine and sage. The air was cool as fresh water. I looked into the small mirrors, windows of sky, the woods, the bright turquoise water far below, they reflected and fragmented everything. It was mesmerizing.

The man said his name was Mystic.

"Of the Donner Party?" He was one of the hikers who'd followed Warner Springs Monty north, skipping the High Sierra.

"Yes."

I'd met him back at Kennedy Meadows, I remembered. I told him it was cool to see him here. I told him, "Cool project. You're really good." He was amazing. He collected his mirrors, zipped them safely into his knapsack, and we walked north together.

Mystic told me the story of what had become of Warner Springs Monty's Donner Party; at last I heard the truth. Up at Donner Pass the group had found only snowfields, vast and trackless, blue sky, the sun blinding. The mountains were as cold and white as the High Sierra, just as remote and without tracks or hiker-made signs. They'd tried to trudge north, through it, stubborn; Monty led the way, ahead, into snow. But they were without a path or clue. The snow was deep; Old BoJo fell. He broke his foot. Monty told him it was fine, to try to keep going.

Of course BoJo couldn't. Donner Pass was endless snow, impassible, even to hikers in good shape with good maps and two feet. BoJo had hoped to reinvent himself on his walk, to become braver, to gain new confidence and pride, to accomplish something big, and in a snap it was over. He was still only a follower, left with the consequence of his foolish choice, the hurt it caused him. Sprawled on the snow, he'd cried. The six hikers who'd followed Monty nearly froze saving him.

But they'd already skipped, and returning to Kennedy Meadows would be costly and shameful, a logistical mess. Skipping farther north seemed like bypassing everything. They couldn't think where they should go. They didn't belong anywhere, felt plucked from the hiker-pack, far away from it. They'd followed Monty blindly and, arriving at more snow, believing it was impossible to cross, their continuous chain of footsteps was now broken. Feeling discouraged, each of them had to decide the next step from here. They dispersed. Most left the trail, returned to homes with roofs. They abandoned their hikes. Stranded on snow, apart from other hikers, so far off the course they'd planned, tired and broken, they quit.

All of them but Mystic. Mystic had skipped again, back south, then way up to Oregon. This was no longer a thru-hike for him, but he kept on keeping on, regardless. Mystic told me he was the last of the Donner Party members still hiking, and though he regretted missing the High Sierra, its beauty, he seemed happy to continue on and leave that gap behind.

The sun was orange, evening light, our shadows long, the soft earth smelling sweet and rich. Mystic hadn't missed everything. Oregon was beautiful, too. Here he was, walking with me, my pace, and I was happy to be with him. "It's good you kept going," I said. I felt high, floating past dark trees, above the perfect turquoise view. "I'm glad."

I was feeling silly. I announced, "I want to live on Wizard Island." I told him: "Imagine."

He smiled, shook his head no, "Can't." It was a national park, he said, illegal.

We walked without talking, comfortably, side by side, the trail

here atypically wide. It accommodated us both perfectly. The dimming woods were tranquil, the perfect turquoise of the lake now
paler, a mirror to the cotton-candy sky. My father had once fostered
fantasies of the same kind that pulled me now. I felt compassion for
my dad, my writing blood, for his desire for life in a wilderness—a
forgiving compassion—he was human and not only just my father. I
smiled, remembering the father he was when he'd been wonderful to
me. I felt my strong alliance with the man he used to be and wished
he saw how close we were connected.

Daylight faded. We skirted Crater Lake, passed Wizard Island,
my own mad dreams of far-flung woodland refuge.

The woods were soundless, dark now. Perfect turquoise: glassy
black. Mirror to nothing. The sky colorless but for a yellow and pale
pink smudge at the western horizon, becoming fiery red, becoming
coal.

That night in the pines I sat at a fire with Mystic and the guys he now
hiked with. Blackfoot, Buddha, Deep, Einstein, and Ass-Scratcher—
thru-hikers whose names and notes I'd seen. It seemed remarkable that
I didn't know them. After he'd skipped north, Mystic had joined them
and they'd formed a pack—six young male hikers who called themselves the Thirty-Eights. They were exuberant and fit, loudly made
known their ambitious daily mileage aspirations—but they were also
easily distracted, sidetracked by lakes and towns and beer. They had
fun. This was a pack of wild men, but a kind one; I felt at ease with
them. I sat with them around the dying fire; branches glowed, burned
out, charred wood and weightless pallid ashes remained, cold.

My place around the fire had shifted, I could feel it. Somewhere
in the quiet miles between Mexico and this fire pit, the social anxiety
that reached back through my childhood had left me. These were
friends—I'd finally found a tribe in which I effortlessly fit. I felt secure
with them, affection for them—exciting *hope* that I could sustain this
confidence, this was how it would be for me from now on. I was no
longer on the outside.

Mystic captivated me with his stories. He was twenty-nine, a pizza delivery boy in a small town in the real world, though he had aspirations of being a musician and photographer. He lived in Keene, New Hampshire, the same town he'd grown up in. I liked him. He was gregarious and bubbly. But then he said, "I miss Sarah. It's killing me."

So that was why he was so happy. The reason he couldn't stop smiling was Sarah, a girl he met at Crater Lake, right before me. He'd only spent two days with her—she was a firefighter at the national park and had to stay—but he was sure something sweet and enduring would blossom from their brief connection. He was *sure*. And life was fantastic.

Mystic's good humor was infectious; Buddha laughed. Soon I grinned too. And then I laughed because we were all preposterous. We had walked nearly two thousand miles from Mexico, I'd walked thirty-one miles today to keep up with Mystic, and I was dizzy with fatigue. I couldn't stop thinking of Wizard Island. I wondered if that house on it was real.

My vision split. I stared at Mystic, his eyes so dark his pupils looked fully dilated, his firelit eyes floated, hovered by the charred log. He looked at once attentive and vacant. Our eyes were meeting, smiling, completely adjusted to the darkness. "Do you love Sarah?" I heard myself say to him. I didn't know why I'd asked it, it was a crazy question.

He didn't flinch or blink. Our eyes held each other's gently. "I do," he said to me.

Morning broke, pearly light fractured by trees, split into bars. I felt gloomy, as if I'd been drunk the night before and now regretted something shameful I had done. Yet I'd done nothing. Mystic seemed happy, he was wide awake and chatty, packed up before I was ready, hiking away. It occurred to me that in night's dimness we had passed the lake; the trail wouldn't return to it. It was there; gone. The other guys were all already up and gone. "We're camping tonight on Summit Lake's south shore," he called back to me, "we'll see you there!"

"I'll be there," I said, knowing that I would, though Summit Lake was thirty-two miles away. I would make it there somehow.

Then Mystic was gone too. I checked the *Data Book*—I was ninety-four miles from the tiny town of Three Sisters, where I'd re-supply. I broke down my tent, packed quickly, walked the trail the way he'd gone.

I walked an hour, two, three, four, alone. The forest was gentle, flat and wide, and I hiked quickly, wanting badly to catch the Thirty-Eights. I liked them. They stuck together, and I would try to stick with them.

I walked into a fire. Pine needles piled in mounds were ablaze, red and orange, smoking, burning. The pines were burned bare, charred, ebony skeletons of trees, their lifeless branches pointed toward the ground. The smoke was low and blue; the ground was literally on fire, orange-red; the charred trees were scrawny, weedy. I was in pure and complete shock. This burning world seemed fantastical, impossi-ble. To think: I'd walked into a forest fire. I was inside a fire, literally, sweating in its heat, tingling in it, and it also seemed impossible, im-possibly lucky, that the only ground not ablaze was the Pacific Crest Trail. It was soft damp clay.

Maybe I'd die. Maybe I'd burn to ash in wind, or blacken like the pines. Charred skeletons, I'd add one to the count. I didn't feel scared. I didn't think to panic. The trail wasn't burning. I was raw, ripe for loving. I wasn't stopping. I was hot, wanting a man's body pressed against me. Craving thick hands gripping me. I was no longer as-sociating sex with fear or shame. It felt euphoric, feeling this heat of desire for sex with someone not specific again: trusting I'd find a good partner.

Just as I was emerging from the burn, the sun still high and white, the day not half over, I caught up with Mystic. He was wandering as if lost, also emerging.

I watched his body walk. He was tanned and stocky, his step bouncy, happy. Meeting Sarah, he thought he'd won the lottery. His eyes were black like India ink. What was he? He looked a frac-

tion Asian, maybe Native American, his cheekbones high and protruding, sweaty, shining, his eyes dark and warm. He was warm to
everybody.

"What was that fire?" I asked him.

"Cool, yeah?" he said, "It's Sarah's, a prescribed burn." As we
walked out back into refreshing cooler air, Mystic explained that
forest-fire departments set fires they can control to reduce the risk
of catastrophic wildfires, decrease natural forest fires' intensity and
damages. They are cooler fires, lower intensity. This burn we'd left
would last only a day or two.

"Oh," I said.

"This one's Sarah's."

We walked away from the burn until it was only blue smoke.

I walked with Mystic, devouring the stories he told, his glad-manic
attitude, which was infectious. He energized me. He saw beauty in
pure blue lakes, in girls, food, birds, common things. In just walking. Before he stepped onto the Pacific Crest Trail, he had hiked
the entire length of the Appalachian Trail from Georgia to Maine.
His stories of that hike thrilled me. He described the Appalachian
Trail as more communal than the PCT, a moving party with nightly
bonfires. Rather than using tents, hikers lay like sardines in wooden
three-walled shelters deep in mossy woods. He described footpaths
through forests that led above stuck towns to ancient mountains the
soft blue color of ice. "It's a fairy tale," he said of the place where the
Appalachian Trail ends, the summit of Mount Katahdin. "You get
higher and higher. Everything gets beautiful."

I pictured the blue-green mountain summit where the two-
thousand-mile Appalachian Trail ended. The view must have been
grand, the high blinding and pure. And then you're at the end.

"Sounds incredible," I said. I asked him where he went after the
trail ended.

"Went back to Keene, to work to save," he said, "to walk again."

He was poetic and charismatic, yet he'd delivered pizzas for the same place in the same small town for thirteen years. He was happy to drift.

I wondered why Mystic was still hiking, what he could be seeking, if he was looking for anything or if he only loved it purely.

I thought of Muir. I thought of Shakespeare, that hostel, the old words painted on the wall burning me. Journeys end in lovers meeting, journeys end in lovers meeting, journeys end in lovers meeting, ending. One spark, flame catching; the world burning. Hard rain falling. Ashes blowing away in idiot wind.

Dylan, Shakespeare, Muir. Alive, dead, dead. Where the hell was I walking to?

I'd planned to resupply in the town of Three Sisters—it was close to the trail and compact, good for walking—but in the morning Mystic told me Bend was the place to be. It was past Three Sisters on the highway, a thirty-mile hitch, but worth it. He was going there. Everyone was. Wasn't I?

I decided that I was, too.

The woods were gentle, uniform, bright green pines like fields of Christmas trees. It'd be easy to lose your way here. I said, "Okay."

Mystic smiled, looking forward at the flat footpath. He seemed excited. "Big miles," he said. "Wild Child, bet we can rip out thirties to Bend."

I'd found already that a thirty-mile day in Oregon is like an eighteen-mile day in the Sierra Nevada, with its cracked, snow-crusted granite culminating in thirteen-thousand-foot-high clouds. The Oregon woods are tame: pine and damp earth. I said, "We can."

I kept up with Mystic until that evening when we caught the rest of the Thirty-Eights. These guys were faster hikers than I was, but I was lonely, and I wanted to be with them, so I hiked faster. I'd wake each day at first light, hike big miles; midday they'd catch me, quickly pass. On my own I passed Elk Lake, Bachelor Butte, the twin peaks named the Wife and the Husband, strode past Midnight Lake and Shelter Cove, over the Old Oregon Skyline Trail, uphill to Maiden Lake Trail junction. I walked alone through the afternoons, hoping to catch them. And I always did. I would hike into the night to reach them, their little tents already standing, fire burning. My knees aching. Making myself make it back to them. Thirty miles, Mystic, fire, happy sleep. Showing myself that I was goddamned strong. Beginning to believe that I really was. With a pack of men in wilderness, and feeling safe. Then the terrain changed. Soft pines and damp earth vanished; pocked pale stones appeared. Distant pale volcanoes rested like mountains of bone. These were cinder cones. This was the Oregon desert, dry white fields of ancient volcanic rubble, blue sky, no moss or rain.

Even though I was starting to see that my rape was not my fault, I was struggling with whether I could trust new friends or not. The fear of being blamed for it, very strong in me, was stopping me. I didn't want to know if they'd be cruel. I liked them too much, I didn't want to risk losing our innocent connection. My rape was still my secret.

Midmorning on my last day on the trail before I reached Bend, I met a Boy Scout troop. I was alone, had woken very early and begun walking in darkness and hadn't seen the Thirty-Eights all day. I assumed they hadn't caught me yet. The boys were twelve or so, each one with a plastic orange whistle hanging around his neck. They were brushing their teeth, not yet packed up. I walked toward them, a girl alone in the woods. They wanted to help me. They asked if I was okay. They bragged to me that yesterday they had walked eight miles. It was ten o'clock in the morning, and I'd already walked more than eight miles. But I didn't tell them, I just walked past.

When I reached the highway at McKenzie Pass—the road on which I'd hitchhike into Bend—the Thirty-Eights still hadn't appeared. It was two o'clock in the afternoon. I assumed I was ahead of the guys, but I wasn't sure. I was about to try to hitchhike into town alone when I saw that the tree by the road had a phone number stapled to it. I called it. An old man's voice answered, "Hello," and stated immediately that he was deaf; he told me there was no need to bother answering him. He'd be at McKenzie to pick me up in one hour. He didn't give me an option.

I decided that if he seemed creepy, if there were anything unappealing about him at all, I wouldn't get into his car. The day was hot, the sky flame-blue, and I sat on my pack on the side of the highway, at the center of an endless sea of snow-white stones.

An hour later exactly, a faded green, rusted old car pulled over. Stones crunched under the chalky tires. The deaf man waved. He looked very old and frail, friendly; I smiled at him. I dusted off my pack and climbed inside.

On the thirty-mile drive east, into Bend, the old man explained how "shuttling" was his thing. All hiker-season, he drove back and forth, to and fro, to Three Sisters, Bend, back to the pass.

I asked him, "How much do I owe you?"

He said this road was repaved in 1997.

"Oh," I said, unsure if there was something I should grasp that I was missing. I pulled out my slim trail-wallet, just a tiny Ziploc baggie with cash and cards and my picture of Jacob, and unfolded a twenty. "For gas?"

He swerved and wheezed, it was his raspy laugh. He did not want my money. "Save it for the old inn," he said.

I didn't know what he meant by that. We putted into Bend, a clean sunny mountain town, and he pulled over outside a big white Colonial. A ten-foot-tall sea foam green model of the Statue of Liberty was propped up on the lawn. Pink and yellow flowers were planted in circles instead of strips. It looked like an eccentric's fortress, an inflated version of my parents' house. The old man put the car in park outside the house and insisted that I go inside.

I didn't know what I should do. I didn't want to stay there. If this white house were a bed and breakfast, it would be expensive, and I didn't want to waste so much money. And if it wasn't a B and B, it was somebody's house.

I felt nervous. I considered my choices. I missed the Thirty-Eights; I wondered where they were, how the hell we'd gotten separated. Maybe they were riding into town now, getting motel rooms. I wished I'd waited for them. But then maybe they were ahead of me, had passed me when I was squatting to go to the bathroom off the trail; there wasn't a way to know. I didn't have any of their phone numbers, how absolutely dumb of me, Bend was a big town. I felt like a shard of cracked plate; I didn't know any of their real-life names.

Faced with the possibility of losing these friends, it suddenly bothered me deeply that none of them knew that I'd been raped. I felt that they had never had the chance to truly see me as I am, and I wondered if I could have trusted them to be kind. My secret began to feel more unbearable to keep than to risk telling. Now, I regretted losing them without them ever *knowing* me and my secrets. I felt lonelier than I had before.

I had come to Bend for the Thirty-Eights, but I was here alone.

I didn't know where I should stay.

I grabbed my pack, nauseated and hot, sun-blistered, and hopped out of the car and started walking, the sun-heated pavement silent, the volcanic rock's dead crunch still echoing in my memory.

BEND, OREGON, MILE 1,989.5

Bend was cut by a calm and winding river, pine-scented, lovely. I checked into the old inn the deaf man had dropped me off at—it *was* a bed and breakfast, $89 a night, a lot to waste but I ached to lie on a bed—and there I was. I didn't have the energy to wander. The inn turned out to be owned by an ex-New Yorker, which explained the ten-foot-tall sea-green model of the Statue of Liberty propped up on the lawn; the bed was plush and clean with soft, smooth sheets. I showered and then collapsed onto it. In the morning I felt good, rested and happy. Breakfast was fresh strawberries on French toast. I devoured it, studying the map of town.

The dining room was white and sunny, well-fed tourists talking quietly. The innkeeper, Gwyn, squeezed my arm as she walked past me, she was carrying a frosted pink glass pitcher of orange juice, I smiled up at her. She slipped back in from the kitchen, over to the small round table I sat at alone. "God girl," she said to me, "you'll be a star." Her accent was thick true-blue New York.

I laughed. I said thank you. I drank my last MRSA-killing pill, it shimmered in my water in bright day's light, the window a shining block of silver, and then stepped outside and met Dash.

I first saw him in Bend's public library. I was sitting behind a big clunky public computer, writing about my hike. He was packing up, squinted at me and said hi. I said hi back. We were both in town to get hot food and a bed, rest our legs and shower, as hikers did about once a week or so. You can always spot a thru-hiker by their filthy clothes. Even after they've been washed and no longer smell pungent, gray dirt darkens the armpits. His were nearly black. He told me his trail name, "Dash," but I forgot it right away. I'm pretty bad with names. I did remember that he was handsome, remembered his slick muscles, his suntan, his big lips, ice blue eyes bright under thick, dark lashes. He had big hands and muscular arms strung with veins. He was tall. I was blinded by him, as if I'd looked at fire and then away, into the dark. Then he left. I tried to get back to work, to concentrate, but couldn't. A few of the Thirty-Eights drifted through; we made plans for dinner later. I stared at the bright screen's blinking curser. Later I noticed a torn shred of paper tucked under my black journal: his number.

When I showed up to the Deschutes Brewery that night to meet the boys, he was having dinner with them. It turned out they were friends. Apparently Mystic had known him since the desert. I sat next to him, close, and his knee brushed mine. He smiled. I smiled, too— tried not to but couldn't help it.

I lifted my hand, moved it slow through the space between us like a teenage boy trying to float unnoticed to second base. I pressed my trembling palm against his sweating beer, squeezed the glass. Lifted and carried it through the air to my mouth. Took a sip. I was nineteen, underage, and he knew it. He looked amused, and contorted his face like he disapproved. I wasn't supposed to be there, didn't have a fake ID.

"What's your name?" I asked him.

He stared right at my eyes, squinted, his eyes were so bright, pool blue. He told me, "You asked me that fifteen minutes ago."

I didn't look away. I could hardly breathe. I felt like my face was on fire, I was burning up. He was so damn hot. "Sorry, I don't remember."

"Stash," he said.

"Stash," I repeated. "Stash, hello." And so I called him Stash, not knowing, the Thirty-Eights all grinning when I spoke, me wondering why. Me drinking Stash's beer, his brilliant smile.

Then, the Thirty-Eights still all around, a happy, shouting pack, we were sitting in the outfield of a baseball field at dusk. Then night. Then it was just us—Mystic, Buddha, and Deep had left for a bar—and the sky was cooled-coal gray and Stash and I were talking, alone, together. I talked to him for hours while it got dark. He was almost thirty, he told me. I was nineteen with that narrow sense of what I wanted.

I didn't know quite how to talk to him. He was an adult. I had no allure. I had no style. My secret fear was that he'd be able to sense that I had never been loved romantically by a boy ever, and find that there was a detectible reason for it. He told me he'd had a six-year relationship, had worked in aerospace and then in finance in Manhattan. I wanted to know everything about him. "What did you major in?" I asked.

"What?" That same big grin, he looked so happy. His lips mesmerized me.

"In college?" I asked. "What did you major in?"

"I haven't thought about it in years."

"But tell me."

"It was math."

It was math. I was disappointed. I was sure that I could only ever love an artist, best of all a writer. "Why math?"

"Because it was easy."

"Oh," I said. I told him that made sense. "I'm just getting over MRSA."

"I have no idea what that is."

I regretted saying it; he'd know I was dirty and think I was disgusting. He would get up from the ground and leave me on the outfield's grass, alone. Yet I answered him, fully and graphically. I told him it was a flesh-eating bacterial infection commonly spread in prisons and in urban gyms. "I had to go home for four days. My mom almost wouldn't let me back."

He looked at me. I felt embarrassed. Young. But I didn't feel he was judging me, his warm gaze didn't falter. Suddenly I knew the one possible way I could have contracted it: from the bed of one of the small-town motels I'd slept in, those non-brand, cinder-block palaces.

We told stories from our childhoods. Stash told me about his old pet rat called Lizzy, named for the Queen of England. She would sit on his shoulder and sometimes try to climb up on his head. But in the 1991 Oakland Hills fire he took her with his family to the car—their house would, like the thousands around it, burn to nothing. When they faced a flaming evergreen dropping lit-amber needles like sparks onto the windshield, blocking the road out, they climbed out of the car and into the burning air and abandoned Lizzy. Lizzy burned to death.

I told him I'd had a parakeet named Alex, the namesake of Alex from my preschool, my best friend. "But no fire, though."

We went for a walk and Stash bought a six-pack of Pabst Blue Ribbon at a gas station, and I took his hand. I didn't really like beer but didn't say anything. In the river park where we stopped and sat I just pretended to sip. Stash had a few while I touched one to my tongue. Lying on wood chips above the water's bank, he kissed me.

"I didn't see that coming," I said.

He pulled back, tilted his chin down. "You didn't?"

I shook my head no, but I was euphoric. "I don't know."

He was grinning. "What do you think we're doing here?" he

asked. He lay on his back and I kissed him. "You know Stash isn't my name," he said.

We lay there by the river, kissing, pressing palms.

When we rejoined our trail-gang at another bar where I wasn't legal, Dash's back was covered with clinging wood. Everyone pointed and started calling him "Woodchips."

I was a little embarrassed. "You guys," I said. "We just only kissed, relax."

But Dash kept smiling and saying, "*Stop* calling me Woodchips," bringing it up long after everyone else had forgotten. That's how I knew he liked me. He wanted everyone to know about us.

The Thirty-Eights found a pizza box left on a nearby table with a plastic baggie full of shrooms inside. Mystic, Einstein, Deep, Buddha, everyone took them except for Dash. "I'm good," he said, grinning like a kid, passing the baggie to me. "I'm good too," I said, also passing it.

As the Thirty-Eights got high, Dash and I slipped away from them, out of the Brewery garden, lit with gold and blue Christmas-tree lights and copper lanterns, out to an overgrown field behind the sprawling shopping mall. The sky was black. We wandered the reeds and tall grasses of the abandoned field, it was huge, felt never-ending, skirted the pines, we could feel their shadowed figures but could hardly see. I had never been so attracted to someone. I hoped he felt it too. I wished on every star I saw that he did.

"I wish," I said, not knowing how I was going to finish the sentence, wishing I hadn't started, wanting to say something smart and wonderful. "I wish that there were more girls on the trail. Sometimes I go weeks before I see another."

He laughed. "That makes two of us," he said. Dash bent and kissed my neck, my cheek, my lips lightly. He whispered, "Where you sleeping tonight, Wild Child?"

I looked at my phone. I didn't know. It was one A.M. and the town of Bend was closed. Mystic had met a rich guy earlier in the night, apparently, and charmed his way into the man's vacant weekend cabin on the town's outskirts. Dash could have stayed with them, but there were only four bunks. There wasn't room for me.

We were walking across the field, wandering. The ground was ink dark; I lifted my feet high and lowered them slowly so I wouldn't trip. I took his hand. "I don't want you to sleep alone," he said. "Do you want to get a motel room?"

I smiled and hoped that, in the darkness, my joy was invisible. "We just met today," I said, swinging his hand, speeding my steps, "Maybe that's a little fast?"

He didn't comment on my pace or pull me back. He said, "Don't worry, I don't want to have sex with you. I just want to see you naked."

I laughed; I was blushing. He was too blunt. "Still no," I said. I was still holding his hand, my palm was hot, I could feel my pulse against him, I was burning up. "But thanks."

He said only, flatly, "Okay." Then his face broke open into a sweet boyish grin. His palm was warm with mine. He said that even if I didn't get a motel room with him, he didn't want to leave me alone here on this dark field in a town we didn't know. He suggested we stealth-it, pitch our tents at the edge of the overgrown field, in the trees.

So we did. I pitched my tent at the field's edge, he put his nearby in the dark trees, and we slept separately, divided by nylon walls and night.

I woke to my tent shaking, someone was pounding on it, mumbling, "We're not allowed to camp here." It was a man's voice, raspy. It wasn't Dash. I peeked outside. A homeless man wearing a blanket like a cape bent over my tent, I stuck my head out, he was squinting, as if I were blinding.

He was saying, "The police don't like it when we camp here."

I was scared, only half-dressed, shocked at myself for camping so exposed. The night before, in darkness, Dash had tried to convince me to come with him into the trees, we'd be hidden there, but I'd been scared, and I'd stayed out in the open on the field, pitched my tent by starlight, drunk on black night air, the Milky Way my roof.

I crawled out of the tent, barefoot, in only my shorts and new light cotton shirt. The dry grass snapped under my foot soles, sharp. "Sorry," I said, squatting to pull my sleeping pad and sleeping bag and knapsack—everything I had—out into the light. I lifted my empty tent, shook out last night's dust, took it down. I glanced into the dark still woods. I felt melancholy, realizing that Dash and his tent were gone.

I was crestfallen. I'd never met anyone like him. I felt a twinge of loss, in a blink robbed of a gem I'd found in all this dirt, its brilliance blinding. Our meeting felt fated. I wished I'd asked him everything. I badly wished I'd asked him his real name. I desperately wanted to know it.

I packed my knapsack, alone again, zipped it up, sad, walked back across the overgrown abandoned field, sun gleaming in thin patches of stray wheat.

I walked, dejected, for a slow minute, down a sandy dirt road until it became paved, heard my name, a man's voice, looked up, around. Tripped and steadied myself in the road. Up on a small nearby hill a man waved. Dash! There Dash was. He'd been sitting, watching; he'd seen the caped homeless man, the whole scary interaction, ready to intervene. I looked down, relieved, embarrassed that he'd been right—the trees were safer—and I'd been caught. Climbing the hill to him, I found a marble in the dirt, a blue and yellow cat's eye. I stooped down as I climbed and plucked it up.

"For you," I said, passing it to him. "A lucky marble."

It was still dusty, and he cleaned it off on his faded plaid shirt. That shirt hung on him, his shoulders, like shirts in Ralph Lauren ads, sleeves rolled, his forearms thick and perfect. He grinned, amused. "Gee thanks."

We walked back into the center of Bend together; I took his hand. He held mine firmly. I told him in more detail the story of my infection, omitting my mother, about how I was fully better now, I hoped.

"Well, if you didn't have it, I wouldn't have caught you," he said.

It was true, if I'd been healthy, he'd have forever been behind me.

I laughed hysterically, though nothing was funny. He laughed with me. I was so happy.

Someone had given us the number of Fluff-N-Puff, a trail groupie-angel who had once been a thru-hiker—when she'd reached the High Sierra, she had quit—and we called her for a ride back to the trail. She met us and gave us kiwis and explained to us that we could eat them like peaches, swallow the skin too, people everywhere except in America do. I tried it; the skin easily broke and tasted like not much. She was right. Dash bit the skin, too. I liked how adventurous he was, how he tried it without judgment or cynicism, just like me. Green juice glistened on his chin. I rose onto my tiptoes and licked it off, like a cat.

We rode the twenty-nine miles back up to the trail in the back of angel Fluff-N-Puff's minivan, not speaking, clasping hands. I leaned against him. He smelled warm, like an infant, like salt, his scent addictive to me. I wanted to kiss his neck, inhale the smell of his hair and skin, but I stopped myself.

"It's here," Dash said, as we reached the pull-off where Santiam Highway met the Pacific Crest Trail, PCT Mile 2,006.9, according to the *Data Book*. But I didn't remember passing the two-thousand-mile mark, which seemed significant. I didn't recognize the place. This wasn't where I'd left the Pacific Crest Trail.

I said, "But, wait." Dash leaned over me and looked down at the book. "McKenzie Pass," I said. "That's where I got off."

And unfortunately it was true. In fact two separate highways that crossed the PCT led into Bend. And I'd hitched into town on the other crossroad—one that intersected the Pacific Crest Trail seventeen miles south of where I now was with Dash and Fluff-N-Puff. I couldn't believe it: Dash and I had been together in Bend, but I was seventeen miles south of Dash on the continuous footpath from Mexico to Canada.

Dash hopped out, tossed his pack on, extended his hand to me. Pale pumice crunched like bird bones under his running shoes. "Skip up with me," he said. It wasn't a question. "It's just seventeen miles."

"Just seventeen," I repeated, though I didn't step out of the minivan.

He told me that the miles I'd miss were hell. It'd be volcanic rubble, desolate and ugly, fields of boulders, the footpath pumice stones on stones. "You keep on rolling your ankle. It's like walking on golf balls."

I blinked at him.

"Seventeen," he repeated. "That's like nothing."

I wanted to go with him. Of course I did. He was so handsome and understated, a quiet strong man who made my whole neck blush. He'd stood at the Mexican border just two days after I had, also alone, and for three months we'd been within a week's walk of each other, trekking north in sync. And now, it seemed, fast as he'd appeared for me, he would be gone. And if I skipped up with him what difference would it make? Seventeen miles out of 2,650 really did seem like nothing.

But it wasn't. I had walked the 1,989.5 miles from Mexico to Bend without breaking my continuous chain of footsteps, even half-miles mattered to me, and I knew that these seventeen miles mattered a lot.

I knew what happened, psychologically, when thru-hikers skipped miles; I'd seen skipping, like a sickness, spread to destroy hikes. A steep mile here, five dry drab miles there, and then pretty soon you're a Yellow Blazer, hitchhiking around the trail, missing the toughest climbs, the views, hopping trail-town to trail-town, highway-coasting.

I'd seen Warner Springs Monty's Donner Party, avoiding discomfort, seduced by ideas of an easier way. None of them ended up making it all the way back down to the High Sierra. They wouldn't finish the trail.

I stepped out of the car. Trembling, I hugged him. His chest was warm. I clung to him, wanting him, wanting to stay. Longing to. Yet we needed to be at different trailheads. I knew I'd regret skipping, breaking my chain of continuous footsteps, wrecking my hike for this man I hardly knew. The trail without him would be lonely, but I had the torn corner of paper he'd left me with his number, back at the library. I'd smoothed the scrap of paper and pressed it into my mesh hip-belt pocket. I would walk at my own pace, knowing I would call him. I knew I'd see him again.

"Slow down for me," I whispered into his chest. "So I can catch you."

Then I let go of him.

CHAPTER 18

LOVE NOTES UNDER ROCKS

I daydreamed about Dash. I missed him. Walking alone felt different now, sadder. For the first time in a thousand miles, I didn't want to walk by myself.

The path entered an open expanse of stones, the earth's infinite volcanic carcass. I snaked unsteadily across white fields of brittle pumice rocks. Dash had been right; these miles were tedious, but I would walk them, despite the discomfort. I felt like the trail was the place I needed to be. I told myself that my separation from Dash was necessary. I couldn't wreck my hike for anyone, not Dash, no one. I knew this now. I knew how powerfully it mattered to me. I'd preserve my walk's integrity—complete *the whole* trail, and enjoy it. I felt the magnitude of my solitude. I was lonely, yes—but it was the healthy choice.

I decided not to rush my pace to catch him. I had his number in my pocket; I would call it once I reached the next town. We would find our way to each other again. I was confident that he wanted to walk with me. I reached in to touch the torn paper with his number. Where it should have been I felt nothing.

I tossed my pack off, checked everywhere—I was frantic. I smoothed my pack's flat interior pocket searching for it, looking in every nook and crease of fabric. I couldn't believe it. I had lost it. It was somehow gone.

I was devastated. I wouldn't be able to call him. My patient loneliness felt suddenly claustrophobic, the promise of the company and all the day's happy dreams I was walking toward threatened.

I walked faster now, jogging soft descents, only half-seeing the unending streak of silver pines as if looking through a scuffed car window, silently crying. I slipped north, fiercely missing what I thought I almost had. The woods were quiet.

It was clear to me my feelings for him were more than only lust. I'd never felt such chemistry with anyone. I wanted to be with him in a way I never had with Icecap; already, I felt Dash fit with me. It had felt so easy to imagine walking with him. Already he was someone I wanted to share my time, my self, with after the trail ended. I sensed he was the one who might be able to see me clearly, the way I most wished to be seen.

Everything about us had seemed destined. We were hiking in sync; we fit. And now, it seemed, fast as he'd appeared for me he would be gone.

I wasn't going to be able to hear his voice. I couldn't feel his hands on me again.

I'd just so briefly met this man that feeling this sad to lose him felt crazy. Yet I felt it. I realized I was so devastated because I liked him so much, because I was so attracted to him. I considered what that meant for me. I was ready to let myself be vulnerable with a man again—*that* was proof of healing. I craved it with him, in a way I hadn't even with Icecap.

As I strode faster, I replayed his voice: "Want to get a motel room?" Shockingly, now I did. I wanted to feel his breath on my cheek, I couldn't stop conjuring his thick hands. I almost wished that in Bend I had said yes. I couldn't believe I wanted that—but I did. I wanted both things: strength in my independence and also this new desire. This felt like the beginning of a new kind of love.

I entered a petrified forest, all the pines were brown, their nee-

dles fallen, padding the footpath. I had expected northern Oregon
to be coastal and pastel, smelling of sunbaked seaweed. But I was on
volcanic rock; I was in dead trees. Black pumice crunched beneath
my running shoes; I was passing through the wreckage of volcanoes
that had erupted thousands of years ago. The path was a bright scar
through the rubble. The woods were pale, then ebony; trees had
burned down, they were charcoal: recent fire. I screamed and I could
hear the echo forever.

"Wild Chiiild," I yelled. "Hello!"

I heard a "hello" back but didn't see a person.

I felt my solitude like a frigid wind. I imagined us reunited, all
the things that could happen. These were daydreams, crisper in my
vision than the rocks and trees. Already I wanted to know what I had
to do to make him keep walking beside me after the PCT ended.

Walking north through still pines, my eye caught on a glint of white
on the ground—a note. It was held in place by three petal-size rocks,
dusty but surprisingly clean white. It was addressed to no one, but no
one had taken it. I bent onto my knees to read it:

IN CASE ANYONE CARES, STASH'S NUMBER IS 646-555-1126.

He wrote he'd be in Hood River, and the dates. He had left this
note for me. I was blissful, the confirmation of my importance to him
in my hands. He wanted extra insurance in case I'd lost his folded,
little slip. He was taking care of me even when he was not with me;
passing these same trees, he was thinking of me, too.

I'd thought I'd been unlucky—struck sick with MRSA, punished,
sentenced to always have to walk alone—but with his note in my
hand, that whole story was different. The place to which my trail was
leading me began to take a more complex form than the woods of
southern Canada, each step and setback I'd encountered filled with a
small, warming new purpose. If I hadn't gotten MRSA, Dash would
never have caught me.

I could see that I was terribly lucky. I realized what exactly I'd met the night before, I felt the weight of it—how important he was. The relief I felt was so tremendous that I laughed aloud.

In the next trail-town, he'd made a date for us. He wanted me, too.

I photographed his note. I kept walking through the forest, and felt strong, sure, consumptive *want* for the first time in my young life—he was different than any man before him. The sky broke into the longest, pinkest sunset of my life, a celestial painting the cosmos made me. Everything I passed became suddenly terribly beautiful, I knew I was sharing it with him, even if he wasn't yet beside me. I was running again—no longer from men, but toward one.

My excitement grew as I took steps; butterflies fluttered over each other within me, building uncertainties. Would I still like him as much? Would he still even like me? It was almost scarier now, it would be more real than when we'd stumbled upon each other and didn't need to ask these questions at all. I didn't want the one man I liked the most to have any reason to disregard me. I wanted him to see me: beautiful, a great writer, strong, able, autonomous—not damaged. I wanted him not only to adore me, but also to respect me.

Dash's note requested that I come join him in Hood River—a larger town, a long hitch from the trail. But I hadn't planned to go there, I didn't want to. If I diverged from my path and hitched there, it would be for him.

In shadowed woods, excited and feeling lonely, I walked toward an old man, white-haired, walking south. I was startled by his sudden presence here. We met; he stopped. "Thru-hikin'?" he asked. Each breath he inhaled softly whistled. I remained some feet removed from him and said yes.

He laughed, then coughed. I was eager to leave and keep on moving north, toward Dash. He told me he was walking south, from Canada. He had traveled 590 miles so far and had, he told me, 2,000-plus to go.

"When you get to the Bridge of the Gods," he said, "say 'hi' to the Berry Man. The Berry Man gives e'ry hiker somethin'."

I was three days' walk north of Bend. I'd hardly seen a person: only a father and daughter out for the weekend; this man. No Dash. I walked north daydreaming about Dash's bright gray eyes and scent. I wanted to show him that I was strong and worthy of respect, a talented poet; I wanted him to declare in shock how overlooked and underestimated I had been ever since I was a child. How lucky he felt to be the one to have discovered me, to have me. I wanted him to look at me like maybe I was magic.

I had planned to resupply in Cascade Locks, a tiny town directly on the trail on the border between Oregon and Washington. I'd call him there, and I was positive that he would come to me. When sun fell that night, I built my tent; I maintained my own comfortable pace. If he wanted to wait for me, he would wait for me. If he wanted me, he would appear for me again.

I again recommitted to my decision to honor my own pace.

It didn't matter how much I liked him or how excited I was when he used our one inside joke—*Stash*—so I'd be sure his number was for me. In fact, *because* I liked him so badly, I needed to continue on my course. I was finally becoming the woman I wanted to be, and *she* was whom I needed to show Dash—and myself. Descending past smudging trees, strong, I decided I would not go to Hood River.

Cascade Locks is Oregon's northern-most town, green and misty, sitting still on the bank of the broad, slow Columbia River. As I hiked closer to it, trail magic resumed, making me happy. A burlap soccer-ball sack of fat furry peaches hung from a pine limb; Macintosh apples flooded a green bucket. A couple out camping to do trail magic gave me a gigantic chocolate-chip muffin—I devoured it—and, as I was leaving them, offered me a thin joint. I thanked them, but declined.

The forest was gorgeous, stained with light. The terrain was no longer hostile but instead easy. I climbed gently to Timberline

Lodge, a tourist resort high above pines, passed it and descended. I slipped behind a violent waterfall along a stone footbridge, the rocks wet, the crisp sheet of falling water gleaming, the hillside vibrantly green. Then the trail dropped abruptly down into the river valley, down toward Cascade Locks.

It was early evening when I walked into town, the water of the Columbia a million tiny silver swells shimmering, blindingly bright.

I got a hotel room on the river, convinced an old hiker named Billy Goat to buy me a bottle of vodka, and bought myself a bottle of Gatorade to mix it with. I shaved my legs smooth and soft in the tub in my little room with a view. In the bed I watched a bad '90s movie—two kids making out on a haystack, the girl blond with boxy overalls. The river was silver in my window. I watched it glisten, then blacken with the night. I remembered *The Breakfast Club* tinting the dark of my new dorm room. I thought of Dash.

I reshaved my legs until they were so smooth my open palms could hardly feel them. I texted Dash to tell him that I was in a hotel room in Cascade Locks, sipping vodka, naked, waiting. My text to him was bold, but not drunken. Drinking now and drinking four months ago, in the desert, felt different. I wasn't masking sadness or shame, losing control of myself. I was telling him to come to me.

He didn't write back, "I told you Hood River." Instead he responded, immediately, "Oh man."

I was euphoric.

Not a minute later my phone screen lit up again: "Getting a cab." He'd get a taxi all the way from Hood River to Cascade Locks, to me.

I mixed more vodka with Gatorade, feeling nervous and a little buzzed, and excited. I dreamed of his fingers on my skin. I was ready, but the idea of sex still scared me, hurt me. It wasn't what I wanted. I wanted the intimacy of him next to me here, naked skin, and trusted him to stop when I wanted him to stop. I didn't know exactly what would happen that night, and I didn't need to. The one thing I felt sure of was that I wouldn't have sex with him yet.

Around midnight there was a knock on my door.

I answered in only a towel. I was bold and deliberate. I wanted him to see me. I felt my most beautiful. I had earned this beauty. He looked at me like I was treasure. He touched my nose gently with his fingertip. It was the second night he'd ever seen me. I felt a tremendous relief.

He looked just as I remembered. His eyes were bright granite in the half-light, his thick lips parted. I lightly kissed them. "Hello," he said. He traced my cheekbone with his finger, back and forth. I hardly knew him, yet he gave me an incredible sense that we were a tribe that extended back through my history, that he was finally back with me now, to stay. I wanted him to look at my naked body and naked face—without makeup, without heavy glasses—and see my potential, how beautiful I was.

We kissed gently, without tongues, our chins bumping, we couldn't straighten them.

He placed his palm lightly on my cheek. It slid down to my neck as he led me onto the bed.

We didn't have sex. Intuitively, he knew I didn't want to. Instead, he was doing something no other man had done—he began asking me questions. "Tell me who you are," he told me, his lips tilting in a goofy smile. He wanted to know everything about me.

We talked for hours. He didn't want to go to sleep. He was so different than any other man I'd met. I felt such tremendous relief, I was at ease with him: we *did* fit. Everything in my mind was also real.

He told me he'd been watching a movie with some hikers at a theater in Hood River when I'd texted. He was normally a cheap bastard, he said, but he'd called a midnight cab to get to me. He was so different from boys at college.

He asked me how I'd decided to hike the PCT. He asked about my personal history. What kind of relationships had I had, and was I single?

Dash asked questions the way I'd always wished a boy would, trying to *see* me—and yet I was afraid to let him. I couldn't give him real answers to his questions. Everything he wanted to know was a truth that I wanted to leave behind. I felt panic at the thought of bringing my past into this moment. I didn't want to ruin this chance at being seen without shame, as whom I had become in the miles since Mexico. When he asked if I was single, my mind flooded with the list of truths about what sex and love had looked like for me:

I'd never had a boyfriend off the trail—Tyler, Never-Never, Icecap; the few boys I'd felt connected with all somehow related to the PCT. I hadn't ever had a boyfriend at my own school in high school or college, someone to wander the campus and hold hands with. Nothing like my mother had with my father.

I'd never had sex that felt good to me.

I'd never had sex with the same man more than once.

I'd never had an orgasm.

I'd never been in love.

I could still count on one hand the number of times I had had sex.

I had been raped.

I had been Debby Parker.

His eyes were lit with intent curiosity as he waited for my words, as if he wanted to find in me someone worth loving.

I didn't want to tell him anything that would ever kill it.

And so instead of answering, instead of telling him about my rape, I evaded his questions about my history and told him with enthusiasm that, more than anything, I loved to write. I was reading *The Best American Short Stories 2008*. I showed it to him. I told him I was walking because I just wanted to have an adventure.

He asked if any of the stories were good. I said, "Most of them."

"What's the best one?"

"Galatea." I told him about my favorite story. It was about a girl who went to Cornell in Ithaca, New York, to the same school Dash had gone to. She married a hermit who lived in the town but didn't go to the school or work, though he called himself an inventor. She was devoted to him. Each time I read it, I wanted things to work out, for their weird intense hermit love to last forever. But it doesn't. They end. I reread and reread and reread the ending, always in denial. I hoped that I could find where they could have salvaged it, the mistake she had made that caused him to leave and see how they could have saved their marriage, what tiny thing she could have done to make it last forever, as intensely as it was in the beginning. But one day the husband disappeared and went into the woods and didn't come back.

I must've fallen back asleep; I woke to Dash reading. He lay close to me, focused, the book propped open on his pillow. I watched morning sun rest on his hand as it turned a page. It felt impossibly natural waking to him next to me, so much safer than I'd felt even the night before. I parted my lips, wanting on that fresh morning to finally tell him about my mother dressing me and years of feeling ugly. About hating my body. About my rape and hating my body even more. I wanted him to tell me that my mother had reacted to my rape without compassion, that she was wrong that I was damaged, my school was wrong that it was my fault—Junior was wrong.

He was still reading, he didn't see I was awake. I said, "It makes me really happy you're reading the stories that I like."

He looked up at me. He said, "And then, you can tell me why they're good."

He was smart, charming. He wanted to know my opinions. He needed to know what I thought, wanted my ideas. We were impressed by each other.

I realized we had so much in common—not only because we had literally physically lived our last four months covering the identical terrain—but by virtue of the fact that we had chosen to. We were caught up, could walk the last five hundred miles together. Miraculously both walking this trail, on the same mile, at the identical place.

I wished I were able to remain entirely myself with him—to be fully honest, to expose my history and shame—for him to know, and to still want me with him.

But I didn't tell him.

From my hotel window, I could see Washington. I wanted to enter the state ahead, together.

I didn't tell him.

He turned the book to show me the story he was reading. "Galatea."

I didn't tell him.

We reawakened to hooting—a pack of voices, cheering. Magically, we stepped out in daylight into a celebration. Along the river people were setting up square green canopies, hammering support cords into the dirt. Thru-hikers of all appearances pitched their tents on the grass along the riverbank. I felt the energy—hikers flocking from all around, hitchhiking back south from all points north on the trail, hopping out at the Columbia's banks for tonight's party. We discovered that we were here in Cascade Locks on Trail Days, the annual celebration for all the hikers who had made it this far on their PCT journeys. Trail Days would be a giant hiker-party, much like Kickoff.

We decided we would stay in Cascade Locks another day together for the party. He also wanted to be with everyone else. He was unlike Icecap. I pitched my tent under a tree, my temporary shelter. Dash didn't pitch his. Our tent was one of hundreds on the big green under tall pines along the river. We'd both heard of the party—both of us had always hoped to attend—but here we were, this was the morning of it, and Dash and I happened by great, good luck to be in Cascade Locks, no need to hitch back.

As afternoon light brightened, a raffle was beginning. Gear and clothing companies gave away tents and sleeping pads, socks, the things hikers needed. Groups convened, quirky characters I'd heard about: the lost boys who hike the trail every year; the "trail celebrities" who set speed records hiking the PCT in just eighty days; the trail legends who had hiked the PCT in its earliest years, half a century ago. Two thousand people filled the green along the Columbia River. Last night it had been quiet.

Someone had set up a projector to play onto a sheet in the woods and a younger mass of hikers was dancing. Sunlight cupped in the river's dimples, shimmering; feet twisted on grass slick with red-brown pine needles, the sky a fierce blue. I was a part of this euphoric celebration of the distances our legs carried us, of making it. We gathered here to say goodbye before bursting northward and finally reaching Canada, proud we'd made it to Washington State. We were high on the anticipation of the final stretch. The raffle began—two bearded emcees with mics calling out trail names, their booming voices quick like giddy kids'.

Dash bought forty dollars' worth of raffle tickets for hiking gear. He was giving them all away to people—ten to a one-eyed ex-con named Yogi Beer; ten to me.

I won a NeoAir, the Cadillac of sleeping pads. It was worth $200 and ultralight. Yogi Beer won an Osprey backpack. Dash won a daypack, the smallest prize among us, yet he seemed completely happy.

I couldn't believe our small group's luck. I couldn't believe my luck.

Together Dash and I wandered past the concrete state park bathrooms, along the river cradling sunlight like pools of gold. My tent was olive green, for two people. It was at our feet.

Wordlessly, Dash climbed in. Camping by the gorgeous borderriver, together we disappeared from the big party that we were so perfectly paced for.

He carefully undressed me, exposing the striking whiteness of my stomach, my pale shoulders tinted pallid by sunlight filtered through the green tent walls. Those first intimacies with him were different than those with others I'd known, even those with Icecap. There was no vulgarity. My body unclenched in his hands, warm and calm. Touched by his lips, how different the things I now wanted were—bigger, absolutely huge, because his warm touch made my nerves finally dissolve into trust.

In the tent next to us a young, muscular guy named Buddha, one of the Thirty-Eights, was fending off an old woman called Sugar Mama. "You must be cold," she said to him, drunk. "Come into my Volkswagen."

"No thanks," he would say politely, always softly.

Dash and I kept cracking up. Buddha heard us, too.

We were still again, lying facing each other. I was euphoric, studying his relaxed lips. I asked him if we had just had sex.

"What?" He smirked, confused.

"Was that sex?" I asked him. Everything had felt so good, so easy—like I imagined sex should—that I actually wasn't sure.

His lips were smiling now, his eyes were bright with tender laughter. "We haven't yet," he said.

The Trail Days celebration was raging and for once I was in the heart of the thru-hiking body. Icecap had forced me to be miles ahead of them all—he was probably in northern Washington now, nearly finished—maybe already done. I was surrounded by people who'd chosen to be homeless for five months, to have stones in their shoes, to sleep on strangers' lawns or just on roots, constantly filthy. All these strangers bonded in the choice to take the cards they were dealt and toss them in the dirt. I had come to see: we all had reasons.

But for now we were in a quiet center. In our tent. The party pulsed around us, but we spent hours inside making out, invisible, the eye of our own storm. We stayed at our spot under the tree beside the Columbia for three days, three exciting nights, sexless.

The Columbia divides Oregon and Washington, states connected by the Bridge of the Gods—once a natural crossing created by a violent rock slide, long ago, though that mythic bridge has crumpled back into the water. Now the Bridge of the Gods is a smooth man-made arc.

Dash and I crossed the Bridge of the Gods holding hands. Cars flashed in both directions, and the metal bridge constantly vibrated. I was walking with Dash at last.

We passed the tollbooth but didn't have to pay. At the northern end of the bridge, a dark Mexican man behind a wooden fruit stand waved to us.

We walked to him.

"You walk here from Mexico?" he asked.

I was beaming. We told him that we had.

The man handed me a fat doughnut peach, then one to Dash.

Later, back in forest, I told Dash, "That was the Berry Man we saw." I said it boldly, as if the statement explained something greater.

"He gave us peaches though," Dash said.

Walking with Dash, everything felt distinctive. Up the trail he found a special pair of jeans, folded neatly on the dirt. Dozens of hikers had signed the pants in black Sharpie. He tried them on, and they made his butt look good. He looked like a gritty advertisement for boyish youth. Everything felt ridiculously flawless. I could not stop dumbly grinning.

We signed them with the black Sharpie, folded them, and left them there.

Our first night on the trail together, I built our tent while Dash set up the stove and cooked us Annie's mac and cheese. For four months I had subsisted mostly on granola bars, cheese, and chocolate. I hadn't brought a stove. Everything I'd eaten on the trail before Dash had been cold.

We sat by a dark lake, night air chilling, smelling the powdered cheese melting. He pulled a navy goose down vest from his pack and draped it over me.

He offered me a spoon of cheesy macaroni and my heart stopped.

That night in our tent he called me pretty, just as I was at my most comfortable, snuggled against him makeupless and dirty, in the woods. It was so easy. I could just be who I was.

I was scared of Dash at first too, but in a tingly way. He wanted me to want him, I felt it vividly.

We kept walking toward Canada together. Each night, I set up our tent; he cooked warm dinners. He always wanted to share, to make me happy. I did some work, he did some, harmoniously. I felt how different this connection was from what my relationship with Icecap had been. We were like a tiny family. If we both did what we should, we would survive.

He began lighting a stick of Nag Champa incense in the tent's vestibule each night, a small tent ritual, our first. Dash fiddled each night with the stove, lighting the flame, lighting the incense he'd stick in the dirt floor of our vestibule to scent our slow evening. Fire is not essential. Fire is warm comfort. From fire, cultures are born.

Sometimes when the air was clear we cowboy-camped directly on the dirt, under the galaxies. One of these nights, sleeping soundly deep in middle-night's early blackness, a chipmunk ran across my face and woke me.

I cried out, "Dash!" I sat up. "A fucking something just ran over me."

He didn't respond, he was still as silence, but then he sprang and tackled me, dashing fingers over my face and body, running them, not stopping. I was laughing. He was laughing too. Happy people have everything to give.

Dash and I trotted up the trail, down a dip like a bike jump, up. Hot rain drizzled, then poured like a sky-wide waterfall, poured out empty. Dripped. Gray-hot mist rose.

Douglas firs and Nootka rosebushes hung in the haze of the rain. Roots bulged like doorknobs I'd turn to open the ground. I was soaked. The rain-weighted air was warm but in two weeks it would freeze into flat crystals of soft snow, burying the way, erasing my good trail. It was seven o'clock, dusk dimmed the forest's details, and we walked, faster. Toward flat ground, camp and sleep.

In the hanging fog and still, I could feel in my wrist and thumb and right eyebrow my pulse, hard, like a beat-drum. This was September in Washington. The bears and squirrels eating huckleberries and nuts, fattening, as is their pattern, as they've been taught, as they will teach their young to do when the days' light shortens and mornings bite with frost. A large squirrel slipped up a thick trunk, her cheeks bulging with acorns for winter, for her babies. I blinked. I stumbled on slick roots, swayed upright, sad. I thought of my mother: she supported me in the way she knew how, had given me everything—but it wasn't enough. My mother provided for me the things she was taught I needed—food and shelter and money and even art lessons—but she didn't know I needed more than these things to thrive. I couldn't find the name for what she'd failed to offer me, but walking now, in fog, through dim green woods, I felt alone. My eyebrow twitched. We stopped hard, nearly collided.

The Canadian couple—we'd been seeing them in towns and on the trail, around their tent in the warm evenings—stopped, stood. Thin and twenty-two-ish and both tall, from rural Alberta, the pair looked as similar as boy-girl twins. Both lanky as branches, and in love. They were hiking south, the *wrong* way, slow. The girl—I couldn't remember her name and had probably never asked it—carried in her twiggy arms a fawn. Tiny. With eyes like dark lights. Bones delicate.

I couldn't look away from its huge eyes; they were infant eyes, yet it was sick and dying. It was striking. It stretched its mouth open but made no sound. It looked like a creature from an old bleak fairy tale in which the knobbed trees are hollowed and full of goblins, and the night might last a half-day or a lifetime. This was September twelfth. This fawn was born months late.

"'S mother left him," the Canadian girl said. She was a marionette doll, her body long bones, untethered to the ground, her stick-arms pressing a fawn to her core, weighing her shoulder blades down. The girl's pointy bones shifted and bulged under her skin at odd angles, a bone-dance, mourning, revealing her heaviness. But the fawn wasn't dead. It quivered like wheat in wind. "We sat there, waiting and waiting just for her to come. He's bleeding outta his hoof, got an infection."

She lifted his infected hoof. It was swollen twice as thick as the other three, puffy and pink and bleeding a pastel, pus-diluted blood. It was trembling. The couple had kneeled ten yards from the fawn for hours, waiting for its mother to return. She hadn't. They'd waited longer, hopeful, then scooped him up.

"You guys have powdered milk?" The veins in her eyes were red, and I could see she'd been crying.

We didn't, we were sorry. I was hollow. A mother had abandoned her new fawn. The fawn had been alone since noon or earlier, needing its mother's milk, dehydrating. Now it shivered, emaciated, its eye-whites yellowed, looking nearer to the bird-picked, sun-bleached carcasses I'd seen in the Mojave than a baby, fat and coddled, learning to live. I couldn't understand. Couldn't the mother just nurse the fawn for a couple weeks until its young body beat the infection? Infections clear; broken bones heal. Evolution gifted us with this ability. Kindness exists in the strands of code spiraling in our genes. This fawn was not good as dead. Where was the mother?

The mother needed to prepare herself for winter, yes, and she was bracing herself, sustaining herself, perhaps not equipped to save a wounded baby. Deer only have a life span of five to six years, less than a chicken's, less than a human child's before she spurts upward into a woman. And who—God, *who*—could be prepared for this? Not my mother. Not any mother; saving the hurt was not a mother's job. Mothers are programmed to teach the fit. They are unequipped to listen to pleas, to alter their patterns. Mothers know how to nurse and nurture those who they have hope for—they coo over babies with infections they can help heal, they give advice for things they know, they protect from the dangers they know to fear. But once their baby becomes so hurt the mother doesn't know how to heal her, she neglects because she doesn't know better. The tricks she knows don't work, she fears, and, eventually, when she is so lost she feels hopeless, she abandons.

Whenever I was injured, my mother was excellent. She would bring me fresh cups of tea before I'd finished the old ones, chicken soup or kreplach soup or wonton soup; she'd buy the soft kind of tissues so my nose wouldn't abrade. She'd sit up with me if I couldn't sleep. She'd rub where it was sore. If I'd broken a bone, she'd always check when I'd last had the Children's Motrin, so I didn't take too much. The right amount, no more. If I had early period cramps, she'd set up the heating pad. She was a constant comfort.

Dash and I held hands. We followed the good couple, back down and up, southbound. The exact wrong way. We walked in silence. The trail crossed a dirt road and we turned onto it, left, east. Toward, we hoped, houses and milk. The place where we could find the game warden. He'd be angry, we knew, would ask why we'd touched a fawn. Why we took him.

We were breaking laws.

The fawn screamed, a weak, infant's scream. A cry like my newborn nephew, Tom, had cried when he wanted his mother. I imagined him—baby Thomas—alone in fog, in woods, wanting. Not knowing how scared he should really be. Needing love and a deep hug, an explanation for his abandonment, a second chance. He was not unsavable. He was not dead.

I spoke: "They'll send you pictures, I bet. After he's better and running around in their yard. He'll get better, and they'll send you pictures of him as he grows."

He peed, dark and yellow-brown and *so much*. Down my new friend's leg.

Her boyfriend pulled a bright bandana out of his drab pants like a magic trick—poof! okay!—and dried his shaking girlfriend. Up and down, patting. Right by her crotch.

" 'S better," the boyfriend said. He wanted to help. "It's good—means he's still enough hydrated." His cheeks were flushed. He turned to Dash and me. "Second time he's peed."

Second time. My new friend was so good.

The smell remained, musky and terrible. "It *is* good," I said. If I were alone, I would never be here. I wouldn't want to—I wouldn't want to know.

We walked again, faster. I tried not to see the fawn's large eyes closing. His constant quiver faded to shivers, less and less frequent, weaker. Every tiny muscle in his infant body tensed—I felt hope!—we were all holding breath—and the baby collapsed in her arms, limp. *Limp.* But its eyes were now fully open, huge black globes, the only echo of its spent youngness, and it remained cute, yet it was dead. It deserved to live, to live a full deer-life. I wondered if it had ever even had a chance to walk.

My friend kneeled, laid him down in the center of the wet, hard dirt road. No mud.

I kneeled, too.

"He's not dead," Dash said. He stood up straight, *straight,* paced. He was going to fix this. "He's *not dead.*"

I believed him. It was easy to believe Dash, I wanted to believe him. Now Dash crouched down, kneeled low, this man, my man above this infant deer. He was searching—his fingers darted too young to understand, frantic, sure they'd find a pulse. Watching his hand's desperate sprint, his trembling pinkie outreached, pleading for a heartbeat, for a happy ending to this walk's story, I fell in love with his vast and noble hope.

"He's not dead," he declared again, the only words he'd spoken. Dash's face was just two inches from the fawn's. The fawn's eyes were vacant.

Dash didn't say anything more. He unfolded himself upright, walked maybe fifteen feet, off the road and into the wet forest. We all followed behind him. The ground here was ancient leaves, wet and so-long-dead, the color of Thomas's wet hair fresh from the tub. Dash shook a boulder back and forth and back, large as an infant's crib and cold. He uprooted it, shoved and rolled it five feet to the side. It exposed a foot-deep hole.

He dug with cupped fingers.

I felt in my warm chest a cavity of loss. My mother, my body, my blood and life: gone. My mother's eyes: vacant. She had gone deaf. She had wanted me to hold rape inside my body like a dark pearl, keep it in there, as it grew, as I grew cramped, as it overtook me as hidden things do. Secrets become lies. I'd carried in every step I took this lie, the shame of it. My mother's mute eyes. They couldn't even cry for me, my loss. Her ability to love me in the way I needed was as gone as my childhood. I'd been her girl, Doll Girl, bleeding, needing her, but now I didn't. Now I had Dash. To nurse me back to health. To love me hugely.

The rain was flowing again—I didn't know when it had gotten this hard—and Dash scooped up the fawn and lay it down in the dirt-hole grave. He pivoted from grave to soil-mound to stone to grave to stone, filling the hole, burying the fawn; he rolled the biggest rocks he could find onto the grave, instinctually following the ceremony of our ancestors, keeping the body sacred.

We three could only watch.

Dusk's shadow swallowed trees, lumped evergreens and sky together in black blotches shaped like house-less roofs, like a giant stooping woman in silhouette. This day was ending. This hike was ending, too, I knew, I felt.

In one week snow would drift down in wide twirls; the ground would freeze, all white, too hard for coyotes or grizzlies to dig into. The fawn would lie dead in peace, well-buried, protected from indignity by Dash.

Dusk had faded into nighttime in the woods. Dash was walking, now, down the road, back west, north on the faithful trail. We followed. The boyfriend kissed the girl. The rain drizzled out again, and I thought I saw a little black sky through the fog. I was still crying, I realized, late that night, Dash asleep, hugging me in his sleep in our taut tent as he had for hours and hours.

Late in night in darkness, still awake, I asked Dash, "Why are you doing this walk?" I finally needed to know his story too.

He told me a story about a mother deer. "When I was a kid, deer used a path behind my house, hundreds of deer every evening. I once threw a pinecone and hit one, there were so many I couldn't have missed. The sound was hollow, it wasn't made of much. It dashed away from me."

"That's your whole reason?" I tried to see him in the darkness. I couldn't.

"That mother looked so big, so solid."

"That's the only reason?" I asked again.

He told me the story of how he suddenly lost his hearing in one ear. For the first time he realized that his body wasn't permanent; it could fail him. I remembered the moment in the desert when my eyes were drying, I terrifyingly felt in my body how I was mortal; I understood.

Jacob had stared, straight-backed, at the ambulance's turning blue-red-blue. I had sat, silent. Inked minutes had passed, my tears dripping on my thighs, on my fingers and crossed wrists, and I'd felt brittle. Hollow, like an excavated crater. I'd felt I had been erased, whited out like an embarrassing typo, smothered slowly by falling snow, my mouth filling. Jacob had looked at me and said, softly, asking, "Do you want me to beat him up for you?"

By then, after the wait, the crash and wreck, all I'd said to him was "No."

I didn't want Dash to see me as damaged, and yet I wanted him to see me.

I took a huge breath in, I slowly breathed it out. My lips were against his neck. I told him softly that on my second night of my freshman year of college, before classes had begun, before I'd removed my colorful construction paper name tag from my dorm room door, I was raped.

He didn't flinch. He didn't ask me "Why?" He didn't ask me how I was alone with a guy, or how it had happened. He didn't ask me any question at all. All he did was almost nothing but exactly everything I'd needed everyone I'd told before him to do: he shifted his body to open his arms. He reacted with absolutely untainted compassion.

I slipped in.

He held me. I leaned into him deeply.

When the weight of my head was on his chest and I was sure he couldn't see my face, my cheek melting into his warm breathing chest, I silently said: *I love you.*

These words felt different this time.

CHAPTER 19

A Hiker's Guide to Healing

Whitman is my daddy.
—LANA DEL REY

A word after a word after a word is power.
—MARGARET ATWOOD

*When a woman tells the truth she is creating the possibility
for more truth around her.*
—ADRIENNE RICH

Writing is a way to make a living dreaming wild dreams.
—WILD CHILD'S PCT JOURNAL

Writing is a way.

We walked through clouds, breathless, above green valleys and into huckleberries, bushy fields glistening with dew. The fruit was ripe and plump, I grabbed at a shimmering bush and half the berries I brushed fell easily into my hand. I gulped them as feasting bear cubs do. I grinned. We dipped back down into soft white pine woods.

He talked of times in the future when we would ski down mountains in Colorado, I'd host a 1920s-themed party for my twentieth birthday; we'd live together in sunny mountains, or in a narrow house in Greenwich Village. The shared future he imagined thrilled me. He was presumptuous, saying "When we," as if the plan had already been made.

I wanted to make it.

Often he talked about the amount of money he'd need to earn before he retired. "Everybody has a nut," he told me. "How much it is depends on who you are."

I didn't fully understand. I asked him, "How much is yours?"

He answered without pausing, "Five million bucks."

I said that was a lot. I thought he seemed so young to me to be planning for the end of work already.

We sang bad duets, "Me and you, I do, I think about you day and night, it's only right, to think about the one you love, and hold her (me: him!) tight . . ." We skinny-dipped in beautiful clear lakes, they were freezing cold; I was awake in my body.

He made us morning tea, the steam dancing like a shadow flame in the bright daylight. There was no snow; there were no trees scorched by fire here.

I was building our home nightly, it was easy. I felt safe and light, my abilities crisp, making camp—tent taut and motionless beneath the rustling pines.

The earth was rich and blooming. Slipping toward Canada, through safer terrain, I felt fit and graceful—recently seemingly unattainable strengths, for me. I felt pretty. The woods were damp and smelled of unseen gardens.

I was falling in love for the first time. My world was providing for me in abundance because I had finally learned to trust it.

I'd entered the bliss of Washington, physically and emotionally: eating huckleberries, feeling beautiful and finally in control of my self. Feeling the changing season, my self changed.

The miles we walked together were beautiful.

We walked without talking. The trail climbed and we emerged from the trees on a viewless ridge, white and wet.

A group of mountain sheep appeared, materialized out of the thick curtain of low-hanging fog. This would be an inconvenient place to twist an ankle, a deadly place to fall. We were climbing up to the Knife's Edge, a tightrope ridge of rock through sky, through this swift wind. Walking closer, we felt the threat of falling. Off the eastern side, a thirty-foot drop. To the west, twelve hundred feet through air to treetops, rocks.

My hair, knotted in a bun, came undone, long curls whipping my face. My voice was a skipping rock over vast wind and rain, nearly inaudible. Frozen rain struck my cheeks and neck and I shivered. I was wearing all my clothes but my hands wouldn't close and my stomach wasn't warm. I couldn't see straight; if I opened my eyes fully ice-rain stung them. And it was all so white. I tripped over my left foot and scraped my right shin.

We traversed the glacier—white snow in white air, the huge height we could fall invisible. Now we walked into a scree field, snow-crusted and foggy. And I couldn't see. And I couldn't stop shivering.

And Dash just slipped—fell—probably twelve feet. Tears froze on my cold cheeks.

I was crying for Dash—I was scared he'd broken a rib or had a concussion.

I tripped out of the rocks and onto the icy alpine brush, to him. He was standing now and said he was all right. He said we should camp. I heard the words but could not move my mouth the right way to speak. I just nodded and shut my eyes and pressed my forearm to my lashes, frozen, brittle like glass casts of themselves. Through blinding ice-fog we lunged down, down. Prayed we didn't slip. Found an island of pine trees, the *only* trees, clinging to the slick and rocky slope. Sheltering a slanted flat of soil. A hundred years ago unlucky seeds blown to this rocky slope had found that one flat spot and been saved. On a ten-by-ten flat soil island, they'd fallen in despair and grown. Four twisted trees like miracle house posts now saved us, gave us a spot of shelter. A place to pitch our tent. Good ground, bulging with roots.

Dash set up the tent while I shuddered and opened and closed my mouth, hands against my stomach. While I waited, Dash said, I should jump up and down. I couldn't.

He got into my sleeping bag.

I couldn't ask why—couldn't talk.

He told me to undress, to get into my narrow bag with him. I was shaking. I felt jittery, like I was on fire, like fire was consuming me but it didn't hurt, like I was drunker than I'd ever been. I tugged at my soaked shirt. I was astonished it came off. I shook myself into the bag with him, went limp. Observed my fingernails, which had become lilac.

My hands heated up against his stomach, and my cheeks warmed against his neck.

That night he nearly froze keeping me warm.

I was warming. And I already loved him.

We woke in the morning on a snow-covered slope, unsure where we were, unsure where the trail passed through. I called my dad on the sat phone, and passed it to Dash—the two of them figured out our route down toward the valley town below.

Descending the steep mountainside, trying not to slip and fall again, he grabbed my hand at times to steady us both. We lunged together down the slope, cold still, but warming, less snow, frost-studded gravel, down and down. We were alive and warm, walking together through the most beautiful world. And then—thank God!—we were back on solid trail.

We descended quickly, made it back into meadowed forest by afternoon. I outreached my arm and with my fingers skimmed the back of Dash's swinging arm. He slowed and stopped for me. I wanted this man. I wanted to be with him forever. I told him this. He kissed my talking mouth, my cold palm.

Stumbling together, tangled in a hug, we didn't get ten steps off the trail, lay on the cold wild grass. Peeled off our worn-thin shirts, our underclothes.

I was scared, tight. I thought of the few times I'd had sex before this—one of them with Junior, resisting him—and I felt my face get hot. I panicked. Yet I wanted this. I knew so solidly that I wanted it, it hurt my body a little bit—I was naked on a grassy mound, freezing and flushed, my heart pounding, bouncing off the walls of me. Like a molecule of oxygen, frantic, its heated state disorder.

Sex had always hurt me until now. It hurt this time too, but less than before—it was bearable now. The pain was giving into pleasure. I felt relief, like sex before him had existed just only to get the pain I'd feel out of the way. I'd never had sex with anyone more than once, but I knew that could change, now.

This was the first time I didn't bleed at all.

Then Michigan Paul walked up on us, saw us through the narrow trees on our green mound. We froze. Another hiker's footsteps clomp-clomped, sped up; he looked away.

Dash said we were zero for one.

Cool soil against my naked side, his heat. The air feverish against my racing heart, my shame passed quickly—I didn't care who saw. I was happy. I kissed him.

He rubbed sunscreen I'd missed into my face. He told me I had the cutest little nose.

"What." I said.

"You have a little nose. It's so cute." He didn't seem like he was joking. I felt I had never seen myself in a mirror.

He traced my face with shiny fingers that smelled of camp and the Cape: my childhood summers. It didn't matter that we'd been seen this way. I cared about nothing as much as us together.

I was starting to fall in love with the attention that he gave me, the way his skin smelled. I felt safe and secure with him. Dash accepted me, made me accept myself more. I told him I was raped; he had hugged me. I felt I could tell him anything, and he would still like me, and he'd have wisdom for me. I had never met anyone like him. I was in good hands.

We lay together in the stillness under the canopy of tall rustling trees. That cool evening on the dirt, in the clean sunlight, all he could do was keep running his hand up and down my body.

We would stumble together off the side of the trail into the forest and make love, and make love, and make love; sunscreen spot I missed, he rubbed it in, making love; it became our ritual.

The verdant town of Trout Lake was dotted with white llamas, they wandered the endless fields of huckleberries. Men in the fields picked them, filling up white buckets. Pounds of berries sat on the general store floor. The gas station sold the "World's Greatest Huckleberry Milkshake," and so did the coffee shop across the road, too.

The town's small hotel was full, and the motel was full. The woman at the general store wherein everything except huckleberries was exceptionally expensive told us that an L.A. entrepreneur who'd become a Buddhist monk opened a monastery in town, and he some-times let hikers sleep there. She called him for us. In fifteen minutes he pulled up in a shiny new white Escalade. We rolled past more huckleberry fields, more men picking, the hills beyond them golden with sun, it was beautiful.

That afternoon, we sat in silence at meditation in the temple, and then climbed spiraled stairs to our bedroom. We made love, even though I was on my period, and, rolling over each other, we imprinted the white linen sheets with blood.

Dash spot-cleaned the sheets with bleach as I walked with the monk, picking snap peas and cauliflower from the monastery's or-ganic garden to cook for our dinner. After we ate, Dash and I began to clean; I confessed I'd never actually done dishes before. My face heated, I feared he'd see me as a child.

The water was steaming, Dash was running it. He smiled, told me, "I picked you underripe."

That night we did the dishes together.

Descending a ridge one chilly morning, Dash told me a true story about the tropical expat phenomenon: young men who move to

Thailand and live off the money they've already made for the rest of their lives. In Thailand they're rich enough to have a girl wash their bodies for them as they shower on the beach. Massages cost only one U.S. dollar.

I wondered what he was telling me in this story. I asked, "That's what you want to do?"

"Their brains get squishy," he said. He grinned dopily. "They rot." He switched topics and told me instead about the work he had done in finance in New York City. He'd been paid a lot of money to calculate the probability of different natural disasters and estimate the value of insurance against them.

He then said that really he was more interested in what I wanted to do. He wanted to show me the hidden swimming holes in the river gorges of Ithaca, in upstate New York where he'd studied math. He wanted to take me to the glaciers in Waterton National Park on the Great Divide Trail in Canada; he told me it was "more beautiful than the American side." The American side was Glacier National Park— revered for its beauty. We'd road-trip up there, it was too stunning a place to look at alone. He wanted to tell me everything he'd figured out, show me all the beautiful places he'd found. We talked about places we might go together at the end of September. We spoke without ever asking if going together was what the other wanted; it was.

I told him of Colorado, where I lived before the trail, below the mountains there: red clay and the smell of dank river mud, and of thunderstorms: dust rising. Pikes Peak snow-faded like a permanent ivory castle. Together we'd ski it. He had ski-raced at Cornell. With him, I'd be fearless.

He seemed intrigued and excited.

He told me he had always wanted to live in Colorado—Co-lo-rado.

I thought it was lucky that I'd lived somewhere he always wanted to go. Anywhere I went with Dash would be good, because I would be *with him*. And really I still loved Colorado Springs. I had always loved the beauty, I hadn't forgotten my childhood memories. The Bluffs, the red rock dirt; I couldn't think of anyplace better to go: I could return, even alone. I understood: *I could*. It couldn't be bad this time, I was immune.

I wouldn't run away from that pain, the rape. I was done running. I felt tremendous. Junior felt like the outsider. Junior didn't seem to belong with my memories of the Springs, he seemed disconnected from Colorado. I understood now that he could have been anywhere, he didn't taint the state. I had nothing to run from. Really I still loved Colorado Springs. It was my childhood Eden, nothing could kill that love.

And for the first time on the trail, I began to feel excited to return to my life off the PCT. I would return to Colorado Springs—with Dash. I saw that I was still in love with it. I grinned at the thought of kissing in winter's cold light in our sparse apartment, cloud light resting on the wooden floorboards, a snowstorm whiting out the world outside. High on the North American continent's continental divide, living inside our glass-walled box of home.

I began to lust after our conjoining life.

One day Dash asked me directly about my mother. "What does she do?"

There were mammoth truths I still hadn't told Dash. I hadn't been in control of my life, my self. In her shadow, I was muted, fainter. We all want to feel like our own people, otherwise we feel chained and trapped and like we are out of control of ourselves. Which in many ways I felt I was.

But I couldn't say any of this yet. No one answer felt it could contain anything close to the truth about her. My thoughts of my mother were wild chaos, I didn't know how to tell him we'd been enmeshed for as long as I could remember. I told him, flatly, "She's a lawyer."

A *lawyer*.

In a way this whole walk felt like an answer to the question, "What does your mom do?" My mother spent my lifetime telling me I was not capable of controlling my life, of taking care of myself, and therefore was forever bound to her.

I told Dash about how my dad spent hours upstairs in my old room, writing, years of his life. He'd written more than a dozen novels, I'd lost count. I'd only been allowed to read "Desk Carvings," "City of Children," A Game for Everyone"—the few written for children. He said he wouldn't want to be edited; he was doing this for himself. He said, "You wouldn't ask someone who learns to play the piano why they don't perform at Carnegie Hall." He was learning to write books. He'd never sent any of them out to try to publish. I told Dash how excited my father sometimes was to go and write.

Dash said, "He sounds like you."

I wished my father could see what Dash could.

I realized none of the wild plans Dash was imagining for us involved my writing. He didn't have any faith in it because I hadn't yet shown him any of it.

I wanted him to see how huge my potential was, to read my stories and the letters in my journal and to see that my writing was brilliant, as my father could in flickers *see*: I was a writer.

If I wanted him to see me as a writer, I would need to finally show him.

"What is your dad like?" I asked him.

He kissed me; through happy kisses he whispered, "He's a physicist."

When I asked him about his mother, all he said was, "Aloof."

I wondered what stories hid beneath his answers.

Dash and I descended toward the Cascade Range town of Packwood. It was drizzling, the sky draped like a blanket of white fog. We climbed over the trunks of massive fallen trees, knocked down by mountain storms. They were seven or nine feet thick, the roots at their bases a tangle like branches, but brittle; old dry dirt still clinging. We were morphed forest creatures.

We fell again, again, again to the other side, landing, landing down onto the damp dirt like dark green clay. We spent more time climbing over tree trucks than walking forward on the path between them.

In my vision, they became the outside of rabbits' houses, portals in my mind into a woodland creature's world.

These northern woods were familiar, as in a dream or an old nighttime story I'd been told. This was true old-growth woods.

When I was little, at bedtime, my mommy would read me the Uncle Wiggily Longears stories, set in a fantastical world inside the woods—beautiful old, illustrated books with cloth covers—faded navy, royal purple, burlap brown.

Uncle Wiggily was an aging "gentleman rabbit" afflicted with incessant rheumatism. Forest inhabitants would work and play. But they were plagued by the wood's "bad chaps," outlandish beasts all bent on nibbling off Uncle Wiggily's little ears. But strong and mean as the bad chaps were, frail old Uncle Wiggily could always escape them.

I loved *The Great Brain* books; tales of two young brothers' escapades, conning other kids and hopping trains—being wild boys. I listened with glee as my mother read me *The Little House on the Prairie*, enchanted by Laura's stories of how her family banded together through winters, tornadoes. Their ingenuity amazed me; subsistence seemed a game they all played as a family, always.

But Uncle Wiggily's was my very favorite world to slip into as I fell into dreams.

Dash and I descended into Packwood, through the looming old-growth trees huge over me, rooted in me.

When I was eight, my mommy gave me *A Walk in the Woods*, the story of a man who attempts to walk from Georgia to Maine, along the Appalachian Trail—a true story.

I felt the damp dirt squish under my running shoes, it was imprinted.

Packwood itself was a damp green town in the damp green woods, a central Washington forest valley.

We got hamburgers and shakes at the Blue Spruce Saloon &

Diner, it was vacant, and the waiter asked us what we did "in the real world" that allowed us to take six months off to hike the trail.

"We're in the real world," Dash responded, not answering. He seemed annoyed. "This is real life."

Our waiter, an older man with pure white hair, looked to me; I blushed for Dash. "I'm just a student," I said softly and then wondered if it was still true.

"I did finance stuff," Dash said; he was too loud. He quickly added, "And I'm retired."

He was acting like he wished for an end—not the beginning. He'd often spoken of investing and his dream of quickly making his five million "nut," but he hadn't yet. "Retired" seemed wrong. He was only twenty-nine, and he didn't have enough money to retire on. He wasn't working, didn't have a job to return to after the trail.

From the place this trail ended, he didn't have a plan, he had nowhere he had to go. He looked like a lost man. His reaction exposed his insecurity.

I felt safer with him in many ways—he was older, felt certain in ways I felt afraid, but in this way I felt this was reversed. While he seemed nervous in our inevitable return to the world off the trail, I was beginning to feel excited. I was ready.

For the first time, I was not afraid.

Early the next morning, I went to the Packwood Public Library to print one of my essays to let Dash read. I checked my e-mail; my dad had sent a picture "from a very long time ago," with a note that said it was "great" and he still loved it.

I opened it to see. It was a photograph of my old drawing of the Animal Ancestors, the creatures I'd imagined we'd evolved from, all grinning. They were faded now, almost invisible, but I could still remember the Magic Marker colors each had been. The one of Human Man had glasses and a curly beard—Man was the image of my father.

My dad wrote me, "Please also remember at all times that I love you very much, that my failures toward you were caused by static in my head and not at all by anything you did or said. . . . My hope (and goal) is that someday, not too far off, we can have a wonderful father-daughter friendship."

I was stunned to find his message. Printing these words from my daddy, knowing they were mine forever, I felt stronger. I was terribly loved. I was rich.

He knew he had been absent—he wouldn't be now. He promised me. I saw new hope for my father and me; closer to equals. This time, maybe we could evolve into friends.

It was heartbreaking to realize how we can fail the people we most love without even trying.

I thought: I'm still young. It's not too late.

I hadn't talked with my brother Jacob since the High Sierra. Our last conversation had been our call long ago when Icecap and I had parted paths and I had found myself alone. I'd been so comforted by his story of first love lost; it meant a lot to me to hear how he understood. In the language of lovesickness, we could understand each other clearly.

I missed him. Completing the entire Pacific Crest Trail required just the kind of dedication Jacob had shown me—I was remembering how important he'd been to me. We shared our childhood, spaghetti with meat sauce and pet names, secret jokes, adventures in our yard under the red canoe. That game he made up that was called Monster.

I remembered how when I was in kindergarten and he was in fifth grade, he'd wanted me to learn Spanish so that we'd have our own language our parents wouldn't be able to understand, like a secret language. But somewhere in my childhood, a fundamental fissure in the foundation of our connection had formed.

We grew up together, and it made me sad to see we'd become strangers.

I longed to tell him how my days on the trail were exhausting but sweet; I'd found a lovely strength, walking thirty miles in a day with ease now. I hiked hard by day and wrote late into nights, feeling like a child playing pioneer for real, young and full of promise. Divorcing my mother, mourning our sweet love lost, I found myself still comforted by the existence of my brother: pro baseball player. Though we had parted paths, our trails seemed parallel and both wonderful, it meant a lot to know he was playing hard too.

I reached deep into my knapsack for my valuables, the place I kept his image. I had carried it with me all this way. When I found the photo, I saw it was white and fuzzy at the edges, dissolving from abrasion against my driver's license. He was difficult to see clearly now.

I loved him hugely; he loved me badly, too.

In Jacob's dissolving image I could see that I'd done more to fuck up my relationship with my brother than I'd ever admitted to myself.

I know it wasn't fair of me, or rational, but I'd been angry at Jacob for more than how he'd reacted after my rape. I'd been angry with him for leaving when I was thirteen to DC, for college. For not wanting me with him as badly as I wanted to be with him. In reaction, I'd become distant with him first.

I was cold, I was rude; he was absent more and more. It was a cycle beginning long before the night I told him I was raped.

I hoped he was doing well. I wondered how baseball beyond Newton felt to him, if he felt that it was right for him, if he'd connected with someone there, a coach or an impressive fellow player. If he was finding it fulfilling and promising and exciting—and if he feared the time when it would end. I hoped he knew that his little sister was thinking of him, hoping that he was finding the fulfillment and beauty we'd dreamed of from the safety of our lawn, so much happiness. I was so curious to know.

From Canada I would call him.

I carried my essay back to meet the man I loved at a coffee shop, still in shock. I was grinning wildly. Immediately he put what he was reading down. He finally read my writing. Dash's validation was necessary and important; I trusted him. I wanted it. I needed him to love it.

I couldn't even look at him as his eyes moved though my story. It was the story of how I'd traversed the High Sierra. For simplicity I'd bypassed Aspen Meadow, the wooden sign and Muir Trail Ranch, Bonnie's kindness there; instead I'd written it as if I'd made it through entirely on my own. I'd hoped to publish the story in *There & Back Magazine* in Colorado, and didn't want people to enter the Sierras unprepared, believing they also could depend on the ranch.

When Dash finished he told me with a solemn stare: he was relieved. "It's incredible. Wild Child. You are a fucking writer."

I felt an intoxicating thrill. He saw in me a genius.

He called me a writer, I was a motherfucking writer. He saw me the way I wanted to be seen, and so would others. I was giddy—euphoric.

I stepped outside, so Dash couldn't hear, and called back home to Newton on the sat phone. I told them I had met a man who was going to move with me to Colorado.

Dash had never said it, it was technically a lie, but I *knew* it would be true. We were a drifting island. We could go anywhere, we had no jobs, no ties, no responsibilities or friends, but we had money, we had no plan at all, and all I felt was glee.

My parents answered me. My father: "It's a pretty wild place to meet somebody." I could envision his eyes smiling.

My mother said, "It sounds like you're in love."

Ascending out of town, rain poured in sheets, softening the trail. The world shone in gray light. Dash and I shouted over the downpour; he asked me "what next" and I answered him: "back to school. I guess." He said we would make it to Canada before it snowed, "And then you'll write a book."

I wanted to kiss him. The sky was white smoke, patterned with inky tree tops. We were drenched and I was so happy, I couldn't speak. The trail was a muddy stream; we splashed through it. The evergreens smelled sweet, of sap and clean wood.

Then Dash asked what my real name was. I almost half-lied and said, "Deb," but then I added the truth.

I asked him back: what was his? He said, "Justin Matis," and I liked the way it sounded.

That day we met a stranger on our trail, and when the man asked me what I did, Dash answered for me: "She's a great writer."

It was startling—he used the same words my father had once used to affirm me, naming me what I wanted to become. He stated so bluntly what my father had seen so long ago: that I was talented. I wished my dad had wanted to cultivate it in me the way he wanted to make Jacob great.

In the deafening downpour, I whispered, "I'm not sure." My doubt was inaudible.

The rain thinned into drizzle, and then only mist.

He told me I could make money as a writer. The wild faith he had in me seemed crazy.

Through the nights in our tent, I wrote. Day's thoughts coalesced; I couldn't sleep. Hiking, writing at night, not stopping—my ambition met talent met hard work, and he saw them all in me, conversing, surging: things no other man had shown a sign of recognizing. With Dash I didn't need the eyeless world: these endless woods.

I no longer needed to peel myself of my skin, or to hide. To Dash the colorless ephemeral things that existed just beneath my surface were as vivid as the beauty marks he traced on my cheek.

We were able to speak about everything in a way I'd seldom talked about anything. Our wildest dreams, our hopes. Our futures.

He told me I should be in New York City. He told me it wasn't as unaffordable as people say. All the fancy grocery stores throw out cheese and bread that's still perfectly good; he would Dumpster-dive for us. He'd forage. "It's worth it for you."

He told me he would read everything I ever wrote.

I felt I'd learned a sneaky trick while walking, something I'd apply to my life off the PCT, for the rest of my life: choose people who don't put you in the position of always saying no. Choose friends you truly want to say yes to. Dash's presence, his age, wisdom—his care for me—opened up so many possibilities. I didn't have to do what was expected of me around him, I could do what excited me.

I hadn't changed my submissive tendency; I'd found someone who could harness it to guide and protect me. I could see that Dash was leading me somewhere worth going, nearer to myself—closer to the self I wanted to embody.

We began to plan a life together. I could see—Dash was the person to get me closer to the person I'd found I wanted to be—a *writer*. He made me feel so secure in his love. He made me feel we were on a team and always would be.

When I was hungry he would set up his stove on a rock and cook me quinoa or pasta or even something with meat. He gave away his best food to me. I was always hungry then.

When I cried (I did, sometimes), he held me. He kissed my head and neck and didn't stop until I stopped.

I wanted to be with this man whom I loved and go somewhere new and exciting, either somewhere really remote in the middle of the wilderness or a metropolis of artists like Manhattan. Nowhere suburban. Nowhere in the middle. No compromises. He made me feel we were living in this society's loopholes, savaging—us against the Man—taking care of each other.

We called ourselves the Twilight Tribe, because we often hiked through sunset, into dusk. Our love grew stronger and stronger. I grew happier.

Together we decided we should rename me: "Like a pen name," Dash said. "You can do better than Deborah Parker." He was right—I knew it the moment he said the words. I realized that I'd been feeling this need for a new name for months now, but hadn't yet understood I could do something about it. Debby was the name of the girl I was before I'd walked. I would find a name that better represented me now. Wild Child was a name I'd taken in the context of who I was when I began this walk through woods—it reflected the girl I'd been when it was chosen.

Living as Wild Child, I could no longer be Debby Parker comfortably—this name that I'd been given at birth that defined me before I'd had the chance to define myself.

Every new person we met, Dash introduced me: "She's a great writer. We can show you her stories. It's the best stuff I've ever found." He believed it.

People were always skeptical. I was young, and maybe because I didn't look quite the way that they imagined writers do. But Dash got people to look at my work—to see me more fully. He saw me as absolutely unique. He saw me as independent, my own girl—just as I'd always wanted to be seen. He wanted to read my writing, all of it, to know everything about me and fully see me.

He gave me certainty in the merit of my work.

Maybe I fell in love with the confidence he gave me, the fury with which he affirmed me. Reflected in his eyes, I saw how beautiful I would be soon. His eyes were lit with incredible warmth.

It seemed he believed in me with an intensity no one I'd ever loved had.

His feelings for me changed the way I thought about my world.

I wondered if my bliss and the gratitude I felt was tied to him, or if it grew from within me.

One night, I saw that Dash had a pair of glasses in his hand. I'd never seen him wear them, but he'd been carrying them this whole way.

"You need glasses?" I asked him where they'd come from.

He slipped them on, squinting, and explained that he had nearly perfect vision. "I carry my glasses on the trail just so I can see stars."

About a week after Packwood I finally tried to answer Dash's question about my mother—who was she—the deeper reason of my walk. The thought of him not knowing who I actually was became more unbearable than my fear. I'd found the person I wanted to love me; I had to confess my secrets. I needed him to know who I was.

I opened my mouth and this time told him about how my mother dressed me until I was sixteen, because she didn't trust me to get to school on time without that help from her. He said flatly, "I'm impressed you're wearing pants." I laughed and he opened his warm arms, let me step in, and closed them around me.

We were walking along gorgeous ridges across Washington, above the timberline: alpine log flower fields in mountains before mountains before mountains. This beauty we'd emerged within felt limitless. I felt fit and strong, we were hiking fast. I stopped to take pictures of an alpine berry field; I wanted to remember.

Dash's neck flopped back; he tightened, hard-angled like cut stone. "Less breaking," he called back to me, "and more walking." His posture had stiffened. He wasn't looking at me.

I knew that the huckleberry photo wasn't really what frustrated him. My pausing captured in a moment the true problem: my walking pace was consistently slower than his. Dash's legs were longer than mine, he was six foot two, and I was five foot four—and his natural speed was about three and a half miles per hour, while mine was closer to just three. Hiking pace determines compatibility on the PCT. He was waiting for me again, getting cold, and once again I felt I should be rushing. He was frustrated. He criticized me, calling me slower.

It wasn't true though. In fact we'd been moving north at an almost identical rate for one hundred days before we'd even met. I told him we were hiking the same number of miles per day, we were just following different rhythms.

He squinted forward. "You're always breaking," he said.

A thousand miles ago, I would have let his frustration hurt me. Now I didn't. This snap of anger couldn't move me. I knew it wasn't about me—

But now I had no time for what I had no time for.

I was hiking to savor, not wanting this part of my life to be over.

"I'm not six feet," I said. "Walk your pace, I'll walk mine. We don't need to always be together." I handed Dash our tent; he took it. I told him, "I'll see you where you want to stop tonight."

His lips parting again, his jaw released its tension. The sun was going down to a big, beautiful blue flat dusk. He took the tent and walked ahead.

I walked the high crest's snaking trail toward shelter alone. The fronts of my toes and my heels were softly throbbing. Lately I had noticed something strange—I'd worn a size eight running shoe since freshman year of high school but now that size was suddenly too small. It seemed impossible—but all the miles of walking had caused my feet to grow. They craved more space.

The valley below inked blacker, gone from my view now. After another hour, I turned a bend and emerged to a prow: a flat of rock, our tent built on it, glowing soft yellow amid dimming rock, the black woods pooled below us. He had pitched our tent unsheltered on that high rock in the cold Washington air.

I noticed a second tent pitched nearby ours: Songbird's. She was a cute Canadian girl who carried a ukulele and sang songs by Macy Gray and Regina Spektor. I stepped slowly up the moon-white and steep granite slab, to the point—our tent very near the brink of the cliff. I took my shoes off. Dash heard me but didn't emerge.

"Dash," I said softly as I entered. He didn't answer. I feared he was still angry. I was hit with the scent of pine sap: Nag Champa burning. Dash had stuck it in the dirt floor of our tent's vestibule. I crawled in where it smoked lovely and sweet.

On that exposed prow, undressing in the smoke—suddenly scared he was changing—not knowing if we were still fighting—I wanted him to speak.

He leaned in toward me. I leaned toward him, too—was relieved to see his eyes were smiling brightly. He said nothing. Then he kissed me. On my lips, they parted, with his tongue.

I hadn't showered in a week, my curly hair was tied up in one dreadlock-knot on the back of my head, and my ankles were brown with dry dirt, my whole face darkened with filth—I smelled like aged sweat, and yet he wanted my scent and my face, my body.

Dash was the first person I ever had sex with more than once. I desired sex with him in the way I hadn't with anyone before him. I

felt safe with him. I'd never been in love. I'd never had an orgasm—
not even from my own touch. It was as if my body wouldn't let me
have an orgasm until I felt love first, until it knew I wouldn't get hurt.
My body was smarter than I was. I was with someone who would
never hurt me, and so I finally relaxed.

It started to feel good. I felt consumed, blinded by his fire. He was
worthy of devotion—I felt devout. I was high on the climb's endor-
phins, fitter than I'd ever been, among the beauty of granite mountains, in *love* and with a man who could finally make sex good for
me. I screamed in pleasure through cool night, my hot call echoing
through the dark blue sky, out to the distant silhouetted peaks.

Afterward, I held his face and kissed him. I wanted to wake up
and have breakfast with this man for all the mornings of my life. We
were nearing the end of the trail, only weeks from the borderline,
and I wanted to cross over with this boy.

Sun broke our dreaming. We kissed each other 'bye and walked at
our own paces; I stopped and took a picture of him, an inky silhouette over blank sky, sun rising. The morning was thick with mois-
ture. Dash was a fleck on the gold sun, drifting. Rumors had been
circulating about an imminent snowstorm, and I could feel the cold
air in my lungs.

I climbed the vertical 3,130 feet to the top of Suiattle Pass—hiked
twenty-eight miles, a big day. Dash must have hiked even faster because I didn't catch him that night. We built our camps separately,
treading our journeys' final stretches independently. The last trail-
town, a tiny lakeside community called Stehekin—our very final
stop before Canada—was nearing.

A sign appeared. It pointed down a forested hillside, toward the
far end of the only road around. Twice daily through the summer,
a stout bus would arrive at an opening in the trees below. Through
evergreens I saw Dash on an old bench, elbows on thighs, looking at
the dirt. I called to him, "Caught you!" It was 2:53—the second bus
would come at 3:00 and I was just barely in time.

Dash was solemn. He told me he feared we might get snowed out of Canada.

The bus arrived promptly, and we stepped wordlessly aboard.

The road wasn't paved, only dirt and mud, and we bumped and swayed down it, chilly, squinting through gold light to try to finally glimpse Stehekin, and sea-blue Lake Chelan. I pressed my fist to the cold glass. The clear wet print of it was a damp window out to trees, green fields bright with dandelions. We saw the faint lake growing, pale blue mountains rising—watching for the tiny pack of villagers living alongside the water—the very last town. We were now at the northwestern tip of America.

Outside a rose-dotted shock of green—a redwood cottage and its simple garden—we parked. This was the town bakery. Dash gorged himself on cinnamon buns, savory puff pastries, bread glistening with huckleberry jam. I wanted it all—but I took only a few bites from his rich pastries. Soon I wouldn't be a thru-hiker anymore.

We found Stehekin had no cell phone reception, and no pavement at all. It was lush, accessible only by floatplane, boat, or foot—and the one bus, down the dirt road, from the clearing we'd both found—just the one way in, from the woods.

There was one main restaurant, a perfect restaurant. Only one country store, and it had hot chocolate, coffee, milk. And Dash.

We set up camp in the town's gorgeous campground, Lake Chelan shimmering through the black trees, long and winding, a blue vein of a lake.

A red leaf danced from a branch like a dropping flame, down into the calm blue lake. A gust had broken it free. There was a cold bite in the wind.

It was now deep autumn in the mountains.

Stehekin is a Columbia-Moses word. It means simply "the way through."

At the post office the woman was stern with me. I'd come just to pick up the package of food my mother promised she'd send, as usual,

along with a final—sixth—pair of running shoes. I hadn't expected
to need this pair, but Washington had proven damp and gritty, the
grainy mud tearing up the sneakers' mesh. At my name the postal
worker smirked. "You," she told me. "*Debby.*"

I stood dumbly. We were the only two people in the small office.
"Just please sit down," she said and disappeared into the back. She
seemed annoyed with me already.

But she produced my package quickly—and then another. And
another, back, another, back, one more; "*There's* more."

She carried package after package after package, placing them
on the floorboards at my feet. I stayed sitting, a little embarrassed. I
wondered if I should offer to help her. I called to her, "I'm sorry."

My mother had sent me eight packages—"*Eight.*" The woman
told me it was a Stehekin town record.

It was also more than I could possibly carry. I couldn't leave town
lugging these extra things. Giving food away, repackaging and mail-
ing everything leftover back to her would stall me—I feared I'd get
snowed out. But I had to. At the picnic table outside, feeling angry, I
broke open the first—

It held running shoes. They were carefully stuffed with tissue
paper so they wouldn't become warped. The shoes I wore were darkened with dirt, another five hundred miles of stones and mud, and
now both toes poked through, exposed in their filthy socks. My feet
ached for support—I needed these shoes desperately.

I noticed one of the other boxes was identical. Inside was a backup
pair of the same shoes, carefully packaged the exact same, a half a
size larger than my normal shoe size.

That pair fit me perfectly.

A larger box was full of wholesome food: freeze-dried strawberries and mango; green beans and foil-wrapped white Irish cheddar;
dark-chocolate calcium supplements and Flintstone vitamins, the
purple ones picked out. The best food of any thru-hiker I knew.

I tore open another—black leather high-heeled pumps, matte
and sleek. I'd purchased them for no reason when I was eighteen, at a
trail-town in central California, back when I'd hiked away, just weeks

after losing my virginity to Tyler, weeks before the rape. Beneath the heels lay a folded cloth that shimmered—a white sequin-encrusted skirt I'd picked out years before that at a teenaged girls' boutique in Newton Centre, a million miles ago. It glittered in the sun. I remembered I'd once loved it. I'd felt lovely in it—the only skirt I had that I had confidently chosen. I stared blankly at the dress-clothes— *remembering.*

Somehow I had forgotten—weeks before, down in Cascade Locks, giddy and silly and wanting Dash to want me, I had actually asked my mother to mail me this pair of heels and sequined ivory skirt. I was ridiculous.

My mother had lovingly obeyed me, regardless.

In heels, I walked through the trees toward a light. A dozen hikers were building a bonfire at the campground. Sparkling in my sequined lace, I fed it branches. My skirt shimmered, the fire leaped, and I pivoted back, twirled; I felt lovely. Songbird plucked at her ukulele, singing Jason Mraz and Macy Gray into the fire shadows, and her voice was agile and sweet. *I try to say goodbye and I choke / Try to walk away and I stumble.* My mom had mailed much more food than I needed, boxes filled with Clif Bars and bags of dried pineapple and blueberries and walnuts—my pack was bloated—and I broke open bags of roasted nuts, and dried cherries and the most wonderful dark chocolate. I felt fortunate. I began giving away this nourishment I wouldn't be able to carry. An old hiker from Berkeley, California named Nobody said, "City girl, look at him looking at you. I see you steal that country boy."

I saw what he saw—Dash watching me, sweetly smiling.

I had never lived in a big city, and Dash wasn't a country boy; he was from Berkeley also. And yet what Nobody said felt perfectly true. Dash and I were stolen away.

We'd married our souls.

I smiled back, into the firelight, bright sparks rising—I was so happy—and saw Jacob was there for me in my last breakup, and he had been right. I could trust my brother. I was so heartbroken that I couldn't trust my brother, that Jacob didn't care about my life anymore—but he did. Connected by an emotion we had once felt in solidarity, I felt linked with him in a way that I hadn't in forever. I felt impossibly secure. My posture had changed—maybe even the muscles of my face, and there was no mirror here, but I was sure: at this moment I would be unrecognizable to anybody back in Newton. Confident in my body for the first time on the trail and perhaps in my life, among sweet friends, I felt beautiful—in control of the direction of my life, where I'd go from the place where this trail ended. I was empowered, finally to have chosen my own outfit—and to have my mom support that.

I thought about the second pair of running shoes she'd sent me here—which fit me better. She cared tremendously. The shoes had reached me just in time to help me complete this journey. I thought, *My mother gave me exactly what I needed*, and the simple statement made me teary, though it seemed silly to cry, to feel so happy. Tears fell into the fallen leaves. I was grateful for the new cushion and support of the clean shoes, but also—more potently—for her.

My mother had been good—remarkable. She'd sent all the packages I'd asked for into the middle of nowhere—it must have been terribly expensive—just as she had delivered me everything I'd needed for this whole walk. Shimmering in my skirt, I felt how my mother had sent what I needed—and now also respected what I wanted, even when it was different from what she'd wanted for herself.

I felt a new sense of freedom that allowed me to see her with empathy, I was no longer stuck.

Touching my zipper, the white sequins twinkling in the campfire's golden light, I felt like I belonged to an ancient tradition of all young people given this same task of finding their own ways through to the futures they wanted for themselves.

The skirt was so wonderfully insane to wear here that it made me shiver—fingering the delicate pearl lace, my strength in my hands.

I passed around all the food I didn't need; my friends took it, they were grateful. My hands free, I fed and fed the fire.

She sent me two pairs of running shoes, knowing my feet had grown.

The truth was that it wasn't just luck that I'd found the way to the sign that led me down to salvation at Muir Trail Ranch. The truth was: I'd remembered that fork. I had been there, at that same signpost, twice before that harrowing day I'd nearly starved: the summer before college, happy, I had followed this same sign—the meadow had been different then, snowless: transformed by spring. I had reached Muir Trail Ranch and picked up my mother's support package from a kind older woman.

And the year before that, lying to my parents about the Outward Bound alumni trip, I had emerged from the woods, to Aspen Meadow and Muir's sign. I'd found the ranch then, too.

My mother had sent me a package there then, too.

I had always expected to be taken care of and unconditionally loved and supported. Childhood is an inherently narcissistic time, and it was as if all my life I had been a child. I had seen my life from only my perspective. I didn't want to remain a child—blind to compassion. I sat in the warmth of my last bonfire, among sweet nomads I may soon never see again, and it was as if I was only just finally remembering that I had a privileged history also.

And my mother had her own history.

I remembered that Grandma Belle, who had always been so fun to play with, had not truly been an overly loving mother to my mother. My mom had once told me about how Grandma hardly touched her or her little sister and seldom told them, "I love you." She was both controlling and distant, would yell at my mom when she was a child for small, ridiculous things, like not offering to vacuum.

Belle was a young mom; she was beautiful, yet cold. She was a stay-at-home mother. Every day, if you asked her, was the worst day of her life.

My mom used to tell me, "I don't like my mother, but I love her."

She cleaned my room, did my dishes and my laundry, shopped for my clothes and put on my socks each morning. She sent me beautiful bouquets on holidays, on my birthday, when I was sick. She supported my every venture. In a thousand ways she was incredibly wonderful. I knew that everything my mother had ever done for me came from the same sweet place as her tremendous love.

My mother became the good mother she wished she'd had.

My mother seemed so pure and vulnerable in her love.

I could finally see that my mother's need to take care of me grew from feeling rejected by her own mother. I saw—my mommy didn't know how to feel loved if she didn't feel needed.

I tried to see my rape from my mother's perspective.

Perhaps my mother saw my rape as a testament to her own failure to be the good mother she'd been my entire life. I wondered if she feared now that she'd sheltered me too much. She told me to remain silent as if my rape were my shame, but now I wondered if it was hers. She had avoided the difficult conversation, as I had. I understood my mother's desire for my silence. She was a basically good mother, muted in pain. What I didn't know was how terribly common that was.

She thought she was protecting our family—and also me. She was trying to protect me from the rape-shaming she saw in her generation. She wanted to do everything right for me—but couldn't understand that I could want different things.

When we apply the lessons we've struggled for our whole lives to learn to the lives of people we love, our love becomes judgment—which is toxic. Our fear our daughters will fail leads us to fail them.

My mother spent eighteen years caring for me and protecting me from hurt, and the minute I left home the worst thing that could have happened *happened*. It must have devastated her, she couldn't face it. She needed to avoid it. Because it hurt her too much, too.

I could feel the heartbreak of the tragedy of the failure of intent, I could see now that mothers who love us can fail us. Her love was still stunningly real.

On this walk I'd had so much time and space to actually figure out who *I* was without my mother's influence. I understood now: the things that my mother had found made her happy were not the same as the things that made me happy. And I understood: that was okay.

I'd asked to walk this trail—which I'd known would terrify her—for the flights and all the money and packages. My mother had done everything I'd asked of her for this walk, right up until these packages in my last trail town. She'd always done just what I'd asked, supported me. So close to Canada, the end, I no longer felt resentment. My resentment became understanding that could also allow gratitude. I saw finally that she was doing all she could.

Vividly seeing that love had always been my mother's guide, I could finally release my anger—let go of it there in the woods—and move past it.

I could see now that her support of this walk, thorough and complete, financial and also logistical—*was* her supporting me in the best way she knew how. She'd done every single thing I asked of her. This was how my mother knew to love. She provided devoted support with hard, tangible things when she couldn't with words, or with her ear—and I felt terribly grateful here. I was amazed to find that her continued loyalty to my requests came to mean much more to me in this last trail-town than simply possessing an old skirt.

I pivoted and spun, adding dead limbs to the bonfire, it surged.

Our parents do their bests.

The fact was this walk would have been much harder, maybe impossible without my mother's care packages. Her support of me had enabled my healing. A colder mother would have let the good world bury me.

Because I feared I couldn't walk to Newton Centre without her, I needed to hike through desert, snow and woods alone.

Childhood is a wilderness.

CHAPTER 20

A GIRL IN THE WOODS

Now Autumn's fire burns slowly along
the woods and day by day the dead leaves fall and melt.
—WILLIAM ALLINGHAM

We write only at the frontiers of our knowledge, at the border
which separates our knowledge from our ignorance and transforms
the one into the other.
Only in this manner are we resolved to write.
To satisfy ignorance is to put off writing
until tomorrow—or rather, to make it impossible.
—GILLES DELEUZE

A cold storm was forming. The PCT's weather window was closing, and if we didn't keep moving north, soon the trail would be buried under snow. My request for the girlish clothing now felt naive and silly. I hadn't planned properly, and didn't think about how having these things sent out here would mean I would have to carry an impossible load for the final days on the trail—or I'd need to shed them. I rushed to the post office to send back the extra weight, but repackaging everything in boxes took all afternoon. I'd told Dash I'd be on the two o'clock bus, but I was too slow. I missed it. When I reemerged onto the porch, the bus with Dash was gone.

But this time his absence felt different. There was no question—I knew our separation wasn't permanent. I had no doubt he would be waiting for me where the trail ended.

And I'd thrive in these mountains. I had been cold before; I could handle myself in the wild. I was an animal learning, instinctively. So little time remained to make this dream real—it would all end soon—and I had just eighty-nine miles to walk from Stehekin to the border. Just three or four more days—my last. It felt fitting and right to walk these final miles alone. Dash had left me free to finish at my own pace, the way I'd started—and beat this storm.

I left Stehekin on the second bus, at five thirty that evening, exhausted; I walked through dusk—determined to reach Canada before snow erased the world. The land became a vast bed of gravel, I was exposed. The trees vanished. I walked swiftly, happy, drinking the vastness of my freedom. Small stones sifted into my shoes' mesh, muddy pebbles; the ground became soft with them. My calloused feet were unbothered, immune. My legs were strong.

That evening, still hiking swiftly, I smelled sugary lilac; instantly I knew it was a day-hiker's perfume. Then I saw the shadow: a lady hiking. High on a ridge we met; she stopped me to ask where I'd come from and where I was going, astonished to learn I'd walked the whole trail from Mexico.

"And what made you decide to do this?" she asked. She was probably forty, and her lipstick matched mine. She said the distance I'd traveled was amazing.

"My parents used to always take me backpacking," I said, "and I still love it."

The woman nodded adamantly. "Yes, *excellent*." She said, "You go girl!" She was looking at my face in the dark air—at my sunglasses. She was trying to see me. I wanted to take the glasses off, but then I wouldn't be able to see her.

I left them on and thanked her, and said goodbye. I kept going.

She called after me to say I was her hero.

My ears rang, I walked away unsteady—

I had transformed my body, I was strong and resourceful—in the woods I had learned I was capable of anything I committed to doing—but I hadn't committed. I could pitch a tent and carry a backpack a marathon a day through mountains—a thousand feats—physically I'd become undeniably confident—I had survived 2,600 miles from Mexico to this cold night in a spill of mossy black forests—but even as I walked alone over the crests of the Cascade Mountains, my inabilities still trapped me. I was her hero who couldn't put in contact lenses, who was still embarrassed I wore sunglasses at night.

I began to run, as I had on the very first day in the desert; I committed: I would beat the snow. I absolutely needed to complete this walk. I crossed mossy rock slabs: northern Washington's granite spine.

It must have been ten or later by the time I stopped, camping directly under the cool spray of stars' pale etching on the navy sea of sky.

That night in my journal I began a new list, like the ones I'd make and throw out as a kid, but this one to keep—*I will*:

• touch my eyes.

And I saw that there was something else I still needed to change.

As my mother wished, I wasn't telling people about my rape, or raising money for RAINN. When asked, I changed my reason for walking back to John Muir, childhood backpacking, my wonderful summer base camp out in Colorado Springs—vague and faded things. I had almost completely stopped speaking about my more recent past. I had stopped telling people the truth about my rape and I had found a crutch in the word "virgin."

I needed to stop it.

"Virgin" surprised men, contradicted everything they had heard and *thought they knew* about me—it got men to back off quickly. It was my shorthand for *innocence*. It told people irrefutably my body was my own, not to persist— the rumors they'd heard were false—but it was *a lie*.

It wasn't who I was.

In those dark hours, tentless and exposed to the night, my mind returned to *The Breakfast Club* ending. I saw the way I'd accepted Junior's joint, giving the college a reason to blame me for what came next. The way I'd told him to leave now, very softly. Before the boy had raped me, I had wanted him to want to kiss me.

More than anything, more than everything, I'd felt guilty.

For this entire walk, my desire had ashamed me, as if my wanting to be kissed that night mitigated the fault of Junior's sudden deafness. I'd been given stacks of reasons to blame myself for an act of violence committed by another. I had blamed my flirting for his subsequent felony. My college taught me: my rape was my shame. Everyone I'd trusted asked only what I might have done to let it happen.

In my gut, I'd always believed I'd caused it.

I finally questioned it.

I wrote through darkness, vividly seeing: my passivity was not a crime; my desire to trust was not a flaw. *Junior* was guilty of forcing me to have to actively fight for my own safety in the first place. The virgin lie was my answer to my painful shame; the lie created its own, new shame. I needed to stop hiding: I was raped. It was time to honestly be exactly who I was. I saw—the shame wasn't mine, it was his, and I could stop misrepresenting myself, and I could accept myself.

Silent snow was falling, faint in the dark woods; the ground beneath my thin foam sleeping pad was a rug of moss; I felt close to the ground, at home here. The ancient moss smelled sweet, and I felt buoyed.

I crossed into a new territory in the woods. I pardoned myself for being passive and paralyzed in the face of danger—whether it was the danger of starvation or of being raped when I was eighteen and painfully innocent. I finally bypassed the wall I hadn't known I was hitting: the wrong conviction that I was to blame for Junior's decision to attack and threaten me.

My rape was not my fault. Old words returned to me:

No one causes rape but rapists.

I believed it.

And I forgave myself for my rape.

I scrawled under galaxies, glancing at night's sky through sunglasses, as I had for my whole walk. I wrote for hours as the clouds cleared and the spray of stars reappeared in the cold blackness, brighter now.

I woke to snow. It was first light, the forest and my sleeping bag shimmering, dusted with powder, enough to make the world gleam, but nothing dangerous: blue dawn.

The snow had stopped. Dark gray rolls of clouds drifted eastward, and I was whitened, glittering and cold. The climate of these mountains was damp, the weather erratic—fierce and fitful. Tomorrow it might snow again and pile higher. I walked, floated, lighter—forty miles, my biggest day yet. I'd lifted the burden of guilt and shame off of my body. I held my new hard-won wisdom, the gift three months of walking in the wilderness had carried me to: compassion for my younger self—forgiveness for my innocence.

I was gliding. My heart beat fast, faster in the dark—still fast when I again collapsed on the dirt trail and rested. That night, my very last on the PCT, my thighs were numb. I had no energy to pitch my tent, and I again slept directly on the dirt, under stars.

I swore to tell the story that those in charge of caring for me had silenced.

Quiet forest lay before me, cold and white—and I would make it: Canada.

In those final eighty-nine miles, I wouldn't once pitch my shelter. Out of exhaustion, or maybe simply in deep comfort, I slept each night directly under evening sky.

The night Junior stayed, my right to myself was taken from me in a way that had felt more final than ever before. Then the school had denied my rape—my word. The subsequent silencing and exile—misplaced shame—were the catalysts for me to finally break free of my mother's grasp and my voicelessness and do what I truly wanted, alone. I wished to prove myself as independent and valid and strong—to my mother, and to the world. I'd believed I had needed something huge and external that no one could deny was impressive, so I could show my family I was able—so they could finally know that I was strong.

Instead I had shown myself.

And it felt wonderful.

I was ending a wild child transition phase, filthy, stoveless make-upless and mapless, but also the fittest I'd ever been—testing myself in a hundred extreme ways, failing until I decided that the consequences of failing myself were too devastating to justify—and the only option I had left was to change, to do the very things I was so sure I couldn't, to survive.

Living in woods, I had sweat and bruised, walked boldly through snow and shame and pain. I faced obstacles and monsters and had some very thirsty miles, dark nights, freezing mornings and dream-like days of fear of starving in which I came close to dying; I'd made it past desert sunspots: my own blindness. I had earned the very self-reliance, poise and self-assurance that I believed would remain for-ever out of my reach as I'd stared at Lake Morena's dirty mirror that morning five months earlier—a country away.

I'd entered a place in my life where I was straddling two names— Debby Parker of my past, Wild Child of a life that was now ending— just as I was straddling my childhood girl and the woman I was becoming. I'd walked away from Debby, and in my darkest despera-tion, at the edge of my death, passed through Aspen Meadow to get to Muir Trail Ranch, to be saved, to save myself. To find my strength.

When I came closest to death, the woods gave way to Aspen. The name brought my gifted future.

I was not forever lost.

The border is defined by a road-wide clear-cut line in the thick pine forest. I stood at the wooden monument that marked the end of my

2,650-mile hike from Mexico to Canada; I stared at the thing with glazed eyes. No tears, no ecstatic dance. I'd accomplished what, five months earlier, I had set out to accomplish.

I took a picture of myself in front of the Pacific Crest Trail's northern terminus and kept walking. Where the trail ends, there isn't anything. I had to walk eight more miles to a highway in Manning Park, Canada, and then I'd have to find something more to do.

I had feared this end, wondered where I would go from it, from the moment I first stepped on this footpath in the desert. But I found I was not afraid of reaching it now. I was happy. I hadn't found every answer for where I was going, but I now had all I needed to take these next steps. I knew I would do what I needed to do to become a writer now.

I was going to be Aspen, without the barriers Debby was trapped by. And I had found a partner who would help me reach where I wanted to go, identify and guide my path in ways I couldn't yet. He told me to write, he told me to do what I loved and what he saw moved me closer to what I wanted most. I could walk forward with him now. He was helping me carve a strong new path that led from this post that marked the end of the path we'd met on, and I trusted it. I could take the gift Wild Child had found and with his hand, walk into Aspen Matis.

I grinned as I stepped. This name felt like home. I trusted where it would lead.

And to get there, I knew how to walk.

At the highway, Songbird, Shell, the Stumbling Norwegian, Bonanza Jellybean, A-Bear, and a few new hikers I'd never met but who must have been always around—and Dash—were clapping.

For me.

Dash ran to me, hugged me. A-Bear handed me a beer and a brownie. Songbird's family had a grill set up, and the smell hit me like wind—charred meat. On the side of the highway, they were making burgers for us hikers, as if we were just any hungry people. Really that was what we were now: hungry people.

Then Dash kissed me. He was here; I was here. I smiled and pressed my cheek against his chest. "We did it," I said to him.

He lifted my hand in his. He said, "Now's the scary part."

It seemed an arbitrary end. I stood in that forest spot and looked to Dash's face. I heard a car's tinny engine and could see through the trees an old Jeep passing.

Standing in the clearing where the PCT joined with the highway, looking from tree to tree, smelling meat charring, burning wood snapping and smoking, I saw the other trails I might have taken, the other yellow dirt ways my life more easily might have gone. In one world, I'd never have known of the Pacific Crest Trail. In another, I'd have flown back home, weak with MRSA and healed there—and never returned to the PCT. Truly I nearly hadn't. In most worlds, Dash would live, and I would live, and our footsteps wouldn't ever have overlapped.

We wouldn't meet. In another, Junior Mason would have stopped when I said stop, and I'd study English at Colorado College, and I'd graduate, not unhappy, not so extremely happy, Debby Parker. I'd become an English teacher or a professor, walking the middle road.

I kissed back the man who would become my husband.

From that unremarkable gap in dense northern forest, I could finally see clearly that if I hadn't walked away from school, through devastating beauty alone on the Pacific Crest Trail, met rattlesnakes and bears, fording frigid and remote rivers as deep as I am tall—feeling terror and the gratitude that followed the realization that I'd survived rape—I'd have remained lost, maybe for my whole life. The trail had shown me how to change.

This is the story of how my recklessness became my salvation.

I wrote it.

In the dim of the Cinder-block Palace I had listed the things I would carry, the things I thought I'd need to survive in wilderness alone.

In Canada I saw the list newly. I hadn't truly survived all on my own. I could see I'd been supported the whole way through.

I saw: The Things That Carried Me:

- John Muir. "In every walk with nature one receives far more than he seeks."
- John Donovan, for showing me that even in death, gifts lie in wait, revealed in storms and snow.
- Trail Magic, for showing me that when you're walking through deserts that should give no refuge, the road will provide, so long as you keep stepping. An unexpected peach could propel me 100 dusty miles.
- Trail Angels unseen and unacknowledged, who provided essential and reliable support, showed me to trust that when I need help it will come. They proved a silent, sightless force aids people on all journeys that matter.
- My father's music—*You're a big girl now, And hard like an oak, Buckets of moonbeams in my hand.* These mantras lulled my mind to solace in Maine's virgin woods and the house my dad imagined for us there. Dad's wilted brave dreams of beauty, abandoned homes of my childhood: constant rhythms of love that that would sterilize the terrible seeds that had stained me.
- The running shoes my mom always remembered to send before my last pair was worn out.
- My trail legs. When I rely on them they grow strong. They carried me through the woods when my mind couldn't.
- My parents, who taught me how to walk.
- The Pacific Crest Trail. It led me someplace worth going, after all.

EPILOGUE

A Chinese proverb says that a journey of a thousand miles begins with a single step. This journey had begun with my terrible passivity and fear. I hadn't trusted myself to be able to do anything for myself without guidance and assistance. Then I took a reckless leap: I *tried to*. I walked boldly into desolate mountains; I lay motionless through black star-etched nights alone. I had taken six million steps in the direction of my grand hopes for myself—and had delivered myself to Manning Park and amnesty from shame. I found my strength and independence. I had contracted MRSA and left this trail for just long enough to come back to meet Dash; I'd beat the winter, and crossed over, my childhood over.

The day after I finished, snow fell like an endless curtain and few hikers behind us on the trail would make it through. It seemed everything had happened just in time, in grace.

I would return to Eden, living in my old college town's beauty, walking under the campus's golden aspens with Dash through the fall. We slept on a mattress on the floor of his apartment, and then in our bed.

On the last day of February we walked together through Colorado Springs's beautiful red rock state park—the Garden of the Gods. Erect pinnacles of rock shot into the pristine blue sky, tiny people clinging to them, climbing. I could smell the clay earth and Dash's hair. I felt very close to him. There, walking that Eden, clasping each other's hands, we became engaged.

I would go back to school, this time not within the Eden of my childhood but in New York City. I would write every day, that was my job now, and I'd publish my stories in the *New York Times*, my favorite literary magazines—journals I'd long-read and daydreamed with but never thought I had permission to submit to.

The next summer Dash and I would return to the Pacific Crest Trail and re-hike six hundred of California's most remote and striking miles. And when we got to trail-side towns we'd eat fresh strawberries and fat cherries shipped from Leona Valley and shower in motels with flower-printed curtains and compile lists of friends and plan our wedding.

We returned to the Cascade mountain, where we'd met, and wed.

I didn't know then if Dash and I would end up with three kids, together forever like my parents, or if the inevitable responsibilities— and normalcy—of our lives in the "real world" would extinguish the fire of this young love. If the heat would slowly cool. Maybe I'd be left in the woods in darkness. Perhaps unformed storms poured farther down our path, unseeable. All I knew was he was the sweetest, most gentle man I'd ever met, and I would let him lead me to New York, back to school.

And if I'd be left alone in woods again, I smiled to think how I'd find new gifts and thrive. At the end of a long trail and the beginning of the rest of my life, I was committed to always loving my self. I would put myself in that win-win situation.

I sat alone in my Greenwich Village apartment with a new determination. Dash had returned to the woods, to walk from Mexico to Canada, again; I'd returned to wearing thick glasses, still believing I couldn't touch my eyes. It had been months since Dash disappeared down some new side-path into his dark woods, and I was done with being bound to glasses, with waiting for him to return to me.

I washed my hands and returned to the mirror over my bed and opened a new box of contacts. I so desperately wanted to be able to change, to just finally *do it*—touch my eye and be seen. I was fed up with being the girl who had to wear glasses. I realized that no, no one would actually come to save or even stop me, I had absolutely no choice. The scale tipped: the moment *not* doing it became more difficult and unbearable than just doing it.

Squatting on my bed—after twelve years of trying and missing, in about two minutes total—I put my own contacts in for the first time. Second try on the right eye, first try on the left. I blinked in the contact, my apartment where I now lived alone and my story coming into focus.

After twelve years of trying, I just decided to stop missing.

I looked straight—a mirror was there. I was shocked by the face I saw. I was looking at my image for the first time since I was a child in third grade, seeing my face without glass and wire adorning it. I felt lovely, seeing my beauty—the beauty Jacob had always told me I had. I had always wanted to see it too, now I vividly could. It was my own. And looking into that mirror at my exposed eyes, I could see with clarity why I loved Jacob so much: as a child, I'd felt that he believed in the brightness of me and saw the way to dreams—he helped me see that I was able to make my own dreams real, too. It was the most exciting thing, those maps we'd made.

It was suddenly Technicolor clear: the only thing holding me from giving myself vision this entire time had actually simply been me.

I saw how in the fall and winter of my childhood, I'd walked through the golden aspens. And then I simply committed and gave myself my own eyes.

I had once again proven that again alone, I was again enough.

I was astounded to find an invitation from Colorado College—the school I'd dropped out of six years before, after I'd been raped on campus. As I read their words, I became unsteady with heat. I'd long ago reconciled myself to the fact of their abandonment. I never imagined I would get a message from them that had the potential to finally prove the past six years of my social shame wrong—after all this time, what I hoped was the promise that they finally believed me, *they knew the truth*. Colorado College was inviting me to return—to speak publicly about the rape they had denied.

Now the school that had silenced me not only acknowledged my rape—they wanted to pay $1,000 plus airfare and two nights in a fancy hotel, for me to come back and speak on campus to current students about what had happened there.

In my tiny Greenwich Village bedroom, I considered their offer and its origin—what had caused it. My upcoming hardcover was listed in catalogs they must have seen. Were they star-chasers only interested because a New York publisher had validated me? I deeply hoped my old school wanted me back to apologize and acknowledge their mistake. Cross-legged on crisp white bedsheets, I painted my nails red. I felt emboldened. My pain might finally be validated. I would do it, I wrote back. Yes.

A week later my grandma Belle mailed me a clipping from the *Colorado Springs Gazette*. The college called me a *"New York Times* correspondent"—a mistake. I was embarrassed. I had published only one essay in the *Times*, no reportage. The college didn't mention I'd been raped there. Instead, they ambiguously said, "a horrific trauma." Instead of a dropout, I was now a successful "alumna" enhancing the prestige of their institution—not myself: a girl who had been raped on campus, who fled.

They were obscuring me again.

I asked for corrections of the misinformation—explaining that I was not a graduate, and the shocking vague "trauma," was actually sexual assault. I'd spent the years searching for the *right words* to talk about what had happened; I'd found how tremendously important it was to find the integrity of words matching my truth. I told them I felt misrepresented by the incorrect information. They said they'd fix their mistakes. Posters with the original mistakes were printed and up all over campus, but online they changed "alumna" to "former CC student" and *New York Times* "correspondent" to "contributor"— but they left "a horrific trauma." Still no rape.

Back at my old college, I stood before one hundred people at the podium in a classroom lecture hall where I used to sit in the back row. The last time I was there I wore heavy glasses, a backpack and sneakers, but now in flowing red silk and my grandma's golden locket and heels—and contact lenses—I felt larger and vivid, ready to be seen. I looked forward. I said it four times: *Rape rape rape, rape.* That's what it was.

Halfway through speaking, I looked up in the room and saw my grandmother Belle. Visiting her in my childhood summers was why I chose that college to begin with. Ever since I was five, I would send her crayon drawings of the Colorado mountains where she lived. At ninety-one now, tiny but still sprightly, she'd surprised me by showing up.

I spoke without interruption for a half hour. They listened. I read to them from my memoir what happened on my second night here at college; I cried for a breath—with my shoulders back, eyes open brightly. When I exhaled, I looked out into the audience to see a woman—she looked like a teacher—was crying. I felt loved and I felt heard.

During the Q and A session, I answered everything all the female co-eds, and boys, and men and women in the audience asked me. I wished the hurt eighteen-year-old I used to be could have seen me back here, at twenty-four, reading—speaking unapologetically.

I was finally having the rape openly acknowledged and discussed at the place where it had first been silenced, it was surreal. The invitation—this talk—made me feel like I was transcending, I was rising like a night star.

The way to self-love and admiration is to behave like someone whom you love and admire. I felt the potential of this euphoric insight.

Toward the end, my grandma raised her hand. The mediator called on her. "I want everyone to know my granddaughter is also a great artist," she announced. The room laughed. She smiled at me with pride.

I'd crossed a border—

Speaking openly, exposing the weak girl I'd been, I was no longer her.

In the power of my newfound strength, I saw clearly—even though I'd been empowered to have my old college finally address my "horrific trauma," make me finally feel heard, this event would never have happened had I not first given myself my own voice, the permission to call my rape *rape* and not *shame*. In telling, I forced the school that silenced me, that minimized my trauma, that blamed me for the rape, to finally respect my voice and give me the platform they should have given me in the first place. I did not need the school to call it by its name; I did it myself, and they listened. *I* was the powerful party who brought the closure and empowerment I'd hoped, in first finding their invitation, that Colorado College would bring.

The next day, a girl who must have been in the audience found me on Facebook and wrote that she was also raped at our school. She still hadn't told anybody. She wrote that now she would.

The bravest thing I ever did was leave there. The next bravest thing I did was come back, to make myself heard.

International Resources

UNITED STATES
RAINN National Sexual Assault Hotline: 1 (800) 656-4673
www.rainn.org

CANADA
Canadian Association of Sexual Assault Centres
www.casac.ca

ENGLAND AND WALES
Rape Crisis England & Wales Hotline: 0808 802 9999
www.rapecrisis.org.uk

SCOTLAND
Rape Crisis Scotland Hotline: 0808 801 0302
www.rapecrisisscotland.org.uk

NEW ZEALAND
Victim Support Hotline: 0800-842-846
www.victimsupport.org.nz/get-help/your-help-lines

AUSTRALIA
National Counselling Helpline: 1800 737 732
www.1800respect.org.au

ACKNOWLEDGMENTS

THE BOOK

I have limitless gratitude for Susan Shapiro, the most passionate, generous professor and friend a young writer could ever meet. Sue, this book would not exist without you. (Sue! I don't know what I'd be doing in New York City without you.)

Thank you to Andrew Blauner, my attentive, kind, and tireless literary agent. I adore, admire, and respect you. Thank you, Matthew Snyder, my intrepid film agent at CAA.

Emma Komlos-Hrobsky, for discerning which of my memories were necessary to share, and which were repetitive or dull. Thank you for helping me find the puzzle pieces that fit well together, for making time for this story, for building this book with me. This memoir might still be 1,208 pages without you and Corrina.

I am endlessly grateful.

This book is the creation of an amazing unflagging pack at HarperCollins—thank you all! I'm especially grateful to my editor Matt Harper, for wise letters rich with wisdoms, the clarity you offer; Dani Valladares, brilliant editor, for teaching me— no matter how lovely, there is nothing poetic about unnecessary scenes. Thank you for making infinite revisions finite, truncating my stresses. What a lucky girl I am to get to learn with you how to write a book; Lisa Sharkey—our benevolent director, sage and guide. My assiduous publicist Joseph Papa. I'm also thankful to my publisher Liate Stehlik, Lynn Grady, Tavia Kowalchuk, Mandy Kain, production editor Shelby Peak (you are truly wonderful), and everyone else at HarperCollins who helped to make my story into a book. Thank you Sara Partridge, for helping this book find its home at HarperCollins.

NEWTON

Mr. Jampol, my eleventh-grade English teacher. Mr. Reinstein, Ms. Marder, Ms. Leslie. Yolande Abramian, my first teacher of beauty. All my childhood friends.

COLORADO COLLEGE

Sarah Eckstat, maid of honor at my wedding, beautiful tumbleweed, and kindred dreamer. Annie Evankow, the sweetest girl. Mary Katherine Southern, I saw galaxies in your freckles. Heather Horton. RAINN.

THE WOODS

The Saufleys, the Andersons, Firefly and Firewalker: for the tree house in the woods and tasty tacos and pulled pork barbecue, and your kindness to strangers in the woods like me. The Dinsmores, for a lawn on which to pitch my tent, and your forest lore. Chuck and Tigger. Daniel. A thousand angels unseen and unacknowledged.

The PCTA, for building and maintaining the Pacific Crest Trail.

Strangers who gave me beer and peaches, and all trail angels and fellow hikers who helped me make it to Canada.

Wilderness Press, for the *Data Book*. Karen Berger and Daniel R. Smith, for *The Pacific Crest Trail: A Hiker's Companion*, which was invaluable to me, both as I walked and as I wrote.

Michael David Smith, Mystic, lost boy. My friend Mystic passed away at only thirty-three. He was the sweetest. I met Justin through him. I'll never forget his stories of footpaths through forests that led above stuck towns to ancient mountains the soft blue color of ice. "It's a fairy tale," he said to me of the place where the Appalachian Trail ends, the summit of Mount Katahdin. "You get higher and higher. Everything gets beautiful."

What Justin wrote on Mystic's Facebook wall:

> *Mystic, the man who sat on pancakes to win an eating challenge. my dad finding your ipod. occupying my couch to shoot occupy. no sleeves, but high, high gaiters. hitchhiking 100's of miles for a little love. throwing a glass off a porch and walking away like it was no big deal. the mirrors you carried. days hiking with you were some of the best of my life.*
>
> *burning a stick of incense in your memory. rip, brother.*

NEW YORK CITY

Cameron Watkins, the kindest woman I know. Thank you for taking me into your overfull home when I had nowhere, for handing me the critical scrap of paper—"It was only when I wrote my first book that the world I wanted to live in opened to me." You didn't allow me to give up. You had copied the statement from Anais Nin's diary, which you happened to be reading. Edison Apple, for showing me how freedom is more exciting than it is frightening. Amanda Messenger, my model for diligence. We have committed, and so the universe conspires to assist us. We have each other, and so New York is kind. Ellie Anderson, philosopher-muse, my lady love.

David Brand, who finds my secret stories like a magician, the first person I can say absolutely anything to. Thank you. Suzannah Lessard, for teaching me that it is in the real idiosyncratic truth of the facts that profundity exists—that the reality is always more interesting than however writers might unconsciously simplify it, explaining truth away. Royal Young, who interviewed me and then transcribed my answers for me to consider, when writing the truth alone seemed impossible. Bryan Hurt, for answering the phone when I called for help and then reading my entire manuscript last-minute, in two days, and assuring me, "This is not a book that needs help." For inviting me back to Colorado College—that return has empowered me. Bonnie Nadzam, you are a magnifying glass and a map, a brilliant storyteller.

Luis Jaramillo, for admitting me to The New School. Laura Cronk, for always letting me talk for forty-five minutes, even when you only really have five. Leonard and Louise Riggio of the Riggio Foundation, for my fellowship. I am forever indebted. And my fellow writing students.

Thank you Andrea, my neighbor, who—when I was prepared to leave New York City—helped me remember why I'd come. She said I'd planted a budding life here and should stay. Thank god, thank god, thank god—*thank* you.

ART WORLDS

John Cameron Mitchell, for plays and movies that make me teary, for your friendship, for giving me a rent-free, gorgeous Caribbean hideaway to write this book in. Thank you. Artists like you make me grateful to call my neighborhood home. B. J. Novak, for showing me your view. Suzanne Heathcote, witty and wise playwright, bright light in L.A. Christine Sneed, I loved our long correspondence.

Thank you for your friendship and your enchanting books and stories. Karen Brown, your writing inspires me. Dylan Hale Lewis, for giving generously to RAINN in my honor.

Fellow writers: Charles Wilson, Sarah Herrington, Danielle Gelfand, Isabelle Forbes, Desiree Prieto—wonderful friends.

Daniel Jones, for publishing "A Hiker's Guide to Healing" in the *New York Times* when I was twenty-two, and still only dreaming. Jill Rothenburg, for the freedom of structure. Shelly Oria, my writing life SWEET mentor; it was thrilling getting to hear a SWEET actor read my life's biggest story. You opened the world—fellowships and residencies, awakening me to a community. Thank you for guiding me through the book-composing wilds. Lena Dunham, you brought me to the set of *Girls* and listened to my stories, and told yours. Thank you for your endless generosity. Your support has affirmed and fueled me more than I can thank you for. I feel so, so fortunate for that day, and for your kindness. I treasure it within me. It was the first time I felt noticed by an artist I admired. Nicholas Kristof, for tweeting my *Times* essay and for your own important work. Cheryl Strayed, for sharing this story, and your own stories, which helped pave my way to creating this book; for your wise art. Greil Marcus, this book began as a folk song in the Old Weird America, written for you. Sigrid Nunez, who once told my New School class that there is no German word for *innocent* and no Hebrew word for *fiction*. John Reed, who taught me: "Cut your problems." Annie Dillard, whom I've never met, whose book *The Writing Life* liberated me from all the pages I wrote to get to the place that was actually the beginning. Now I delete freely. Rob Spillman, for opening the door to the great *Tin House* for me. I adore the *Tin House* family: Elissa Shappel, Lance Cleland, and others I've worked with and talked to. Willing Davidson at *The New Yorker*, for your encouragement. Allen Houston, Greta Gerwig. Salman Rushdie, for always writing me back. Dayne Pillow, who published my stories first—this was the beginning—thank you.

Kerri Kleiner, Mark Lipson, Zara Lipson, Farhad Parsa, Jane

Nussbaum, David Lockwood, Tom Benedik. Marielle Henault. Leigh Newman.

All my English teachers and teachers of language, official and unofficial.

I wrote this book in the cafés and hotel lounges of New York. I have to thank: Caffe Reggio, Stumptown, the Mondrian, the Marlton, the Third Rail, McNally Jackson, HousingWorks, French Roast, Whynot Bistro, and Jack's, and above all Joe Coffee at Gay Street and Waverly—my office. The most magical paths grow from Joe.

In Berkeley, the Elmwood Café.

THE HOME

Mike King, who worked on the California Construction Corps and built the trail I walked. For your tenderness. When your kindness surprised me and I asked you, "How are you always so sweet?" you answered, "You should always be treated this way." On your days off from fighting fires, you showed me the beauty of the northern California coast.

Justin Matis, who believed in this book. Thank you for accompanying me to the place that made magic possible. You scavenged the streets of New York for materials to build the bed we shared.

The Matis Family: Howard Matis, Mary Matis—fellow writer. Kenneth Matis, Bea Matis, Irving Matis. Newfound timeless family, for taking me in and never letting me go. Small but great. I love you all, for always.

In the time since Dash left us, I have intermittently lived with his lovely parents, in his post-fire rebuilt Berkeley home, without him.

Mary and Howard—after Justin left to walk from Mexico to Canada again, you welcomed me back into your sunny home in the Berkeley hills, and made it ours again. Your love is truly remarkable. We missed Justin together, mourned his silence, and bonded wonderfully in our love.

The Parker Family

Mom, you're generous, a great mother, the kind who's always there, who acts always out of love. I know you've always wanted only the best for me. Your marriage with Dad is fiery still, what I aspire to find. Thank you for teaching me how to be a partner, for showing me that it's possible to build a life around love.

Also—thank you for buying me my ticket back to the trail. It pained you, and you didn't have to. Many other mothers wouldn't have.

And for giving to RAINN, often and generously.

Jacob, my big brother, for protecting me, wanting the best for me, wanting to help guide me and pull me through. For seeing the beauty in me before I could. For wanting me to find what you had.

Robert, my big brother, the smartest man, and a great dad. Thank you for "publishing" my first "book." I love you.

Kelly, for confiding your own stories, and listening to mine since I was two.

Wellesley, for teaching me how to wear eyeliner for the first time, framing my eyes and making me feel beautiful, and for your kindness.

Tom Parker, my incredible nephew—I love you dearly. You will be wildly great.

Dad. The best storyteller I know. In the time since, for giving me all the love and affection I craved as a girl. When things fell apart again, you rushed to New York. "Yours will not be a tragic life," you promised me, and I believed you—and now I cannot allow it to be. You wrote me a poem about the Animal Ancestors you remember me drawing, regretting the carousels we didn't ride together—we're riding them now.

I love you and it's not too late.

I am a writer because you are a writer.

Thank you for calling me a writer when I was only a kid.

Mom and Dad, for teaching me how to walk.

And for allowing me to finish this book in the place where it all began.

MY TRIBE

Tess Johnson, poet of angst and desire, rising rockstar. My Hell-flower and my safety—and I am yours, always and forever. You make all days better. I'm terribly excited for this summer. Tessie—I love you.

Corrina Gramma, goddess girl. We found each other in a Greenwich Village café in the middle of the night; from the dark you lit my way to sobriety and the clarity that followed—the earthy place where I learned that I am tall enough to reach up high and turn on the light myself.

Thank you for your grace, your perceptive convictions clear as water, your quiet power to sway your friends in healthier directions. You teach me the morals of the stories I've been telling all my life. This book is peppered with your gems, shimmering with Gramma.

You show me the way to empowering autonomy—solid ground from where I can see my younger self with compassion. Every question that you ask me leads to answers that show and show once again how capable we all are of making our dreams real.

You are your own sun.

You are a truly great thinker, and woman.

You are the Aerialist.